I0817207

Music in the Flesh

NEW MATERIAL HISTORIES *of* MUSIC

A series edited by James Q. Davies and Nicholas Mathew

ALSO PUBLISHED IN THE SERIES

Musical Vitalities: Ventures in a Biotic Aesthetics of Music
Holly Watkins

Sex, Death, and Minuets: Anna Magdalena Bach and Her Musical Notebooks
David Yearsley

The Voice as Something More: Essays toward Materiality
Edited by Martha Feldman and Judith T. Zeitlin

Listening to China: Sound and the Sino-Western Encounter, 1770–1839
Thomas Irvine

The Search for Medieval Music in Africa and Germany, 1891–1961: Scholars, Singers, Missionaries
Anna Maria Busse Berger

An Unnatural Attitude: Phenomenology in Weimar Musical Thought
Benjamin Steege

Mozart and the Mediation of Childhood
Adeline Mueller

Musical Migration and Imperial New York: Early Cold War Scenes
Brigid Cohen

The Haydn Economy: Music, Aesthetics, and Commerce in the Late Eighteenth Century
Nicholas Mathew

Tuning the World: The Rise of 440 Hertz in Music, Science, and Politics, 1859–1955
Fanny Gribenski

Creatures of the Air: Music, Atlantic Spirits, Breath, 1817–1913
J. Q. Davies

Music in the Flesh

AN EARLY MODERN MUSICAL PHYSIOLOGY

Bettina Varwig

The University of Chicago Press CHICAGO AND LONDON

The University of Chicago Press, Chicago 60637
The University of Chicago Press, Ltd., London
© 2023 by The University of Chicago
All rights reserved. No part of this book may be used or reproduced in any manner whatsoever without written permission, except in the case of brief quotations in critical articles and reviews. For more information, contact the University of Chicago Press, 1427 E. 60th St., Chicago, IL 60637.
Published 2023
Printed in the United States of America

32 31 30 29 28 27 26 25 24 23   1 2 3 4 5

ISBN-13: 978-0-226-82688-2 (cloth)
ISBN-13: 978-0-226-82689-9 (e-book)
DOI: https://doi.org/10.7208/chicago/9780226826899.001.0001

This book has received the Weiss-Brown Publication Subvention Award from the Newberry Library. The award supports the publication of outstanding works of scholarship that cover European civilization before 1700 in the areas of music, theater, French or Italian literature, or cultural studies. It is made to commemorate the career of Howard Mayer Brown.

This book has been supported by the Donna Cardamone Jackson Fund, Martin Picker Fund, and General Fund of the American Musicological Society, supported in part by the National Endowment for the Humanities and the Andrew W. Mellon Foundation.

Library of Congress Cataloging-in-Publication Data

Names: Varwig, Bettina, 1978– author.
Title: Music in the flesh : an early modern musical physiology / Bettina Varwig.
Other titles: New material histories of music.
Description: Chicago : The University of Chicago Press, 2023. | Series: New material histories of music | Includes bibliographical references and index.
Identifiers: LCCN 2022052885 | ISBN 9780226826882 (cloth) | ISBN 9780226826899 (e-book)
Subjects: LCSH: Music—Physiological aspects—History—17th century. | Music—17th century—Philosophy and aesthetics. | Music—17th century—History and criticism.
Classification: LCC ML3820.V27 2023 | DDC 781.1—dc23
LC record available at https://lccn.loc.gov/2022052885

♾ This paper meets the requirements of ANSI/NISO Z39.48-1992 (Permanence of Paper).

To my family

Contents

Part III: Ensoulment

Figures

Musical Examples

A Note on Musical Examples and Translations

Where feasible, I have reproduced my musical examples from an original source of the time, in order to bring my readers a bit closer to the experiences of early modern musicians interacting with these scripts. In the case of excerpts originally published in part books or involving a large number of parts, or where an original source was not accessible to me, the musical examples have been newly typeset.

In my foreign language quotations, I have retained the original spellings and punctuation. All translations are mine unless otherwise noted.

Acknowledgments

"Did it ever occur to you that there's no limit to how complicated things can get, on account of one thing always leading to another?"[1] Looking back over how this book has come into being over the past decade or so, I find myself responding to E. B. White's astute observation with a resounding yes. It would be impossible to retrace how one thing led to another, how the numerous conversations I've had with colleagues and friends, the books I've read, the talks and concerts I've attended, the music I've played over the years somehow resulted in what you have before you now. But I would like to thank at least a few of the remarkable thinkers, musicians, critics, and kindred spirits I have been fortunate to work amongst. I am hugely grateful to Roger Mathew Grant, Alan Howard, Alana Mailes, Kate van Orden, Stephen Rose, and David Yearsley, who offered their generous advice on parts of the manuscript. Jeremy Begbie read every word of it and inspired me to do better at every turn. My brilliant PhD students Peter Elliott, Fatima Lahham, Paul Newton-Jackson, and Mark Seow also read significant portions in draft and kept me on my toes with their critical acumen. Additional thanks are due to Paul for typesetting the musical examples. My valued colleagues John Butt, Delia Casadei, Eric Clarke, Arnie Cox, Ellen Exner, Maggie Faultless, David Ganz, Matthew Head, Wendy Heller, Marie Louise Herzfeld-Schild, David Irving, Julian Johnson, Michael Marissen, Peter McMurray, Daniel Melamed, Susan Rankin, Jesse Rodin, and Ruth Tatlow all shaped my thinking and writing in their own ways, through thought-provoking exchanges, joint projects, unstinting advice, and empathetic listening. Mina Gorji's sparklingly imaginative ways of beholding the world made me look at things differently time and again. Emily White generously shared her wisdom and expertise in

1. E. B. White, *Quo Vadimus? Or the Case for the Bicycle* (New York and London: Harper, 1927), 26.

Baroque trombone playing; so did Geoffrey Burgess for the oboe. My stalwart coworker Anne Faulkner kept me writing at her kitchen table in all weathers. My father, Freyr Varwig, provided unfailing assistance with untangling bits of Baroque Latin; Marion Colombani kindly lent a hand with some idiosyncratic French. Finally, a heartfelt thanks to Marta Tonegutti, Kristin Rawlings, and Nicholas Mathew at the Press, for their steadfast support and expert guidance throughout the publication process.

I gratefully acknowledge the financial support of the British Academy in the form of a Mid-Career Fellowship, during which this book was completed; of the Newberry Library in Chicago in the form of a Weiss-Brown Publication Subvention Award; and of the Donna Cardamone Jackson Fund, Martin Picker Fund, and General Fund of the American Musicological Society, supported in part by the National Endowment for the Humanities and the Andrew W. Mellon Foundation.

Preamble

Facts about what it is like to be an *X* are very peculiar,
so peculiar that some may be inclined to doubt their reality.
THOMAS NAGEL, "What Is It Like to Be a Bat?" (1974)

"Music is joy in the heart, pleasure in the mind; music is honey in the mouth, melody in the ear."[1] So begins a poem by the Nuremberg lawyer Hieronymus Ammon, published in 1643. The kind of music invoked by Ammon infiltrates the body's sensory and internal organs: the ears, but also the mouth and the heart, as well as the mind. It is somehow liquid, yet intangible. A string of mellifluous poetic metaphors: but how metaphorical were they? In a wedding sermon of 1621 dedicated to the praise of music, the Greiffenberg preacher Wolfgang Silber mused: "the natural spirits of our soul and our blood have a special affinity and closeness with the tunes and sounds of music."[2] In Silber's world, both the material and immaterial constituents of human beings related to, were drawn to, tuned in with music. The Lutheran pastor Christoph Frick affirmed in 1631 that the singing of the faithful was a "heart-bell, which . . . penetrates all the blood vessels of the heart and awakens its affect."[3] In his *Musurgia universalis* of 1650, the Roman Jesuit Athanasius Kircher proposed: "If someone should know the proportion of the sound of an instrument in relation to the spirits, muscles and arteries of the human body, they could awaken and bring about any effect in it they wanted."[4] Some decades later, the French writer M. de Vigneul-Marville wrote that "music and the sound of instruments contribute to the health of the body and the spirit, they aide the circulation of the humors, purify the blood, dissipate the vapors and dilate the vessels and pores."[5] Musical dissonance, meanwhile, according to the Berlin cantor Martin Heinrich Fuhrmann, caused "your throat to contract like from a sharp-sour vinegar."[6]

Taken together, these statements sketch out a physiology of music that seems at once alien and enticing. They make me wonder: What was it like to be a musicking subject—to compose, play, or hear music—in the early modern period? How could music penetrate the blood vessels of the heart or dissipate the body's vapors? What did those acidic dissonances taste like? How did it feel to be out of tune? In this book, I set out to explore how music operated within and upon early modern European body-souls to produce those effects that contemporary writers often described as moving, ravishing, painful, ecstatic, curative, miraculous.[7] Music's potential to "move the affections" had been a prominent topic already in antiquity, and during the period under consideration here (ca. 1580–1740), it re-emerged as a pervasive precept that fundamentally structured attitudes to and experiences of music. But what exactly was being moved, and how? In order to address these questions, I have sought out a diverse range of historical materials. Some of these have been known to music scholars for a long time and are returned to here in order to build a picture that reaches across different locales, communities, repertories, and practices of the period; others are drawn from less familiar discourses. In combination, these sources open up new insights not only into the nature of these affective motions and how they flowed within and between the body-souls of early modern subjects, but also what music was and how it could so strikingly transform people's bodily-spiritual makeup.

These are not easy issues to grapple with, and they can hardly be streamlined into a single linear narrative. They implicate fundamental philosophical debates—prominent at the time, and continuing to the present day—regarding human nature and the relationship between body, soul, mind, and spirit. They also demand engagement with the period's anatomical and medical knowledge and assumptions regarding the human body and its workings; with theoretical and practical writings about music, concerning its nature, function, production, and effects; and with the religious beliefs and practices in which all these discourses and experiences were embedded. These questions challenge us, furthermore, to look again at musical scores, those material traces of past musical activities, which hold their own kind of evidence about early modern modes of being in and using the body. In particular, I argue that approaching scores as *somatic scripts* allows us to recuperate the ways in which many standard musical features for which we can typically supply cogent technical explanations—such as dissonance, repetition, melisma, timbre, arpeggio—harbored crucial physiological dimensions that have tended to get lost in later commentary.[8] In drawing together these different strands, I offer a kind of historical phenomenology that outlines a set of parameters within which musical experiences unfolded for early modern composers, performers and, especially, listeners.[9] I thereby hope to show not only how certain foundational metaphors of the body reached across different spheres of music-making, scientific inquiry, and devotional practice, but that music can serve as a unique point of access to the experiential realities of these early modern bodies in action.

"Experience" has become a buzzword among certain groups of historians over recent decades, with subdisciplines such as the history of the senses or the emotions setting out to recover the felt dimension of past times and events.[10] My own project taps into some of these productive currents. But the notion of experience has also sat at the heart of certain much older problems concerning human nature that emerge as central matters of concern here. As Isaac Newton put it in a letter of 1672, "to determine . . . by what modes or actions [light] produceth in our minds the phantasm of colour is not so easie."[11] With "phantasm," Newton was referring to the subjective experience of a phenomenon whose physical properties failed to explain that experience (which Newton located in the mind). His remark anticipates what the philosopher David Chalmers in 1995 famously termed the "hard problem" of consciousness.[12] Our experience of the qualities of color, of music, of having or being a body, is underpinned by certain physical givens—light frequencies, sound waves, cells and molecules, the laws of gravity and mechanics—which the science of Newton's age made great strides in investigating. Today these investigations have advanced to the level of identifying neural correlates for particular experiential states. But still the question of where or how these experiential states arise remains curiously unresolved. As neurologist Steven Sevush has put it recently with reference to the proverbial redness of a rose: "Chemicals may churn and electricity may flow, but nowhere will the redness itself be found."[13]

The problem is compounded further when history enters the frame. As Jill Anne Kowalik has noted, the "radical postmodern assertion of discontinuity between discourse and experience" would preclude any possibility of a meaningful historical investigation into past experiences. Conversely, she finds, "the assumption that discourse 'mirrors' experience destroys our critical distance to a text and prevents us from differentiating between doctrine and affective praxis."[14] In response to this conundrum, I would venture that music, as a nonverbal mode of expression that took shape in both practice and discourse, can help mitigate that discontinuity. The fact that written records necessarily constitute one of the primary routes for historians to access past experiences certainly means that we will only ever gain a mediated picture of the object of investigation; the actual feel of their ways of perceiving the world, the lived experience of their bodies, minds, hearts, spaces, and communities will ultimately remain out of reach. But musical scores constitute a peculiar type of written record that arguably inscribes acts of bodily engagement more determinedly than many others. Hence, while I draw extensively on verbal discourses, what follows is not primarily intended as a history of ideas. Instead, I use these discourses, in all their entangled multiplicity, to move toward illuminating the past bodily actions and reactions afforded by musical notation. For although we can never fully know the experience of someone from the past—just as we cannot know what it is like to be a bat, or, for that matter, the person living next door to us—this ignorance is a matter of degrees: most human interactions take place on the grounds of an assumed sense of shared experience, and people command sophisticated strategies for inferring another person's experiential state by taking in contextual, verbal, and bodily clues. Those shared assumptions and clues no doubt become harder to read as we move into the past, but they were still operative in all their historical-cultural specificity. Even though some of these early modern ways of being-in-the-world were indeed different—sometimes strikingly so—I propose that we can use a focus on music-making practices as a way to delineate, quite closely, some of the structures of feeling within which these experiences unfolded.[15]

Such an endeavor entails taking seriously the science, language, metaphors, and explanations put forward in those discourses, even if they seem outlandish or flawed by present-day standards. In doing so, I unearth a widely shared assemblage of ideas and feelings around bodies and embodiment that amalgamated inherited Galenic physiology with more current philosophical ideas, anatomical discoveries, religious sensibilities, and everyday experiences of music and sound. My approach also entails embracing music's odd status as a historical set of practices and faded sonic utterances that nonetheless retain currency in performance today. In one sense, this continued presence complicates matters, since we have come to relate to these musical repertories in particular ways that potentially obstruct a clearer view of their nature and effects in the past. But this continuity also poses a productive challenge, by inviting us to use these historical insights to try to retune our own ears, bodies, and minds; to adapt and enrich our engrained habits of performing, hearing, and analyzing this music. Unlike Elisabeth Le Guin's inspirational study of Boccherini's music, I do not explicitly draw on my experiences of performing the repertories I discuss here; but I am mindful of how my own bodily-mental habitus might shape—and be reshaped by—my engagement with these past musical practices and ideas.[16] If my project constitutes a kind of "carnal" musicology, then, it primarily aims to recuperate the historical dimension of that carnality, albeit in a way that ultimately may end up refashioning our own musicking selves as well.

In particular, these past modes of being carnal in music mount a renewed challenge to the Cartesian anthropology that has underpinned the dominant conceptions of human nature in Western modernity. The sheer number of studies I have encountered over the years that claim finally to have overcome the legacy of Descartes's mind-body dualism and its associated binaries makes me suspect that we are in fact quite a long way yet from doing so. But what this study hopes to show is that early modern musicking practices persistently disrupted these binaries by stubbornly resisting reduction to one or the other side. A renewed engagement with these early modern musics encourages us to practice modes of thinking and feeling outside a dualist frame: aspective, dialectical, paradoxical, or spectrum thinking, say, all of which are put to work at different points in this book. In this I follow the lead of the feminist writer Elizabeth Grosz, who regarded the body as "the threshold or borderline concept that hovers perilously and undecidably at the pivotal point of binary pairs."[17] The bodies I grapple with ultimately emerge as neither fully constructed nor entirely natural; music cannot be positioned as just material vibration or disembodied aesthetic object; the literal and the metaphorical exist along a spectrum rather than as categorical opposites; and the duality of body and mind is broken up by the interference of spirits and/or souls. Thinking about early modern musical experiences thus urges us to entertain a more integrated anthropology, in which human subjects may be made up of discrete material/nonmaterial aspects, but ultimately their ways of being human can only be explained holistically. The early modern musical physiology reconstructed here thus necessarily enfolds a psychology as well, held together by the wet and vaporous flows of spirit that governed the vital functions, moral proclivities, and interactions with the world of these historical subjects.

Who, then, are these subjects whose physiology I am after? I use the term "early modern" pragmatically to delineate a time frame that to my mind evinces a certain continuity in Christian European attitudes to music and bodies, though aspects of these continuities could no doubt be tracked further back as well as forward in time. I take physiology in the comprehensive sense instituted by the sixteenth-century French physician Jean François Fernel to be concerned with body parts and their functions but also with temperaments, spirits, humors, and the faculties of the soul.[18] My main focus falls on music-making bodies in early modern Lutheran German lands; not only because these are the people I know most about from my past research, but also because this musicological subfield notably lags behind compared to scholarship on Italian, English, or French repertories from a carnal perspective. At the same time, many of the ideas and experiences traced here had a trans-national and trans-confessional reach that this study seeks to elucidate, in the hope of inspiring increasing crossover among our still nationally divided historiographies. On the one hand, there is no way to tell a unified story even just of Lutheran German music of the period, composed of numerous disparate places, repertories, and communities; yet, on the other, the lively exchanges and patent commonalities across regional and national boundaries urge a broader purview and greater integration of different Latin and vernacular sources. I would argue, furthermore, that certain Lutheran approaches to questions of music, bodies, spirits, sin, and grace prove particularly enlightening in my pursuit of this historical physiology, given not only the elevated status of music as a gift of God in Lutheran theology, but the "sea change" in relations between matter and spirit that the Reformation initiated.[19] In making such claims for the wider relevance of my project, I do not presume to achieve comprehensive coverage in any respect, but aim to offer a set of concepts and tools that could be fruitfully brought to, and modified in relation to, specific repertories and practices.

On the whole, I focus less here on individual musicking subjects and their ego-documents (letters, diaries, etc.) than on shared underlying patterns of bodily engagement and experience. Yet I am also keen to avoid the construct of an "ideal" performer or listener, which would erase the numerous levels of differentiation that existed along gender, religious, ethnic, or class lines. While this book does not pursue a historical phenomenology of how different groups of non-Christian or non-white inhabitants of Europe and beyond experienced their own embodiment, it remains alert throughout to the ways in which these (imagined, feared, subjugated) bodies of others shaped emerging notions of the dominant white male body of Western modernity. And within the broad category of early modern Christians, I advocate for attending closely to difference and multiplicity of experience: not only were women wetter musicians than men, but aged bodies behaved differently from children's, the bodies of those attending a church service potentially responded differently when those same bodies entered an opera house, and so on. Ultimately, though, all the bodies I deal with here—of listeners, singers, instrumentalists, composers, dancers, improvisers—emerge as purposive, volatile, spiritous, in flux, and permeated by sin and a yearning for salvation. Needless to say, no MRI scan could reveal this kind of crucial information about the body-souls that this study seeks to get inside. Still, throughout the book I reference relevant illuminating aspects of current research in neuropsychology and embodied cognition. In doing so, I in no way profess full expertise in these areas, but only wish to point out some of the striking resonances between certain early modern views and their present-day formulations. In highlighting the dialogic, partial, and evolving nature of these different bodies of knowledge, such resonances might further encourage us to read the historical testimonies presented here seriously and sympathetically.

The book unfolds as a series of reflections on interlinked themes. Its three parts are divided into a number of smaller subsections, each dealing with a particular issue, metaphor, body part, or piece of music/moment of performance. Taken together, the subsections form a larger overarching argument, but they can also be read in isolation. In order to facilitate engagement with the numerous early modern witnesses I cite, I have included a biographical register within the customary inventory of works cited. Overall, the book's three parts move from an exposition of some key terms that frame my historical exploration to the finer nuances of the musical physiology that the book intends to bring to life. Detailed discussions of individual pieces take up some sections entirely, but are also woven into the fabric of the argument throughout. I thereby hope to test out different ways of integrating the study of musical scores and the bodies they enfold more directly with other types of historical sources, and to allow the historical insights that emerge here to transform—to carnalize—our analytical approaches and vocabulary. Ultimately, then, what follows is intended as an open invitation, to feel our way into these musics with ears, limbs, and hearts not quite our own.

I

Embodiment

1
Words

I begin where most respectable studies of modern Western music history have begun: with Claudio Monteverdi's proclamation (via his brother Giulio Cesare) of his "seconda prattica" in 1605, a proclamation later hailed by twentieth-century musicologists as encapsulating the spirit of the so-called Baroque age. In this "Dichiaratione," Giulio Cesare famously asserted that in Claudio's newly invented second practice of composition, the "oration is the mistress of the harmony and not the servant."[1] Roughly four hundred years later, the eminent music historian Claude Palisca referred to this declaration as "one of the most important manifestos in the history of music."[2] But I do not return to this assumed watershed moment in order to tell yet another version of the familiar tale concerning the enthronement of words over music and its concomitant stylistic revolutions (the invention of monody, opera, figured bass, and so on); nor to remind my readers that, notwithstanding the Monteverdian rhetoric of radical innovation, the eminent Italian theorist Gioseffo Zarlino had already made a closely related claim almost half a century earlier, when he stated that "harmony and rhythm are to follow the oration."[3] Instead, I propose to re-evaluate the declaration in terms of what I perceive as the lasting restrictive effects it has had on our appreciation of certain musical repertories and practices that in the later musicological estimation came under its spell: from Claudio Monteverdi's own output to German composers from Heinrich Schütz to Johann Sebastian Bach, from Reformation hymnody to aristocratic *Tafelmusik*.

I am by no means the first to propose such a re-evaluation. As Tim Carter has argued, Giulio Cesare's argumentative strategy in the declaration was born out of the need to get his brother out of a tight spot. After Claudio had been publicly reprimanded by the conservative critic Giovanni Maria Artusi for breaking the established rules of counterpoint, Giulio

Cesare's polemic "usefully pulled the rug out from under Artusi's feet" by asserting that Claudio's compositional practice operated in a parallel universe where Artusi's rules did not apply. As Carter asserts, the declaration therefore "did not necessarily form the basis of a consistent aesthetic position"; yet its catchphrase about the words governing the music has been taken as "one defining feature of Monteverdi's output, and indeed of his entire period," viewed as "ushering in a new musical age."[4] I do not intend to enter here into the intricate debates over what exactly the Monteverdis may have meant by this phrase; others have addressed this question with great insight and finesse.[5] I also do not mean to set (either) Monteverdi up as a straw man, to be blamed for everything that subsequently went wrong with Baroque music scholarship. What I wish to reflect on are two fundamental interpretive habits that arose from the more or less wholesale musicological adoption of Monteverdi's pronouncement. The first of these concerns the tendency to regard "the music" in vocal compositions of the time principally as a secondary bearer of meaning, tasked with re-presenting the semantic content of its associated text. The second results from the specific terms in which the declaration was couched ("oratio"—"harmonia"), inducing us to keep our attention focused on the score and the relationship of its textual elements, that is, words and notes, at the expense of the performed, enacted, sounding dimension of music.[6]

In order to illustrate the deep-seated effects of this scholarly enthusiasm for Monteverdi's dictum, I turn to the piece that for many modern commentators has exemplified this "second practice" at its best, namely the lament from his opera *Arianna* of 1608. A lot, of course, has happened since Gary Tomlinson's classic account of the piece from 1987, which celebrated it as a perfect union of verbal and musical declamation.[7] Tomlinson offered a deeply perceptive yet decidedly text-based account: "Monteverdi derived the overall organization of his music from the rhetorical shape of Rinuccini's three periods . . . He filled out this structure with gestures reflecting the poet's finer rhetorical details . . . On all levels the music responds to the syntactic structure and rhetoric of the text."[8] Where Tomlinson's analysis construed this relationship of music and text as detached from any performed instantiation or the corporeal presence of its participants, the new musicologists of the 1990s set out to redress this formalist orientation, aiming to bring those participants with their historically shaped subjectivities and bodily-spiritual resources back into the picture. Hence Suzanne Cusick attended to the cultural significance of the tears that Arianna's lament produced in its female listeners, and Bonnie Gordon brought the vocal cords and uteruses of early modern female singers into close focus.[9] While Cusick reminded us that the performance of Monteverdi's lament was bound up with patriarchal politics, Gordon noted that, since "song embodies female desire," Arianna's singing voice in fact "counteracted the message of the words she sang."[10] Most recently, Emily Wilbourne has shined a revealing spotlight on Virginia Ramponi Andreini, the commedia dell'arte actress who took the part of Arianna in the opera's premiere.[11]

My own project gratefully builds on these advances. Yet, more than that, it hopes to address the gap that still remains between some of the corporeally grounded approaches proposed by these scholars and current mainstream historical-analytical discourses around Baroque music. Those historical bodies—their materialities, genders, and dispositions—have not, I think, sufficiently infiltrated the ways in which most early modern musical practices and repertories are habitually heard or interpreted. Even Cusick's own approach, though centered on female bodies and their disciplining, produced a musical analysis that remained both score-based and grounded in the assumption of music as representational: the lament's opening phrase depicted the two sides of Arianna's nature, she wrote, with its rising elements "representing Arianna's uncontrollable passion" and the subsequent descent portraying the public castigation that returned her to female submission.[12] If the notes no longer necessarily follow the words of the libretto in Cusick's interpretation, their primary function is still to signify, to illustrate a broader set of meanings. Gordon's reading of vocal ornamentation in some of Monteverdi's madrigals comes much closer to embedding aspects of physicality in her analytical approach and language. Yet the details of the female physiology she invokes often remain sketchy: no early modern writer is cited in support of the assertion that the "rapid closing and opening of the glottis" in virtuosic female singing was understood to parallel "the opening of the uterus imagined to accompany orgasm."[13] And even Wilbourne's attention to Andreini's "dominating physicality" on stage does not quite capture those sonic-emotive effects which, to my mind, this anonymous contemporary sonnet in praise of her performance makes uniquely palpable:

> Co la bocca di rose, d'onde uscia
> Il nettare che inebria alma e l'senso,
> Mentre disacerbava il duolo intenso
> Arianna gentile i cor rapia.
>
> Ma mentre accompagnava l'armonia,
> La man stringendo al sen, co'affetto immenso,

Spremeva l'alme e, se ben dritto io penso,
Gli angioli istessi a un tempo anche feria.

[While gentle Arianna assuaged our intense pain, she stole our hearts with a mouth of roses, from which poured forth the nectar that inebriates soul and sense. Accompanied by harmony, her hand pressed against her heart with intense affect, squeezing our souls, and at that point, if I am right in thinking it, the angels themselves were wounded.][14]

"The music," you may note, is barely thematized in this poeticized recollection, and no attention is paid to its rhetorical structures or representational function. Music and words hardly seem to constitute separable entities at all. Instead, their joint outpouring, figured as physical action accompanied by harmony, enacted a mode of intensely haptic communication, in which the singer's voice, mouth, and hands connected tangibly with both her listeners' souls and those survivors of the old universal harmony, the angels. No doubt Monteverdi's intricate music-rhetorical strategies contributed significantly to this sense of immediacy. But the sonnet brazenly annihilates the physical and intellectual distance that most modern-day analyses tend to preserve from their object. As Carolyn Abbate put it, "metaphysical mania encourages us to retreat from real music to the abstraction of the work."[15] This distancing strategy is evident in philosopher Peter Kivy's description of the lament's opening phrase: "The musical line can be, and was, thought of as a kind of musical icon, resembling a piece of human emotive expression."[16] His formulation betrays an analytical process that starts from (and ends with) the notes on the page. In contemplating a score of the piece (fig. 1.1), one might indeed read that opening vocal gesture and dissonant accompanying harmony as an "icon," representing the despair communicated in the text. If, however, one sought to address first and foremost the performed reality of the piece made audible in sound by human agents, it would seem rather strange, I think, to describe that sonic experience as "resembling" a piece of human emotive expression. In a moment of performance, I would venture, what a singer performed and an acculturated listener encountered *was* an emotive utterance in its own right, made up of sounding words (their phonetic profile as well as their semantic potential) bound up with music (its sonic qualities and gestural shapes as well as the meanings that these elements might have conveyed). Decoding its meanings may no doubt have formed an important part of a listener's response to such an utterance; but that decoding process does not by far exhaust what those sounds may have been doing to or for anyone hearing them.

FIGURE 1.1. Claudio Monteverdi, *Lamento d'Arianna* (Venice: Gardano, 1623), excerpt. Ghent University Library, BHSL.RES.0671/13.

What I want to suggest, then, is that only when we embed our considerations of musical rhetoric or representation fully in these performed, corporeal dimensions can we begin to appreciate what that "nectar" flowing from Andreini's lips may have tasted like for its historical performers and listeners: how it materially affected their bodies, souls, and spirits in the act of singing or listening. In order to do so, we are in need of a more detailed, fleshy historical physiology, and we need that physiology to permeate more fully our modes of hearing and analyzing. I hasten to add that my plea for a (yet) more embodied approach to these musics in no way intends to deny the importance of text in musicking practices of the long seventeenth century. There is no doubt that the words which composers set, performers intoned, and listeners heard formed crucial components of these practices. Here, in fact, may be a first opportunity to step out of an instinctively binary framework, by challenging the supposed duality of meaning versus embodiment, or text versus sound. "More body" does not necessarily imply "less meaning," but more body underneath, within, against, around, or as meaning. Over the course of this book, I pursue two main strategies to undercut this particular duality: first, by paying attention to those aspects that made musical performances a meaningful form of sonic-emotive communication beyond the textual content they carried. Second, by embracing the notion, all but commonplace in the study of (early modern) poetry, that words also have (or are) sounds, and that their sonorous qualities of rhythm, assonance, and flow can operate alongside, in conjunction with, or in opposition to semantic content. These sonorous, corporeally produced, experiential qualities of both music and words have tended to be muted in those representational readings of early modern repertories grounded in the twentieth-century embrace of the "seconda prattica" doctrine. My attempts in these pages to recuperate some of these qualities lead me, moreover, to propose two key concepts to elucidate alternative processes of meaning-making in acts of musicking: the notion of "emergent" meaning, by which a musical utterance can be perceived as meaning-ful without that meaning necessarily being specifiable in words; and the notion of "defamiliarization," by which a musical utterance can unsettle and reshape, rather than simply affirm, the meaning of any associated verbal content. Across the book I explore different ways in which these concepts can help us gauge this fuller sense of meaningfulness in early modern acts of music-making, grounded in the embodied sense-making capacities of their participating body-souls.

✷ 2 ✷

Affektenlehre

It is well known that one of the most prominent formulations of a representation-based approach in modern music scholarship arose not in relation to Monteverdi but in the context of twentieth-century interpretations of early modern German music. The 1910s saw the discovery (or rather invention) of the so-called *Affektenlehre* in German musicology, subsequently billed as the dominant aesthetic theory of the German Baroque. It posited that the compositional practice of the period was built on a coherent system of affective representation, in which particular musical gestures were associated with particular affective or semantic content. The notion that such a coherent system existed was persuasively debunked by George Buelow in the 1980s; but I have found the analytical and listening habits instituted by this system to have been startlingly persistent.[1] As a student musicologist in the early 2000s, I encountered the lineaments of *Affektenlehre*-thinking more or less fully intact; it was that encounter, in fact, that sowed the first seeds for what would eventually become this book. My sense already then was that this analytical mindset fell frustratingly short of capturing what I felt was most striking in some of the music of a Buxtehude or Bach. Ostensibly, once you had labeled your musical gestures, your job was done and you had safely encompassed the music's affective potential. Buelow described this approach as an interpretive "straitjacket," a term that captures that sense of restrictiveness to which many of my own students now still readily seem to submit, habitually approaching this musical language as an extended form of word-painting, as a code needing to be deciphered.

Hence in the opening chorus of Johann Sebastian Bach's cantata *Herr Christ, der einge Gottessohn* (BWV 96), the "incessant figuration of the recorder set in a very high register . . . [is] surely meant to illustrate symbolically the sparkling of the morning star."[2] Downward modulation in Bach's *St. Matthew Passion* represents "the passive sufferings Jesus undergoes."[3] The chromatic contortions in the vocal line of his aria "Es kommt ein Tag" in Cantata 136 "describ[e] the 'annihilating' . . . power of God's wrath."[4] Much of Bach's music, contends Mark Ringer, "does not aspire to superficial physical beauty. Its beauty lies in its truth to the concept it is depicting with unsurpassed specificity."[5] In Barbara Strozzi's cantata *Ardo in tacito foco* (published in 1654), a rising melisma "depicts the opening word *ardo* ('I burn')," while "dissonant suspensions represent the meaning of the word *aspro* ('bitter')."[6] Fugues "often represent legality and certainty of events"; a fugal section in Dietrich Buxtehude's organ prelude *Wie schön leuchtet der Morgenstern* expresses "the joy of marital union."[7] Georg Frideric Handel's instrumentation and chromaticism in the chorus "He sent a thick darkness" from his oratorio *Israel in Egypt* (1739) "represent the covering gloom."[8] Jean-Philippe Rameau "depicts the horrors of the underworld with a series of half-step modulations that descend chromatically" in act 2 of his opera *Hippolyte et Aricie* (1733).[9] In Heinrich Schütz's motet *Reduc, Domine Deus* from his *Cantiones Sacrae* (1625), we find a "madrigalian representation of sweetness" in the prominent parallel thirds, while "in melodies that ascend and descend over an octave, the stretching out of Christ's body is represented in all voices. The soprano line . . . is a musical-rhetorical *hyperbole*, representing the excesses of torture by overstepping the musical ambitus."[10] I could easily go on: examples of this analytical mindset permeate many past and current accounts of these repertories. To be sure, I am not claiming that any of these readings are necessarily incorrect; some of them strike me as entirely plausible or even incontrovertible. But, to my mind, they seem to be missing (out) something essential: something to do with the agency, power, excitement, and pleasure of musical sound beyond its signifying function. These interpretations rely on what Nina Sun Eidsheim has called the "figure of sound," that is, the assumption of a direct representational relationship between musical figurations and their affective or semantic content.[11]

The use of the term "hyperbole" in Isabella van Elferen's analysis of Schütz's motet points to the close relationship between the alleged "doctrine of the affections" and the *Figurenlehre* (doctrine of figures), derived from rhetoric, which scholars found operating in close conjunction. The newly codified discipline of "musica poetica," as it emerged in German writings in the decades around 1600, set out to codify how to compose pieces of music, in part as a response to some of the challenges of form and style arising from contemporary stylistic innovations. And those first theorists (Gallus Dressler, Johannes Nucius, Joachim Burmeister) looked to the established teachings of rhetoric as a model for a musical poetics. In particular, they used the names of rhetorical figures to label certain common musical figurations. In later twentieth-century readings, these musico-rhetorical figures were once again widely understood to be primarily text-related, that is, aiding the expression of pictorial or affective content. This is perhaps not surprising, given that the terms were taken from the domain of oratory, principally concerned with words. But a rereading of those historical sources shows that much of these writers' interest in rhetoric resided simply in its capacity to provide a terminology for common strategies of combining musical phrases into syntactic units that "made sense" on a musical level. While rhetoric offered a useful set of established terms, in other words, there was no inherent meaningful connection between the rhetorical and musical uses of those terms. In his 1606 *Musica poetica*, Burmeister described most of his figures, including "hyperbole," without any reference to textual content; and many of his musical examples are printed without the words.[12] Any of those figures could, of course, be used in the service of text expression; but they were not primarily conceived as strategies for conveying semantic content. Overall, Burmeister and his contemporaries were simply not as text-focused in their approach to the art of musical composition as our analyses of the repertories associated with this tradition later became.[13]

Only two of Burmeister's figures, hypotyposis and pathopoeia, were explicitly described as word- and/or affect-related. Hypotyposis referred to the kind of word-painting devices familiar from sixteenth-century madrigal composition (that is, not specifically linked to the "seconda prattica" moment). Burmeister called it "that ornament whereby the sense of the text is so depicted that those matters contained in the text that are inanimate or lifeless seem to be brought to life."[14] Burmeister's phrase echoed Martin Luther's assertion that just as a sermon was "the living voice of the Gospel," so in music "the notes bring the text to life," implying an orientation toward music's performed, live dimension.[15] Burmeister identified examples of hypotyposis in a number of motets by Orlando di Lasso, primarily in passages setting the words "joy" or "pain." We might add to this much later examples, for instance when the pizzicato strings in the bass recitative in Bach's cantata *Nun komm, der Heiden Heiland* (BWV 61) offer an aural simulation of the knocking on the door referenced in the text. In such instances, the music could indeed act as a way to render textual meaning more vivid and immediate—although even these examples open up all sorts of tricky questions about the status of mimesis versus the "real," or about how such devices felt in ears and bodies. Some seventeenth-century "musica poetica" writings even included handy lists of words suited to this direct translation of textual meaning into music. Andreas Herbst advised that composers needed to consider the words initially in terms of their accent, prosody, and number of syllables, before attending to the "verba affectuum" (affective words), "which all need to be expressed in sound through variation and alternation of the notes."[16] Most writers, however, acknowledged that compositional craft should extend beyond the localized translation of individual words. The Italian theorist Vincenzo Galilei had already cautioned against an excess of literal word-painting, since if the text already presented its meaning, the music did not need to "re-present" it.[17] A hundred years later, the German lexicographer Johann Gottfried Walther agreed that "when an affect is to be expressed, a composer should pay more attention to it than to individual words," that is, capturing what rhetoricians called the "scopus" (rather than the "sensus") of the words.[18] Such an approach could form the foundation, of course, for the extended exploration of a single affective state in the eighteenth-century aria.

Pathopoeia, meanwhile, in Burmeister's description, was a "figure suited to generating affects," specifically by introducing semitones foreign to the mode.[19] Burmeister did not explicitly characterize it as a text-related figure, but many of his examples involve textual passages referencing weeping or grief. Dissonance, and chromaticism in particular, indeed served as a key device for evoking sad or harsh affects across the period; and as "moving the affections" evolved into the central mandate in contemporary writings on music, pathopoeia in a certain sense emerged as *the* fundamental compositional objective. Yet Burmeister's description—a figure suited to generating affect—left open whether this strategy was thought to operate primarily via a direct relationship of signifier and signified. If this has often been assumed in later musicological discourse, such a reading would arguably render the musical formulation ultimately redundant; its usefulness ended once you had deciphered the intended meaning. But commentators across the long seventeenth century made it abundantly clear that this was not all that music's affective potential amounted to, an impression I have found confirmed in my own listening experiences. Take Johann Sebastian Bach's soprano aria "Wie lieblich klingt es in den Ohren" (How beautifully it rings in my ears) from his Cantata 133. The singer repeats the opening textual phrase five times over 23 measures before a listener gets to hear what that phrase referred to, namely, "this word: my Jesus is born." I would venture that those of Bach's congregants without access to a libretto print would not have sat through those opening 23 measures simply waiting for the words to tell them what should be ringing pleasantly in their ears, since those ears were being filled with pleasant musical sound all along. The crucial words, once they arrived, potentially added to that pleasurable experience and could be absorbed into the mind and heart as sounding truth. But the performed enactment of this unusually long aria—over seven minutes even in the fastest recordings available—could not be justified simply as a more elaborate way of getting those words across. In a 1999 performance by Emmanuel Music conducted by Craig Smith, the piece extends to almost ten minutes: a long time indeed to enunciate a four-line poem.[20] What was all that musical sound doing there, ringing in people's ears?

3
Melisma

Ben, bene, tutto è zolfa, tutto è zolfa.

CLAUDIO MONTEVERDI[1]

One major complication besetting early modern music's supposedly straightforward relationship with words and their meaning is its sonic overabundance. This is evident not only in the experience of hearing, say, several voices intoning a madrigal text ostensibly uttered by a single poetic self, or choirs of instruments amplifying the voices in a polychoral motet, but even on the local level of what could be done with (or to) individual words and their component parts. Why would one want to sing—or compose, or hear—several notes to one syllable of text? Or, in the words of the German theorist Gaspar Stocker, writing around 1570: "How does it happen that we find more notes than syllables?"[2] Melisma, from this perspective, emerges as perhaps *the* primal moment of sound getting in the way of, or away from, words. Melismatic elaboration certainly had the capacity to enhance the meaning of those words; but its surplus sonic stimulation potentially ended up impeding their delivery. While the term "melisma" was adopted as a common descriptor for this phenomenon only in early twentieth-century scholarship, the practice of singing several notes to one syllable reached back to some of the earliest forms of Christian liturgical chant. It persisted into the Renaissance contrapuntal style, critiqued by the sixteenth-century Italian theorist Nicola Vicentino as "brutto udire" (ugly listening); for him, syllabic setting should be the norm and starting point.[3] Across the long seventeenth century, as monodic singing entered mainstream musical practice and individual virtuosity became highly prized, such passages of florid singing were called different things, but they were considered primarily an improvised, performed phenomenon: something that a singer (or instrumentalist) did, first and foremost, even if from at least the time of Giulio Caccini's *Le nuove musiche* (1601) or Luzzasco Luzzaschi's *Madrigali* of the same year, composers frequently notated them in order to instruct performers how to do so. The variety of contemporary terms used to describe the phenomenon—"passaggi" or "diminutioni" in Italian, "roulades" or "traits de gorge" in Jean Millet, "Coloraturen" in German singing treatises—all referred to throats and vocal cords (or fingers and bows) producing chains of notes to pass between, break up, or decorate a plain (syllabic) musical line or contrapuntal framework.[4] The term "melisma" only appeared sporadically in the period, as in a 1719 treatise by the Bohemian theorist Mauritius Vogt, whose taxonomy of different styles included an entry for the "stylus melismaticus," described as "soft, airy, rhythmical, [and] maximally expressive of the work and art of the singer."[5]

Contemporary sources rarely discussed melisma in relation to textual meaning, instead usually presenting tables of figurations for singers (or instrumentalists) to apply in syntactically appropriate places. The Italian doctor and musician Giovanni Camillo Maffei, in a 1562 letter on the art of singing, did hold up a distinction between those melismas applied "with the intention of signifying something, that is, inferring the sentiment of the words," and the kind of "voce passaggiata" solely intended to "please the ear." In the former, Maffei noted, the "syllables of the words are carried in the mouth," whereas the latter was "singing with the throat."[6] By the time of Caccini, and in the wake of the "seconda prattica," many writers insisted that performers should employ the ear-tickling type of "passaggi" with discrimination, in order to avoid a "laceration of the poetry."[7] And composers did of course use melisma routinely in the service of text expression. Melismas could depict things that are long (by elongating the word) or fast (by filling up temporal space with lots of notes). In the fourth movement of Johann Sebastian Bach's Cantata 25, brief melismas decorate the words "lebenslang" (lifelong) and "flieh" (flee) in an otherwise syllabic recitative, while melismatic elaboration of increasing length and complexity marks the repeated word "eternal" in Henry Purcell's *Music for a While*. Melismas could signify other things, too: in the bass aria "Gewaltige stößt Gott vom Stuhl" from Bach's Cantata 10, Markus Rathey finds the wide-ranging figuration serving "the celebration of male strength."[8] "Canto," "riso," "giuoco," "fiori," "ardori," as Nino Pirrotta has pointed out, "unfailingly give rise to the response of vocal melisma" in Monteverdi's seventh book of madrigals.[9] It would indeed be possible to explain the majority of melismatic passages in the vocal works of early modern composers in terms of such significatory function.

Yet, at the same time, melismas also did other things. They could direct a singer's or listener's attention to the sonic dimension of the voice; they could distract from or hamper the audibility of the text. They introduced excess airy noise that needed to be filtered out around consonants and vowels if they were to be received as meaningful verbal utterance. With its outrageous opening melisma on "Sa-," the aria "Sag, Amor" from the third act of Reinhard Keiser's opera *Adonis* made a mockery of the requirement for text audibility in front of its Hamburg audience in 1697 (fig. 3.1). Mona Spägele's enraged performance of 2001 freely traverses tonal space in a flagrant disregard for any listener's desire to know what word they might be hearing.[10] According to Vogt, a syllabic style, which he called "cantus choralis," was most gratifying to God, since it "does not evacuate the sense of the words, but feeds it."[11] And yet most composers summarily failed to stick to this plain model, instead perpetually giving in to the lure of melisma, even as its airy bursts tore the ear away from the words and their sense. The elaborate melismatic singing styles that developed in the decades around 1600 seem to have been driven at least in part by a sense of enjoyment derived from unfettered vocal sound, from the resonance of dismembered phonemes wafting through the ether. This sonic dimension formed a standard part of musicians' training, too. As Georg Quitschreiber outlined in his 1598 singing treatise, a musical line may be studied in three

FIGURE 3.1. Reinhard Keiser, aria "Sag, Amor," from *Der geliebte Adonis* (premiered 1697), excerpt. Staatsbibliothek zu Berlin—Preußischer Kulturbesitz, Musikabteilung mit Mendelssohn-Archiv, Mus.ms. 11480, f. 65v and 66r.

ways: by using solmization syllables, as pure sound ("nur am Klange") in the manner of instrumentalists, or with words.[12] A hundred years later, the Mühlhausen musician Johann Rudolf Ahle still confirmed that a boy "first had to learn to sing and solmizate without the text" and then "underlay the text nicely and pronounce all the syllables properly."[13]

But there was a difference, of course, between boys and women producing such unfettered vocal sound. Any music performed by women—unruly voices issuing from abjected female bodies—harbored the threat of overstepping the boundaries of sanctioned text-based expressivity.[14] As Suzanne Cusick has suggested, in the teaching practice of Francesca Caccini it was especially songs in Latin that allowed an escape from the "culture of word-dominated song, to create songs that celebrate the music itself." Cusick contends that "in Latin, the language of spiritual and scholarly retreat," Caccini's female pupils could "practice extravagantly melismatic singing and call it ecstasy."[15] Although one might maintain that the melismatic elaborations in Francesca's or her father Giulio's monodies simply served to enhance their texts, the sonic outbursts at the end of the latter's *Amarilli, mia bella* arguably did more than emphasize the name of the beloved. They performed a syntactic function, not least, creating an effect of pre-cadential intensification and delayed gratification as the melisma shifted from the "i" of "Amarilli" to the more open and resonant "o" of the final word "amore" (fig. 3.2). If Susan McClary's reading of this tension-release pattern as a "wordless orgasm of sorts" seems rather vague, at least it aims to capture some of the potential bodily impact of that rush of air.[16] The breath and throat control required of a singer to deliver this final melisma could indeed have—pleasurably, perilously—increased the heat and tension in their own and their listeners' bodies.

Already Maffei had singled out "o" as the most suitable vowel for applying passaggi, while cautioning against "i," which produced the sound of a wailing baby animal, and "u," which generated the impression of a wolf howling.[17] More recently, in his discussion of early modern English soundscapes, Bruce Smith harnessed this power of the "O-factor" as a way to capture "all the things that make the voice strange: lungs, larynx, and tongue." In Smith's description, [o:] is "a burst of energy from within," an "act of aggression, a projection of one's body into the world."[18] His formulation reminds us that "pure sound," as a disembodied and/or meaningless entity, is, of course, a myth. The resonance of melisma remained as entwined with bodies as with signification, in shifting constellations that leaned variously toward the sonic, the semantic, or the carnal. As a wordless but word-carrying gesture, melisma could take listeners straight into that liminal space between materiality and signification, opening out any

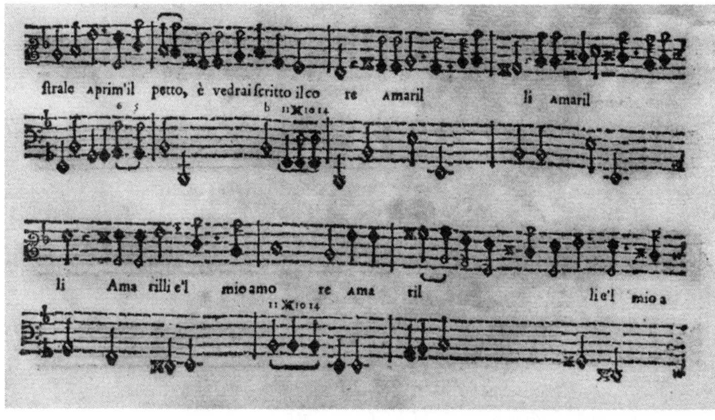

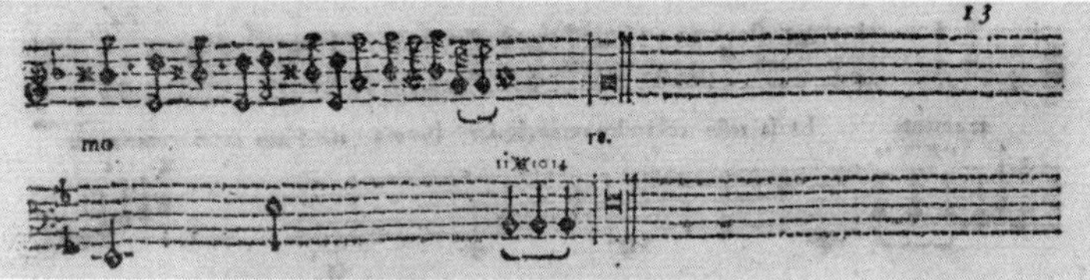

FIGURE 3.2. Giulio Caccini, *Amarilli, mia bella*, from *Le nuove musiche* (Florence: Marescotti, 1601), excerpt. Bayerische Staatsbibliothek München, 2 Mus.pr. 1347.

specific textual meaning into a more vaguely grasped "meaningfulness" or an unspecifiable yet keenly felt sensation.[19] This emerges in an early commentary on melismatic singing by the church father Augustine, in which he discussed the singing of the "jubilus," a melismatic extension attached to the alleluia chant: "One who jubilates does not speak words. It is rather a sort of sound of joy without words, since it is the voice of a soul poured out in joy."[20] Melisma, as a wordless emanation of joy, subsequently became the prototypical way of generating joyfulness in music: Cusick notes the "accumulating musical energy" of melisma "burst[ing] free of ordinary language" in Francesca Caccini's motet *Haec dies*, while the number of "Freude" melismas in Johann Sebastian Bach's cantata output is too large to enumerate here.[21] Again, such figurations could plausibly be heard as representational, easily decoded by listeners acquainted with the stylistic conventions. But "alleluia" passages in particular are striking for the way in which the word itself can seem on the verge of dissolving into sound, combining soft l's and a plethora of vowels in a manner that threatens to shade into lallation. The German composer Johannes Lindemann exploited this proximity in his 1595 contrafactum of a secular song by Giovanni Giacomo Gastoldi, easily transforming the vernacular nonsense word "falala" into "alleluia."[22]

Though the Gastoldi/Lindemann setting is in fact syllabic, perhaps Johann Sebastian Bach's organ prelude on Lindemann's hymn from a century later (*In dir ist Freude*, BWV 615) could be heard as a large-scale instrumental composing-out of that vocal outburst of joy. The organ, as the French writer Pierre de La Primaudaye noted, operated in close analogy to that bodily organ, the voice, as in both cases sound is produced by air flowing through a windpipe and past an apparatus that produces audible sound.[23] In melisma, vocal sound came closest to those wordless sounds emitted by the organ—each generating a flow of air carrying a potential for meaning that may be more or less realized in any specific performance or listening situation. In Ulf Norberg's 2015 rendering of BWV 615, the potential for a carnal expression of joyfulness afforded by the score is—to this listener—persuasively instantiated in an exquisitely calibrated interface of tempo, articulation, phrase shape, and animated bodily demeanor.[24] When looking at the score of a Bach cantata, likewise, an analyst might easily identify a group of notes above the word "Freude" as an obvious instance of word-painting and move on. But in its sung realization—the form in which most of Bach's congregants would have encountered this music—that pleasing cognitive insight may not have constituted the only or defining aspect of their listening responses. As Augustine had adumbrated, melismas did something beyond what words could do, and the verbal signifier "joy" fell short of encapsulating that unspecifiable extra. In one medieval formulation, the term to capture that effect was "pneumatize": "because the praise of eternal life will not resonate with human words, certain churches pneumatize the sequence mystically without words."[25] The ancient classical concept of pneuma (or "spiritus" in its Latin form), which retained its currency into the early modern period as a legacy of the Hippocratic tradition, did not solely denote the breath expelled in order to vocalize. Pneuma was an animating force, the locus or vehicle of soul. In melisma, what flowed was not just breath, but vital spirit; it was body and soul distilled in voice.

✴ 4 ✴
Quemadmodum desiderat cervus

How might we begin to trace the vital current that flowed between performers and listeners in any particular moment of performance? Our analytical methods have become very well honed to extract copious information from a few notes on the page; but so far they have not, on the whole, fully implemented Bonnie Gordon's call for the body becoming "the central unit of analysis."[1] Over the course of this book, I will attempt to move closer to that objective, by trying out different ways of engaging with scores less as "symbolic representations of affects" than as somatic scripts that inscribe the memory of and potential for a set of bodily actions and reactions from performers and listeners.[2] If melismas can be heard as a projection of the body into the world, I propose to treat pieces of music as melisma writ large, as extended sonic expressions and interactions of musicking body-souls. While I might not go as far as Daniel Leech-Wilkinson's claim that musical works exist solely in performance, since the histories and material traces of such performances tend to coalesce into ostensibly coherent shapes (or "works") that subsist apart from individual performed instances, these shapes need to be recognized as the fragile and easily transformed entities that they are.[3] Though the neat, authoritative appearance of modern-day printed scores seems designed to bestow fixity, most notated pieces of early modern music were "supersaturated" with the performance event.[4] Our sense today of the identity of a musical work arguably arises principally from its specific oral (and, more recently, recorded) history, made up of layers of remembered and forgotten performances that collectively determine its sonic identity. If much philosophical and analytical discourse over the past decades has assumed to be examining "the music" apart from the vicissitudes of individual performances and the bodies they involve, such an approach tends to rest on deep-seated assumptions about how it—the music—is meant to go. This shines through, for instance, in Jenefer Robinson's commentary on Henry Purcell's choral anthem *Hear my prayer, O Lord*, which she finds "most notable for the way in which it slowly increases in volume and intensity until the end."[5] Robinson's appraisal of the work's emotional effects is evidently based on a specific (if widely shared) performance tradition that enacts a particular expressive contour. There is no doubt that Purcell's score plausibly affords such a reading; but the realization of this potential only happens in situ when a group of singers employs their collective bodily-spiritual resources to that end.

Rather than privileging either score or performance to the detriment of the other, therefore, I propose to treat them as inevitably commingled and co-constitutive in acts of music-making: scores put bodies "into play."[6] I turn to Dietrich Buxtehude's chaconne aria *Quemadmodum desiderat cervus* (BuxWV 92) in a first attempt to tease out some of the forms of bodily-spiritual engagement afforded by this score. We do not know much about the specific performance situations in which this type of piece may have been heard in the late seventeenth century, but any listener's ears would have been struck first of all by a brief instrumental introduction, a descending bass motive whose ostinato repetitions would turn out to underpin the whole piece. When the voice enters, it almost immediately launches into an extended word-effacing melisma on the syllable "si" (ex. 4.1). For at least some listeners in Buxtehude's circles, the opening text may have been instantly recognizable as Psalm 42, though presented here with added passages from the soliloquia of Augustine. Strikingly, all references to negative emotions of "tristitia" or tribulation are excised in Buxtehude's version, narrowing the textual "scopus" to a sense of longing for the sweetness of God's grace—unlike, say, Heinrich Schütz's setting of the same text (SWV 336), whose opening section is saturated with grating chromatic imitation that sounds particularly bittersweet in the beautifully cultivated rendering by the Choir of New College, Oxford.[7] That opening melisma in Buxtehude's work, in an inspired performance by Marc Mauillon of 2015, spills luxuriantly over the two-measure unit of the continuo bass, though in this first iteration it still joins in decorously with the bass's next cadential arrival back on F.[8] The musical phrase is complete, in other words, though the textual phrase is not: leaving the first half of the sentence ("As the hart desires") hanging, the two violins present a wordless extension of the melisma, the sonic residue of a (semi-)meaningful vocal utterance. The notation then prompts the singer to take a bigger breath in order to repeat the opening phrase in amplified form, with the melisma expanded by a half measure. If the intensity of desire may seem to be growing as a result, this sense of longing, as it spreads between Mauillon's own body and those of his co-performers and listeners, seems only loosely attached, at best, to the specific textual image of the thirsting hart.

EXAMPLE 4.1. Dietrich Buxtehude, *Quemadmodum desiderat cervus* (BuxWV 92), mm. 1–7.

As the ensemble moves into the following phrase, that free-flowing breath is problematized. The closely spaced rests between repetitions of "ita" and "ad te," filled by the instruments, afford alternative ways of sonic realization, with differing corporeal implications (ex. 4.2). Contemporary singing primers agreed on the function of rests to demarcate syntactic units of text and music, and to allow performers to take a breath—hence their common designation as "suspirium" or "soupir." As the Berlin musician Martin Heinrich Fuhrmann explained, rests existed "so that singers can breathe, and instrumentalists, especially wind players, can periodically refresh themselves, for continuous singing, bowing and blowing would exhaust the musicians too much."[9] And, according to Giulio Caccini, a singer's breath was intimately tied to expressivity, as respiration control was necessary "to give greater spirit to the increasing and diminishing of the voice, to exclamations and all the other passions."[10] If a singer actually took up Buxtehude's invitation to catch a top-up breath in each of these gaps, the effect would be one of overexcited hyperventilation, counteracting the cooling effect of the breath on the inner organs and further unsettling the body's equilibrium. Mauillon instead opts to smooth over the gaps to maintain an overall sense of mellifluous ease. Yet the notation

EXAMPLE 4.2. Buxtehude, *Quemadmodum desiderat cervus*, mm. 19–25.

prompts a further rise in intensity, in reaching up to g in this melisma on "desiderat," which pushes the singer's voice to exceed the vocal compass circumscribed by the mode and voice part (middle C to f1). And then the "o" of "o fons" arrives, that primal sonic gesture charged with potential meaningfulness (surprise, sadness, sympathy, joy, depending on how it is uttered) (ex. 4.3). The musical figuration here will take on its particular affective shade depending on how it materializes in a singer's mouth, becoming "legible" principally in a gestural, embodied way, especially as the interspersed sixteenth-note rests cut the sound loose from any surrounding meaning-giving phonemes. The prominent e-flat inflections in the vocal line, meanwhile, would have drawn a singer and their vocal flow into the "mollis" (flat and soft) region of the tonal spectrum, bestowing additional mellowing qualities to the sonic outpouring. A carnally attuned hearing of this passage might posit that an acculturated listener thereby encountered not only a sonic representation of the sweet waters referenced in the text, but an embodied experience of this grace-bestowing flow—a tangible instantiation of that which the text can only formulate conceptually as a desire.

In other moments, Buxtehude's early modern listeners may have begun to feel thirsty. The singer's multiple iterations of "sitivit" (thirsteth) and, later, "sitio" (I thirst) also threaten to rob those words of their sense,

EXAMPLE 4.3. Buxtehude, *Quemadmodum desiderat cervus*, mm. 39–45.

EXAMPLE 4.4. Buxtehude, *Quemadmodum desiderat cervus*, mm. 60–63.

dissolving them into a series of closely spaced "s"s and "t"s punctuating a persistent "i" sound (ex. 4.4). Their pronunciation would potentially have varied across different performance locales, but in any variation these chains of consonants not only disrupted the flow of vowel-borne melismatic air, but could generate a physical sensation of dryness from the friction produced between the tongue and the roof of the mouth. This connection between moisture levels and vocal production is pinpointed, for instance, in Athanasius Kircher's mid-seventeenth-century taxonomy of voice types and their dry or wet qualities, as well as in recent research showing that languages in drier climates tend to use fewer vowel sounds, owing to the effects of dry air on phonation.[11] Paying attention to what Susan Melrose has called "the bite and taste of the words in the mouth" in this way can help open up the physical, sensory dimensions of these musicking acts, as articulated in Bertrand Bénigne de Bacilly's 1688 instructions on vowel formation involving different shapes of the mouth and throat.[12] In Buxtehude's piece, as the subsequent reiterations of "sitio" accentuate more explicitly the dotted rhythm inherent in the word, they could begin to stir a skipping joyfulness, pushing those performing or listening body-souls toward the affective state of "gaudium" afforded in the final section of the piece (ex. 4.6). Once Maullion has negotiated the quick-fire declamation of measure 97, maintaining control over his tongue and jaw and finding a place to breathe (not a mean feat at his chosen tempo), he can launch into those concluding melismas that once again carry him beyond the modal ambitus to his top g, interspersed with numerous giddy reiterations of "gaudium," before just about winding down the accumulated energy in the final moments of the piece. The prominent "circulatio" figures in these closing melismas might, of course, have been intended or heard as a sonic representation of waters flowing (ex. 4.5). But the figure also constituted one of the primary "passaggi," the so-called "groppo," enabling an ultimately senseless display of vocal prowess. In the context of contemporary Lutheran theology, such a musical outburst had the capacity to move beyond a representational function toward offering an actual foretaste of those eternal heavenly "alleluias," enabling an ecstatic form of sonic immersion that Veit Erlmann has called a "folie de l'écoute."[13] In Maullion's rendering, even the continuo players, whose parts instructed them to repeat the same two-measure phrase no fewer than 64 times, seem swept up in this large-scale sonic-affective surge.

Numerous luxuriating "o"s reverberated across seventeenth-century vocal music, each affording subtly different modes of corporeal-spiritual immersion. The English actor-singer Anne Bracegirdle's enactment of love gone mad in John Eccles's play *Cyrus the Great* begins with a string of "o"s interrupted by rests that set the tone for an erratic musical outpouring beyond sense or reason. The published version, though claimed to have been "exactly Engrav'd" by the printer, most likely did not capture precisely what and how she sang to produce those primal nonsensical sounds, which Amanda Eubanks Winkler has described as a kind of creativity of the body (fig. 4.1).[14] In Alessandro Grandi's setting of "O quam tu pulchra es," that classic song of spiritual-erotic desire (published in 1625), listeners encountered an opening "o" sound fixed in place as the accompanying

EXAMPLE 4.5. Buxtehude, *Quemadmodum desiderat cervus*, mm. 107–111.

FIGURE 4.1. John Eccles, *Oh, take him gently from the Pile* (England: Cross, 1697), excerpt. © British Library Board, Music Collections K.7.i.2.(42.). Image produced by ProQuest as part of Early English Books Online. www.proquest.com. Image published with permission of ProQuest. Further reproduction is prohibited without permission.

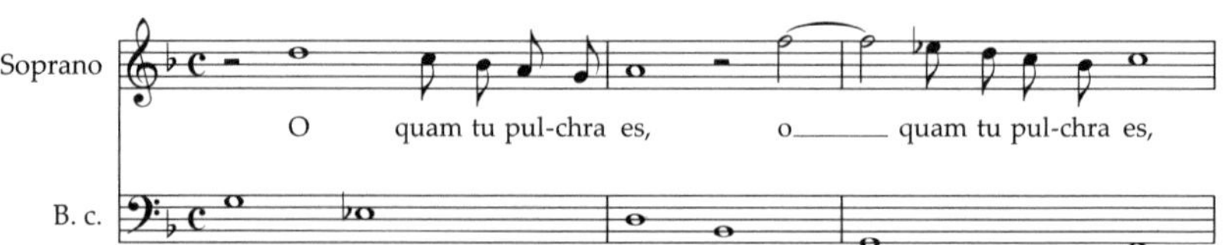

EXAMPLE 4.6. Alessandro Grandi, *O quam tu pulchra es,* from *Ghirlanda Sacra* (Venice: Gardano, 1625), mm. 1–3.

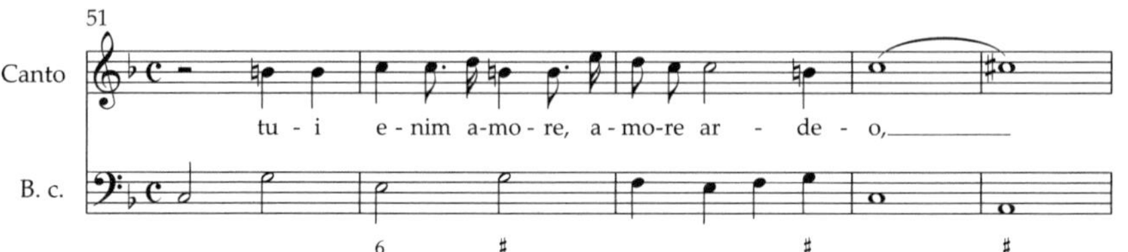

EXAMPLE 4.7. Stefano Bernardi, *O dulcissima,* from *Seconda raccolta de' sacri canti* (Venice: Vincenti, 1624), mm. 51–55.

EXAMPLE 4.8. Bernardi, *O dulcissima,* mm. 42–47.

chord progression rendered it first consonant, then acutely dissonant, allowing a singer to explore the changing feel of the open mouth as it dwelled in these contrasting environments (ex. 4.6). If the initial "o" of Stefano Bernardi's *O dulcissima* (1624) was less harmonically adventurous, the striking upward chromatic shift on the last syllable of "arde-o" later in the piece made up for it, affording performers and listeners an intensely dislocating experience as sense was allowed to drift away as sound (ex. 4.7). Meanwhile, the extended "o" melisma in measures 44–47 of the piece, hijacking the final sound of "erg-o" (ex. 4.8), to this listener encapsulates the way in which melisma can be heard as, in the best sense of the word, gratuitous: not just in such extreme cases as the infamous vocal roulade on the article "la" in Seneca's aria from Monteverdi's opera *Poppea* (1643), which Wendy Heller finds "meaningless," but in each instance offering a moment of excess noise, of sound doubling back on itself.[15] Yet where Heller's commentary once more seems to invoke a binary of sound versus meaning, I would contend that any such sonic excess still retained the capacity for the production of meaning, whether corporeally or cognitively routed. In Victor Zuckerkandl's words, reflecting on the process of turning words into song, "for the singer, words acquire a very special plenitude and depth of meaning. Something that remains silent in words merely spoken begins to flow, to vibrate; the words open and the singer opens to them."[16] In any specific performance and its listening reception, both sound as sensory stimulation and sound as a source of meaningfulness might have operated in more or less conjoined fashion. Those moments when only a "sort-of-meaning" might be emergent—arising from what neuropsychologist Stefan Koelsch has called music's "musicogenic meaning quality"—remain difficult to capture in words, not to mention in precise analytical terms.[17] Yet my sense is that we can only begin to appreciate the potential richness of these historical musicking experiences if we endeavor to grapple with exactly those liminal moments.

5
Representation

Music's capacity for representation may best be figured as a case of both/and. In the context of early modern stylistic and performance conventions, a piece or passage of music could be heard as representing something (an image, action, or emotion) and, simultaneously or alternatively, be experienced as a moment of nonrepresentational sonic stimulation. Such a non-representational sonic encounter would not necessarily have been perceived as meaning-less, however. Where Charles Nussbaum asserts that nothing "means anything unless and until it is pressed into representational service by an interpreter," I would caution that such a narrow definition of the meaningful can end up excluding those curious moments of "emergent" meaning that early modern acts of musicking seem to have been so adept at conjuring.[1] Any sonic utterance, such as a vocal melisma, may well have remained representationally opaque vis-à-vis an interpreter, and yet have done something to or for them that felt distinctly meaningful. These moments of emergent meaning can form a starting point for reconsidering the foundational role of representation in Western modernity's view of the world. In the familiar Foucauldian narrative, it was around the beginning of the seventeenth century that the Renaissance episteme of "resemblance" was replaced by a modern episteme of "representation." For Foucault, this arrival of the representational paradigm cast asunder the pre-modern seamless interconnection of the micro- and macro-structures of the cosmos. The notion that Western modernity was constituted through a process of irreversible divisions—splitting body from mind, humanity from God, music from language, and so on—has been reiterated numerous times. Hence Mauro Calcagno proposed that music's capacity for "overvocalization," as in the extensive "la" melisma intoned by Seneca in Monteverdi's *Poppea*, arose as the result of a primal split between signifier and signified. As language became detached from the reality it related to, Calcagno argues, this enabled a "legitimization of sound in itself."[2] Gary Tomlinson has identified far-reaching implications of this schism for early modern singing practices: in his account, voice and spirit, reconfigured as matter, were no longer insolubly joined to the immaterial realm of soul, but only corresponded to and with it by means of an inexplicable predetermined harmony. The early modern voice, as a result, "conveys a dualistic subjectivity in which it does not touch the soul"; its materiality, wrote Tomlinson, "will not permit it to cross the Cartesian divide."[3]

Critiques of the ideology of representation have multiplied in recent decades, perhaps most radically from the new materialist perspectives of, say, Jane Bennett or Christoph Cox. Hence Cox asserts that the sonic "eludes analysis in terms of representation and signification"; he proposes to go "below" the level of representation in order to access the "perceptible plenitude of matter."[4] Rather than getting caught up in centuries-old philosophical debates pitting realists against idealists, I propose here to assess the issue in specific historical terms: Did the schism that Tomlinson and others have detected in musical thought and practice around 1600 indeed take place in the cataclysmic way in which it has often been portrayed? The term "representation" did have some currency in seventeenth-century musical discourse, in particular in the "stile rappresentativo" designation first recorded on the title page of Giulio Caccini's *Euridice* (1600). Although in the 1630s the Italian theorist Giovanni Battista Doni tried to delimit the term as applicable only to stage music, it was also used in relation to other genres, such as madrigals or sacred concertos, referring broadly to "music that (re)presents a text in a particularly dramatic or emotional way."[5] But these instances appear to confine the term to a rather more specific context than the fundamental paradigm shift referenced by Tomlinson. In order to avoid an indiscriminate blending of these nested notions of representation, it seems crucial to disentangle some of the different levels at which representation operated, and to assess how music was implicated in each; not as a means of establishing conclusively whether music was indeed (heard as) representational or not, but in order to gain a better sense of the possible modes of interplay between sound and meaning in these historical acts of musicking.

Most fundamentally, perhaps, in the Cartesian worldview invoked by Tomlinson, representation referred to the mechanism by which the human mind or soul related to the outer world. This outer reality, in Descartes's conception, was represented via the sense organs of the body to the mind, which remained separate from both body and world. Verbal language came to form part of this broader system of representation, which was seen to determine the very structure of human experience in and of the world, including any experience of music-making. As the rationalist philosopher Christian Wolff put it, the human soul was defined by the "power to represent the world to itself."[6] Current neurophysiological explanations of the human faculty of hearing invoke another version of this representational process, in the translation of mechanical vibration into electrical signals along the basilar membrane of the ear, to be decoded by the brain. It is worth recalling, however, that Descartes's model was neither wholly unprecedented, nor was it unanimously adopted by others at the time. Many pre-modern conceptions of human nature, from Plato to the Christian tradition, harbored their own dualist tendencies that split mind (or soul) from body and the rest of the material world; though not all relied on representation as the mediating mechanism. Various modern-day commentators have questioned, therefore, the supposed "great epistemic upheaval that divides Shakespeare from Descartes."[7] Of Descartes's contemporaries, meanwhile, such influential figures as Gottfried Wilhelm Leibniz, Baruch Spinoza, or Claude Perrault all resisted his model in different ways. Though many early modern writers did end up subscribing to a fundamentally mechanistic view of human nature and the universe, Descartes's theory of representation put an improbable burden on the small pineal gland at the back of the brain to communicate external realities in all their detail and texture to the immaterial mind. Moreover, Descartes himself, not surprisingly, failed to be consistent over a lifetime of evolving philosophical activity: in his early music treatise, for instance, the locus of not just sensation but judgment often still appears to be the ear. Phrases such as "in the end or close of each Tune, the eares be so fully satisfied, as they expect no more," may not denote an unintentional foreshortening of the cognitive process, but indicate that Descartes indeed "began his philosophical career in the body."[8]

One of the challenges pursued in this book, then, would be to think and feel oneself into an early modern not-yet or not-quite Cartesian mindset.[9] The notion of a fundamental rupture around 1600 carries the danger of assessing the musical practices of this period in terms of a system that by all accounts remained either hotly contested or broadly irrelevant for much of the following century. As John Cottingham has attested, "[Descartes's] attempts to demonstrate the distinctness of soul from body were widely rejected as invalid even in his own day."[10] Other commentators agree that the Cartesian invention of Western disembodied rationality only stabilized as the philosopher's key legacy around the mid-eighteenth century. A retro-projection of this legacy onto musicking practices across the long seventeenth century risks tuning out modes of composing, performing, and listening that operated against or outside any emerging dualist certainties. The resulting monochromatic readings of these musical repertories as primarily representational in intent or effect confirm Mary Ann Smart's suspicion that an approach couched too comfortably in Tomlinson's panoptic framework can "flatten out the most interesting features of musical works into mere instances of some broad historical condition."[11] Even more, such readings end up obscuring the possibility that these early modern acts of musicking could have actively disrupted any neat partitioning of mind and body/world, in ways that, arguably, music continued to do throughout the subsequent period of European modernity. Perhaps, in the history of Western music-making, the Cartesian moment never fully arrived: perhaps magical incantations never quite lost their power.

Certain present-day scientific trends can be brought into productive dialogue with these historical routes of inquiry.[12] If the cognitive sciences have traditionally treated the mind as a computational system, recent models of human cognition as embodied and ecologically embedded have posed certain fundamental challenges to this approach. As Eric Clarke has discussed, the standard information-processing account of cognition "relies very heavily on the idea of mental representations," yet "the nature and existence of these representations is purely conjectural." Additionally, Clarke points out, they tend to be "disembodied and abstract, as if perception was a kind of reasoning or problem-solving process." In Clarke's alternative account, the sounds emitted when, say, a piece of hollow wood is struck are "a direct consequence of the physical properties of the wood itself"; they are an "imprint" of its physical structure. An organism, Clarke posits, "does not have to do complex processing to 'decode' the information within the source: it needs to have a perceptual system that will *resonate* to the information." Clarke concludes that "the construction of musical meaning through language and other forms of representation is undeniable, but it does not proceed independently of the affordances of musical materials."[13] In the context of early modern music-making, Clarke's account invites us to reconsider any meaning-making processes as always inseparably entangled with music's material, corporeal, affective affordances.

In a narrower sense, musical representation has commonly been figured as a type of mimesis, underpinning the early modern notion of art as a "reasoned imitation of nature."[14] Going back to Aristotle's description of tragedy as "mimesis of an action" in the real world, this idea was invoked in Claudio Monteverdi's search for a "natural manner of imitation" of the words; a century later, it was recapped by the Hamburg writer Johann Mattheson under the heading of "locus descriptionis," denoting the imitation of extramusical concepts as an aid to compositional invention.[15] Although in one letter Monteverdi famously complained about the impossibility of translating certain concepts—such as the wind—into music, in this sense his musical aesthetics might indeed be characterized as straightforwardly representational.[16] In a theatrical context, in particular, these layers of representation quickly tended to multiply, as an operatic plot might imitate a real-life occurrence, an opera singer represented a character in the plot, and the music re-presented the verbal content of their utterances. The English theorist Roger North hence famously called music "a true pantomime or resemblance of humanity in all its states, actions, passions and affections," with the power of putting a listener "into the like condition, as if the state represented were his owne." Unlike Monteverdi, North found the winds easily portrayed through the vocal technique of "messa di voce," as "the swelling and dying of musical notes . . . wonderfully represents the waiving of air, and pleasant gales moving, and sinking away."[17]

Yet while these various layers of representation were clearly operative in, say, a seventeenth-century operatic performance, music's sonic presence could at the same time complicate or override them: even Mattheson agreed that music should not merely "imitate or mimic" human nature and actions, but "rectify and improve them."[18] If, as Erin Sullivan has argued, art had the power to be world-creating rather than just world-reflecting, there may well have been more to an early modern operatic experience than a perceived re-presentation of an external reality.[19] As I hope to show repeatedly in these pages, in the moment of performance music could produce effects on acculturated listeners' ears, internal organs, nervous system, and spiritual disposition that did not require mediation through a cognitive system of representation. This was not solely a matter of suspended disbelief as, say, Virginia Ramponi Andreini strode on stage pretending to be Arianna, but more broadly of music's capacity as material vibration to circumvent, undercut, or interfere with any assumed representational process. As Holly Watkins has posited with reference to Peircean semiotics, music "does not submit willingly" to such semiotic systems; rather, it persistently seems to critique them from within.[20] We might single out, with Tim Carter, the early modern convention of conveying the affect of love through a choice of triple meter—"scarcely a plausible mimetic gesture," Carter points out—as one way in which music generated its own, twisted strategies of producing meaning.[21] For, in addition to signifying a particular concept or feeling, these metric manipulations would also have had the potential to affect a habituated listener's body-soul more immediately than via a system of decoding conventional signs.[22] Even if representation was (and is) deeply woven into the fabric of everyday human experience—as Michael Taussig has put it, "we know in our heart of hearts that the way we picture and talk is bound to a dense set of representational gimmicks"—acts of making and hearing music could reveal and outstrip the limits of these Cartesian modes of picturing, talking, and being.[23]

✷ 6 ✷

Music

"Musica est ars bene canendi" (music is the art of singing well): thus ran one of the commonplace definitions of music in sixteenth- and seventeenth-century European writings. In different variations, it featured especially in teaching primers, ranging from Nikolaus Listenius (1533) and William Barley (1596) to Georg Falck (1688); and in dictionary definitions, such as Christian Ludovici's 1706 English-German-French dictionary, whose entry on "Music" reads "singekunst, the art of singing or playing on musical instruments."[1] Other writers instead adopted versions of the Augustinian formulation "music est scientia bene modulandi," for instance the Lutheran cantor Michael Altenburg in his manuscript treatise *De musica*, which defined music as "an art of modulating well"; or the English writer Charles Butler in his *Principles of Musik* (1636): "Musik is the Art of modulating Notes in voice or instrument."[2] All these definitions marked music out as an activity, their gerund forms chiming with the "musick-ing" preoccupations of much current thinking about music.[3] By presenting that which a singer or instrumentalist did as the essence of what music was, they emphasized the performative moment, the act of making rather than what was made. They contrasted with those contemporaneous approaches in the Pythagorean tradition that considered music a mathematical construct, taking as their object of contemplation the sounds produced through performative action or imagined in abstract number play. This tradition, transmitted via Boethius and Gioseffo Zarlino, reached at least up to the German theorist Andreas Werckmeister, who in 1687 affirmed that music was a mathematical science that dealt with sounding number.[4] Throughout the long seventeenth century, this perspective also shaped the experimental tradition extending from Vincenzo Galilei to Francis Bacon, Marin Mersenne and Jean-Philippe Rameau, all of whom helped consolidate the notion of music as an empirically grounded investigation of sound: Music, wrote Rameau, "is the science of sounds; therefore sound is the principal subject of music."[5]

This conceptual split between music as performative act versus music as sounding number or object was captured to some degree in the traditional categories of "musica practica" and "musica theorica": in Pablo Nassare's music treatise of 1700, "theorica" is identified as "all those things pertaining to the speculation of the mind," whereas "practica" comprised "all that which is executed with one or more body parts, such as singing or playing instruments."[6] In German seventeenth-century writings, "musica poetica" had been introduced as an intermediary third term: on the one hand, it chimed with the concerns of "musica practica" by emphasizing the activity of making, yet, on the other, it arguably laid the foundation for the modern-day preoccupation with the musical opus as the product of this act of making. Nonetheless, the opposition between "practica" and "theorica" ended up shaping some of the fundamental binaries that still structure current debates about the nature of Western art music: one view regarding music as text, gnostic, of the mind, signifying; the other, re-embraced more recently, considering music as act, drastic, of the body, pre-significatory. As Linda Phyllis Austern has put it, "Western thinkers have traditionally positioned music somewhere in the shifting space between mathematical abstraction and corporeality, between reasoned creation and emotive response."[7] But if her formulation might imply that the two poles of this spectrum were neutral, value-free places to occupy, this masks a long-standing historical bias that valued one side over the other. This hierarchy underpins Athanasius Kircher's definition of the "musicus theoricus" as one who "judges and evaluates everything that can occur in harmonic music just with the intellect," whereas the "practicus" "relies exclusively on their sense of hearing."[8] Following Boethius, Kircher portrayed the former as superior to the latter, an evaluation that resonates with the dominance of the "music as text" paradigm in Western modernity. His views corroborate Austern's characterization of sound in the modern imagination as a "disembodied emanation": as sound exits the bodies of singers or instrumentalists, it "leaves their materiality and concentrated localization behind."[9] Yet, thinking back to that sonnet about Arianna's hands squeezing her listeners' souls, it appears that musical sound could also very much carry elements of that materiality with it. Only if imagined as cut off from the bodies of those producing and receiving it could music morph into the body- and odorless vehicle of meaning that it became in later constructions of the musical Baroque.

I do not wish to suggest that, in counteracting this tendency, we should rush to embrace Carolyn Abbate's much critiqued notion of the "drastic," which, at her own admission, might prevent us from articulating much beyond statements like "doing this really fast is fun" or "here comes a big jump."[10] As Karol Berger has pointed out, even in the heat of the performative moment there is no such thing as pure carnal experience: "We are hermeneutic creatures through and through."[11] Abbate's programmatic binary of drastic and gnostic conceals the fact that any "drastic" response by a performer or listener would already have been shaped by their acquired habitus, their bodily-mental dispositions as determined by their cultural-historical environment. Not only do the "material presence and carnality" sought by Abbate have histories, but those histories enfold the gnostic, the meaningful, within them, be that in the knowing fingers of an early modern keyboardist or in those female listening bodies that produced tears when they should. Nonetheless, Abbate was right to point out that in our "rush to metaphysical signifieds," the physical, sensual, embodied dimensions of musicking have tended to be pushed aside. Many early modern musical repertories, in particular, have extended a strong hermeneutic invitation to modern-day analysts, still in thrall, one might say, to that fear of "senseless" music articulated in Fontenelle's famous rejection of the instrumental sonata. That fear, as John Hamilton has argued, arises in response to music's physical force beyond rational control: the "indomitable potency" of music left free to "exert its violence" on a listener.[12]

In its suspicion of the carnal, the hermeneutic approach condemned by Abbate epitomizes the disembodied nature of Western aesthetics since Immanuel Kant. Even if Alexander Baumgarten's initial formulation of aesthetics attended to people's sensory interaction with the world—as Terry Eagleton affirmed, aesthetics was indeed "born as a discourse of the body"—Kant's reinterpretation shifted the emphasis to the detached contemplation of artistic objects.[13] Bolstered by the mimetic theory of art advocated by Christian Wolff and Charles Batteux, this enshrined a notion of the aesthetic as "an objectifying act of consciousness."[14] The perception that music, in Kantian terms, was merely an "inoffensive pleasure of the senses" was grounded in the notion of a transcendental subjectivity that left little room for acknowledging the bodily moorings of such a subject, or for music developing active agency in shaping experiences of the self. Kant's dismissal of music as a trivial source of sensory pleasure was of course turned on its head soon after with the emergence of the idea of "absolute music" after 1800; but by that point the art form had been effectively transposed into that metaphysical realm, in which the material realities of the body had little traction. In the wake of persistent critiques of the Kantian paradigm from Eagleton to feminist critics, current aesthetic theories have again become more body-conscious, often drawing on

Maurice Merleau-Ponty's alternative vision of aesthetics as an embodied way of knowing.[15] Yet this historical removal of bodies is still immediately apparent in Western concertgoing etiquette as it evolved right around the time of the consolidation of Kantian aesthetics: neat rows of musicians dressed in body-veiling black, facing neat rows of immobile listeners trying to suppress their bodily urges as much as possible. The body-effacing strategies at work here are made explicit in a 2020 statement issued by the Cambridge-based music society Camerata Musica in connection with a high-profile concert series at Peterhouse College: "Because of the small size and exceptionally clear acoustic of the concert hall, any noise made by a member of the audience is highly disruptive to the artists' concentration and to that of the rest of the audience. Any member of the audience suffering from a cold or from any other malady likely to cause coughing is requested to return their tickets and not to attend the concert."[16]

Ideally, it seems, listeners would not be there with their noisy, spluttering bodies at all, but would attend as disembodied minds, perfectly still and mute in meeting that disembodied emanation of sound. Both the individual consumption of music through headphones and the remote listening protocols that emerged during the Covid-19 pandemic of 2020 and beyond might be regarded as close-to-ideal instantiations of this conception of music as a metaphysical transaction.

There is, of course, a much longer, pre-Kantian history of suspicion toward the (musicking) body, reaching from Plato's awareness of music's dangerous affective potential to the Christian fear of the sinful desires of the flesh. These suspicions spawned a range of containment strategies over the course of Western music history, from Renaissance theories of music as abstract harmonious proportion and seventeenth-century music-rhetorical systems to Antonio Vivaldi's Venetian nuns performing behind grates and Romantic ideologies of musical transcendence. Yet in a parallel history, one might see the body continually reasserting its vital presence: in those spiritual practices of medieval mystics traced by Bruce Holsinger, say, or in James Davies's exploration of how nineteenth-century musical virtuosity "acted in the cultivation of bodies."[17] As Deniz Peters has argued with respect to electronic music, even the most seemingly disembodied forms of music-making necessarily implicate the body, which appears "via extension in listening activated by bodily knowledge all listeners have acquired during a lifetime experience of everyday touch-sound relationships."[18] Yet it was across the long seventeenth century in particular, at a time when new models of composing, performing, and listening aimed to recuperate those mythical powers of ancient music, that bodies and their physiologies became a prime locus for enacting and explaining music's capacities to move. In this sense, certain early modern musical practices offer an especially revealing window onto music's corporeal dimensions, before they became more concealed in later aesthetic discourse.

An approach that aims to recapture these historical modes of musicking will therefore need to take seriously the notion of music as bodily doing prior to its consolidation into a set of display pieces in an imaginary museum. Yet if early modern music was widely figured as action, it was in the form of the sounding matter produced through that action that it could "flow into ears and hearts."[19] Not all of it flowed as effervescently as the "champagne" of French recitative, perhaps; but it was when musical sounds "flooded" Augustine's ears or "flowed" as Matthesonian melody that they could unfold their remarkable effects on a not-quite-Cartesian body-soul.[20] In accounting for early modern music's capacity to act as a catalyst for psycho-physiological change, then, we may do well to avoid positioning it exclusively as either action or object, and instead imagine it as a kind of vital matter emanating from and infiltrating performing and listening bodies. If this intermediate conception ultimately rendered music difficult to contain—"unsearchable, Divine and Excellent," in John Playford's apt precis—it also holds the promise now of offering certain unique insights into the nature of these early modern body-souls.[21]

✵ 7 ✵
Bodies

A man is a substance, but if you dissect him, what is he? Head, heart, stomach, veins, each vein, each bit of vein, blood, each humor of blood?

BLAISE PASCAL[1]

How can we gain a more textured, tangible sense of what these early modern musicking bodies were, how they felt, how music operated within and upon them? Suzanne Cusick's hard-won insight in 1994 that music is "an art which self-evidently does not exist until bodies make it and/or receive it" came on the back of a resurgence of scholarly interest in the body from feminist, anthropological, and literary perspectives.[2] This cross-disciplinary engagement with bodies has arguably been especially productive with regard to the early modern period, given its inclination to propose bodily explanations for phenomena that might now be regarded as "of the mind."[3] Hence Gail Kern Paster explored the "agency, purposiveness and plenitude" of the early modern body as a site of gender construction; Jonathan Sawday probed the cultural politics of Renaissance anatomical dissection; and many more recent contributions have rethought the body in the context of early modern reading practices, illness narratives, image theory, or Reformation theology.[4] The concurrent wave of interest in the history of the emotions and the senses has further contributed to the development of increasingly holistic approaches, charting the diverse manifestations that the seemingly "basic and intimate reality" of the body has produced in different times, places, and contexts.[5] The resulting portraits of early modern corporeality have often been compellingly vivid, aspiring to recreate a sense of "what passions of many sorts might have felt like in a penetrable body containing wriggling animal spirits."[6] And yet the body has a vexing tendency to absent itself. As Sarah Coakley has asked with some exasperation, "why, then, are 'bodies' simultaneously so ubiquitous and yet so hard to get our 'hands' around?" Her answer posits that any conception of what "the body" might be is always already ideologically freighted: in materialist philosophy, the body may be "everything else except the brain"; in Freudian or Foucauldian accounts of sexuality it "becomes the site of either forbidden or condoned pleasures," and so on.[7] At least some of the literature just cited has shared a focus on the "semiotic body" as a locus where discourses of power and identity were inscribed, engendering a continuous deferral of "embodiment" to the level of hermeneutics.[8]

While acknowledging the necessarily mediating quality of language in capturing any felt experience, I would venture that a focus on early modern musicking practices can aid in bridging this gulf between bodily praxis and discourse: not through a naïve quest to recreate past experiential realities, but through a somatically attuned reconstruction of certain historical parameters that delineated different possible modes of experiencing and using the body. Musicking involved distinct forms and habits of sensing, feeling, and moving that can not only help us reimagine these bodies as material-spiritual entities, but which posed persistent challenges to any straightforwardly dualist and/or mechanistic conceptions of human nature. There is room, in other words, to "flesh out" David Yearsley's astute account of Johann Sebastian Bach's organ-playing feet and hands, in which those limbs can still seem more like those of a Cartesian mechanical contraption.[9] We need a better sense, I feel, of bodies animated by those "wriggling" spirits, as hinted at in Cusick's analysis of Bach's organ prelude BWV 686 from his *Clavierübung III*. Cusick suggests that the most challenging moment in the piece, in which an organist might have found themselves physically thrown off balance, marked the (inaudible) moment at which grace was conferred on the performer.[10] Her reading can be grounded in the continued relevance in Bach's time of the biblical story of the prophet Elijah, transmitted through Luther and the eighteenth-century pastor Christoph Raupach, in which Elijah asked to have a "Spielmann" brought to him for inspiration. According to the scriptural account, it was only when "the hand of God" came upon the musician—which, as Raupach clarified, meant the Holy Spirit—that his newly en-spirited performance allowed Elijah to prophesy, by "cleansing and freeing his soul" from all unrest and sadness adhering to it.[11]

But if Cusick's analysis was alert to spirit, her imagined performing bodies remained largely unhistoricized. How could an early eighteenth-century organist's body-soul find itself suddenly full of spirit? If the vast and growing literature on early modern bodies has confirmed one thing, it is that these bodies were fundamentally different entities from the autonomous, scientifically charted body of Western modernity. As Elisabeth Le Guin has argued, one can no doubt identify certain basic commonalities of response, such as jerking away from an unexpected pin prick; but any individual experience of such a sensation is subject to historical fluctuation.[12] I would add that one may well profitably draw on, say, current neuropsychological research to elucidate some of early modern music's kinesthetic affective force. If these past acts of music-making could perceptibly alter the bodily disposition of its participants, this notion is bolstered by the "mimetic hypothesis" in current cognitive discourse, which posits that certain motor actions executed by performers are replicated in a listener's neural networks.[13] As a singer's throat tightens when they reach for higher notes, a listener may experience this tightening sensation vicariously, generating increased tension in their own bodies. In conjunction, these historical and scientific perspectives throw serious doubt on the Cartesian conception of a disembodied mind inhabiting an impassive body. As the German physician Christian Friedrich Richter affirmed in a 1705 anatomical treatise, the body had its own ways of knowing unconnected to rational cognition, enabled by "those nerves inside the body through which nature attains knowledge of that which has entered the body."[14] Richter's assertion chimes, too, with a directive by the twentieth-century Polish theater director Jerzy Grotowski for his actors to "think, but with the body, logically, with precision and responsibility. You must think with the whole body by means of actions."[15] If taken literally, Grotowksi's formulation can stand as a compelling portrayal of how an early modern body may have been understood and felt to operate.

Yet these suggestive convergences should not distract us from the need to adjust many of our current bodily habits and assumptions in order to get behind or inside the ears and bodies of early modern performers or listeners. One might certainly argue that the rapid scientific advances over the course of the seventeenth century, coupled with the intensification of European colonial encounters and anxieties, helped produce many of the defining narratives of Western rationality, subjectivity, and bodiliness. The mounting pressures of radical empiricism and colonial otherness rendered the European body and its habits fundamentally problematic, thereby shaping the conditions for the invention of Western reason and its associated mechanisms of corporeal and mental discipline.[16] Yet a teleological reading that regards the early modern body simply as a staging post en route to the emergence of the white bourgeois European self risks overlooking those bodily (and musical) practices that disrupted or exceeded these incipient ideological certainties. Commentators across the period continually grappled with music's capacities to affect bodies, minds, and spirits in ways that eluded rational control, as in the German physician Michael Ernst Ettmüller's description in 1714 of the effects of hymn singing: "Hymns have their singular sweetness, out of the pleasing harmony of numbers and also the melody, so that they are not only sung with the greatest pleasure and delectation, but also penetrate miraculously into the souls and hearts of listeners, and inflame feelings of true piety, elation, and ardent joy in the breast."[17] His account not only reaffirmed music's powers as a body- and mind-bending force, but reminds us that those body-souls existed within—and indeed embodied—a moral and religious framework of sin and grace whose foundational relevance became obscured in the (ostensibly) secularized body of later modernity.

In order to reimagine how an early modern performer or auditor may have experienced the interaction between musical sounds and the ear, the heart, the bodily fluids, the imagination, and the rational soul; or how music's power to envelop every fiber of one's being operated in situ, we need a fully carnalized musicology of historically situated bodies. Le Guin's coinage of "carnal" rather than "bodily" is felicitous in emphasizing the moist, squishy dimension of the flesh permeated by both bodily fluids and sinful impulses. Such a music-centered physiology needs to bring the intellectual trends of the age, as uncovered in the work of Penelope Gouk or Linda Phyllis Austern, into direct contact with actual musicking bodies and performance situations.[18] In the process, we may even come to question that central term "embodiment," proposed as a paradigm for the study of human culture by Thomas Csordas, which in bringing issues of the body back into focus nevertheless seems to preserve the assumption of the soul or mind as prior, housed in a material shell.[19] In order to move past an attitude that both takes the body for granted and considers it a secondary appendage to the self, we may need to look instead at "ensoulment" as the principle underpinning the early modern conception of human nature as a "corpus animatum": that animated, living body inherited from the medieval tradition and revived in a different guise by eighteenth-century vitalists.[20] As the Prussian physician Georg Ernst Stahl proposed, the task was to understand the "temperament of a living body [Leib] and not simply the complexion of a body [Körper] composed out of lifeless materials."[21]

The distinction between the terms "Leib" and "Körper" introduced here, which became fundamental to the twentieth-century phenomenological tradition, appears crucial in capturing the notion of an animated body and its experiential qualities, as opposed to the passive object of empirical investigation that the body became in modern scientific thought. As Barbara Duden has argued, early modern bodies operated in ways not easily captured by current medical vocabularies and technologies: "blood, skin, bodily orifices cannot be reduced to anatomical organs" when they appear in eighteenth-century texts.[22] In numerous early modern writings, whether anatomical, theological, or devotional in nature, the Cartesian primacy of the mind is challenged by alternative models of the human body as active, willful, and cognizant. In different ways, ensouled bodies populate Thomas Wright's account of the passions as much as Claude Perrault's seminal investigation into the nature of sound, *Du Bruit* (1680), which assumed "the agency of some kind of 'reasoning' force in every part of the animal organism."[23] Certainly the continuing vogue for anatomical dissection in some ways furthered an understanding of human bodies as mechanical systems made up of pulleys, pumps, and liquids. Yet the body as portrayed in many contemporary anatomy treatises still ultimately remained a body of wonder, with public dissection spectacles enacting a "sacred ritual" to admire God's handiwork.[24] And certainly when music entered the picture, the human self revealed itself not as an immaterial entity enclosed in an inert physical container, but as a body-spirit-soul composite with the capacity to be conjointly affected in all its aspects.

8
Flow

"All bodies are Transpirable and Trans-fluxible, that is, so open to the ayre as that it may easily passe and repasse through them," observed the English writer Helkiah Crooke in 1615.[1] His French contemporary Étienne Binet agreed that the "substance of man" is "all breathable and evaporable due to its rarefication and the openings of the pores that puncture the skin and outer membrane."[2] As historians from Gail Kern Paster to Ulinka Rublack have shown, early modern bodies were systems of flow, governed by the four humors (blood, phlegm, black bile, and yellow bile) inherited from Galenic medicine, but incorporating a plethora of other fluids too.[3] In Christoph Heinrich Keil's enumeration, the liquid components of the body included blood, lymph fluid, serum, sweat, urine, chyle, milk, semen, nerve fluid, tears, ear wax, mucus, saliva, glandular juices, gall and joint fluid; constituting a complex system of watery and viscous substances that percolated, intermingled, and transformed into each other.[4] In Binet's words, they "all flow together down the veins and the sanguine matter."[5] The particular qualities of each of the four main liquids or humors (hot/cold; wet/dry) linked them to one of the four elements (air, water, earth, fire), and their admixture determined everything from an individual's outward appearance and constitution to their character, morals, and emotional life. Writing in 1705, Christian Friedrich Richter summarized the common assumptions associated with the four temperaments: choleric people are of a "fast, hot and fiery" nature; the excess of gall in their system means that they are active, quick, impatient, fickle, sensitive, disagreeable, distrustful, wrathful, arrogant, daring, talkative, unforgiving, cunning, and clever. They have a "lean body with large veins," are usually somewhat red in the face, and have thin, volatile blood; therefore, they "easily get hot from a small amount of movement," and their dense flesh feels hard to the touch. Phlegmatic people, on the other hand, are "cold, lazy and slow"; they have "the weakest minds" and are disorderly, piggish, sleepy, feminine, voluptuous, fickle, and fearful. They have a pale and slightly bloated face and small veins, feel soft to the touch, and have thick, slimy, watery blood ("Geblüt").[6] Analogous descriptions are provided for the sanguine and melancholic temperaments. A range of mixed temperaments and subtypes could be derived from these; in a singing treatise of 1715, Martin Heinrich Fuhrmann identified a "Pilatisches Geblüt" in people whose constitution of flows meant they could not tolerate the truth.[7] A 1730 treatise on human nature by the German Pietist Peter Friedrich Detry further specified color and taste preferences for each temperament (sanguine persons like sweet foods and the colors red and green, and so on), as well as types of music: sanguine listeners, "according to their sense of hearing," prefer lively, leaping music in triple meter such as minuets and courantes, whereas cholerics appreciate loud trumpet and drum music.[8] It was only later in the eighteenth century that the notion of taste became chiefly defined through qualities of refinement and connoisseurship.[9]

Food, colors, and music were all things that could enter the body from the outside, though in the case of music the body also had the capacity to reverse that process and send out musical sound from within. As indicated in Crooke's description, the body-souls within which these humors flowed were not the bounded, closed-off containers of the self that the modern body became, but porous and permeable, and hence fundamentally open to the environment. Timothy Reiss has proposed "passibility" as the guiding metaphor through which to view the pre-modern subject;[10] a position that, incidentally, chimes with current understandings of postmodern subjectivity, too, which regard identity and self as always "passing," decentered, and in flux.[11] In 1749, the French medic Jean-Baptiste de Sénac still attested that "the body is thus open in all parts to the substances that surround it."[12] Processes of ingestion and excretion—involving air, water, food, feces, menstrual blood, and so on—formed part of a broader cyclical exchange between body-souls and their surroundings. Early modern physicians usually considered these processes under the heading of the six "non-naturals": air, motion and rest, sleep and waking, food and drink, things excreted, and passions or emotions. Contaminated air, for instance, could have an immediate deleterious effect on the body's flows: "There is no thynge excepte poyson that doth putryfye, or doeth corrupte the bloude of man; and also doth mortyfye the spyrytes of man, as dothe a corrupte and a contagyous ayre," wrote the English author Andrew Boorde in a popular sixteenth-century health almanac.[13] Such contamination was not just a matter of pollution from noxious fumes, but could be caused by fog, air that was too cold or hot, or air corrupted by "meteors, thunder and lightning."[14] Events in the heavens and astrological patterns affected the humoral flows in human bodies not merely by analogy: since the sun warmed and the moon made moist, their movement, according to the Lutheran reformer Philipp Melanchthon, directly shaped "certain qualities of animated bodies."[15] The planets exerted a tangible influence over earthly matter, often figured as "influxus." Johann Popp's *Thesaurus medicinae* of 1628 claimed: "When the starry firmament pours out its poisonous rays . . . onto the soil of the earth, or in the water, or in the air, so then not only the fruits of the earth are poisoned . . . the water and the fish will be poisoned and die, the air is corrupted. And just as the earth, water and air are corrupted, so the little world is corrupted: . . . the heart, liver, brain also receive through the inhaled air a change or mutation of the inner powers of the vital spirits."[16] Numerous scholars and physicians, including the great empiricist William Harvey, subscribed to the Galenic view that the brain shrank and expanded with the waxing and waning of the moon.[17]

Music was directly implicated in these processes through the Platonic idea of universal harmony. As the Lutheran theologian Caspar Calvör affirmed, the seven planets "with their incessant motion perform a pleasant heavenly music and dance, day and night, without our deaf and thick human ears being able to hear it."[18] Andreas Werckmeister explained this process of "influxus" in greater detail in his commentary on a treatise by the Italian theorist Agostino Steffani: "Just as sounding harmony enters into our ears, and the fluxes that are incited by a sound incite another body or string and make it sound, if it accords with that sound and stands in the same proportion: thus the harmony of the constellations enters into our soul [Gemüt], and reigns and propels it. . . . And just as the constellations change from time to time, so the souls are changed through this spirit and harmony of the stars, so that from one time to the next the humors and morals of the people are altered."[19] Food and drink likewise intersected with music in affecting the constitution of all parts of the body, including the vocal tract: Wolfgang Caspar Printz's singing treatise of 1678 advised singers to avoid consuming sour and bitter things because of their adverse effects on the voice.[20] Singing and music thus occupied a curious position among and across the non-naturals, being carried in or out of the body by air, but also perceived as honey in the mouth or vinegar in the throat, and experienced as a strong stimulant or appeaser of the passions.

Yet while in certain ways their open bodies left early modern subjects at the mercy of these external influxes, individuals did have some agency over directing and balancing their bodily-spiritual flows. Available medical procedures included purging, bloodletting, and administering drugs that diluted or thickened the fluids, thereby speeding up or slowing their flow and drying out or moistening the body. Over the course of the seventeenth century, the Galenic belief in *crasis* (humoral balance) as the body's ideal state was easily incorporated into the emerging conception of the body as a hydromechanical system, consolidated by Harvey's discovery of blood circulation in 1620 (though the Arab scholar Ibn al-Nafis had already proposed a theory of pulmonary circulation back in the thirteenth century). In conjunction with the incipient Cartesian separation of the thinking "I" from its physical manifestation, these developments shaped a physiology that considered the heart as the engine of a hydraulic machine: the heart, wrote the German medic Johann Helffrich Jüngken in 1699, is "the most important component of our pumping apparatus or hydraulic display."[21] Or, as the Dutch physician Steven Blankaart put it, the body is like "an artful water display," comparable to the elaborate fountain systems installed in aristocratic pleasure gardens.[22] Gender distinctions—imagining women as wetter, colder, leakier, and more volatile than men—could ostensibly be as easily explained in these terms as class, ethnic, or racial differences. Detry claimed, for instance, that sanguine people were most suited to a bourgeois life, whereas sanguine-choleric people flourished in courtly environments.[23] The Jesuit philosopher Athanasius Kircher, meanwhile, offered a typology of national character in relation to vocal quality: "The manner of singing is unique to each country and people. Each has their own particular style, according to the natural complexion of its inhabitants and the country's conditions. . . . The Germans have a cold country and therefore a cold complexion and rough voice. The French are of a joyful, carefree nature; hence they love the hyporchematic style most, in dancing, leaping, galliards and courentes. . . . The Italians have the greatest advantage in music, because they have the most temperate country, and therefore the most perfect and temperate style, according to their nature."[24] According to the Italian theorist Giovanni Battista Doni, inhabitants of Northern Italy spoke with lower voices than their Southern neighbors because of their large arteries and moister bodies.[25] A hundred years later, the German writer Meinrad Spiess propounded the chauvinistic idea that his countrymen did not need to travel to Italy to learn from their musicking: "the fire of the Germans is for the most part such that it emits a continuous stable heat, neither too strong nor too weak, and therefore it does not go out or is scattered," whereas the "tramontani" tended toward a vivacity that readily degenerated into "barbarism."[26]

Such descriptions easily shaded into ethnic or racial prejudice, as when Johann Wilhelm Albrecht in a medical treatise on music's effects on the body complained about the "lamentable dissonances" of the Turks and other "barbaric" peoples;[27] or when François Le Gallois attested that the Turks produced "violent" chords since "their passions are of that nature";

such a love of violent music, he claimed, arose from "the grossness of their humor."[28] Rebecca Earle has highlighted the belief among European colonizers that "living in an unfamiliar environment, and among unfamiliar peoples, might alter not only the customs but also the very bodies of settlers," due to changes in climate or food intake. The fear that their bodies might "cease to be a European body at all" confirms that normative ideas about the body at the time were fundamentally shaped by those encounters with non-European others as well as the "quite-other" of, say, the Southern Mediterranean.[29] Hence Kircher affirmed the superiority of the bodies (and music) of those inhabiting the earth's temperate regions, whose climatic characteristics produced temperate voices, whereas the damp heat of "Neu-Hispanien" and other areas of the "zona torrida" made for rough and obtuse voices—a hierarchy that mapped neatly onto the assumed inferiority of wetter female bodies as well.[30] As Justin Smith has argued, such characterizations were not necessarily conceived as inborn traits in the terms of later modernity's constructions of race, but often constituted "relatively reversible and contingent features" of the populations they described.[31] If environmental factors determined these traits, a change in those non-naturals could potentially reshape them—hence those spectacular early modern accounts of women turning into men overnight. Contemporary descriptions of blackness, meanwhile, frequently overlaid humoral and racial connotations. A medical-theological treatise by Johann Jacob Schmidt of 1743 surmised that

> Human skin goes black partly from the sun . . . as when the hot climate of the Moors, Indians, and other peoples living beneath the Equator causes such a transformation in their color and external appearance, which black skin they cannot change; . . . partly from melancholy and sadness, when the thick, viscous blood coagulates, so to speak, or gets stuck in the outermost blood vessels and causes a blackness in the external translucent [layer of] skin; partly from an inner cause of illness, when sharp ulcers that eat through the skin cause the light rays to enter and be swallowed up rather than be reflected.[32]

While each person was assumed to be equipped with a particular complexion of flows, fundamental aspects of which they shared with their community, a variety of external forces could corrupt or enhance this humoral makeup, with male European whiteness as the assumed norm and apex of a healthy, civilized body.

If such explanations seem to veer close to a fully material-mechanistic explanation of human nature and difference, it is worth remembering that they were still embedded in a Christian theological framework that on the whole did not treat questions of soul, spirit, or virtue as separable from the body's materiality. As Jessica Riskin has pointed out, even a wholly mechanical conception of the body ultimately relied on the theology of a prime mover, invoking God (that is, Descartes's third substance) as the first cause of life and motion.[33] The German physician Friedrich Hoffmann restated this well-worn argument in 1716: "Our unfathomable Creator has created in each thing a certain power to move itself and to effect things. . . . But just as in an artificial machine there must be something that initiates and causes all movement . . . thus also the same is encountered in a human body, as long as it is alive, and indeed doubly so, that is, spiritually with regard to the soul and its powers, and physically with regard to the body and its constitution."[34] Moreover, the early modern Christian body was never a neutral material assemblage, but in the very matter of its fluid and solid components constituted a moral entity, and an ambivalent one at that. On the one hand, the flesh—conceived in opposition to spirit as a sinful orientation toward the world—was condemned as the cause and, in its material form of muscles, bones, and cartilage, the locus of original sin. Yet, on the other hand, it was only through Christ's incarnation, through the Word made Flesh, that the grace of God could descend in embodied form to save mankind. Perhaps this paradox might be reckoned as the ultimate overcoming of the primordial opposition of logos and matter, mind and body.[35] It certainly can help explain the medieval Christian obsession with the body of the crucified Christ, carried over into the early modern Lutheran tradition in musical works like Dietrich Buxtehude's cantata cycle *Membra Jesu nostri*. After all, in early modern Lutheranism, the communion bread still *is* Christ's body ("in, with, and under" the form of bread); and their theology in that sense affirmed the material body as a gift and sacrament, notwithstanding the widespread rhetoric of denigration and mortification of the flesh.

An early modern body's economy of flows, then, not only governed an individual's health, looks, personality, and social status, but for Christian believers determined their path to salvation or damnation. In the psychological materialism that underpinned early modern experiences of the world, excessive dryness constituted a route to death, and not just the death of the body: a dried-up, hardened heart was unable to hold faith, to let Jesus dwell inside, and hence spelled a believer's spiritual death as well. These precepts run through devotional pamphlets and prayer books as well as medical primers at the time, shaping collective structures of feeling and piety among laypeople. They compel us, I think, to answer in the affirmative Rublack's searching question concerning the nature of early modern bodies: "may it have been the case in the early modern period not only that bodily existence was conceived of differently from today, but also that this body actually *behaved* differently?"[36] In acts of music-making, much can be gleaned about these different patterns of behavior. As a gift of God that nonetheless could unfold dangerous sensual powers, music in many ways shared the ambivalent status of bodies; and as a kind of flow that both emerged from bodies and entered into other bodies, music revealed its uniquely double nature—an outpouring of a bodily-spiritual substance that in turn could condition and transform the bodily-spiritual entities it penetrated.

9

Sound

Would that it would, would that it could, come clean, this true real.

MICHAEL TAUSSIG[1]

In later eighteenth-century physiological discourse, the language of flows gradually ceded to a focus on solids, on the fibers and tissues investigated in Albrecht von Haller's pioneering experiments on sensible nerves and irritable muscles. Sensibility subsequently became a key term in musical writings as well, often grounded in an understanding of vibrating nerves as the body's strings.[2] This shift was not a linear process, however, since visions of the human body as a resonator had circulated throughout the long seventeenth century, drawing on ancient theories of harmonic proportion as well as the Boethian idea of *musica humana*, the well-ordered relationship between the soul and the body and its parts. These vibrational models often coexisted with flow-based accounts in what David Trippett has called a "delicate dance of vibration and physiology," generating a variety of sometimes perplexing combinations of nerves understood as tensed fibers yet with nerve fluid (or spirit) flowing through them.[3] Friedrich Hoffmann, for instance, described illnesses caused by an adverse "tonus" or tension of the nerve fibers alongside those arising from a corruption of the spirits contained in those fibers.[4] The Zurich-based doctor Johann Jakob Scheuchzer asserted that sadness caused nerve strands to tense too much as well as too much nerve juice to flow; music could exacerbate these symptoms yet further.[5] Even after the discovery of electrochemical signals in the body, initiated by Luigi Galvani's research into "animal electricity" in the 1780s, languages of flow persisted in different ways, and still do—electricity, after all, also flows.[6] Though this may seem to stretch the metaphor too far to remain useful for historical analysis, it does connect to certain current modes of scientific enquiry in revealing ways. As Fay Bound Alberti has pointed out, the twentieth-century development of endocrinology, for instance, provided "a materialistic account of the mind-body relationship in ways that echo the humoral interpretations of the ancients," also harnessing the language of flow.[7] Recent accounts of musical emotions as well as the psychobiology of affects as "dynamic flows" equally rely on it.[8]

Flows have emerged as fundamental, moreover, in current new materialist thought, not least Manuel DeLanda's sweeping *A Thousand Years of Nonlinear History*, which explains all natural and cultural phenomena as flow-based.[9] His approach informs Christoph Cox's theory of "sonic flux," which positions sound as "an immemorial material flow to which human expressions contribute but which precedes and exceeds those expressions." Cox draws on Gilles Deleuze's notion that "one can . . . conceive of a continuous acoustic flow . . . that traverses the world and that even encompasses silence . . . A musician is someone who samples something from this flow."[10] Deleuze, of course, had a documented affinity for "Baroque" modes of thinking; and Cox, too, invokes early modern writings, in particular by Gottfried Wilhelm Leibniz, in developing his notion of an elemental sonic flux. Not unlike certain current theories of affect that ground themselves in Baruch Spinoza's philosophy, Cox's work thus exemplifies the ways in which particular strands of postmodern thought appear to link up effortlessly with early modern insights, cutting out two centuries of modernity in the process. Also typically, however, Cox is quick to dismiss the theological dimension of Leibniz's arguments, co-opting him for his secularized narrative by finding "an alternative understanding that relinquishes the theological posit."[11] Cox should of course be free to make use of Leibniz's ideas as he sees fit in the service of his "antihumanist" project. Yet his dismissal of "auditory culture" in pursuit of the "sonic real" seems to enthrone a reckless kind of materialism in search, one might say, of its own God: the capacity to assume an outside perspective onto human existence in the world.[12] Cox urges humanities researchers to recognize any manifestations of auditory culture as secondary to this dimension of the "real": "I only challenge auditory cultural studies to acknowledge the sonic flux (and flows of matter-energy-information in general) as real and primary, preceding any particular social coding and always disrupting, decoding, and overflowing such human interventions."[13] Paradoxically, such a claim can read as a deeply modernist attempt at resurrecting a romantic ontology of (musical) sound as immersive and ineffable, grounded in the assumption of a normative white male subject.[14] As Michael Taussig put it cheekily, "I so badly want that wink of recognition, that complicity with the nature of nature. But the more I want it, the more I realize it's not for me. Nor for you either. . . ."[15]

Yet, as Taussig also points out, we do tend to live our lives as if we command full access to the real; and for early modern listeners and commentators, too, some version of the sonic real was very much available as an experiential and discursive category, even if as a historian I will need to conclude that any sense of that real was always already imprinted with cultural specificity. Here is Athanasius Kircher's account of sonic flux: "Thus all things are moved in a continuous motion: out of this everlasting motion arises the collision of bodies: out of this collision, depending on the quality of the sonorous bodies, arise the innumerable varieties of sound, which are not always perceived, but could be if the ear could be supported and strengthened either through divine power or a particular ear instrument."[16] Like Cox, Kircher argued that human sampling of this perpetual sonic flow was limited, but claimed that it could become all-encompassing by means of a divinely or technologically enhanced—that is, transhuman—capacity for hearing. A world devoid of this primal motion, meanwhile, was unimaginable for Kircher: "for if there were no motion in this material world, there would be no collision of bodies, no movement of the air, absolutely no sound or noise. Everything would be immobile and condemned to remain in an eternal, entirely unnatural silence."[17] Sound, in this model, was expressly not a phenomenological issue but an ontological force only partially accessible to human consciousness. And since air flowed—in Hoffmann's words, air was a "liquid and extremely mobile entity"—sound as material force relied on this flow of air particles in order to arrive at the places where it might be felt, comprising not only the eardrum or the auditory nerve, but other parts of the human body too.[18] For although most commentators located the faculty of hearing squarely in the ear, sound as colliding air particles could flow through entire bodies like water through a sieve. As Kircher wrote: "our whole body is aerated and blown through with air, and the nerves as well as the muscles receive the impression or feeling of external sound or resonance just like a string strung over light and resonant wood."[19] The German medic Michael Ernst Ettmüller offered a more detailed physiological account: "But it is not only the organ of hearing that music affects in humans, but it seems most probable that the very swift motion excited by musical instruments is communicated to the skin and then to the blood and nerve fluid, through which the fibers are curled up, the membranes, nerves, and muscles made to leap, and the humors are altered and brought into different motions."[20] Accordingly, the English physician Richard Mead explained the healing effects of music on bodies poisoned by a tarantula bite in terms of full-body vibration, as the sound waves "by immediate Contact" shook "the Contractile Fibres of the Membranes of the Body."[21] Sound could therefore directly affect those bodies it permeated, and not just the bodies of auditors, but also of those producing (musical) sounds, by causing particle collisions in their lungs and throats: vocal music "openeth the Breast and Pipes."[22]

So far, then, sound in the early modern imagination appears to have figured as a wholly reckonable material force. Yet it was also hard to pin down. Writers continually debated its ontological status, including Johann Mattheson, who disputed its existence outside of human perception: "sound does not reside in the air, as we believe," nor do the "sounding bodies hold it within them." Instead, following John Locke, Mattheson proposed a fully phenomenological account of sound: "it happens nowhere but in ourselves, after the ear has been touched and shaken."[23] Other writers freely admitted the ambiguous nature of sound, offering a refreshing counterpoint of doubt to the certainties expounded by some present-day new materialists. Mattheson's contemporary Caspar Calvör mused:

> Nay, tell me, what kind of a thing is sound, which seems to come alive from the dead, so to speak? Is it a spirit that lies in the air and sleeps and therefore wakes up when the air is moved by external instruments and answers to that which the musician seems to ask it through the movement of their voice or instrument? Or is it rather . . . merely a touching and pulsation of the acoustic nerve, or of the naturally inbred air in the ear, which awakens the auditory instruments when they are moved by the external air, which then awaken the common sense or the internally residing spirit, which then responds in the brain to the externally caused commotion with an internal sound? Does the spirit of the musician communicate with the spirit of the auditor in this way? . . . Or, finally, what is it? You say, I do not know: and I do not know it either. Behold! The arcane nature of music and sound.[24]

Vibration, touch, moving air, spirit, an animated entity that carries soul: sound might be any or all of these. And in its multiple nature, sound could work astonishing effects. How could it be so diverse, informative, and textured if it was simply a case of moving air particles? The English philosopher Francis Bacon wrote: "it is one of the strangest secrets in Sounds; that the whole Sound is not in the whole Air onely, but the whole Sound is also in every small part of the Air. So that all the curious diversity of Articulate sounds of the voice of Man or Birds will enter into a small crany, inconfused."[25] Sound acted in ways that did not match other natural phenomena, Bacon pointed out, since in sight, perceptions do not mingle, but "Voices and Consorts of Musick do make a harmony by mixture."[26] The theologian Johann Julius Hecker marveled similarly: "Who else . . . but the eternally wise God could have invented and made such a splendid and beautiful medium, able to take on any and every impression and movement." Those movements were all it took to allow living creatures to express their thoughts and feelings to each other, whether in shouts or whispers, and to "carry to the ear the melody of any string that has been struck or the harmonic beatings of any living voice or pipe and other musical instrument." Most miraculous, Hecker claimed, was the fact that "through the curious position of the auditory nerves the vital spirits can be stirred into fast motion, that the affects can be greatly moved or assuaged again . . . and that music not only delights the imagination, but also rids our hearts of sorrow and distress, as well as calming all those raging passions of the soul arising from excessive fermentation and flow of our blood."[27] Sound thus pinpointed the problematic nexus of body, soul, and spirit in affecting them precisely and conjointly. The German theologian Theophil Großgebauer outlined this process in a pamphlet of 1667, drawing on an account by the sixteenth-century humanist Joseph Scaliger:

> Sound or noise moves people internally and leads them with it to such things that cannot stem from the sense of hearing, such as mercy, murder, fornication, laziness, madness, stillness. . . . This is because the spirits that work within the heart bring the trembling and bouncing air into the breast, and because they are of the same nature, merge with it. The other vital spirits in the other parts of the body follow along and move the muscles or stop them after the sound is moderated . . . just like when on a violin or another stringed instrument a string is moved.[28]

The alarming insight that sound could produce mercy or murder through its impact on the human body chimes with the agency ascribed to (sound as) matter in much recent materialist discourse. Yet, although construed in ostensibly mechanistic terms of cause and effect in Großgebauer's account, there remained a margin of the marvelous in grappling with sound, which music in particular seemed to occupy. As Agostino Steffani affirmed, for a musician sound was ultimately not merely a "percussio aeris," but the "principle or origin of harmony."[29] The sonic "real," then, at least for those commentators aligned with the Platonic tradition, was not grounded in the chaos of quantum particles but in the *musica mundana*, the harmonious, God-given order of the cosmos. Such a conception puts a different spin on the relationship between the modern-day disciplines of sound studies and music, inverting the assumed hierarchy of sound studies incorporating music as simply another species of sound; instead, any sounds took place within or were anchored by that everlasting harmonic hum of matter and spirit. This was the foundation from which music could acquire its unique status as a cure for body, soul, and spirit, as the sonic realization of a well-ordered musical composition not only made that cosmic vibration audible to human ears, but instilled it palpably in every fiber of their body-souls.

✷ 10 ✷
Voices

The human voice was a particular kind of audible flow. The French empiricist Marin Mersenne likened a full and harmonious voice to a "canal which is always full of water when it flows."[1] In seeping out of a humoral, spiritous body-soul, voice carried that body's attributes with it and transferred them to the surrounding porous body-souls of those listening. As the German writer Barthold Heinrich Brockes put it in his extended poetic account of the five senses:

> In des Mundes Purpur-Höhle,
> Die das Paar der Lippen schließt,
> Zeiget sich die kluge Seele,
> Die in süssen Worten fließt,
> Und in diesen engen Schranken,
> Nehmen geistige Gedanken,
> Wenn wir reden, Körper an;
> Daß man sie begreiffen kann.[2]

[In the mouth's red cavern, closed by the pair of lips, the rational soul emerges, flowing in sweet words. And in these close quarters, as we speak, mental ideas take on corporeal form, so that they can be grasped.]

Voice figured as a surge of moving particles and yet, in Gina Bloom's words, destabilized any "easy assumptions about the category of matter."[3] Its material qualities were tied to pneuma, breath, those "winds . . . of the heart and the lungs."[4] Giovanni Camillo Maffei's 1562 pamphlet on the voice described breath as constituted by two opposing movements, namely the expansion and contraction of the chest and diaphragm, with the inbreath "tempering the heat of the heart" and the outbreath "moving all the fumes outside, as well as all inner excretions." Maffei continued: "They say the matter of voice is the outbreath, but more properly it is a very copious outbreath, if it is driven out with some vigor."[5] Song, as Katherine Larson has put it, harnessed this "invisible capriciousness of the air."[6] Vocal skills such as articulation or ornamentation were grounded in the operations of breath and lungs. The Catholic choirmaster Johann Peter Sperling described staccato articulation as a moment in which the vowels are "puffed out" ("aushauchen"). His Lutheran contemporary Wolfgang Michael Mylius called the "trillo" a "swishing" ("sausen") or shaking of the voice, grounded in bodily practice: in order to master this difficult ornament, boys had to practice it determinedly, "so that the chest, throat and gorge become accustomed to it."[7] Common faults in vocal production equally arose from physical features. Martin Heinrich Fuhrmann identified a "vitium tremuli," caused by a stiff throat that generated the sound of a bleating goat, as well as a "vitium anhelitus," in which a singer "took too large a mouthful," meaning that the airstream emerged not from the throat but from the cheeks.[8]

The sonic profile of an individual voice was directly shaped by the state of the internal passages by which it exited the body. Mersenne affirmed that "the qualities of the voice can be reduced to three differences, namely soft and loud, clear and hoarse, low and high: A loud voice is produced by the violent movement of the muscles of the thorax, a clear voice by a well-tempered humidity of the cartilages, membranes and muscles of the larynx, and a rough voice by excessive humidity or dryness of those parts."[9] Athanasius Kircher elaborated further: "The natural quality of the larynx, which consists in its shape, size, placement, contour, and surface, produces different voices: if it is long and round, it produces an even, bright, direct, straight voice; if the passage through the larynx is wide and broad, a big and deep voice results . . . The air also makes different voices: rough air makes a rough voice, clear air a clear voice; therefore voices are rougher in winter than in summer."[10] This was one reason, according to Kircher, that the time from May to October was much better for making affective music, because of the dry and thin quality of the air; or that people in wine-drinking regions sang their hymns with hoarser voices than those who drank beer, as the German theorist Daniel Speer affirmed.[11] If we might be tempted, with Dagmar Glüxam, to dismiss such diagnoses as "over the top," we may end up looking past exactly those ways in which these early modern bodies or voices behaved or felt differently.[12]

Since the body's vocal sounds emerged "from the depths of its interiority," as Richard Leppert has put it, a singer's timbre revealed much about their internal fluid makeup, disposition, and character.[13] The nexus between bodies, voices, and selves in many ways seemed as problematic then as it remains today: Where within any individual body and/or voice could a sense of selfhood or identity be said to arise? Kircher claimed that "if the temperament is moist, without influx of other fluids, [the larynx] produces a dark, unclear, and confused voice; but if it is filled with other humors, it makes a rough and hoarse voice. If the temperament is dry, it produces a bright, clear, well-sounding voice."[14] In a 1600 treatise on the voice, the Italian anatomist Julius Casserius linked those temperamental/timbral differences directly to personality traits: "If a voice is without force, it shows that the man is weak and timid; if it is hoarse, that he is deceitful and haughty; if it is clear, that he is clever and talented; if it is heavy, that he is brave and persevering; if it is tremulous, that he is envious and lazy," and so on across the full spectrum of human attributes.[15] That these categories underpinned the appreciation of actual singing voices is suggested, for instance, in Giulio Strozzi's appraisal in 1644 of the famous Italian operatic soprano Anna Renzi, noting that for a "full, sonorous voice" such as hers, "much warmth is needed to expand the passages and enough humidity to soften them and make them tender."[16] These qualities helped constitute the aesthetic appeal of female voices, as the Lutheran pastor Johann Meißner confirmed: "For since women, especially virgins, naturally have a purer and lighter voice than men, they can sing more pleasantly, move the heart and soul much more," especially when they are also beautiful to look at, since "song coming from a beautiful body is more pleasant."[17] And this "moving" capacity relied in part on the material transmission of certain wet or dry, harsh or soft qualities, by which a speaker's affective state was imprinted in their vocal output. According to Kircher, "this is how it happens that those who are very afraid produce no other voice but a small and broken one; for in such a state of fear, the body's warmth travels to the lower region of the heart and away from the upper parts, which deprived of this heat begin to cool and subsequently to weaken, and ultimately give out a weak, small voice."[18] People with a rough, shouty voice, meanwhile, shared their disposition with a donkey:

> Those people who shout roughly with a big voice are counted by Aristotle among the donkeys, indicating that they are difficult, stubborn, and petulant, i.e., mean-spirited people: for the donkey has a very big and rough voice, and is very uncouth, mean-spirited, and wanton. The cause of such a strong voice is the large windpipe, through which much air is blown out; the cause of the rough voice is that much air is expelled from the windpipe very slowly. Hence a strong voice is associated with a large, wide chest, a big artery, and a thick neck . . . . A rough, low voice arises from coldness

> and slowness, revealing a cold and dry . . . temperament; those who have this are avaricious, fearful, uncouth, rough, and proud.[19]

This "phonognomia," as Mersenne and Kircher called the method of determining a person's character from their voice, arose in analogy to the Aristotelian art of physiognomy, which had recently been updated in Giambattista della Porta's 1586 treatise *De humana physiognomia*. And just as della Porta famously relied on animal likenesses to determine people's dispositions from their facial features, so Kircher reaffirmed a web of resemblances connecting human timbres to the animal world, based on a kinship of blood, humors, and vocal matter. Such an ecologically grounded conception of human nature challenged any firm separation between human/animal, mind/body, or body/environment. Voice appeared as an outflow of what in current cognitive discourse might be termed an "embodied" and "embedded" mind, with different timbres arising from the interaction of an individual's psychosomatic makeup and broader environmental factors including food intake and climate. A brash vocal profile did not merely represent someone with a spiteful disposition, and its asinine and earthen characteristics were not just a matter of analogy, but bespoke a fundamental seepage between elements of the micro- and macrocosm, continually interpenetrating and in flux. Hence Wolfgang Caspar Printz stipulated that "a vocalist, especially a discantist or altist, should live in a chaste and virtuous way and certainly should not come too close to women or converse with them; for nothing is more detrimental to the high voice than the conversation of women."[20] The French anatomist Guichard Joseph Duverney explained this effect of another's voice on one's own physiology by pointing to the connection between the auditory nerve and the vocal tract: "the Vibrations of the Nerves of the Ear, being communicated to the Nerves of the fifth Pair, causes the Spirits which flow from the Brain into these Nerves, which proceed to the Parts which form the Voice, to dispose the Muscles in such a manner that answering the Impression which the Voice hath made in the Brain, they are put in a Method of forming a Voice quite like it."[21]

The assumption that some kind of transmission of inherent qualities could take place through exchanges of voice or touch shaped much of Kircher's natural magic, who upheld that venomous animals could, with their poison, spread their affective disposition to their victims: so a certain species of Egyptian snake would instill its fear of light into those it bit, according to a "hidden magnetism or a blind similitude in nature."[22] Descartes, too, at least in his early years, was not immune to such habits of thought. In the opening paragraphs of his 1618 *Compendium musices*, he claimed that "this only thing seems to render the voice of Man the most gratefull of all other sounds; that it holds the greatest conformity to our spirits. Thus also is the voice of a Friend more gratefull then of an Enemy, from a sympathy and dispathy of Affections: by the same reason, perhaps, that it is conceived that a Drum headed with a Sheeps skin yeelds no sound, though stricken, if another Drum headed with a Wolfs skin bee beaten upon in the same Room."[23] Francis Bacon similarly put his faith in the powers of wolfishness when reporting that "the Guts or Skin of a Woolf being applied to the Belly do cure the Colick. It is true, that the Woolf is a Beast of great Edacity and Digestion; and so it may be the parts of him comfort the Bowels."[24] Of course, these vestiges of an older cosmology could simply be dismissed as "anachronistic murmurs" gradually passing into metaphor or oblivion in an advancing rational worldview.[25] But their widespread reappearance in different contexts suggests that they retained some power to shape early modern attitudes to music's efficacy. As a flow of spiritous particles, a song of voices or instruments (which, via touch or airflow, also transmitted those affective properties) could materially touch others. Arianna's voice, her "ecstatic production of text, air, soul, spit and attitude," flowed as nectar into her listeners' ears and bodies, carrying affect, squeezing their hearts and souls.[26] Virginia Ramponi Andreini's singing managed to elicit tears out of women's body-souls not solely by representing to them the powers of the patriarchal system that subdued them, but because she produced an overly wet "ayre" that stimulated an outflow of liquid from their already excessively wet constitutions. An early modern musical voice could thus enact and manipulate what was feelable within the bodies that generated it and which it touched. It enabled the emergence of specific modes of subjectivity through directing the bodily-spiritual flows that kept these body-souls alive and alert. It could give material shape to affective experiences of grief or compassion, to gendered dispositions of the body, even to what Susan McClary has called the "soaring sensation of ecstasy" that liberated bodies "from the constraints of gravity."[27]

And although material explanations of these effects abounded, many commentators retained a sense of an (uncanny) immaterial presence in the operations of the voice. "Always just out of reach," as Richard Wistreich has written, the voice was a "fulcrum" of breath and sound but also, crucially, soul.[28] Ultimately its production could not simply be the result of different types of air particles passing over different surfaces, for that vaporous current emanating from singers' mouths was animated. A determinedly dualist conception of human nature, like the one put forward by Christian Wolff, would insist that the mechanical human body was able to produce those meaningful sounds without the involvement of a mind or soul, since it required only an appropriate movement of tongue, jaw, and lips. It seems incomprehensible to most, Wolff wrote, "how a body, which is just a machine and itself does not have any reason, still can speak reasonably." Yet since, in Wolff's anthropology, all mental motion (i.e., thought) had a bodily correlate, the mouth "out of the power of the body" could generate the necessary motions to produce sensible language "without the soul becoming involved."[29] But other writers instead reached for a language of wonder when pondering the transmission of affect, thought, and sense via the physical apparatus of the voice. Brockes marveled at the process by which the tongue turned thoughts into corporeal entities that could then be "incorporated" ("einverleibt") by other souls.[30] Andreas Werckmeister, too, called it "miraculous" that "through such a small, slight movement of the tongue and an even smaller movement of the throat and larynx, the air can produce word, sound, song, and tones, in various different ways, depending on how the soul guides and directs it, powerfully and strongly, so that far and wide, all around, it is not just heard by everyone, but also understood and taken in."[31] In this context, Steven Connor's recent reminder that "there is no way of short-circuiting the operations of fantasy in relation to [the voice]" seems to take on particular historical relevance.[32] Voice as matter and voice as soul or spirit remained intertwined throughout the early modern period, bound together by the language of flow. Hence, in Johann Friedrich Agricola's translation of Pier Francesco Tosi's singing treatise of 1723, we find a detailed description of the physical aspects of sound production, of air pushed through the windpipe, glottis, teeth, and lips, coexisting with an explication of the "extraordinarily powerful and sweet impression that music . . . makes on the heart, so that we almost believe that it would form a part of the bliss of eternal life."[33] The compelling sense of animation that music could bestow upon sound—in Holly Watkins's words, "not biological but not merely illusory either"—became most immediately palpable in vocal production.[34] As Julius Hecker affirmed, "when we hear an artful melody being sung, this necessarily has to issue from the voice of a living creature."[35]

11
Fili mi, Absalon

Wake the Lute from gentle Slumbers, Charge the Flute with sounding Air.

SIGISMUND COUSSER[1]

Instrumentalists, like singers, produced animated voices. As the Lutheran theologian Gottfried Arnold affirmed, commenting on 1 Cor. 13:1 ("If I speak in the tongues of men or of angels, but do not have love, I am only a resounding gong or a clanging cymbal"), instruments were dead without being brought to life by those who played them. "A sounding bell or cymbal is a musical instrument upon which a judicious musician can play such a heart-burning melody or dance that all who hear it can hardly keep themselves from dancing. Yet the cymbal has no life: the music does not come from it, but from the art of him who plays it."[2] Instruments needed to be filled with resonant, spiritous air, they needed life breathed into them, like that divine breath animating the original gathering of dust that made the first human. According to the preface of a 1723 hymnal, the musical instruments named in the Bible stood for "the God-praising mouth and heart of a true Christian, indeed their whole body and all its limbs, which like an instrument is breathed into, struck, or moved by the Holy Spirit." The sounds of "lifeless" instruments only "tickled the external ears" unless they were produced from a faithful heart. Only in properly heartfelt singing and playing did the Holy Spirit "tune the hearts of the faithful, like so many harps, citharas, trombones, and other instruments according to their specific kind, so that everything is harmoniously set up for glorifying the divine majesty."[3] In this manner, the whole human body could become a harmonious resonator. As Caspar Calvör put it: "What else are you, first of all, with body and soul, with eyes, ears, hands, feet, mouth, lips, and tongue, in their thousand-fold movements, when you raise your voice and breath in a musical sound, but a well-disposed, well-sounding harp?"[4]

How, then, did the sound of instruments, as a flow of resonant air emanating from fervent hearts, affect their believing listeners? Like countless other sacred vocal concertos of the time, Heinrich Schütz's setting of *Fili mi, Absalon* (SWV 269), the biblical David's lament for his dead son, opens with an instrumental sinfonia. What was the function and effect of this textless musical utterance? Hans Joachim Moser found that the sinfonia was "word-engendered," that is, generated by the words that gave shape to the subsequent vocal melody.[5] Yet, while this is no doubt a plausible claim from a vantage point of compositional process, in a performance context that vocal entry would not have reached listeners' ears for a while: in a ponderously paced 2010 recording by Pro Cantione Antiqua, not for over two minutes.[6] As in the case of Buxtehude's *Quemadmodum desiderat cervus*, it is not clear from the historical record in what sort of settings this kind of piece would customarily have been performed, but semi-private devotional or liturgical occasions at the court in Dresden where Schütz worked at the time seem most likely. *Fili mi, Absalon* was printed in 1629 as part of Schütz's first volume of *Symphoniae Sacrae*, and hence presumably achieved some degree of wider distribution too. But since it required the participation of four trombonists (though the print indicates that the top two parts could alternatively be taken by violinists), this made it suitable only for those aristocratic or civic establishments that could supply such an ensemble. What is clear, in any case, is that, for the vast majority of seventeenth-century listeners, their encounter with this music would have been exclusively aural rather than mediated by access to a score. They would therefore most likely have been unaware of what was to come after the instrumental sinfonia. Even if they had been able to glean the piece's title and hence its biblical content, this still raises the question of how they would have engaged with those opening sounds of the brass ensemble, accompanied by the organ as the specified continuo instrument. Lest we assume that they simply waited for the instrumental racket to pass, how did it feel to enter into this particular sound-world? And how did it feel to produce it?

In order to gain some sense of these historical modes of engagement, an analyst now needs to perform a kind of triangulation between different kinds of evidence, none of which offers unimpeded access to this past sonic transaction. First, there is the score, that supposedly neutral repository of "the music"; though this collection, like most music at the time, was published in parts, thus offering separate sets of instructions for habituated performers rather than a record of the work as a consolidated object. Second, present-day (recorded) performances offer sonic realizations of that notated text, but of course these performances, however "historically informed," will have been shaped by accumulated modern-day assumptions about this music's particular sound and feel. Finally, we might draw on historical documents as well as objects (such as original instruments) to gain insight into numerous aspects not revealed by the musical notation, such as performing and listening habits, the possible meanings of different musical sounds and gestures, and so on. Any reimagined version of a historical performance will be situated somewhere at the intersection of these elements, and will need to assume a spectrum of possible listening responses among past audiences. If this strategy seems to veer close to a classic performance practice approach, I should clarify that, where the latter has tended to be primarily interested in working out the right things to do to a musical object (the score), I instead hope to reconstruct some aspects of how it felt to do these things, as well as their impact on those participating as listeners. Such a reimagining exercise will need to embrace a mode of what Jerrold Levinson has called "concatenationist" listening, assessing musical effects as they arise and coalesce during a piece's gradual unfolding in time, as opposed to the more common scholarly mode of structural-hermeneutic listening, which tends to adopt a bird's-eye view in order to identify larger or deeper structural features and the meanings they might hold.[7]

For anyone who has previously heard Schütz's *Fili mi, Absalon*, perhaps repeatedly, and/or has had the opportunity to study its score, such a shift in listening attitude is not easy to accomplish. But it seems fairly uncontroversial to imagine that what would have struck Schütz's listeners' ears most immediately would have been the distinct timbral profile of layered trombone sounds as they gradually rose from a low register (ex. 11.1). Of course, even a basic claim such as this could inspire an immediate rush to signification. "The trombones at the outset . . . symbolize the *Affekt* of King David's deep and powerful grief of his son with their dark and rich sound," wrote Charlotte Leonard.[8] Or take Mark Radice's reading of this passage for its purported message: "The solemn opening for trombones and continuo only makes it clear that the message we are about to hear is a gravely serious one."[9] Certainly there is some historical documentation that supports an association of trombones with gravity or mourning. "Take the sorrowful grief-trombone and with its mournful sound blast out a universal anguish," demanded a pamphlet on the death of Emperor Charles VI in 1740.[10] The trombones used in the underworld scenes in the Florentine intermedi of 1589 and Claudio Monteverdi's opera *Orfeo* (1607) provide sonic reference points closer to Schütz's time, but this Italian theatrical tradition seems to have had limited impact in German lands. The Wolfenbüttel musician Michael Praetorius called the lower range of

EXAMPLE 11.1. Heinrich Schütz, *Fili mi, Absalon* (SWV 269), from *Symphoniae Sacrae* I (Venice: Magni, 1629), mm. 1–3.

the instrument "stately and splendid," a fitting description, perhaps, of the divine call to attention that opens Schütz's other piece for trombone ensemble in the collection, *Attendite popule meus*.[11] The 1723 hymnal cited above attested that the trombone means "confession and victory of faith."[12] Trombones could be paired with trumpets and kettledrums for battle music, could double or replace choirs of voices in polychoral compositions, or combine with cornetts for a genteel kind of chamber music. In that grouping, they often figured in courtly festivities and carnival processions. The trombone could function as a metaphor for missionary work, through which "the sound of the evangelical trombone has been heard all the way to the utmost ends of the world."[13] And, in the Lutheran vernacular tradition at least, it was the trombone that would resonate across the earth to announce the arrival of the Apocalypse.

In aiming to move beyond a circular argument that asserts that the music means what the text says, the endeavor to identify an unambiguous message in the opening sounds of *Fili mi, Absalon* therefore proves rather challenging. If anything, perhaps its timbral-motivic profile most immediately evoked the sounds of *Turmmusik*, those musical markers of festive occasions and/or the hours of the day performed by bands of Stadtpfeifer across German towns at the time. Johann Heinrich Zedler opened his entry on the trombone in his *Universal-Lexicon* with this reference: "It is used by the Stadtpfeifer on the towers, in town hall passages, in church pieces and on other occasions."[14] Dresden had maintained some version of such an ensemble since 1420. Johann Pezel's volumes of *Turmmusik* from the second half of the seventeenth century, scored for a five-part band of trombones and cornetts, include a number of pieces that betray the roots of the genre in the fanfare as the primal musical call to attention (ex. 11.2). Pezel's preface to his 1670 collection *Hora decima* called this practice of "Abblasen" a "true Christian work, which above all else fires up Christian hearts to praise and honor God." He proposed that it mirrored the custom among "Persians and Turks" to "call to each other every morning from high towers: 'La alla elle alla' . . . how much more should we Christians be entitled to remember God's honor each day, even each hour?"[15] We might imagine, then, that those trombone sounds in SWV 269 recalled that sonic ritual of the praise of God wafting across urban spaces and igniting faithful Christian hearts. But instead of necessarily triggering a full-blown hermeneutics on the part of Schütz's listeners, this may have been a moment of "emergent" meaning, more felt than articulated, eliciting a meaning-ful affective response from habituated body-souls. As Anthony Gritten has put it, timbre may indeed often be the place "where listening starts,"[16] which in the case of an early modern trombone ensemble meant "not such a sharp sound as trumpets but more mellifluous."[17] Marin Mersenne agreed that

EXAMPLE 11.2. Johann Pezel, Sonata No. 39, from *Hora decima musicorum Lipsiensium* (Leipzig: Frommann, 1670), mm. 1–8.

"a skillful musician has to blow it in such a way that it does not imitate the military trumpet, but assimilates itself more to the sweetness of the human voice or the other instruments."[18] In the context of a piece involving a solo bass vocalist, Schütz's trombonists may well have heeded this injunction, as presumably would those Stadtpfeifer regularly playing in consort with the softer tones of cornetts from the tops of city towers.

One might go even further and point out that the triadic outlines of Pezel's Sonata seem to approximate quite closely the opening motivic material of SWV 269. Yet such a score-based comparison of pitch content would once again neglect the crucial caveat that the particular "grain" or timbral-affective character of these motives would only have emerged in the act of envoicing them. As Marco da Gagliano's description of Jacopo Peri's performances claimed, the "sweetness and power" of Peri's airs could only be fully appreciated by those who actually heard him sing; it was in the act of performance that he "so impressed in others the emotions of the words that one was forced to weep or rejoice as the singer wished."[19] Those printed notes in the parts for SWV 269 may indeed have afforded a certain mournful expression, if they were animated by performers who let their spiritous breath flow softly and dolefully out of their lungs and through the metal tubes attached to their lips, as in that long-winded rendering by Pro Cantione Antiqua. A performer of SWV 269 may have been inspired to adopt such a demeanor by the text incipit printed in each part, indicating the "scopus" of the piece to be one of lament. They may have used that information to produce a nonverbal call of distress, communicating in sound a corporeal-spiritual state of suffering that, according to the Lutheran writer Sigismund Scherertz, often emerged from the heart wordlessly, as "pure sighing."[20] It is in that sense, perhaps, that we can mobilize Steven Connor's insight that a musical instrument is "a sounding posture of the body."[21] Whether Schütz's trombonists would have tried to "declaim" those opening notes in line with the verbal syntax, grouping them into threes by means of articulation and micro-dynamics, or whether they would have opted for a more sustained flow of spirit-as-sound, remains an open question. But in either scenario, a well-tuned rendering of this series of concords would initially have produced that unique experience of "mellifluous," solemn-but-soothing sonic immersion offered by such a brass ensemble. Alongside or beyond any specific semantic connotations, the opening sinfonia thus held the potential for a more generalized restorative, harmonizing effect on a listener's body-soul—notwithstanding the ever-present threat of audible interference from the burbling that inevitably occurred when spirit-as-spit filled up the instrument's bends and curves.

The subsequent unfolding of the motivic material in *Fili mi, Absalon* may have nudged our imagined historical performers further in a downhearted affective direction. Schütz's cumulative stacking of thirds gradually bent the classic triadic fanfare gesture out of shape: after six beats, the first trombonist intoned the seventh degree of the scale (f), and then the ninth (a), rather than the more appropriate octave. This effect is amplified further in the vocal entry, where the trombone's minor-third d–f, entirely reasonable in the context of a G-Dorian mode, is chromatically altered to d–f-sharp, pulling the progression from its soft ("mollis") opening of b-flats into the sharp ("durus") realm (ex. 11.3).[22] Further chromatic alterations mar the subsequent chain of falling thirds in the voice, now squashed into diminished-fifth shapes. As Praetorius noted, unlike the trumpet, the trombone with its slide mechanism was particularly suited to playing "in all sorts of keys through tones and semitones"[23]; and hence the instruments, too, end up producing chromatic alterations further on in Schütz's piece, especially in their second sinfonia. And these chromatic shifts potentially disturbed the harmonious, praise-inducing potential associated with *Turmmusik* fanfares. As Ernst Gottlieb Baron outlined in a 1727 treatise on lute playing: "So much is certain, that when one moves into chromaticism on an instrument, it cannot but be the case that through such a slow and harsh motion the vital spirits are subdued and consequently the circulation of the blood is slightly obstructed, so to speak, or halted in its usual fast movement, and [the spirits] are brought to a grave kind of attention."[24] When Daniel Speer described a progression such as b-natural to e-flat (navigated by the singer in measure 26) as "durchaus falsch" (thoroughly wrong), this was wrong not just in terms of the abstract rules of counterpoint, but because it produced a viscerally experienced disruption of flows.[25]

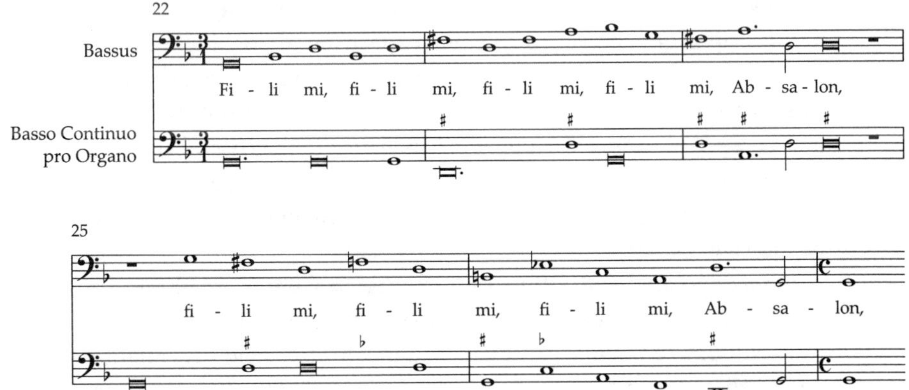

EXAMPLE 11.3. Schütz, *Fili mi, Absalon*, mm. 22–27.

A 2017 recording of Schütz's piece led by Hans-Christoph Rademann brings out some of this potential for disruption.[26] His ensemble gets through the opening sinfonia in half the time taken by Pro Cantione Antiqua, lending a jauntier shade of stateliness to those opening fanfares, with a buoyant, almost staccato articulation for the subsequent quarter-note scales and an audible increase in collective airflow as the trombonists approach the cadence. The bass soloist Felix Schwandtke then subtly leans into those chromatic (mis)steps on the downward portion of his opening statement, exploiting the discomforting effect afforded by the notated intervals. The subsequent shift to duple meter in this recording brings with it a palpable slackening of pace, creating a kind of aural slow-motion effect that lends a particular intensity to the singer's repeated "Absalon" exclamations. The ensemble sound really blossoms here, achieving one version of that vocal-instrumental blending championed by Mersenne. In a recording with Musica Fiata, the bass singer Wolf Matthias Friedrich instead projects a gripping intensity by taking a breath between each of the initial "Fili mi" statements, an immoderate physical effort that interferes with the unfolding of a more sustained musical phrase.[27] His breathing pattern accentuates the awkwardness of ending these short upward snippets on the vowel "i," generating an aural impression of strenuous sobbing or gasping for air through a tightened throat. Friedrich's rendering of the subsequent "Absalon" calls, with his hard aspiration on the opening "a" vowel, bespeaks an equally urgent physical force, an approach that contrasts markedly with the smooth, sustained quality of a 1991 performance by Harry van der Kamp with Concerto Palatino.[28] Both the singing and trombone playing in this version instead project a muted, resigned quality, with no audible inhalations interrupting the wider arc of legato phrases. Van der Kamp's heart-rending sighs of "Absalon," too, maintain that silky, floating sensation, seemingly detached from the bodily moorings of diaphragm and larynx. A similar spectrum of possible sonic realizations is afforded by that second instrumental sinfonia: depending on the speed at which the section is taken, the shift to eighth-note figurations may have posed an increased physical challenge to the ensemble players, who could have chosen to either accentuate or conceal the bodily effort expended in stretching and contracting their arm muscles in order to hit the indicated pitches.

Schütz's notated text—the intervals, gestures, phrasing, physical action, and respiration patterns it inscribes—thus provided the basis for a range of different sonic expressions in an affective field that might be broadly characterized as a kind of grave solemnity. But this emotive potential was and is only ever activated in actual embodied acts of performing and listening. However palpable the differences between these recorded versions may seem in the listening process, the unique timbral-affective profile of each eludes full verbal capture, notwithstanding recent attempts by performance studies scholars to measure and quantify some of these elements. In these distinct acts of envoicing the same notated text, music as embodied and emergent in performance reveals its ability to impact eardrums, bodies, and hearts in nuanced ways that a verbal category such as "sadness" or "grief" can only crudely summarize. In any individual seventeenth-century instantiation, David's lament may have sounded and been heard differently—languorous, acquiescent, vehement, regal, uplifting, or any combination of these. Some of these performances, instead of simply saying musically what the words said, may have helped defamiliarize those words for their listeners, inviting them to experience their affective force in novel ways. Though potentially giving rise to a range of emergent meanings, and thus registering as wholly meaning-ful among Schütz's listeners, such sonic experiences ultimately affirmed that music could do things with, to, and for early modern body-souls that words could not.

II

Inspiration

✷ 12 ✷
Spirit

"And now," wrote Isaac Newton in his "General Scholium" (first published 1713), "we might add something concerning a certain most subtle Spirit which pervades and lies hid in all gross bodies."[1] It is time, then, to come to grips with that elusive early modern notion of spirit. Bad air, as we heard from Andrew Boorde, could "mortyfy the spirites" of a person; and Theophil Großgebauer's account of how sound infiltrated human bodies relied centrally on the idea of spirit.[2] Yet any attempt to pin down these spirits quickly finds itself entangled in a complex web of physiological, philosophical, and religious beliefs and experiences surrounding this ancient and richly evocative term. A number of scholars have ventured to offer broad genealogies of spiritus/esprit/Geist (and their plural forms) from Greek philosophy to Galen, Descartes, and beyond; but, as George Rousseau wisely concludes, the spirits remained "fundamentally Ovidian in their metamorphic status."[3] In Penelope Gouk's lucid synopsis, the early modern meanings of spirit could range from "an alcoholic liquid which had gone through the process of distillation" to "a wholly incorporeal entity such as the Holy Spirit, an invisible demon, the animating principle in man and animals . . . or the soul at the moment of death."[4] The German medic Sebastian Wirdig affirmed in 1673 that spirit stood for three things: "1. For that which is immutable, i.e., God; 2. For that which is void of matter, such as angels; 3. For a thin and very subtle body."[5] In the shape of "vital" or "animal" spirits ("Lebensgeister"), this last kind of spirit occupied a "middle nature" between soul and body, and constituted the central ingredient, the bonding agent, of the early modern physiology traced in this book. Recovering this centrality of spirit and understanding its operations within human body-souls is thus crucial to my attempt to get "beneath the skin" of these early modern musicking experiences.[6] As Gail Kern Paster affirmed, spirit is indeed the place where "semantic differences between past and present discourses of the body may work most powerfully to occlude early modern habits of bodily sensation and self-experience."[7]

The spirit(s) of the early moderns owed the possibility of their existence to a commonly held conception of matter and non-matter as arranged along a continuum, with spirit hovering near the non-material end of the spectrum. In accounting for early modern experiences of being "spirited," we need to assume such a gradated notion of matter, reaching from the most solid earthen objects to the immateriality of angels, rather than, or at least alongside, a Cartesian binary of "res cogitans" and "res extensa." The fluid intermingling of physiology and psychology (as we might call them now) in much early modern discourse about bodies, souls, emotions, and music evinces the persistent appeal of these alternatives to dualism in both learned and vernacular writings. Even if in certain ways Christianity may indeed be characterized as an "insistently dualistic religion," as Richard Sugg has written, its early modern instantiations embraced and harnessed that intermediary notion of "spirit" in a variety of ways.[8] We encounter it, for instance, in the Pietist theologian Peter Friedrich Detry's 1726 essay on human nature "according to spirit, soul and body," which affirmed that "spirit is the third part of human beings, by which man is essentially differentiated from animals. It is that part in which resides the image of God and of which after the Fall a spark still remained."[9] In more scientifically oriented accounts, these theological connotations of spirit still resonated. Soul, as Paster has noted, "could not be found in anatomical dissection," but its operations via the medium of vital spirit(s) still fundamentally shaped the living matter of human bodies; it made them alive.[10]

Usually figured as a subtle, volatile liquid and/or as the hot vapor of Stoic pneuma, the vital spirits formed the prime instrument—or, for some writers, the very seat—of the soul. They enabled the body's basic functions, including sensation, movement, and consciousness. In Helkiah Crooke's 1615 definition, spirit was "a subtile and thinne body alwayes moouable, engendred of blood and vapour, and the vehicle or carriage of the Faculties of the soule."[11] Over a hundred years later, Johann Heinrich Zedler's *Universal-Lexicon* testified to the continuing validity of this spirit-based anthropology: "The vital spirits are thought to be the spirited, fine, volatile and extremely mobile particles of the living body, which are . . . replenished every day through the intake of food, secreted from the blood in the brain as well as partly in the spinal cord, distributed via the nerves to all parts of the body, and transformed in different parts in multiple ways. They are the origin and efficient cause of the movement of the senses, the emotions, and all functions that occur in a living body."[12] These spirits were generated by the body through a process of increasing distillation of the blood, gradually refining its particles along that spectrum of matter toward immateriality. A medical handbook of 1694 outlined: "The most lively and speedy particles of the blood, as the vital spirits can be understood, rise from the left ventricle of the heart . . . through the blood vessels into the ventricles of the brain, where they are turned into a subtle flame or wind, which is usually called the animal spirit."[13] The Dutch physician Herman Boerhaave presented a more fully liquid-based account, neatly falling in line with what Paster has called the early modern "civilising narrative of purification":[14] "The Matter from whence the Juices or Spirits of the Brain are prepared, is the viscid and tenaceous Serum of the Blood, which by passing thro' many Degrees of Attenuation, at length acquires the Subtility of a Spirit, after its Particles have been moulded or formed by passing frequently thro' the smallest Series of Vessels in the Body; passing from Blood into Serum, from Serum into Lymph, and from Lymph of the first Order in all successive smaller ones, till at least losing the Nature of Lymph it acquires the subtle one of a Spirit."[15] For the Prussian educator Johann Julius Hecker, this life-giving process of increasing rarefication of gross matter into the essence of human nature even had measurable anatomical consequences, since for him the only way to explain the exceptional size of the human brain was in its function of secreting "nerve juice": "It is easy to discern that in the brain a necessary liquid serving the preservation of life has to be secreted from the large volume of blood that flows up to the head. For otherwise one cannot adduce another sufficient cause for such a large apparatus, instrument, and part."[16]

Hecker's choice of terminology—"Nervensaft"—points to the growing interest in and understanding of the nervous system in eighteenth-century physiology, a process that eventually spelled the demise of the animal spirit doctrine by the following century. Yet at this point the notion of a liquid filling the nerves still preserved a fundamentally flow-based conception of human nature, even if some writers disputed the assertion (made by Descartes, among others) that the nerves were hollow tubes, given that no fluid could be seen to spill from them when cut. Already William Harvey had called the notion of animal spirits a "common subterfuge of ignorance"; and in the decades after 1700, the voices dismissing those nerve juices as fictitious became increasingly numerous.[17] But many anatomists and philosophers still sided with Boerhaave, who upheld the veracity of "nerve juice," even though it could not be "exhibited to the Eye either by Ligatures, Wounds, Punctures, Suction, the Air-pump, or Injections"—a comprehensive list of failed attempts to make those spirits empirically graspable.[18] An alternative model of nerves operating by means of irritation or vibration, which Jan Swammerdam's experiments on frogs in the 1660s had strongly pointed toward, was endorsed by some of Boerhaave's contemporaries. The Scottish physician George Cheyne, for instance, imagined the nerves as toned, elastic ropes that ended in the brain and, on being touched or pulled, transmitted that external impulse to the soul that resided there.[19] Cheyne's vision of the human body as a well-tuned instrument harks back, of course, to the Boethian model of *musica humana*. But Boerhaave rejected this model on the grounds that the "soft, pulpy and flaccid" nature of the nerves with their "many Inflections and Incurvations" rendered them incapable of resonating like a taut string.[20] The discovery of electrical currents in the nervous system, which would ultimately confirm Swammerdam's theory, was still decades away at this point.[21]

In the popular imagination, spirits thus continued to flow through bodies as more or less fully material entities, in line with the ongoing materialization of the sensitive soul traced by Katherine Park.[22] The natural, vital, and animal spirits formed the most liquid components of the body's hydraulic machinery, continuously coursing around its parts like the blood propelled by the heart. And yet the immaterial dimensions of soul often remained directly implicated. Hence Christian Wolff asserted that "the glandular substance of the brain is the workshop where the spirits are abstracted from the most subtle blood of the arteries. And this therefore reveals a new reason why all nerves originate in the brain, since they receive the vital spirits from there, by which the body is enlivened or ensouled, if you will." According to Wolff, since the spirits "evaporate" ("verrauchen") constantly, vast quantities needed to be constantly produced.[23] In these remarks, Wolff's spirits seem to approach that edge where the materiality of the soul's operations ends and the immaterial soul starts: "In this nebulous transitional zone," writes Sugg, "hard logic and organic tissue slowly dissolved . . . into that strange incorporeal substance which otherwise sat so uncomfortably against the crude and stubborn matter of human flesh and bone."[24] The Paracelsian physician Franciscus Mercurius van Helmont, whose father Jan Baptist had famously found the soul to reside in the mouth of the stomach, articulated this transition as a direct link between the food ingested by the body and the thoughts produced by the mind:

> And for as much as the Food we eat must nourish and maintain the very least parts of the Body . . . therefore it follows that the same must be changed into a Spiritual water, to the end it may pierce into all and every least part of the Body: Yea what is more our Food must be reduc'd to that high Degree of Spirituality as to be a fit Nutriment for our Thoughts . . . .

> the Food wherewith we are nourished must be changed into such a spiritual Essence, as is that out of which our Thoughts and Ideas are formed.[25]

We might note this passage's resonances with certain models in present-day embodied cognition research of how cognitive structures arise. As Francisco Varela, Evan Thompson and Eleanor Rosch explain: "The nervous system does not process preexistent information in the traditional computationalist sense; it creates information in concert with the rest of the body and the environment. . . . Cognitive structures and processes emerge from and constitutively depend on recurrent sensorimotor patterns of perception and action . . . a cognitive being's world is . . . a relational domain enacted or brought forth by that being in and through its mode of coupling with the environment."[26] We may also note its sympathies with the radical materialist positions that emerged over the course of the seventeenth century (most famously in Thomas Hobbes), which held that those spiritual flows in the brain in fact *were* the thoughts. The German physician Urban Gottfried Bucher asserted that the "processus intelligendi" happens when the sensory organs cause a movement in the fibers of the brain; those movements in the brain, Bucher claimed, are the ideas themselves.[27] This "astonishing hypothesis," as Francis Crick termed it almost three hundred years later, forms the (often tacit) foundation for the dominant strands of cognitive neuroscience today, as well as for the current new materialist trends in the humanities;[28] yet it continues to be decried by others as a "greedy" reductionism that views human consciousness and actions as determined by the haphazard movement of chemicals around the brain.[29] Unsurprisingly, Bucher's contemporaries feared the God- or soul-destroying implications of his position, and most of them held on to a model in which the flow of spirit(s) enabled but did not fully encompass the immaterial dimensions of human nature. As Bucher's erstwhile teacher Friedrich Hoffmann wrote, "above all the body gains this special splendid benefit from the flow of its liquids, that thereby body and soul are most firmly conjoined and tied together," so that "the actions of our soul are found to be the same as the blood flows through the brain. When the latter flows quickly, the soul also hurries along speedily."[30] Without providing clear answers to the question of how this spirit-based conjunction was achieved, most commentators in this way took a position somewhere between the extremes of Bucherian materialism and Cartesian dualism.

The fluid interchange between material and nonmaterial entities that the spirits enabled is articulated in the English philosopher Francis

Bacon's musings on "transmission" in his *Sylva Sylvarum*. His account ranges from the transmission of odors or infectious air to the operations of "sympathy":

> If you desire to super-induce any Virtue or Disposition upon a Person, you should take the Living Creature, in which that Virtue is most eminent and in perfection; of that creature you must take the parts wherein that Virtue chiefly is collocate. . . . and then you must apply it to that part of Man, wherein that Virtue chiefly consisteth. As if you would super-induce Courage and Fortitude, take a Lion or a Cock; and take the Heart, Tooth, or Paw of the Lion; or the Heart, or Spur of the Cock: Take those parts immediately after the Lion or the Cock have been in fight, and let them be worn upon a Mans heart or wrist.[31]

Hecker similarly affirmed that "the bite of an enraged person" could "put the other in such a state of fury that they die from it."[32] This belief in the transmission of moral, emotional, or healing qualities through material contact was not too distant, either, from certain Catholic miracle practices, in which, for instance, a nun might apply the hair of a Madonna to her fingers that had become damaged while playing the theorbo.[33] The emanations from these material objects could be either physical or spiritual, as Detry confirmed in relation to toxic substances; some physical poisons, he related, are "very subtle and come very close to a spiritual nature, such as those distributed in and through the air." Just as one body could infect another with disease, Detry claimed, the "spirits or souls of people can feel the emanation of spiritual powers at an even greater distance and can be infected thereby."[34] This is what the German Pietist Johann Conrad Dippel (Democritus) called the "Dunst-Kräys der Seele" (vaporous orbit of the soul).[35]

And these processes of fluid interchange underpinned the operations of God's Holy Spirit in the material world as well. As a spiritous entity, it could act directly on a believer's internal flows. In Paul's letter to the Romans, God's love is described as being "poured out into our hearts through the Holy Spirit" (Romans 5:5); and for the Lutheran reformer Philipp Melanchthon, this flowing nature of the Holy Spirit aligned smoothly with the Galenic doctrine of spirits. Hence he affirmed that in faithful people, God's spirit mingled with the bodily *spiritus* in the heart and brain, causing "the knowledge of God to become clearer, the agreement firmer, and the motions towards God more ardent."[36] As Volkhard Wels has pointed out, this "pouring out" of the Holy Spirit was thus not merely a metaphorical process for Melanchthon; like the dual nature of the wine in the Lutheran

Eucharist as both wine and grace-bestowing blood, the nature of spirit in the human body-soul could be both/and.[37] Over a century later, the Lutheran theologian Heinrich Müller again described the effects of the Holy Spirit on the human body in such mixed material-moral terms: "Just as water is warmed up by fire, thus the Holy Spirit through faith renders the heart warm, mild, and flowing towards virtue."[38]

The early modern hydraulic model of human nature thus fundamentally relied on spirit(s); but the ambivalent agencies of spirit also revealed the limits of a wholly mechanical model, in particular when it came to questions of consciousness or religious faith, as well as the operations and effects of music. The "spirited" singing of the faithful, according to the Nuremberg theologian Johannes Saubert, was enabled by their body-souls being flooded by a more-than-material spirit: "It is the spirit of God that tunes up so the song can be continued, that is, that it goes through the heart . . . . Hence it is not us who sing or speak spiritually in this way, but it is the spirit of our heavenly Father that lives in us."[39] Like spirit, music occupied a shifting position between material force and immaterial agent, with the same curious powers of transmission and transformation. As the German occult writer Heinrich Cornelius Agrippa put it,

> Singing . . . arising by an Harmonial consent, from the conceit of the minde, and imperious affection of the phantasie and heart, easily penetrateth by motion, with the refracted and well tempered Air, the aerious spirit of the hearer, which is the bond of soul and body; and transferring the affection and minde of the Singer with it, It moveth the affection of the hearer by his affection, and the hearers phantasie by his phantasie, and minde by his minde, and striketh the minde, and striketh the heart, and pierceth even to the inwards of the soul, and by little and little, infuseth even dispositions; moreover it moveth and stoppeth the members and humors of the body.[40]

Music operated upon and within human body-souls both analogously to spirit and by means of spirit. It thus reconfirmed the fundamentally ambiguous nature of spirit, confounding those who insisted either on a fully immaterial soul or a radical materialism. It offered a constant audible reminder of the divine resonances of spirit even as it flowed through the physical vessels and orifices of the human body.

13

Aus Liebe will mein Heiland sterben

How did the spirit-based anthropology that underpins so many early modern accounts of music shape historical experiences of actual musical performances? In what ways did the flows of musical sound, the singing voice as exhaled spirit, interact with the spirited body-souls of those listening? As the German physician Daniel Sennert asserted in 1641, "the matter of the voice is air or spirit";[1] and one "air" that springs to mind as harnessing that spiritual dimension of the voice is Johann Sebastian Bach's aria "Aus Liebe will mein Heiland sterben" from his *St. Matthew Passion*. Many modern commentators have marveled at the rarefied quality of this setting, with all the heavy particles (in the form of low vibrating bass notes) filtered out to leave only an ethereal soprano voice, paired with the breathy sounds of flute and oboes da caccia. Bach scholars have interpreted the absence of a bass part in this movement in a variety of ways. Markus Rathey and Isabella van Elferen both read the scoring as symbolizing the absence of Christ or God, with the sixteenth-note chains in the flute, for Elferen, representing "the abundance of Christ's love while at the same time expressing his suffering in a chromatically descending gradation."[2] Eric Chafe associates the *Bassettchen* texture with "the opposition of God's judgment and mercy," whereas John Eliot Gardiner comes closer to addressing the piece's striking sonic effect when commenting that the "weightless pulse" of the oboes da caccia "allows the ethereal grace of the flute arabesques to fly free."[3] Gardiner's description harks back to an older commentary by Alfred Heuss, who also attempted to capture that sense of severance from gross matter: "A bass is lacking because all earthly burden has ceased; the piece soars over the earth." Subsequently, though, Heuss felt compelled to settle on a more specific representational reading: "Did Bach have in mind the image of a dove?"[4]

Some of these layers of meaning may indeed have informed the responses of Bach's congregants in the Leipzig Thomaskirche on Good Friday 1727. But I want to focus here on how the aria's voices and sounds might have acted on their body-souls in meaningful ways alongside or beyond cognitive interpretation. In foregrounding the physicality of the piece's peculiar sonic-affective profile, I adapt Matthew Head's astute observation, made in relation to Carl Philipp Emanuel Bach's keyboard works, that such music can project "a form of inwardness that also knows about innards."[5] First of all, this means putting to one side the dominant modern performance tradition of the piece, grounded, as Daniel Melamed has shown, in nineteenth-century performance traditions.[6] The slow tempo at which the aria is usually performed nowadays (lasting over six minutes in some modern recordings) certainly lends credence to John Butt's impression that the piece creates a "slowing-down of the sense of time," transporting listeners to a spiritual realm above the uncouth worldliness of murderous mobs.[7] Yet, as Melamed concludes, the tempo choice in a 2006 recording by René Jacobs, which gets through the aria in well under four minutes, is entirely plausible in light of the historical record, and is the tempo at which the autograph staccato indications in the oboe parts make most sense. Moreover, Jacobs's less drawn-out version can help bring out some of the joyfulness that Elferen has found inscribed in the aria's musical features, such as the flowing sixteenth-note figurations as well as the 3/4 time signature, which can only unfold its potentially uplifting effect when its triple nature becomes perceptible in performance.

How, then, might any kind of transmission of spirits have proceeded in a performance of this aria? As those spirits exhaled by singer and wind players wafted through the Thomaskirche, on the borderline of dissolving into immateriality, the interior air quality as well as the church's architectural features would have shaped their progress en route to congregants' ears and bodies; Athanasius Kircher's readers may have noted that it was not yet May.[8] Wind instruments, and the reed-less flute in particular, participated more directly in this economy of airy music-spirit exchange than those of the string family, with their intervening matter of hair and gut. But wind players also had to breathe, grounding any ethereal effect in the wet and fleshy operations of the lungs. As the German theorist Michael Praetorius noted, "the sound and harmony of viols and violins continues ever more with peculiar pleasantness, without any respiration, which cannot be avoided on trombones and other wind instruments."[9] In this aria, Bach's notation perhaps prompted his flautist to pretend to overcome the human need for respiration: after a brief eighth-note rest in the third measure, there is no further space indicated for taking a breath until the pre-cadential fermata in measure 11. If in practice players will of course snatch one here and there, the notation would suggest doing so in as covert a manner as possible. The fermata then obliged the flautist to prolong

EXAMPLE 13.1. Johann Sebastian Bach, "Aus Liebe will mein Heiland sterben," from *St. Matthew Passion* (BWV 244), mm. 1–14.

their outbreath yet further (indefinitely?), seemingly defying the corporeal limitations of human earthly existence (ex. 13.1). But would this have struck those listening as a transcendent reaching for the divine, or made them feel uncomfortably like they were running out of air? The oboes da caccia "exhaling" their regular staccatos may at least have steadied congregants' pulse rates, as well as mellowing their ears and hearts with their muted timbre—though those performers, too, may have struggled with the physical challenges of producing that steady, softly articulated pulse. Then the soprano singer entered, intoning a freewheeling phrase made up entirely of "naturales" pitches (equating the white keys on the piano). According to Johann Georg Ahle, they were called "naturales" because "they are principally contained in nature, which also implanted them in each human being for sounding";[10] they were the pitches that Orpheus sang and that Pan's flute played. As the singer gradually twisted those "natural" pitches into the sharpened chromatic contortions that also periodically passed into the flute part, for habituated listeners this process may have offered a sonic experience of purity inflected, of natural flows obstructed. The resulting tormented quality—especially in a not fully well-tempered tuning—of voices and melodies bent out of shape is often mitigated in modern-day recordings, such as Elin Manahan Thomas's rendering on her album *Eternal Light*, in which she maintains an unfailingly smooth, equal-tempered legato line unfolding at a serene pace.[11]

The details of tuning, timbre, affective shading, and so on ultimately depended, of course, on the particular performers enacting the piece on the day. While we do not know the individual who sang Bach's aria that Good Friday, we can be certain that it would have been a boy soprano. Present-day descriptions of this voice type tend to map neatly onto the perceived qualities of "Aus Liebe": "pure, tremulous or ethereal," in a recent report in the *New York Times*.[12] Listening to Christian Fliegner from the Tölzer Knabenchor perform the piece, I am struck instead by a vocal grain that, compared to a professional soprano singer, seems to make the precariousness of the airflow through lungs and larynx more palpable.[13] Given the uncertainties surrounding the onset of male puberty in Bach's time, very little can be ascertained about the vocal qualities of the boy singers that would have taken on a demanding piece such as this. Prior to breaking, boys' voices presumably hardly differed from girls.[14] The Lutheran pastor Christoph Frick considered the timbre of young girls taking the upper octave in communal hymn singing especially affectively charged: their subtle voices were "drills of heaven and awls of the heart," with which they could "dig through God's heart."[15] Some decades later, Martin Heinrich Fuhrmann similarly lauded the voice of a "proper" (male) discantist as that of an "incarnated angel."[16] Yet in mutation, as Fuhrmann's contemporary Johann Mattheson commented, a boy's voice tended to lose its smooth and agile qualities.[17] Contemporary theories held that this happened due to the greater heat produced in the male body during puberty, leading to the expansion and hardening of the internal passages (including the windpipe), with any residual wetness channeled into the sperm vessels.[18] Ann-

Christine Mecke has reminded us that mutation was a complex psychophysiological process that left boys' voices in a protracted liminal state before full transition to manhood. During this prolonged transition process, boys' voices also often "cracked" to sound a fifth higher.[19] Bach's congregants hence most likely witnessed an array of adolescent in-between vocal types and qualities as his boys sang their way through his music each week, with all the attendant anxieties of youth potentially registering in timbre and respiration.[20]

On this basis, hearing "Aus Liebe" did not necessarily offer a straightforward experience of spiritual purification or transcendence. Contemporary singing primers certainly aimed to mold boys' voices in this direction, advising that they should cultivate a "naturally beautiful, pleasant, tremulous voice disposed to vibrato," a "smooth round neck," and a "continuous long breath without much respiration."[21] Boy singers should avoid opening their mouths too wide or making their voice lighter the higher they went.[22] But these primers also reveal that this ideal was not always, if ever, achieved: young singers routinely got thrown off the tune by unfamiliar words; they did not listen to the organ properly, leading to poor intonation; they added rude or nonsensical sounds by altering the words or pronouncing certain consonants too harshly; and those that were mutating might squeak. Some boys did not control their breath properly, so that they had to take a new breath before each note; or they sang "through the nose" or clenched their teeth.[23] Wolfgang Caspar Printz complained, moreover, that "they scream so loudly that they turn black and roll their eyes like a slaughtered goat," sounding "more like the shouting of drunk peasants or wailing dogs than an artful music."[24] In many instances, such descriptions related more to collective hymnody, or perhaps the noisy chorus sections surrounding "Aus Liebe," than to those singers chosen to perform solo arias. Yet if, in Steven Connor's terms, all voice is in some way "a straining of the air," these boys' voices could make the physicality of that straining urgently palpable.[25]

Crucially, too, the audible exhalations produced by a singer would have been shaped by their inner corporeal-spiritual state. Good singing, Printz contended, was contingent on an earnest devotional attitude, whereas "lukewarm" devotion resulted in uncouth and clumsy singing.[26] According to the Danish physician Georg Heuermann, this correlation was enabled anatomically by a direct nerve connection between the heart and the larynx; the quality of voice produced by a vocal tract depended on the affective state of the heart to which it was tied.[27] A boy's best means of preserving the purity of his prepubescent voice longer-term was, of course, castration, but lifestyle choices such as exercising before meals, not sleeping too much, and avoiding the company of women also helped. Vocalists should protect themselves from "impure, foggy, very cold or hot air, north winds, smoke, and dust (particularly that from flax and lime)," and keep their chests warm.[28] Blechnum, borage, fennel, anis, raisins, colts-foot, and other plant extracts, when boiled and consumed morning and evening, aided vocal production and lung capacity.[29] Similar recommendations for keeping lungs healthy and mucous-free appeared in numerous health almanacs and medical handbooks.[30] Vinegar, wrote Mattheson, purified, cooled, and dried the vocal passages.[31] Consuming sweet syrups, on the other hand, caused a "slimy, viscous, impure slipperiness" in the throat and brought "dense and thickening juices" to the lungs and windpipe. Mattheson furthermore urged singers to shout into a hole in the earth at top volume in order to expel the impurities in their voices and render them "smooth and pure."[32] In the early modern world of theater acting, too, such respiratory calisthenics were deemed desirable: according to the English writer Charles Gildon, vocal exercise "augments the natural Heat, thins the Blood, cleanses the Veins, opens all the Arteries, prevents every Obstruction, and hinders the gross humours from thickening into Distempers."[33] Taken together, what these instructions for vocal cures and enhancements seem to suggest is that a human body—even the unadulterated one of a child—was ultimately incapable of producing "pure" spirit (as voice), which remained an aspiration and, in practice, an approximation.

Nevertheless, adult listeners may still have benefited from the less corrupt emanations issuing from a boy's lips and chest. In a 1675 medical treatise, the Austrian writer Wolf Helmhard von Hohberg restated the common claim that the milk which a child received from their wet-nurse shaped their morals: "Often they drink in evil and iniquitous affective motions with their milk, which adhere to them for life and can even cause serious and incurable illnesses."[34] Conversely, older people could profit from imbibing bodily fluids from those younger than them. The English physician John Floyer asserted that "old men may suck the milk of a Young Woman" to improve their state of health. Taking advantage of this "natural Transfusion of Chyle," according to Floyer, was "more natural than the Blood of Young Children, as Ficinus advises."[35] In current scientific parlance this might be called "rejuvenation . . . by exposure to a young systemic environment": an experiment carried out at Stanford University in 2005 tested the hypothesis that introducing serum from young mice into the bloodstream of older mice could slow their aging process.[36] For Bach's congregants, a young woman's breast milk, or the voices of young boys (as spirit distilled from blood), may well have offered comparable benefits. Any troubling implications of violence or consent did not seem to dampen Floyer's enthusiasm for such measures.

On the other hand, in light of early eighteenth-century Lutheran attitudes to musical styles, the elaborate figurations that the notated text of "Aus Liebe" asked a singer to produce may have had a morally deleterious effect on listeners. Even if Bach's soprano in 1727 did not add many ornaments of his own to the notated line, the florid melismas both posed specific physical challenges for the performer and offered a kind of aural titillation for listeners that could corrupt a congregant's body-soul by inviting the enjoyment of worldly pleasures. The German composer Johann Samuel Beyer affirmed in 1703 that "in singing today the variation of notes, where one adds many ornaments to the notes in places where the composer did not indicate them, is no longer in use."[37] Based on such commentary, we can assume that practices of ornamentation had by this point largely sedimented into notated form. Beyer's older contemporary Johann Quirsfeld, meanwhile, specified the corporeal labor involved in producing such melismatic figurations, stipulating that the individual notes should not just be "exhaled" ("heraus hauchen") but clearly articulated, and that this effect should be produced not from the chest but in the throat.[38] These notated ornaments, then, offer one clear demonstration of how scores inscribed both the memory of and potential for specific physical action on the part of a performer. Although this particular aria is much less virtuosic than many others by Bach, it certainly fell under the heading of what the Dresden composer Christoph Bernhard had called the "stylus luxurians," characterized by an abundance of decorative figures. And it was this newly abundant Italian style that Lutheran and especially Pietist-leaning writers at the time denounced for its potential to feed the desires of the flesh. Already the Lutheran theologian Johann Conrad Dannhauer had demanded: "Away with the new ridiculous Italian leaps and siren songs that aim not at spiritual joy of the heart but at voluptuous worldly pleasures!" Johann Georg Ahle accordingly called the luxurious style "fleshly, voluptuous" and "all too colorful and confused."[39]

Ultimately, then, it might have been more the spirit of human frailty

EXAMPLE 13.2. Johann Sebastian Bach, "Quia respexit," from *Magnificat* (BWV 243), mm. 1–2.

than anything approximating the divine that percolated in the Thomaskirche on Good Friday 1727, produced and received by fallible, sin-drenched human body-souls. Each individual realization of this aria would have occupied a different position on that spectrum of spirit as material or immaterial, pure or corrupted. As Jonathan Gibson has noted with regard to the physically challenging arpeggios in the viola da gamba part of "Komm, süßes Kreuz," another aria from the same Passion, a skilled performer could endeavor to execute these with maximum ease, or else decide to emphasize the harsh timbre, gestural intensity, and metrical displacements afforded by the notation.[40] Even on the smallest scale of note-to-note progression, we can find those physical affordances inscribed in notes. When realized in sound, the two bass notes that open the aria "Quia respexit" from Bach's *Magnificat* can emerge as strikingly different entities despite their shared pitch (ex. 13.2). This is due not simply to their notated difference in length, but to their respective placement in the measure as well as the surrounding harmonic framework: while the first note grounds and affirms, its reiteration transforms it into a bouncing-off point, leading onward. Crucially, where the notation suggests this differentiation, the actualization of this potential only takes place in the physical act of performance, as the timing, weight, speed, and direction of the cellist's bow strokes produce a particular sonic effect that "makes sense" of the notated text through bodily engagement. These scores thus do not simply represent inert musical objects that different performers treat in different ways; rather, they distill in notation the potential for certain kinds of affectively charged bodily action. In a performance of "Aus Liebe" that sets out to conceal the piece's corporeal challenges in order to produce a maximally smooth or "spiritual" effect, we might indeed be tempted to imagine listeners' spirits moved in a pattern of untarnished delight, as described by the Dutch anatomist Steven Blankaart: "In delight or pleasure, the brain juices are in a pleasant and softly stroking flow, by which they communicate to our soul a pleasant motion . . . so that all parts of the heart and various other bodily limbs are pleasantly moved by such a precise accord of the nerve strands; equally the circulation of the bodily juices proceeds in a much more orderly fashion than usual, through which a pleasant warmth is generated in the body."[41] Yet alongside this corporeal-spiritual transmission of delight, we also need to account for the potential for disruption or defamiliarization within any individual performance of the aria, as spirits failed to flow freely, as voices creaked and devotion remained lukewarm.

14
Hearing

L'oreille est, pour la Musique, la porte du coeur.

PIERRE BOURDELOT[1]

Taste buds can smell.[2] Even if you hold your nose, your body can normally still detect odors by means of olfactory receptors in the taste cells located in your tongue. And the tongue is not the only part of the human body that can taste: receptors for bitter, sweet, and umami tastes are found in the digestive system, the respiratory system, the brain and, for men, the testicles.[3] While the function of these distributed receptors remains unknown, they complicate our inherited taxonomy of the five senses, which may mask as much as it reveals about processes of human perception. For a start, there is that sixth sense, proprioception, traditionally overlooked because it cannot be assigned to a specific organ. And some senses are more closely interrelated than others: taste and smell are both forms of chemosensation (assessing chemical components in the environment), whereas hearing and touch are forms of mechanosensation, transducing mechanical stimuli into neural signals. Where the classical system of five senses suggests a neutral set of distinct entities, in practice they intersect in multiple ways beyond explicit instances of synesthesia. Human bodies engage in acts of perception that we may not be fully conscious of at all times, offering striking confirmation of the early modern paradigm of the knowing, active, self-directed body.

Although most early modern writers embraced the classical system of five senses, they were often particularly interested in these instances of overlap and interrelation. While some sided with Plato and Aristotle in asserting the primacy of sight (based on its association with reason), others, like Francis Bacon, championed hearing as the sense that "striketh the Spirits more immediately, than the other senses."[4] This, Bacon continued, explained music's remarkable effects on people's bodies and emotions. The French scholar Marin Mersenne similarly ascribed to hearing a higher emotional capacity as well as a spiritual dimension that was absent from the other senses.[5] Johann Mattheson, too, posited that hearing offered "immediate access to the spirit"[6]; and although it shared that immediacy with smell, the latter sense was "more corporeal" and thus further removed from spirit's immaterial dimensions.[7] By around 1700, the macroscopic elements of the auditory mechanism were by and large mapped. The cochlea had been named by Gabriele Fallopio back in 1561, and in 1683 the French anatomist Guichard Joseph Duverney proposed an explanation of hearing close to Hermann von Helmholtz's later resonance theory. Yet older conceptions of hearing persisted, in particular the ancient notion of an "internal air" filling the ear cavity, which was more rarefied and thereby facilitated the sound's transmission via the spirits to the brain. The Prussian writer Johann Julius Hecker seems to have been unaware of contemporary critiques of this theory when affirming that in auditory perception, external vibrations "compress the inner air under the eardrum."[8] This notion of a purer air implanted in the inner ear lent further support to the conviction that the ear could offer unmediated access to the spirit(s). As many early modern religious reformers recognized, this made the ear a uniquely potent pathway for instilling theological truths.

In many ways, the mechanics of hearing could seem straightforward enough. Georg Heuermann's explanation employed a characteristic combination of vibration and flow metaphors: the air in the inner ear "makes an impression in the nerves, by which the nerve juice is shaken and brought to the brain, where the representation of the sound takes place."[9] You could even on occasion hear those spirits flowing in your ear, especially when they were subject to contamination. The German medic Johann Helffrich Jüngken suggested that "ringing and swishing in the ear" was most likely caused by "badly disposed spirits, when they are mixed with flatus or when they . . . are driven apart and moved strongly through forceful pressure."[10] Most instances of hearing loss or impairment were explained as such spiritual or humoral disturbances. A medical compendium by the Swiss physician Theodor Zwinger stated that tinnitus arose from "humors collecting and stagnating in the aural tubes."[11] Philip Barrough's *Method of Physick* identified "windie vapour" or "grosse and clammie humours" as the cause of "noise and tinkling in the eare," which could arise from cold, heat, a blow to the head, or eating "windie meates"; symptoms could worsen when the patient was hungry. Deafness resulted from "chollericke humours flying upward," or from "crude and grosse humours stopping the hearing."[12] Both aural perception and its disruptions were thus figured as amplifications of that constant gentle flux of spirits around the ears, head, and body.

But such explanations hardly accounted for the experiential reality of a listening body-soul making sense of the complex sonic world—the "polyphony of experience"—around them.[13] Heuermann did attempt to locate music's remarkable effects in the operations of the nervous system. He posited that upon "hearing a pleasant thing, the movement of the spirits flows not only into the auditory nerve, but from there also more strongly through the intercostal nerve, into the nerves of the heart, lungs, etc.," thereby causing various psycho-physiological transformations in listeners.[14] The German poet Barthold Heinrich Brockes marveled at this distributive capacity of the auditory nerve in his extended poem on the human senses:

Hier bey dieser kleinen Sehnen
Soll man mit Verwundrung sehn,
Wie viel Aest aus ihr sich dehnen,
Ja den gantzen Leib durchgehn,
Die nicht nur in Gaum und Munde,
Zähnen, Augen, Nas' und Schlunde
Sich zertheilen; sondern auch
In der Brust und in dem Bauch.

Ja so gar bis in die Füsse
Sollen kleine Zweige gehn,
Wannenher ich leichtlich schliesse,
Wie die Wirckungen geschehn,
Welche die Music erreget,
Da der Ton das Ohr uns schlaget,
Und im Nervchen, das er rührt,
Durch den gantzen Leib sich führt.[15]

[We should marvel at this little (nerve) strand, how many branches extend from it and go through the whole body, parting not only in the mouth and palate, teeth, eyes, nose, and throat, but also in the chest and stomach. Little branches are even said to extend into the feet. From this I easily deduce how the effects arise that music incites, when a sound hits our ear and passes through the whole body via the nerve strand that it touches.]

Among other things, Brockes here seems to offer a poeticized explanation for the phenomenon of feeling compelled to tap your foot when hearing certain rhythms. Nonetheless, as Christian Wolff attested, it remained surprising that the eardrum "can transmit so many different sorts of sound clearly." Even more surprising was the fact that the ear thereby could become "the entrance of another's soul into our own," in the sense that human language, containing another person's thoughts, could enter another body-soul through the ear and be comprehended by the receiver.[16] How the bodily sense organs allowed for this contact between souls, via words or music, remained, as Hecker put it, "miraculous."[17]

What these accounts reveal collectively is that, in the early modern imagination, the process of hearing was not confined to the ear, but could materially affect the whole body. This was due not just to the multi-modal nature of sound perception, which could also take place through visual or tactile modes (for instance by observing a vibrating string). More than that, a human body's innards could hear. In a dedicatory poem to one of Mattheson's treatises, his Hamburg colleague Georg Jacob Hoefft located hearing in the chest: "Nothing can prepare us better for devotion, and no delight provides greater joy, than when our breast perceives the sound of sweet strings."[18] Before we dismiss his formulation as one more instance of Baroque metaphorical excess, let us recall that the early modern heart did in fact have ears, both anatomically and theologically. The "aures cordis" were two "small membranous ventricles" at "the widest and uppermost part of the heart" through which blood was channeled into and out of the heart.[19] While scientifically these ears were understood as non-hearing, in devotional practice the (Augustinian) "ears of the heart" constituted a crucial pathway for absorbing God's Word and grace. As the Lutheran theologian Gottfried Arnold warned in 1700, "those who do not open the ears of the heart to hear the voice of the Lord are hardened and deaf in the heart, they are a corrupt instrument on earth and stand under the judgment of damnation."[20] The Catholic cleric Simplicianus Watzel commented that the Holy Spirit "blows through the ears of the heart" as a gentle air.[21] Corrupting matter, meanwhile, could enter the heart through the actual sensory organs of the human body: as Heinrich Müller put it, "the doors of your heart are your eyes, ears, and mouth, they are wide open during the day, and through them frequently those things enter that destroy the inner devotion."[22] And music had a unique power to operate these doors. In the evocative language of the English lutenist Mary Burwell, "if the heart be closed, [music] openeth it and if it be too much opened, it gently shutteth it to embrace and keep in the sweetness that the lute inspires into its sensible concavities."[23]

The foundation of these processes of external and internal hearing was touch, the haptic transmission of material impact. The German anatomist Lorenz Heister confirmed the widely held opinion that "the sense of touch is the most general, and the other senses are different species of it, so to speak," in that all sensory perception involved the stimulation of nerve papillae on the surface of the sense organ.[24] Isaac Newton also figured sense perception as haptic transmission in his corpuscular theory of light, which imagined "a great number of little Globules striking briskly on the bottom of the eye."[25] With regard to hearing, the German poet Barthold Feind stated: "When the compressed air touches the eardrum, or the sun rays the nerves of the eye, or rough, heavy, cold, and warm particles the skin, and press themselves into it and reach the nerve juice, then the latter through this external touch necessarily has to be indented, pushed forward, and raised . . . to the innermost part of the brain."[26] It was for this reason that hearing could happen through vibrational impact on bones and internal organs, as when the French scientist Claude Perrault asserted that "the agitation caused by sound is capable of moving the diaphragm," or the Swiss scholar Johann Jakob Scheuchzer wrote that "often our bodies and hearts tremble from the sound and tone of the trumpet or a large organ."[27] Other writers outlined more specific modes of non-cochlear hearing that complicate any straightforward process of music entering the ear and traveling to the brain to be represented and decoded there. If this still tends to be the guiding assumption in neuroscientific approaches to musical hearing today, as outlined in Stefan Koelsch's recent comprehensive volume on music and the brain, such an approach risks tuning out more holistic modes of sound perception.[28] A 1734 treatise by the Erfurt medic Johann Wilhelm Albrecht laid out three ways in which music could penetrate the body and cause emotional transformations within: via the nerve fibers of the ear, leading to the brain; by means of adjacent nerve strands vibrating sympathetically with the auditory nerves; and through sound waves agitating the fibers of the whole body, "without the intervention of the auditory organs." These sonic "tremors," Albrecht asserted, "produce various and determined mutations of the solid and fluid parts, and out of this the effects of music on the living body can be explained."[29]

If present-day approaches in sound studies have highlighted the (potentially harmful) physical force of sonic vibration, many early modern accounts of music were already closely attuned to this power.[30] Giovanni Battista Guarini encapsulated it in a poem on the sixteenth-century bass singer Giulio Cesare Brancaccio:

> Quando i più gravi accenti
> Da le vitali sue canore tombe
> Con dilettoso horror Cesare scioglie,

Par che intorno rimbombe
L'aria, e la terra. E chi n'udisse il suono,
Senza veder chi'l move, e chi l'accoglie,
Diria, forse il gran mondo
E che mogge con arte? E dal profondo
Spira musico suono?

[When with delightful horror, Cesare unleashes the lowest notes from the living depths of his sounding sepulcher it seems as if the earth and the air are reverberating around him. And whoever should hear and enjoy the sound without seeing who is producing it and who is receiving it would say, "Perhaps the whole world is rumbling artfully? And breathing musical sound from the deep?"][31]

Such musical reverberation seems to have little to do with any kind of "res cogitans." As Veit Erlmann has elaborated, resonance indeed posed an awkward challenge to the hegemonic claims of early modern reason.[32] Music's haptic impact short-circuited the representational process via the brain by letting sounds infiltrate porous human bodies to immediately affect the airy spirits contained therein. Scheuchzer stated that "the sensory spirits are awoken, so to speak, by a loud or particularly ordered sound, so that they drive out the poison stuck in the blood, or cause other motions in the body in concordance with the sounds."[33] His Lutheran contemporary Christoph Raupach described this process of music inducing bodily-spiritual transformations in a listener in more detail:

> The sound of music, which is much more spiritual than material, spreads together with the air it moves and is transported to the ear. It penetrates even solid bodies, but all the more so our human bodies, which are very porous and full of holes. It does not simply go in the ear, but also to the heart itself, which is the workshop of the vital spirits, which are dispersed throughout the brain, in and around the heart and through the remaining parts of the body. These vital spirits consist in a very subtle and mobile blood vapor and are very easily moved by air that is moved harmonically or musically; this motion, because it is felt by the soul, produces different affective motions according to the different motions of the spirits.[34]

In the body imagined by Raupach, the material transmission of external stimuli did not stop with the skin. The pervious human body, "full of holes," responded to music not solely as an aural stimulus that communicated a representational notion to the brain, but through a full-body immersion in sound.[35] We might be tempted to dismiss this model as grounded in a "nativist fallacy" of music directly eliciting emotions, which modern research into the psychology of musical emotion has shown to be misguided.[36] But Raupach's commentary drew on a commonly shared framework within which at least some of these historical listening experiences unfolded. As the English writer Richard Braithwait put it, human hearing has "a distinct power to sound into the centre of the heart."[37] In Athanasius Kircher's vision of the resonant human body, "when we hear a pleasant and agreeable music, song or sound, we feel a tickle or pleasant itch, so to speak, in our hearts and souls."[38] In these accounts, music is envisaged as a kinesthetic entity that exerted tangible pressure on all parts of the listening body, affecting auditors down to the innermost fibers of their beings. As Steffen Schneider has summarized, the early modern spiritus-based model of sense perception functioned not as a "coding, transmission, and decoding of signs, but as the transmission of particles, as pressure, heat, even as immediate guiding intrusion in the innermost parts of soul and brain."[39] Raupach asserted, moreover, that this took place without those affected necessarily being conscious of it or understanding its causes. A composer who knew the right musical strategies to evoke different affects would achieve any effects they wanted in their listeners, "even though they did not prepare themselves to receive the impression."[40] Without any need to understand the words or decode the affect represented in the notes, these listeners were being permeated by the material-spiritual force of music, from head to toe, from skin to heart.

✵ 15 ✵

Attention

Listening—the opening stretched toward the register of the sonorous.

JEAN-LUC NANCY[1]

If early modern music was experienced not just as a vehicle for expressing the words it set, but as a force that impressed itself on living bodies, this positioned the art form on a knife-edge between efficacy and perilousness—hence the widely divergent reactions among theological authorities at the time, veering between extoling music's powers of persuasion and banning it as a source of illicit gratification. This was music that "wants something of its listener," as Rolf Dammann once put it, and that something was not (only) aesthetic contemplation.[2] In the standard formulation of many English and French commentators, music was out to ravish or rape its targets. "No other rape can be divine," wrote the churchman Robert South in his fantastical poem "Musica incantans" of 1700; "Tu ravis l'ame par l'orreille," went a French poem about the lute songs of Etienne Moulinié.[3] In certain ways, listeners could do little about these sonic acts of violence, about how music infiltrated their body-souls. An individual's innate disposition determined much of their susceptibility to musical sound: as Thomas Morley stated, "divers men are diversly affected to divers kinds of music."[4] While his pronouncement centered the (white Christian) male listener as the assumed norm, the reactions of women or non-white auditors to musical stimulation were similarly taken to be governed by their particular, deviating humoral makeup. Notwithstanding their own essentializing tendencies, these writings thus offer a useful caveat against scholars now envisaging a coherent category of "the listener" or "the ear" in gauging any music's historical effects, instead suggesting the need to delineate a spectrum of potential responses among different groups and individuals. The German physician Michael Ernst Ettmüller affirmed: "Not all people are equally affected by all musical concords . . . for there are those who delight in this or that musical instrument, this or that musical mode. The cause of this is the diverse nature, texture, constitution, and temperament of diverse human bodies, that is, the different volatility of the spirits, the liquidity of the humors, the tension of the solid parts."[5] The divergent anatomies of people's ears resulting from these different bodily flows likewise affected their musical proclivities. Some singers, wrote Martin Heinrich Fuhrmann, had "thick" ears and therefore struggled with intonation; those who wished to add ornamentation to a piece of music needed to have "thin" ears, correlating with the kind of thin, agile brain substance that allowed for quickness of thought.[6] As the Dutch medic Johan van Beverwijck put it, "in a thin brain the spirits can move better, whereas they get stuck if it is thicker."[7] Ears that were too large or round announced a person's dim wits, while well-proportioned ears came with a subtle sense of hearing, good memory, and so on. Whether you paid proper attention to the music played at a wedding, Fuhrmann concluded, fundamentally depended on whether you were of a "noble" or "asinine" disposition.[8]

Human ears, then, in many ways simply figured as impassive entry points for penetration and ravishment. Yet the condition of one's ears was not static, and the "musical catarrh" that prevented some people from appreciating music owing to the clammy humors in their ears could to a certain extent be cured.[9] Moreover, perception was—and, indeed, still is—not understood as an entirely passive process. As Eric Clarke asserts, "when humans and other animals perceive the world, they do so actively."[10] In an early modern context, perhaps the most conspicuous instance of an active notion of perception was the Platonic "extramission" theory of vision, which held that seeing happened as beams emitted from a viewer's eyes touched an object and carried it back to the soul. Though disproven already in the thirteenth century by the Arabic scholar Alhazen, the idea continued to circulate in the Western popular imagination as well as in some learned quarters, not least in Francis Bacon's explication of envy involving "an ejaculation or irradiation of the eye."[11] A moral primer by the French playwright Le Boulanger de Chalussay of 1669 affirmed: "It is certain that there is in our eyes a source of light, and that it incessantly pushes rays to the outside. . . . these luminous traces are nothing but the spirits."[12] These spiritual outflows could then enter the eyes of others and thereby penetrate another's body to imprint themselves on the heart. Barthold Heinrich Brockes's poetic anatomy of the eye still upheld this notion of the eye "exhaling" flames of spirit.[13] Touch and taste, too, were often figured as active processes, as in an account by the Danish physician Georg

Heuermann: "At the fingertips and the toes of the foot, where the sense of touch is primarily located and the nerve papillae are found, one finds that upon touching an object those papillae always extend and come out further, in order to enquire all the more precisely after the nature of the object."[14] The same "reaching out" of the nerve endings took place when the tongue sensed something tasty in the mouth, causing the taste buds to elongate in order to "move themselves closer to the food."[15] Brockes's poem even proposed an analogous extramission model of hearing, musing that the soul must travel outward from the ear in "rays" in order to meet those sound waves emitted from external objects.[16]

Other writers discussed this outward-directed impulse of hearing in terms of attention. Vogt claimed that, aside from a well-disposed fluid economy, proper attention was required if music was to arouse pleasure and other affections.[17] And this capacity for attentive hearing was not merely a mental exercise but a physiologically grounded process. Unlike in some animals, human musculature did not allow the ears to be actively moved; but listeners' ears could still "prick up," be erected ("dresser les oreilles"), pointed ("Ohren spitzen"), or thinned ("assotigliar le orecchie"). As Johann Julius Hecker affirmed, the eardrum could stretch more tightly upon encountering quiet murmuring, a process that enacted in the flesh the etymology of "attendere" as tensing or stretching.[18] But this feat of stretching, of "extending [the self] toward other selves," as Holly Watkins has put it, required continuous effort.[19] Christoph Raupach cautioned that "our hearing and our devotion are precious things that easily tire and flee."[20] He observed a spectrum of greater or lesser attentiveness among those listening to music in church: although he stipulated that congregants should aim to listen "from beginning to end, with attention," he found that some listened only "so obenhin ein bißgen"—a little bit, superficially.[21] An especially intense instance of Raupach's model of attentive listening appears in those early modern Italian practices of "spiritual listening" documented by Andrew Dell'Antonio.[22] Composers, too, could do their bit to raise and keep their listeners' attention, with strategies ranging from introducing unexpected rests to textural devices such as unison writing or genre-specific sonic markers, for instance the opening dissonant chord of a recitative.[23] As the German medic Ernst Anton Nicolai argued, well-placed dissonances increased a listener's attention to the consonances surrounding them, and this kind of attentiveness generated a stronger emotional response.[24] The music theorist Friedrich Erhard Niedt praised variety as a composer's best tactic, since "all sensing consists in a kind of touch, and the senses are worn down chiefly from the constant touching of the same thing, which renders them dull to the extent that it not only causes a dearth of animal spirits but often a complete numbness." He therefore advised that "the ear finds no greater pleasure than in the alternation of so many tones, songs, and melodies: in that case, the ear never hears its fill."[25]

Devotional listening in particular required active effort in order for the faithful to assimilate the doctrine they heard. According to the French writer Jean-Baptiste de La Salle, "the finest adornment for the ears of a Christian is to be well disposed and ever ready to hear attentively and to receive submissively any instructions concerning religion and the maxims of the holy gospel."[26] For Lutheran congregants, preparations for receiving Gospel and grace started in their own homes with routines of praying, washing the body, and purifying hearts and minds.[27] And music could aid the process of ingesting and incorporating the religious truth received by the ears, ensuring that "the doctrine of salvation, might more easily pearce the hearts and minds of the hearers," as the English writer Leonard Wright noted in 1589.[28] In Raupach's view, the frequent repetition of biblical words in motets, concertos, or arias helped "implant God's Word very deeply into people's hearts with great pleasure and emphasis."[29] Although there was wide agreement that listeners often could not understand much of the texts that were being sung in church, especially in pieces that used the newer "theatrical" Italian style with its virtuosic elaborations, such repetition nonetheless ensured that their spiritual gist was more effectively transferred to a listener's innards.[30] Heinrich Müller articulated this precognitive effect of music when claiming that "the loveliness of singing means that the usefulness of the words is grasped by the ear before we ourselves notice it."[31] In this regard, a musician's powers potentially outstripped those of a preacher, since the sounds they produced carried listeners both beyond and deeper into the words. As the Bavarian composer Meinrad Spiess affirmed, a well-arranged piece of music could bring about effects that even "the most eloquent and industrious preachers" could not elicit "with the most extreme threats or promises": namely, "melt ice cold hearts and soften hard ones so that finally in the stillness tears break forth with full force."[32] The insinuation of violent impact here is notable in the context of early modern missionary efforts by Christian colonizers, who found that indigenous people often converted more willingly for the sake of the music rather than the preaching; for these missionaries, teaching singing to indigenous populations formed "a potent force in conveying their own metaphysics," as Gary Tomlinson has written.[33] Other contemporary commentators similarly noted the "pleasant violence" of music that compelled "attentive souls as if by violence to a comforting, amorous, or devotional sorrow."[34] Yet this powerful force worked at its best when it formed part of a reciprocal flow between performers and listeners: according to Wolfgang Caspar Printz, musical performances needed the attention of those listening in order to unfold their full effect.[35] The main task of an auditor, Vogt stipulated, was therefore "to attend well and peacefully."[36]

Conversely, there were wrong ways to use one's ears, with potentially grave effects. We know from Tanya Kevorkian's work that early eighteenth-century Leipzig congregants often failed to listen quietly with full attention.[37] We also know that their Christian bodies were not neutral entities, but saturated with sinful desires. As already Augustine had articulated, the threat of "Fleischeslust" (fleshly desire) loomed large in any encounter with musical sound. According to Niedt, an "orderly and measured gratification of the soul" was entirely permissible, yet immoral persons might easily give in to the darker side of "Wollust" and its craving for "insatiable gratification."[38] This pertained to excessively virtuosic or sensual singing in church as much as lascivious music-making at feasts and weddings. Among a list of "shortcomings and weaknesses of the ear" in Johann Jacob Schmidt's *Biblischer Medicus* (1743), we find an entry on "itching of the ears," a phrase that chimes suggestively with contemporaneous descriptions of sexual desire as an "itch." This aural itch could lead "lustful listeners" to want to be "pampered with gratifying speeches and such sermons that are fashioned according to vain human wisdom, which caress the flesh but leave behind all the more pain in the soul."[39] In a musical context, such listeners abused the art form as "kindling for desire and fleshly cravings."[40] Those Protestant theologians around 1700 who condemned the new "operatic" cantata style held that it had been instituted only to feed this craving for sensory indulgence. As a pamphlet by the Göttingen schoolmaster Joachim Meyer put it, listeners' ears "itch for something new, and where the audience is not being kept amused with the variations of a fleeting and thrilling composition, which is more suited to the theater and to which it is easier to dance than awaken one's devotion to the praise of God, they soon turn up their noses and leave the church."[41] Hence, while music itself figured as an unequivocal gift of God in Lutheran theology, bad listening habits could turn it into a source of vice, by transforming its mellifluous substance into a toxic one. Raupach denounced those people who listened to church music not for devotional purposes but to reminisce about their worldly pursuits, "like those spiders who suck the nectar out of sweet flowers and it afterwards turns into poison." They listened "from the flesh," he lamented, whereas true devotional music passed "from heart to heart."[42] We might note here how the bodily dimension of human nature appears to become increasingly bifurcated, into carnal sinfulness on the one hand and an ever more metaphorical heart on the other as signifier for an inner, nonmaterial sphere. Certain modes of devotional interiority fostered in, say, early eighteenth-century Pietism in this sense may have prefigured something of the disembodied listening paradigm of the later modern concert hall. While all those physically present at a Christian worship ritual—or, indeed, a wedding ceremony—were sounded through by music's airy emanations, only those listeners who pricked up their ears and opened their hearts could experience the full grace-bestowing power of these sonorous flows.

✵ 16 ✵

Affections

Across the long seventeenth century, the terms "affect," "passion," or "Gemütsbewegung" were often used interchangeably or side by side. Although some philosophers did offer more or less rigid terminological distinctions (such as Baruch Spinoza's splitting of "affect" and "affection"), overall I have not been able to trace the consistent differentiation between "affect" and "passion" that Thomas Dixon has postulated for the period.[1] Yet Dixon's account offers a crucial reminder that the term "emotion" was not widely used before the nineteenth century, and that its emergence marked the transition from a theologically charged concept of the passions to a secular psychological category. There is, then, no single term available to encompass the range of early modern experiences that we might now describe as "emotional." If I speak primarily of "affects" or "affections" in this book, I do so as a way to keep the theological and moral dimensions of these past phenomena firmly in view. Nevertheless, in methodological terms, my approach aligns more closely with the recently flourishing field of emotions history than with its portentous sibling "affect theory." More precisely, I endeavor to bring the former's salutary historicizing impulses to the latter's often universalizing embrace of the body. In trying to account for early modern experiences of music "moving the affections"—that is, to illuminate what was being moved and how—we need to pay much closer attention to bodies, for sure, but not without treating those bodies as historically and culturally situated, mutable entities.

The rapid consolidation of the history of the emotions as a discipline over recent decades has been accompanied by intense methodological reflections about the (im)possibility of reconstructing past emotional experiences.[2] Efforts to reimagine what grief, love, or shame felt like in particular times and places have been hampered by the fact that language always necessarily intervenes: written records, which form the main point of access to these historical phenomena, invariably mediate any "actual" felt experience. Whether such "actual" experiences exist(ed) beneath the words that attempt to capture them has formed a particular bone of contention.[3] I would suggest, however, that this issue in part rests on the modern psychological construct of an "inner" self versus its "outer" expression, a construct whose validity must be recognized as limited in an early modern context. No doubt its roots extend well back into this period, as evident, for instance, in those Puritan or Pietist discourses of interiority in the decades around 1700 noted in the preceding chapter. Yet that premodern "inner" was not commonly construed as a disembodied entity, but made up of viscera and spirit flows and a soul somehow distributed among or infusing those innards; and all these parts that made up a human body-soul—inner and outer, material and immaterial—remained in constant sympathetic interaction.

A consideration of music, in the guise of spiritual flow, likewise complicates any neat separation between an early modern body-soul's interior and exterior dimensions. Surprisingly, although emotionality has long been celebrated as one of the defining features of Western music since 1600, leading historians of the emotions have so far not drawn extensively on music as a source of insight. Perhaps it is precisely music's reputation for carrying a suspicious surplus of the stuff—its "somewhat suspect . . . or slippery qualities"—that explains this absence.[4] This slipperiness seems either to invite a dubious kind of psychohistory, where pieces of music supposedly offer direct access to the inner life of their creators; or it pushes us to locate music's emotional content squarely within the structural features of the object, detached from the circumstances of its production and reception. The analysis of those structural features is something from which, for good reasons, historians outside of musicology have tended to steer away. Hence neither Jan Plamper's nor Rob Boddice's recent introductions to emotions history mention music as a possible source to consult, while the chapter on "music" in a 2017 volume on early modern emotions retreats to a narrative of music as representation of verbal content.[5]

Yet, as a nonverbal form of affective transmission, music potentially presents a uniquely revealing source of insight into past emotional experiences. This is not to claim that music can somehow grant the unmediated access that language precludes, but rather to propose a fruitful convergence between the performance-centered approach to music I pursue here and a theory of emotions as a kind of practice, recently outlined by Monique Scheer.[6] Of the four kinds of emotional practice identified by Scheer, early modern acts of musicking arguably instantiated at least three: they *mobilized* emotion in their participants, they *communicated* it among those participants, and thereby *regulated* their emotional states.

Regarding Scheer's fourth kind of emotional practice, *naming*, most music notoriously falls short on that front. Some early modern writers certainly made valiant attempts to attach specific emotion labels to particular musical features, as in Johann Mattheson's famous typology of dances, where the courante supposedly expressed "sweet hope," the bourree "contentment," the minuet "moderate joy," and so on.[7] Potentially such naming could indeed help early modern subjects recognize and contain particular bodily-spiritual states, by offering a template for what hope or contentment might feel like. But other commentators instead highlighted the ambiguous or unarticulated emotions a musical performance might elicit, by giving voice to the "unspeakable joy" of God's love, or the "unutterable sighs" of a repentant soul.[8] Here, then, lay one of the sources of music's peculiar affective powers: making audible the complexity, intensity, and malleability of emotional states that may be difficult to put into words. The sonic-affective profile of, say, Johann Sebastian Bach's penitential aria "Erbarme dich" from his *St. Matthew Passion* can hardly be summarized in a single emotion label (remorse? anguish? wistfulness? consolation?). But in unfolding "an inchoate understanding of an experience that has not been named," as Naomi Cumming aptly put it, a performance of the aria could still affect its listeners in ways that were palpable and real: it mobilized their spirits and regulated their emotional states by permeating their attentive body-souls.

In the common understanding of the time, an affective motion consisted in an alteration or disturbance in a person's bodily-spiritual flows. As a "mixed motion," an affective motion involved body and soul in ways that were often closely intermingled and made it difficult to distinguish between causes and symptoms. In the English writer Thomas Wright's summary, "Passions ingender Humors, and Humors breede Passions."[9] These mixed motions troubled the Cartesian binary model of human nature, to the extent that Descartes himself failed to give a persuasive explanation of how this "intimate union" between body and mind worked.[10] Most accounts in the devotional and scientific literature of the time presupposed a model of body-soul interaction that remained nebulous in its details but relied on the mediating capacity of the spirits. Their liquidity directly determined one's corporeal-mental condition. In pleasurable affects such as joy, love, and hope, the spirits expanded and flowed easily, causing sensations of warmth and delight; in negative emotions such as fear, hate, or disgust, the spirits drained from the extremities and contracted around the inner organs, resulting in coldness, pallor, and feelings of trepidation. These alterations in flow could be caused by either internal or external factors—an idea in your head, the food you ate, or an environmental stimulus. Here is Johann Jacob Schmidt's account of the process: "When the mental image of something pleasant or unpleasant enters into us, on account of the conjunction of soul and body the spirits flow out and flood all parts of the body, like an outpouring of rain, according to the different passions being agitated. . . . thus the equilibrium between body and soul, or between the influx of spirits to the extremities and the movement of the blood, nerves, and arteries, is disturbed by these agitated affects."[11]

Schmidt's descriptions of individual affections, which draw on standard formulations encountered across European writings in the period, are worth quoting at some length here in order to convey the psychosomatic tangibility of these motions. In a state of love, Schmidt wrote,

> the vital spirits are roused in the brain and flow out into the whole body, the eyes, ears, and other instruments of the senses, which is why you see sharply and stretch out the ear; and they are often channeled to the heart and breast, so that the heart can apply its powers to effect a stronger expulsion of the blood, which is why in love the face often reddens and a pleasant warmth is felt in the breast and the whole body, since love's nature is to be fiery. . . . Because the blood is expelled from the left heart chamber into the arteries with great force and vigor, the pulse is strong and the heart beats vigorously. . . . Oftentimes love is very painful . . . and then the vital spirits or nerve juice become master over the heart and drive the blood back from the outer parts, so that the face goes pale, the body faints, or otherwise grows ill and weak.[12]

Envy, according to Schmidt, was a "secret hatred mixed with sadness." As a sinful affect, it stemmed from the flesh: it was "an emaciation, which consumes the marrow in the bones and eats away at the body day and night," leading to disrupted sleep and loss of appetite as sharp gall juices flooded the body.[13] According to Mattheson, this was an affliction suffered predominantly by women.[14] Grief, said Schmidt, gave rise to similarly detrimental bodily-spiritual symptoms:

> For if sad thoughts arise in a person, the so-called vital spirits gain predominance in the heart, because it is flooded, compressed, and tightened by an excessive influx of blood, as if the chest was constricted with ropes . . . . The blood circulation in the outer vessels is muted and slow, especially as the blood grows increasingly thicker and clogged. Hence the skin contracts, so to speak, as if it wanted to flee from the imminent evil and bring itself to safety: the whole exterior body goes pale and cold, shrinks and withers

> away. . . . the whole face grows dark . . . The hair grows stiffer and light gray. . . . the mind has no liveliness in it, the speech consists of sad words, the voice is plangent and mixed with constant sighing.[15]

Finally, in joy, the heart

> expands with a strong expulsion of blood into the external limbs, filling up all the furthest hollow blood vessels, which also brings with it a speedy circulation of the vital spirits and hence increased liveliness of the whole body. Hence in joyful people everything rejoices and leaps (Luke 6:23). They feel a pleasant warmth in the whole body; the face is nice and red in color, the voice is clear, the mouth speaks more than usual, and sometimes sings and jubilates (Es. 16:10, Ps. 65:14). . . . the thoughts are filled with nothing but the pleasure one enjoys, and all actions are directed toward enjoying this pleasure to the full.[16]

Schmidt's holistic take on affective phenomena resonates with present-day scientific definitions of emotion as involving "physiological arousal, expressive behaviours and conscious experience."[17] It chimes with perspectives from embodied cognition research and its conception of emotions as a process where "sensations impinge upon our bodies as chemical and neural responses that temporarily change our internal milieu (that is, our visceral environment, the autonomic nervous system, and the flow of hormones in our blood)."[18] Meanwhile, like Schmidt, Francis Bacon also regarded joy as by nature a musically inflected affect: it caused "a Chearfulness and Vigor in the Eyes, Singing, Leaping, Dancing," as well as "sometimes Tears."[19]

Whereas Schmidt considered the affections primarily as arising from the soul and transforming the body, Sigismund Scherertz outlined the opposite process, for instance in experiences of fear or shock: "For when the blood is corrupted from the obstruction of the mesenteric arteries and the pancreas, the vital spirits and the heart as well as the brain are badly damaged. . . . . Out of this all sorts of unhealthy humors or moistures arise, which take away the air from the chest, and rise up to the head like clouds or fog, injure the organ and instrument of reason, and generate all sorts of sad and even monstrous thoughts in the soul."[20] This distributed bodily-mental agency in generating affective motions was widely recognized. Johann Wilhelm Albrecht outlined how lascivious thoughts could guide the blood toward the sperm vessels, thereby increasing the influx of nerve juice and the number of sperm; conversely, if an external stimulus pushed the fluids toward that region, libidinous thoughts could arise in the mind. In a similar way, Albrecht claimed, religious faith entered more easily into the hearts of those who had first been softened by music.[21] Most writers agreed that musical sound, as an out- or influx of spirit, formed one of the most potent sources of affective disruption or regulation. As Bacon surmised, "Tunes and Airs, even in their own nature, have themselves some affinity with the Affections."[22] Hence Athanasius Kircher proposed that "those who fully comprehend this consensus between the animal spirits and affect, as well as between the external and internal air, would be able to stir any person with just their voice into any affect they wanted."[23] If current embodied cognition research on music is still occupied by the question of why "a musical leap somehow feels something like an actual leap," an early modern listener might have answered that, as a singer or instrumentalist set their own spirits a-leaping in producing a kind of merry, leaping music, those spirits exited their bodies with the voices or sounds they emitted and, upon penetrating an auditor's ears and bodies, made their spirits and hearts leap as well.[24]

This kind of leaping affect is afforded, for instance, in some of the foot- and soul-stirring saltarellas intabulated in Gasparo Zanetti's collection *Il scolaro* (1645); their potential for bounciness does not obviously leap off the printed page, but emerges irrepressibly in an animated 1992 rendering by Musica Antiqua.[25] A more sublimated version of this urge to jump up and down might be the rising upbeat motives in the opening ritornello of Antonio Vivaldi's "Et exultavit" in his *Magnificat* (RV 610a) (ex. 16.1). In realizing in sound the potential for a bouncy sort of joyfulness inscribed in the notated text—with bows hopping across strings at a brisk Allegro pace and syncopations generating an energizing friction with the underlying pulse—those string players had the power to make the spirits in their listeners' limbs surge outward and flow along vivaciously. To my own ears, this effect is captured nicely in Rinaldo Alessandrini's sprightly 2016 recording, which—as Brockes predicted—compels me to at least wiggle my toes as I sit tethered to my laptop by a headphone cable.[26] Actual bodily movements of dancing or leaping could occur as one manifestation of such a process of spiritual transference, but even in their absence these transformations unfolded palpably, in inner organs as well as outer limbs, in the brain as well as in the ideas it produced. As Mattheson commented, "for even though you do not actually leap and jump with your feet in church, still in many listeners their heart leaps and jumps in their body when they hear an affective, vivacious harmony and imagine even just a semblance of the eternal glory and grandeur alongside. . . . What else does the frequently encountered biblical word 'exultare' mean but to dance, leap, jump up, jubilate."[27]

EXAMPLE 16.1. Antonio Vivaldi, "Et exultavit," from *Magnificat* (RV 610), mm. 1–5.

A joy-filled musical performance, then, did not just offer a representation of that "heavenly round dance" that Martin Luther imagined hearing in contrapuntal music. As both Protestant and Catholic writers emphasized, such music could generate an actual bodily sensation that anticipated the experience of heavenly delight—a "foretaste" of the indescribable sweetness of heavenly music, produced, according to Kircher, by the liver sending up "sweet vapors" throughout the body for ears, heart, and soul to savor.[28] As Kircher mused, "thus, when a person is in their devotion, in the contemplation of heavenly things, and this same sweetness and loveliness is evoked by means of a beautiful harmony invented for that purpose, then one will observe how suddenly they are moved to external affects and mental rapture through this harmonic sweetness."[29] For some, like Mattheson, this process relied primarily on strategies of representation that appealed to the rational soul, such as depicting the expansion of vital spirits in joy through large intervals.[30] He shared this representational approach with contemporaries such as the French philosopher Jean-Baptiste Dubos, perhaps the most illustrious proponent of what Roger Grant has called "*Affektenlehre* in its mimetic phase."[31] But even though Mattheson resisted the notion that music could move its listeners through "mere sound," the concepts that the soul drew from this sonic stimulation were still "sensory concepts," derived from sensory input that traveled through the body via its flows of spirits, which musical activity could affectively shape and transform.[32] The greatest use of a properly joyful music, Mattheson argued, was the praise of God; and he deemed "joyful singing and sounding in church or at home" the best means to bring about "this expansion of our nerve-spirits and tensing of our fibers." As a mixed motion, this musically generated expansion of the viscera then simultaneously engaged the rational soul through the "skillful, constantly newly invented and inexhaustible combination, alternation, use and mixture" of harmonious sounds.[33] In this fashion, as Hector Mithobius put it some decades earlier, the joy of God could indeed "penetrate people's marrow, bones, heart, soul and spirit."[34]

✷ 17 ✷

Lament

The material-affective impact of music on surrounding body-souls could be felt in a number of interconnected physical, spiritual, and cognitive ways. Music could tickle the ears, stupefy the senses, agitate the bodily fibers, liquefy the blood, contaminate or purify the soul, and carry verbal or pictorial content to the mind and heart. In 1737, the Hamburg critic Johann Adolph Scheibe captured one version of this multilayered process when recounting his response to a Passion chorus by Georg Philipp Telemann. Its skillful musical invention, he wrote, "causes in its listeners a motion that takes hold of the heart, bewitches the senses, freezes the blood and finally, upon recovery, induces wonder, thereupon reflection and ultimately a quiet sense of awe towards the infinite and eternal love of the Creator."[1] Scheibe's account traces a clear progression: once the initial bodily effects had set in, wonder (the primary passion in Descartes's taxonomy) could arise, culminating in the experience of a religious version of the sublime. The French Jesuit Étienne Binet offered a similar description of witnessing a lute player improvising a fantasia, which induced his listeners to drop their chin to their chest and stare with open eyes or mouths, deprived of all senses except hearing, "as if the soul had retired to the edge of the ears." Yet upon a change in the player's chords, Binet reported, these listeners were revived, their "heart returned to their abdomen," leaving behind a sense of amazement.[2] In both these accounts, the affect of wonder constitutes a nexus where the physiological and the psychological converged. Linda Phyllis Austern pinpoints this sense of musically induced wonder in her reading of Thomas Weelkes's madrigal *The Andalusian Merchant* (1600). "The island volcano Fogo, off the west coast of Africa . . . burns slowly with remarkably unexpected harmonies," she writes, forming part of "a series of distinct acoustic impressions of things seen, felt, and perhaps smelled." Yet these are not just pictorial representations of distant places, argues

Austern, but a multi-modal sensory evocation that induced physiological change, making the "ever-kinetic" heart "beat more quickly."[3]

According to Descartes, wonder resulted from "the impression formed in the brain" of a rare object, as well as "from the movement of the spirits," which rushed to the brain and sensory organs to keep the attention on the object.[4] But if it was spirit that held together the self in these intense sonic-affective experiences—causing the blood to freeze and the jaw to drop as much as awe to spread through the soul—this anthropology made it difficult to determine exactly where corporeal effects ended and cognitive or representational patterns began. In Gary Tomlinson's recent biosemiotic account of affect, there is no such transition point: a deep-historical perspective on human evolution, Tomlinson suggests, reveals the emergence of non-linguistic signifying practices among pre-human life-forms, thus rendering any affective engagement with the world fundamentally semiotic in nature.[5] In other words, in trying to establish the extent to which musical experiences were (or are) grounded in the representational capacities of the mind, we may ultimately be asking the wrong question, since the corporeal dimensions of affect in themselves form part of human sense-making processes in encountering the world. Yet while Tomlinson's account is salutary in counteracting the reification of the body/mind binary in current affect theory, its vast chronological sweep renders it less suitable for capturing specific historical experiences. In considering those listeners who heard that 1737 Passion oratorio by Telemann, say, the challenge resides in delineating a historically plausible spectrum of intermingled mental, spiritual, and corporeal responses, with Scheibe's own experience positioned as one among many possible ones.

The striking dissonance opening Arianna's iconic lament in Monteverdi's opera may similarly have registered in different parts of her listeners' historically conditioned body-souls. According to the Italian composer Agostino Steffani, dissonant intervals affected the flow of spirits directly: whereas the simple numerical proportions of consonances such as octaves or fifths caused the spirits to expand, those proportions that deviated from those larger ratios caused the spirits to contract. The smaller the proportions got, the more they inspired a sense of disgust, so that a piece made up entirely of dissonances would drive away "not just humans, but even animals."[6] Such affective reactions, then, were built into the God-designed proportionate bodies of living beings, who could not help but respond viscerally to sonic stimulation. For sure, this number-based system quickly revealed its limitations, since it failed to explain, for instance, the clear affective differentiation between major and minor thirds in contemporary practice; Steffani had to resort to a vague characterization of a minor third causing "I don't know, a more mixed sensation" than a major third.[7] His Dutch contemporary Joan Albert Ban more determinedly described the minor third as "soft, bland and languid," versus the "agitated" major third.[8] Most kinds of contemporary meantone tuning would have exacerbated the difference between pleasant "in-tune" major thirds and unpleasant minor thirds. Christoph Raupach wisely qualified, however, that music's effects arose not solely from sonic proportions, but from the arrangement of all its other elements, such as rhythm, melody, dynamics, timbre, instrumentation, and so on.[9] Even without a purported grounding in numerical proportion, the "squeezing" sensation caused by that opening minor ninth intoned by Arianna could have been felt physically as a contraction of inner organs and spirits, as the soul "draws back and foldeth it self up" upon encountering an unpleasant stimulus (see fig. 1.1).[10]

We might ascribe analogous effects to the numerous other dissonant laments that floated across the seventeenth-century operatic stage and the private chambers of the social elites. The chromatic opening of Barbara Strozzi's solo cantata *Lagrime mie* springs to mind as another such "soul-squeezing" instance, especially in the luxuriant rendering by Emanuela Galli of 1998, in which her voice wavers between the opening consonant e and its dissonant neighbor d-sharp to prolong the grating effect, each time constricting a listener's heart and spirits a little bit more (fig. 17.1).[11] Yet wholesale immersion in this encounter with a soprano's haptic voice would not have constituted the only plausible response. As objects of the (male) aural gaze, these gut-wrenching performances of lamenting women could also serve as sources of aesthetic pleasure, inviting the appreciation

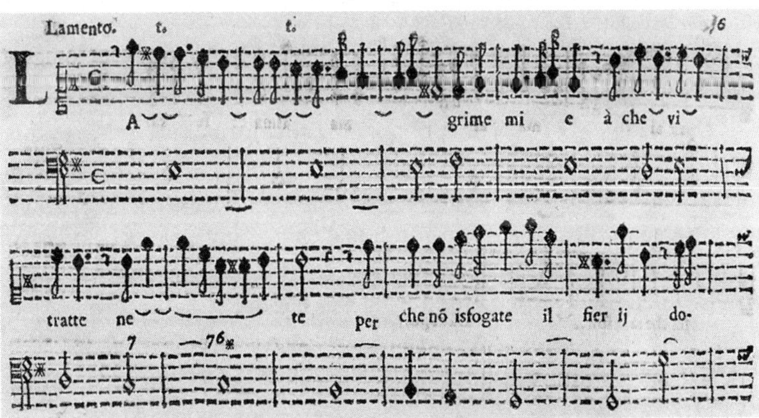

FIGURE 17.1. Barbara Strozzi, *Lagrime mie*, from *Diporti di Euterpe* (Venice: Magni, 1659), excerpt. By permission of University of Glasgow Archives & Special Collections, Euing R.c.17.

of beautiful sounds and forms. That pleasure, too, could come in more carnal or more cerebral guises, but it tended to operate at one remove from an immediate experience of co-suffering with a performer. The French theorist Marin Mersenne addressed this reflexive dimension of musical listening when arguing that "music in a certain way separates the spirit from the body and puts it in a state where it is more suited to contemplation than to action." Even if that spirit was very much still conceived as a material entity, whose "downflow" in moments of sadness rendered one's limbs heavy, the "slow movements of sad tunes" could also "bring back the spirit to itself," leaving it "at greater leisure to contemplate the beauty of the voice." Hence, a mournful piece could afford an overriding sense of pleasure or bliss in "inciting [the spirit] to a more profound speculation."[12] This seems to have been what happened to Scheibe when listening to Telemann's Passion chorus, a meditative "ecce homo" moment at the climax of the crucifixion narrative.[13] Significantly, Mersenne eschewed Steffani's proportion-based system in favor of a concept of habituation in explaining the pleasure aroused by consonant sounds, which, he noted, certain non-European populations did not share. Since we cannot perceive the exact configurations of the animal spirits that carry external stimuli to the common sense, Mersenne argued, we "do not know why one configuration or movement seems more pleasurable than others."[14] Why dissonances might make the spirits contract, or else induce a state of contemplative delight, ultimately remained a mystery, but for Mersenne these effects only worked in those body-souls acculturated to this particular musical tradition.

This layering of potential listening responses—physiological, psychological, emotive, contemplative—appears to be taken to another level in Monteverdi's later *Lamento della Ninfa*, whose narrative design left its listeners in the twice-removed position of observing a group of shepherds observing a lamenting nymph. The piece's descending tetrachord ground bass, that "emblem of the lament," potentially contributed further to this distancing effect: not only did it constitute a conventional sign by this point, thus enriching or disrupting the process of material sonic transmission by interposing a representational device, but its repetitions underlined the theatricality of the situation by creating a kind of aural frame within which the nymph's outpouring was contained.[15] This bifurcation of the musical fabric thereby offered a duality of perspectives on the subject as simultaneously unfettered and disciplined in its affective expression.[16] Yet I would want to resist a teleological narrative according to which the nymph's lament is situated past a supposed point of rupture that separated a resemblance-based model of musical expression from a later representation-based one.[17] Rather, as Scheibe's and Mersenne's accounts suggest, levels of (habituated) carnal and mental appreciation, of resonant and representational impact, continued to co-constitute listening experiences well into the eighteenth century, determined not only by listeners' temperaments, but by the location and context of a performance in church or on stage. The ground bass in the *Lamento della Ninfa,* while clearly inviting a representational reading, simultaneously afforded the possibility of intense corporeal engagement, involving that "bodily memory" invoked by Descartes as an explanation for why different musics made people want to dance or cry.[18] A listener's in situ experience of that bass pattern, with its inexorable pull toward the tonic that nonetheless denied any sense of repose by continuing to descend ever more, may well have been as much visceral as cognitive: it engaged their bodily habitus, shaped by the expressive patterns of tonal harmony as they consolidated at the time. In Marko Aho's words, acculturated listeners can come to appreciate such stylistic features "intimately with our felt living bodies."[19] As the nymph's upward sighs strained against the downward drag of the bass, or as Purcell's Dido was propelled to take yet another breath by a bass line droning on past her vocal cadences, those pulls and pushes could be felt in the very stuff of a habituated listening body, while simultaneously offering tingles of sensory pleasure derived from the beauty of a particular vocal grain, as well as a rational appreciation of the unfolding spectacle.

In some early modern instances of musical lamenting, these layered bodily-spiritual effects could induce moments of profound cognitive (or corporeal) dissonance as well, as in Heinrich Ignaz Biber's lament in his *Battalia* of 1673. Following the larger-than-life musical depictions of drunkards and soldiers earlier in the piece, would the drawn-out chromatic descents in the concluding lament for the wounded have left listeners crying or amused—or both? Music's indeterminacy in such cases could generate an experiential amalgamation of affective strands that in verbal language would need to be separated out into distinct emotion labels. A generation later, Telemann exploited this potential for multilayered affectivity in his instrumental suite on Miguel Cervantes's novel *Don Quixote.* In the fourth movement, "Ses soupirs amoureux" (his amorous sighs), listeners heard the conventional (downward) musical sigh motive subjected to critical inspection through relentless exaggeration, offering a sonic parody of the solipsistic tendencies of the modern self.[20] As the sigh was uttered at least 66 times across the movement in ever higher, more urgent registers, the primordial bodily-vocal expression of woe from which the motive initially took shape revealed itself as fully sedimented into conventional, detachable, and recyclable musical gesture. Rather than just instigating an unmediated intercorporeal affective flow that permeated per-

EXAMPLE 17.1. Georg Philipp Telemann, "Ses soupirs amoureux après la Princesse Dulcinée," from *Burlesque de Quichotte* (TWV 55:G10), mm. 1–10.

formers and listeners, these notated gestures perhaps enticed Telemann's string ensemble to adopt a more aloof position of knowing about and commenting upon the bodily-mental states of those they represented with their hackneyed formulas (ex. 17.1).

Any individual performance of Telemann's piece might have ended up emphasizing or concealing this potential for hyperbolic play-acting; and any listener would have had to find their own degree of suspension of disbelief or ironic detachment vis-à-vis the spectacle. In exploiting the potential gap between affective flow and performative simulation, Telemann's score afforded the possibility for undermining a "nativist" paradigm in which even feigned emotion was understood to be produced from a real flow of spirits within. By the time of Gotthold Ephraim Lessing, an actor could indeed appear "animated with the most intense feeling" when it was in fact "nothing but mechanical imitation."[21] In the realm of music-making, an analogous process meant, on the one hand, the gradual relocation of music's affective capacities to the notes themselves, leaving the performer merely as a vessel through which that affective content was channeled; and, on the other, an invitation to listeners to attend with a degree of "disinterestedness" that placed them at least partly outside the spirit-fueled affective circuit of score-performer-(instrument-)sound-listener. Telemann's listeners might have found themselves moved to pity by the lovesick musical subject of "Ses soupirs amoureux"; but they might (simultaneously or alternatively) have been able to crack a smile at its caricature. Smiling and laughter, of course, were and are corporeal phenomena, too: in laughter, according to Laurent Joubert, the pericardium, "the sheath or cover of the heart pulls on the diaphragm."[22] Nonetheless, in capitalizing on this potential for a more reflexive encounter with a sonic utterance, such modes of musical expression may well have facilitated the gradual transposition of certain kinds of European art music to the ostensibly disembodied domain of the Kantian aesthetic.

18

Pulse

For all we can tell, there is no straightforward correlation between specific musical features and a listener's heart rate. Studies to date have ascertained that heart and respiratory rates tend to increase in response to exciting music compared with calm music, and that they decrease in response to "unpleasant" music compared with "pleasant" music.[1] The evidence for a direct entrainment of heart rate to musical beats is inconsistent. According to one study, musical listening increases synchronization among various cerebral and cardiovascular rhythms, which may underlie the "pleasurable and palliative effects of listening to music."[2] Another study similarly found that autonomic responses can be synchronized with music, which "might therefore convey emotions through autonomic arousal during crescendos or rhythmic phrases."[3] These effects seem greatest when music is self-selected according to taste, suggesting a strong element of habituation in determining listeners' responses. Here is the Lutheran theologian Caspar Calvör musing on this phenomenon in 1717: "It is a strange thing," he wrote, that a musical melody "affects the soul very differently when it is sung or played in a low, middle, or high register, slow or fast, with a soft or muted voice rather than a loud voice, in duple or triple meter, in major or minor, with smaller and closer or larger, more widely spaced intervals."[4] Calvör explained these differences as stemming from "the different motion of the external air, in that it is either strongly forced or softly stroked, so to speak, and set into motion quickly or slowly, and so on, and thereby brings the corresponding air into the same motion together with the acoustic nerve it touches and the associated spirits and affects."[5] A soft and sedate affect, he claimed, arose from a choice of low to medium register, slow tempo, soft timbre, duple meter, and a minor key with small intervals; a high, fresh, and strong voice in triple meter, using hard or sharp intervals, incited the soul to wild, exultant motions.

Calvör's explanations veer surprisingly close to current trends in the psychology of musical emotions, recently summarized by Patrik Juslin, who, for instance, lists fast tempo, major mode, medium to loud dynamics, high pitch, smooth and fluent rhythm, and so on as indicators for happiness.[6] Where Juslin carefully grounds his multivalent model of emotional arousal in the latest neurobiological insights, however, Calvör happily embraced that nativist fallacy of assuming that, through vibrational contact, musical sound could directly generate affective states in a receiving body-soul. Yet, while Calvör's account undoubtedly falls short in terms of present-day standards of intellectual rigor, it offers a counterbalance to the tendency in much current psychological research to locate musical emotions primarily in the interaction between listener and musical object, with performance treated as a more or less dispensable add-on. Although Juslin acknowledges that hardly any musical feature will invariably arouse a certain emotion, he puts this down primarily to variations in listener disposition and listening context.[7] His taxonomy presents a set of emotion-generating features inherent in a musical work or passage, some of which may be "modulated" in performance. For Calvör, instead, it was the performative moment, the impact of airflow on a listening body-soul, that formed the source of any potential affective arousal. As Juslin explains, even a full-blown "arousal theory" of emotion today will tend to assume a process of the brain decoding certain evolved or conventional signals, which may then produce states of mental and physical arousal. Calvör rather imagined the process as directly, materially contagious.

Calvör's position chimes with attempts by some of his French contemporaries to locate music's expressive capabilities in the air-bending qualities of the voice. Descartes affirmed that "to the Creation of an acute sound, is required a more forcible emission of the breath, or spirit in vocall Musick; or a stronger percussion of the strings in instrumentall"; those emissions then strike the ear more forcefully.[8] On this basis, as Catherine Gordon-Seifert has explored, French commentators such as Jean-Léonor de Grimarest discussed vocal gesture, *accens*, tone, and strength as generating different passions. Hope, wrote Grimarest, expressed itself with a strong voice, jealousy with a bold one.[9] Even though Gordon-Seifert's project ends up primarily considering how composers represented different passions in their settings, she reminds us that for writers such as Bertrand Bénigne de Bacilly, it was in fact the singers' responsibility to "animate" their voices so as to generate passionate expression.[10] In that act of animation—of "humoring" a piece of music, as Thomas Mace put it—the notation served as a script that afforded certain modes of emotional enactment, which fueled but also potentially outstripped the representational process.[11] Even if a performer was "merely" play-acting, an early modern spirit-based anthropology rendered it difficult to maintain a clear separation between a performer's inner state and outward expression. Such an anthropology also blurs the distinction often upheld in current emotions research between perceived and felt emotion, or "raw feeling versus reflective consciousness" in responses to music.[12] As Thomas Wright asserted, if one intended to "imprint a passion in another, it is requisit first it be stamped in our hearts: for thorow our voices, eyes, and gestures, the world will pierce and thorowly perceive how we are affected."[13] His advice harks back all the way to Quintilian's instruction for orators, to "feel those emotions oneself" that one wished to instill in others, necessitating an act of holistic impersonation that rendered such "feigned" emotion, in Joseph Roach's analysis, "indistinguishable from genuine feeling."[14]

As an animated and animating process, then, music-making affected air and flesh in ways that hardly abided by those emotional taxonomies proposed by either Calvör or Juslin. Bacilly tried to encapsulate this hard-to-capture effect of an ensouled performance with the notion of "mouvement":

> Mouvement . . . is a certain quality that gives soul to the song, and it is called Mouvement because it stirs up, I may say it excites, the listeners' attention, in the same way as do those who are the most rebellious in harmony; . . . it inspires in hearts such passion as the singer wishes to create, principally that of tenderness. . . . I don't doubt at all that the variety of Mesure, whether quick or slow, contributes a great deal to the expression of the song. But there is certainly another quality, more refined and more spiritual, that always holds the listener attentive and ensures that the song is less tedious.[15]

Not unlike the relationship of (immeasurable) *mouvement* to (countable) *mesure*, pulse in the seventeenth-century imagination constituted something more than the modern quantifiable value of heart rate. Though empirically accessible (by touch) and widely used in medical diagnosis, pulse constituted a moral as well as a physiological entity. This is hinted at in William Fenner's take on the affections as "the soules pulse," whereby, as his subtitle proclaimed, "a Christian may know whether he be living or dying."[16] In an early modern Hippocratic-Galenic anthropology, pulse formed a central element of a person's bodily-spiritual constitution, revealing their state of health and virtue to the expert hand of the physician. Beyond its frequency, its felt qualities—strong or weak, hard or soft, full or empty, intermittent, redoubling, ant- or worm-like (formicans, vermicularis), wave-like (undosus), and so on—revealed bodily-spiritual equilibrium or disruption.[17] A "small artery" in a healthy person indicated a cold temperament, in a sick person a "withering of the body and a sad heart"; if the pulse in a healthy person was "small and fast," it revealed a "hot and pressing nature" with an irascible temperament.[18] The qualities of an individual's pulse were determined by their humoral disposition as well as the influence of the non-naturals; Georg Heuermann noted that "running, jumping, strong movements" as well as "spastic contraction of the arteries as in fear, shock or excessive joy" altered the pulse.[19] Medical practitioners were to take a patient's pulse only when both parties found themselves in a calm state. The voice, meanwhile, figured as "an echo of the pulsating arteries [Puls-Adern] in the air, via the lungs," thereby sounding out a person's "natural morals" as grounded in their "whole inner complexion."[20]

Music's connections with pulse had been well established since antiquity. They ranged from the representation of different pulse types in musical notation by the Polish physician Joseph Struthius (fig. 18.1) and later Robert Fludd to the analogy between pulse and musical tactus.[21] This analogy was invoked increasingly in the wake of the more "pulsating" styles of music-making emerging after 1600: "The tactus was invented . . . from the movement and pulsation of the heart," wrote Johann Georg Ahle in 1704.[22] Music's "modulations of the air," as the Lübeck medic Hermann Grube called them, could alter the quality of a listener's pulse through their metrical ordering.[23] The French writer Nicolas Bergier developed a complete system of rhythmic ethos on this basis, charting the soporific effects of spondees and the bellicose pyrrhic that made soldiers march.[24] These effects were indeed most easily observed in military music, as well as in dance tunes, whose "titillation we regularly sense in us at the beats of instruments, especially when the body is lightened with wine and rejoices with more vivid and subtle spirits"; in this scenario, a participant "can hardly refrain from dancing in the presence of a musical consort."[25] More generally, the basic notion of tactus was firmly tied to bodily motion: as Johann Samuel Beyer wrote in 1703, tactus is "the correct lowering and raising of the hand, with which both vocal and instrumental musicians have to align themselves."[26] And this motion then transferred itself to surrounding bodies: numerous writers confirmed Descartes's observation that "a slow measure doth excite in us gentle, and sluggish motions, such as a kind of Languor, Sadnesse, Fear, Pride, and other heavy, and dull Passions," and a swift measure the nimbler passions of joy, anger, or courage.[27] Triple meter, suggested Calvör, was particularly apt at rousing lively or exulted affects, because "as the tactus is divided into two unequal parts, and leaps along in a limping way on three feet, so to speak, thus the spirits leap and limp together with the bodily feet with particular levity." He claimed that this

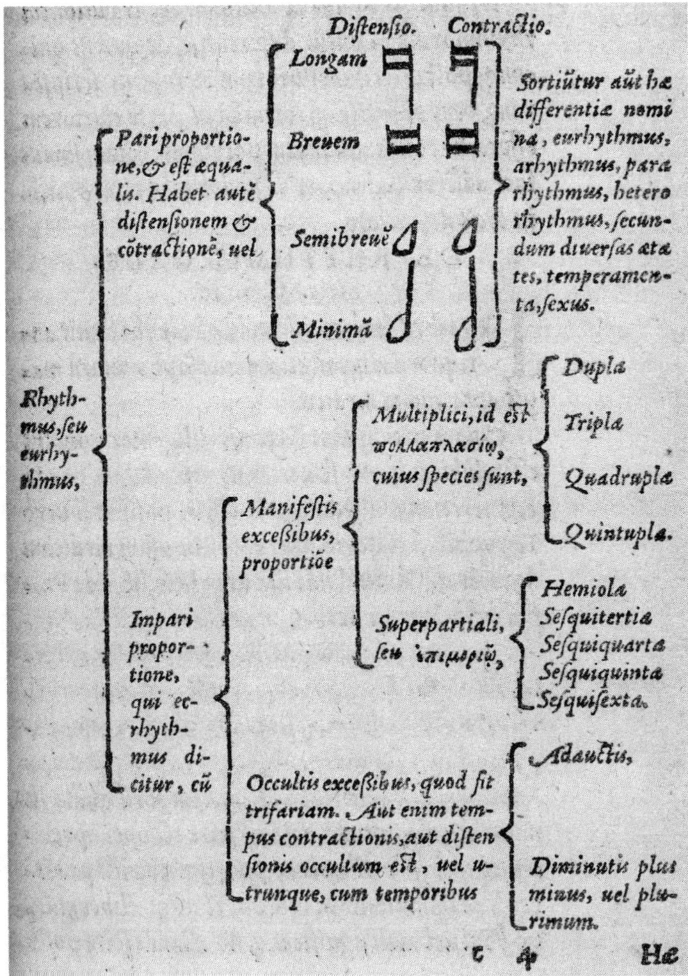

FIGURE 18.1. Heart rhythms shown in musical notation. Joseph Struthius, *Sphymicae artis jam mille ducentos annos perditae et desideratae Libri V* (Basel: Oporinus, 1555), vol. 1, 23. © British Library Board, General Reference Collection DRT Digital Store 775.e.2. Courtesy of the British Library, digitized by the Google Books project.

effect could be observed even in those lower-class attendees at wedding celebrations who knew little about the finer art of dancing, based simply on the "great correspondence and harmony" between the motion of the external and internal air. Hence, he observed, "when the violin produces a slow and decent sound in its middle register," a dancer would automatically moderate their bodily movements.[28] Guichard Joseph Duverney reported a commonly held explanation for this effect of sound on pulse rate:

as the nerves of the outer ear "communicate with those of the Heart and the Lungs, it is from hence that we feel the same Alterations in the Pulse and in Respiration."[29]

The regular pulse that usually underpinned these acts of music-making appears amplified in some pieces—not necessarily intended for dancing—through the insertion of consistent rests between beats, which can increase the sense of a two-part systole/diastole configuration. The free-flowing sixteenth notes produced by a keyboardist's right hand in Johann Sebastian Bach's Prelude in D Major from the *Well-Tempered Clavier* I are anchored by this pulsating sort of bass pattern in the left hand, to which the inner air of a performer (and listeners if present) may have become "entrained" as their spirits resonated with its regular impulses (fig. 18.2). Depending on a performer's choice of tempo, weight, and bounciness of attack, as well as their listeners' internal dispositions, the experience might have been either enlivening or calming, worm- or ant-like; but in any case, exposure to this music could have had a regulating effect on the body's internal rhythms, bringing about that "recreation of the spirit" famously invoked by Bach in reference to his keyboard music. In abandoning this steady bass motion seven measures before the end, coupled with increased chromaticism and smaller note values, a performance may have offered a pleasurable moment of rousing the spirits before relaxing into the closing concord (fig. 18.3).

FIGURE 18.2. Johann Sebastian Bach, Prelude in D Major (BWV 850), from *Well-Tempered Clavier* I, excerpt. Staatsbibliothek zu Berlin—Preußischer Kulturbesitz, Musikabteilung mit Mendelssohn-Archiv, Mus.ms. Bach P 202 (4).

FIGURE 18.3. Johann Sebastian Bach, Prelude in D Major (BWV 850), from *Well-Tempered Clavier* I, excerpt. Staatsbibliothek zu Berlin—Preußischer Kulturbesitz, Musikabteilung mit Mendelssohn-Archiv, Mus.ms. Bach P 202 (4).

Sustained irregular rhythms, on the other hand, could engender a disorderly state of the heart and affections. If Mattheson defined an aria as a "große Gemüthsbewegung" (a great motion of the soul), this quality becomes immediately tangible in Thomas Quasthoff's gripping enactment of Judas's raging despair in "Gebt mir meinem Jesum wieder" from Bach's *St. Matthew Passion*, in a staged performance of 2010 directed by Peter Sellars.[30] As Tom Huizenga commented in a review for NPR, it was "practically impossible not to feel emotionally spent" after participating in this affective transaction.[31] I have not assessed whether my own pulse rate is consistently affected by viewing Quasthoff's performance on DVD, but I have found its sensations of raging despair less represented in the notes than distributed and flowing between his voice and body (often in close focus in the video production), the solo violinist's moving fingers, bow, and torso, the forceful musical gestures and figurations collectively produced by the ensemble, their timbre and sonic impact, and my own bodily and mental kinetics. Here is the English Puritan writer John Downame on the "mixed motion" of anger (considered a less intense form of rage):

> It maketh the hair stand on end . . . . The eyes to stare and candle . . . . The teeth to gnash like a furious Bore. . . . The tongue to stammer, as being not able to expresse the rage of the hart. The bloud ready to burst out of the vaines . . . . The brest to swell, as being not large enough to containe their anger, and therefore seeketh to ease it selfe, by sending out hot-breathing sighes. The hands to beate the tables and walles . . . . The feete to stampe the guiltlesse earth . . . . So that anger deformeth the body from the hayre of the head to the soale of the foote.[32]

Johann Jacob Schmidt reported even more violent psychosomatic symptoms, including the pulse being agitated so much by the influx of hot gall that "eventually blood flows out of the mouth, nose, ears, womb, or from wounds," and "occasionally even the soul is driven out of the body."[33]

None of these drastic symptoms, we must assume, afflicted the participants at Bach's Leipzig performances of his *St. Matthew Passion*. But an account that merely enumerates those features of the aria's score that may have depicted anger—according to Juslin, that could be fast tempo, minor mode, dissonance, high sound level, high pitch, staccato articulation, complex rhythms, and sharp timbre, among others—potentially falls short of capturing where and how this "große Gemüthsbewegung" unfolded its effects. The conventions of the eighteenth-century operatic rage aria indeed comprised some of those stylistic markers.[34] Yet their emotive force, I would suggest, arose from the ways in which these features were brought to life in different constellations in individual moments of performance. That opening downward motive in Bach's aria (ex. 18.1) only becomes a resolute foot-stamping gesture in the hands of an ensemble that embraces the heaviness of this first downbow and its rebound. In terms of pulse, the opening potentially registered as a shock to the system, with the instant syncopation in the upper parts laboring against the two quarter-note beats of the bass, which then failed to settle into a steady pattern, shifting to an eighth-note pulse with a syncopation over the bar line, and stopping abruptly at the end of the phrase.

In some recordings available today, I feel that initial plunge of the upper strings into the gap between the two bass notes in the pit of my stomach: less, perhaps, in the Dunedin Consort's version of 2008, whose players let the second note fade away politely, and more in the earthy rendering of the Dresden Staatskapelle in 1987.[35] The vocalist in the Dunedin recording, too, seems to aim for a beautiful legato line more than a full-blooded activation of the affective force afforded by the notation. But rather than conclude that their performance somehow does the wrong thing to a stable and legible musical object, I would suggest instead that it is simply too schematic to classify this piece as a "rage aria" based on certain stylistic markers discernible in the score. In practice, that score offers a script for a range of subtly divergent emotive utterances that instantiate and intermingle different affective strands, from outrage to pleading, despair, or shame. In any given performance, any of those affective strands may only emerge in a sort-of-meaningful way, and each sonic realization may bring out affective layers that work against a habitual reading of these words and notes. The abrasive energy and rasping gut-string timbre exuding from Philippe Herreweghe's 1998 recording with Dietrich Henschel encapsulates that

EXAMPLE 18.1. Johann Sebastian Bach, "Gebt mir meinen Jesum wieder," from *St. Matthew Passion* (BWV 244), mm. 1–5.

potency of anger to deform the body perhaps more grippingly than the clipped, bouncy version led by Françoise Lasserre in 2015.[36] But in the latter performance, too, the vigorous disjointed octave- and string-crossings produced by the solo violinist to me offer not just the specific image of money thrown to the ground, as a representational reading might have it, but a sonic experience of something (air, spirits, innards) being torn apart and tossed about. In Sellars's performance, moreover, the way in which the violinist looms over the seated Quasthoff as he unleashes his aggressive brand of virtuosity pits the two soloists of the aria against each other, in a manner that makes the singer's seemingly confident verbal demands appear in a rather less familiar light.

Feelings of disruption and overexertion are afforded by the notated text in other ways, too, starting with the repetition of what seems a tonally settled opening statement in G major up a step in A minor, with the continuo players destabilized by having to start on the third of the chord and then drop down a diminished fourth. For the voice, that opening syncopated nosedive on "Gebt" is an awkward way in, later compounded by increasingly wide leaps in the opposite direction, with Quasthoff's voice audibly breaking on the octave jump to d in measure 39. Excess energy spills out in the meticulously notated, gratuitous embellishment in measure 15; in the forceful on-the-beat exhalations of "seht," rising agonizingly higher on their repeat; in the syllable "zu" breaking in too early each time it is pronounced; and in the way that vocal phrases break off at different points in the measure. The shifting, stop-and-start progress of the bass line would also have allowed a growing sense of deformity to creep under a listener's skin. If that opening phrase did not quite let participants settle into a regular pulse, its repetition could have generated expectations for a higher-level regularity—only for that expectation to be confounded by the shift to another rhythmic pattern from measure 5, and again from measure 7, which could drop listeners into a sonic pothole on the third beat as the preceding bass pattern was disrupted. Another one of these bass-line potholes loomed at the missing first beat of measure 23, enhanced by Bach's dynamic indications for the rest of the string players: the notation asked them to play *piano* from measure 22 and not shift to *forte* until the second beat of measure 23, thereby further discouraging any first-beat accentuation. Even the final cadence is overrun by a wanton extra quarter note.

In many ways, then, Bach's aria offered an opportunity for performers to enact and inflict on surrounding body-souls some version of the perturbation articulated in Schmidt's description of anger, of "the poor body with its solid and liquid parts being thrown or tossed between two endpoints, so to speak."[37] Yet any such effect would have come down less to *mesure* than *movement*; that is, to the kinetic energy of a performative experience, with its multivalent flows and unquantifiable admixtures of affect. And, once again, a straightforward transfer of that performative energy to anyone attending, as imagined by Calvör, would not have been the only possible mode of response. Some of Bach's listeners may have had an unmediated experience of sonic impact altering their pulse rates and enfolding their body-souls. Others might have participated more dispassionately, in line, perhaps, with Mersenne's description of French musical practice as opposed to the more "violent" Italian manner: "Airs are not made in order to excite anger and several other passions, but to give enjoyment to the minds of the listeners, and sometimes to incline them to religious devotion, as in church music. I do not wish to deny that certain airs . . . may move to pity, compassion, regret, and other passions, but only that this is not their chief aim, which is to give enjoyment."[38] A performance of Bach's aria may have had the power to elicit many of these affective motions listed here, plus the pleasurable thrill of a virtuosic musical spectacle; as well as, ultimately, a tangible intensification of his congregants' devotional fervor.

✷ 19 ✷
Contagion

Men are made, not born, Christians.

TERTULLIAN, *Apology*, xviii

"What if religion is not only about language, books, or belief?" asks Donovan Schaefer in his 2015 book on *Religious Affects*. "In what ways is religion . . . about the way things feel, the things we want, the way our bodies are guided through thickly textured, magnetized worlds? Or the way our bodies flow into relationships—loving or hostile—with other bodies?"[1] As part of a broader materialist shift across the humanities, affect has become a catalyst for refiguring human beings as bodily assemblages rather than reasoning selves. Based on Gilles Deleuze and Felix Guattari's conception of affect as "a prepersonal intensity corresponding to the passage from one experiential state of the body to another," affect has come to designate the "visceral forces beneath, alongside, or generally *other than* conscious knowing."[2] In the shape of, say, Steve Goodman's "ontology of vibrational force," affect promises to reverse Western modernity's privileging of the cognitive over the somatic in dealing with sonic phenomena.[3] Of course, as Brian Kane and others have pointed out, the claim that affect operates prior to regimes of signification ultimately serves to prolong rather than overcome this dualism, by continuing to reify the mind as disembodied consciousness lodged in a container of vibrating matter.[4] As a historian, I remain suspicious of the universalizing tendencies in certain strands of affect theory, which hold that affect *is* a nonsignifying, nonconscious intensity of "the body." I also share Suzanne Cusick's concerns regarding the "dystopian political possibilities" implicit in a vibration-centered model of human sociality. Nevertheless, this re-emergence of affect offers productive impulses for recovering that "very liquid materiality" of Baroque music recently invoked by Marie Thompson and Ian Biddle.[5] Early modern notions and experiences of affect destabilize the normative listening subject of the modern concert hall, with its "strong sense of separateness, of uniqueness from all other persons . . . whose emotions are felt to be known in their entirety and complexity only to him or herself."[6] The affects I investigate here deny the boundedness and privacy of an intangible inner self, as they spilled out of bodies and souls, voices and instruments. They were distributed and contagious, passed on from parents to offspring via their semen, or to nursing infants via the affectively charged milk they drank.[7]

Contagion, as Albrecht Koschorke has outlined, formed the "vital principle" of pre-modern social cohesion before modernity's gradual "drying up of the interspace between individuals."[8] Musical contagion operated along those same damp material-spiritual pathways. Martin Heinrich Fuhrmann's own ontology of vibrational force pointed out the capacity of a 16-foot sub-bass on the organ to "shake and rattle" several thousand people in a church by reverberating below the deepest reaches of human vocality.[9] Congregational singing held comparable powers. Our standard accounts of Reformation hymnody have tended to sideline the practice's affective dimensions in favor of a narrative of word-centered desensualization: "Even if the proliferation of songs in a certain way signified a return of the affects to the liturgy," the Reformation historian Susan Karant-Nunn has argued, "the main emphasis even in the songs was on the words."[10] There is no doubt, of course, that the texts were crucial to the function and appeal of these hymns. Yet, as the music theorist Andreas Werckmeister wisely concluded already in 1691, this was once again a matter of both/and: "For this reason we have a variety of precious hymns and psalms, which move the hearts of people with both the words and also with their song and sound."[11] The corporeal-affective work performed by communal hymn singing, in its conjunction of words, melodies, and the act of intoning them, formed a key source of their contagious efficacy. As the German hymnwriter Johann Olearius affirmed, the potency of congregational song arose from "the power of God's word which, together with the pleasant melodies that awaken the spirit, penetrates the heart and accomplishes incredible transformations in people."[12] Hymnody here emerges as a collective process of bodily-spiritual renewal, with music providing the crucial link between cognitive and affective appreciation. In the words of Christoph Frick, sacred songs "infuse and imprint the Christian doctrine so deeply into the hearts of people both young and old that it can no longer be eradicated from there."[13] If the notion that knowledge retention in humans worked by leaving physical imprints in the body was widespread at the time, it also chimes with certain current readings of emotional memory as operating outside of standard cognitive pathways, instead taking place at the level of enfolding affects into the body.[14] Communal singing, as Frick suggested, provided the degree of affective intensity necessary for enabling this bodily inscription of memory.

In this respect, singing could develop powers that outstripped those of speaking or, specifically, preaching. Frick affirmed: "These songs have the peculiar capacity and nature that they embed a thing deeply into people and make it appealing. Therefore, when the singing comes from the heart, it can happen in some people that through a Christian song something is accomplished that the sermon could not do."[15] Such heartfelt singing did not merely proclaim religious belief, then, but instantiated it as a felt reality. It could bring about a merging of divine and human spirit, as "there is a power of the Holy Spirit in hymns, and when this power touches a human spirit, one spirit ignites the other, and spirit in spirit boils and burns."[16] And this effect was not confined to an individual believer's experience; it spread outward, touching and transforming other bodies. As the Lutheran preacher Hector Mithobius put it, "through music everything that lives is moved, because the heavenly soul that bestows life on all takes its origin from music."[17] His assertion that music could not but "stick" (haften) to its participants resonates with Sara Ahmed's recent theorization of the "stickiness" of affect as it moves between people and objects in any given affective economy.[18] From such a perspective, music could appear less as a tool used by humans for their own ends than as a pre-personal, even numinous force that worked through them inexorably. But early modern hymnody was, of course, a deeply human, political practice, serving the coercive purposes of Reformation rulers or Jesuit missionaries. The newly disciplined bodies of converted colonial subjects were subdued by the contagious power of singing no less than by the actual diseases imported by the colonizers: the "hearing of the infidel [is] mellowed with sonorous voices . . . their proud brutality appeased with the sweet arms of instrumental and vocal music."[19] Like the foods Amerindians were urged to consume in order to acquire a European complexion, hymns altered not just the content of their religious beliefs but their corporeal-affective disposition to accord with missionary power structures.[20] The insight articulated by the first Bishop of New Spain in 1540, that "more than by preaching the natives are converted by the music," formed the foundation of a centuries-long process of "soft" acculturation: unlike infectious illnesses or certain food stuffs, singing did not routinely kill off its subjects, but offered an ostensibly innocuous tool of bodily-spiritual coercion.[21]

Early modern Lutheran believers, fixed into place in newly erected pews to face the pulpit, were subject to analogous—if in no way existentially threatening—measures of musical disciplining, cajoled into joining in the song through sonic contagion. Jennifer Linhart Wood has traced this process of attunement in the context of early modern theatergoing, where "sound impacts bodies present at sonic events, calibrating them to the same frequencies through vibration and forming networks of connection among them."[22] Athanasius Kircher outlined the process as follows: "For since the heart is the home and residence of the spirit, the animal spirits receive and channel the trembling and moving air to the breast and come to accord with the sounds they carry; and the spirits in the other body parts then follow them accordingly. . . . For the spirits that reside in the heart are moved according to the motion of the external sound . . . . And this must be assumed to be the reason why people, when they hear others sing, want to join in by singing or humming along."[23] This was a vibrational ontology enriched by the assumption that sonic contagion operated across bodily, spiritual, mental, and moral domains as meaningful affective flow. In Frick's account, communal singing "penetrates all the blood vessels of the heart and awakens its affect . . . . Thereby the Holy Spirit prevents much evil among people and ignites their hearts with true devotion, heartfelt thanksgiving, a joyful attitude towards their work, and various other Christian virtues."[24] Religious feeling appears here not simply as an accompaniment to the cognitive dimension of faith, but also not detached from or prior to it as mere vibration of the flesh. The Pietist-leaning Heinrich Müller vividly described this integrated psychosomatic nature of faith: "For when God reveals himself to the soul as the highest sweetness, he rips like a fire through body and soul, through all senses and faculties, touches every droplet of blood and ignites it in burning love. And as our love is, so all our other motions will be; love draws the whole soul after it, with its hope, fear, joy, sadness, etc., and whatever the nature of these motions is, thus flow the psalms we sing."[25]

Congregational song as an outflow of true faith relied on a physiology of circulating blood and spirits, by means of which the singing voice could supposedly emerge directly from the heart. The Lutheran preacher Paul Gottfried Praetorius asserted: "God demands that in songs of praise mouth and heart are both kept engaged: in the heart, true devotion and spiritual joy from contemplating God's merciful deeds should be stirred: and then these should break out through the voice, mouth, and tongue."[26] The role of vernacular song in the "aural contestation of the worship space" between confessions thus extended to the very bodies occupying that space, tying them together by flowing through and between them.[27] As in the case of infectious disease, such contagion relied on a degree of bodily porousness that allowed entry to the infecting agent. In reference to the transmission of syphilis, the Italian physician Carlo Musitano found that "it is not enough that the poisonous vapor touches the flesh, but the vital spirit has to feel it."[28] Communally produced sound waves traveled to the insides of neighboring bodies to inflect their spiritual makeup. As the Rostock theologian Theophil Großgebauer claimed, referencing Paul's letter to the Ephesians (5:18–20): "Singing psalms in your mind . . . does not help to bolster the community, but when the whole congregation sings in the spirit and speaks to one another through psalms, this improves them and leaves them full of spirit."[29]

Of course, musical contagion was not a foolproof process, notwithstanding its vibrational grounding by which it ostensibly shook bodies indiscriminately. These early modern listeners were not merely vibrating passively like "jellyfish wobbling on the beach," in Michael Spitzer's memorable formulation.[30] Contemporary complaints regarding congregants' actively non-compliant behaviors were plentiful, ranging from people singing at different speeds and altering the words to the organist disrupting the proceedings with excessive interludes. Moreover, the music's sensual appeal—its sugary sweetness—could distract from the content it was meant to instill. Mithobius cautioned: "We do consider it sinful and wrong, when singing and playing music, to pay more attention to the melody and the sweet sound of the voice than to the text and words themselves, for the harmony and delight of the song is only created for the purpose that the gracious word of God can infiltrate the heart all the more; just like one tends to sugarcoat a medicine, when the only point is the medicine and not the sugar."[31] Often, wrote the Lutheran theologian Johann Meißner, "you find only a few among hundreds who practice [singing] correctly"; many people participated "alieno animo," with their thoughts "fluttering about the church, their workplace, in India and the New World."[32] As Müller surmised, in those cases the bodily-spiritual symbiosis of heart and tongue had broken down: "Many sing, but without spirit and devotion: the mouth is present, but the heart is far away; they speak the words, but do not feel their power in their heart: therefore they stay cold and dried up inside, and because they never feel a certain heat and sweetness in the song, they soon lose their desire to sing."[33] Although the church historian Christopher Brown has found that, overall, congregational singing became rather successful in the Reformed confessions, there seems to have been significant affective interference from a widespread sense of embarrassment about raising one's voice publicly in song.[34] Werckmeister admonished that "musicians and others should be delighted at the opportunity to call to God with their full voices and to praise him; nobody should be ashamed of it. But in this we often experience resistance; indeed there are evil people who make fun of those congregants who sing along loudly."[35] Shame, it turns out, could be its own "contagious disease of the soule," or one form of what Richard Shusterman has more recently called "intersomatic attunement."[36] The multivalent affective experiences afforded by early modern hymnody rested on this permeability of human body-souls as they produced, absorbed, and amplified the sonic-affective charge of communal song.

✷ 20 ✷

Memory

Memory was an imprint. As one of the faculties of the soul, it left physical traces in early modern bodies. "The human body can suffer many alterations and yet keep the impressions or traces of objects," wrote Baruch Spinoza in his *Ethics*.[1] For many early modern writers, the locus where this impression took place was the brain. The French writer Pierre de La Primaudaye laid out the process in his encyclopedic *French Academie* (first published in 1577):

> Therefore hath God assigned [memory's] seate and lodging in the hindermost part of the braine, to the end, that after such things as are to be committed unto it, have passed by all the other senses, they should be committed to it to keepe, as to their secretary. And for this cause that part of the braine is lesse moist, and most solide and firme. . . . Forasmuch as the memory is as it were the Register & Chancery Court of all the other senses, the images of all things brought and committed unto it by them, are to be imprinted therein, as the image and signe of a ring or seale is imprinted and set in the waxe that is sealed.[2]

In Primaudaye's view, then, memory resided in the head, but was not exclusively a property of the immaterial soul, since it involved the material substance of the brain. Descartes's theory of memory, too, was fully embodied, and has recently formed one of the foundations for reclaiming an "embodied Descartes" over and above his dualist legacy.[3] In his *Treatise of Man*, Descartes affirmed:

> Imagine that . . . spirits pass through tubes . . . and into the pores or intervals that occur between the filaments . . . of the brain. And [assume] that they are forceful enough to enlarge these intervals somewhat and to bend and rearrange any filaments they encounter, according to the differ-

ent types of movement of the spirits themselves and the differing degrees of openness of the tubes into which they pass. . . . Which is why in such cases these patterns are no longer so easily erased, but are retained there in such a way that by means of them the ideas that existed previously on this gland can be formed again long afterward. . . . And it is in this that *Memory* consists.[4]

Although Descartes's account, like Primaudaye's, centered on the brain, the fluid physiology of memory formation outlined here could in fact apply equally well to the popular alternative scenario that saw memory residing primarily in the heart, a view perpetuated in numerous devotional and literary writings at the time. In his 1624 poetry treatise, the German author Martin Opitz articulated the hope of poets to be widely read by their contemporaries and "leave an eternal memory in the hearts of their descendants."[5] Johann Sebastian Bach's librettist Picander penned the following exhortation to the faithful: "Even if you forget everything else, my heart, remember this continually, that your Savior lives."[6] Christoph Raupach drew on a widely shared trope when extolling music's power to "implant God's word very deeply into people's hearts."[7] And those memory traces could spread through other parts of the body too. A 1687 medical handbook described how, when the "footprints" of the images stored in the channels carved by spirits "are brought to the heart through the small arteries, and their rays permeate the whole blood flow, then it can happen that the fetus is marked with certain markers or birthmarks."[8] If this now reads as a rather abstruse model of intersomatic attunement, it is worth pointing out that it in fact goes back to Descartes, too, who discussed how "the traces of these ideas pass through the arteries toward the heart and thus radiate through all the blood," and how "they can sometimes even be caused by certain actions of the mother, to be imprinted on the limbs of the child being formed in her entrails."[9] The idea that memory could be located in bodily fibers, rather than form the exclusive property of a computational mind, is taken up in present-day research on embodied, procedural, or "muscle" memory. As Richard Shusterman has outlined, "in demonstrating that intelligent mind extends beyond clear consciousness, muscle memory . . . makes manifest the mind's embodied nature and the body's crucial role in memory and cognition."[10] Of course, from a neurobiological perspective, the claim that memory is somatically based is not at all surprising, given that it is constituted through the activation of neurons in the cells of the brain. A recent hypothesis moreover proposed "cellular memory" to be responsible for the curious effect of heart transplant recipients experiencing a transfer of donor personality characteristics, although the author recommended that further research is required.[11] Opitz, Raupach, and their fellow believers in the heart as a material memory store would presumably have taken such findings in their stride.

As a somatically grounded phenomenon, the faculty of memory was directly affected by an individual's corporeal disposition, that is, the specific arrangement of matter and flows in their body. As Primaudaye outlined, "therefore it is needefull that the matter of the instrument of Memorie should be so well tempered, that it be neither too soft nor too hard. For if it be too soft, the images will bee soone ingrauen, but they will not stay there any long time, as they that will be quickly blotted out. Contrariwise, if it be ouer hard, it will be a harder matter to imprint them therein. But when it is well tempered, it receiueth the images easily, and keepeth them well."[12] According to Johann Helffrich Jüngken, a weak memory arose primarily from "poorly disposed animal spirits, as when they are too thick, sluggish, and slow and cannot take up and grasp the objects well."[13] The capacity for and quality of memory, then, was shaped by the state of a person's insides; but those memory imprints also reshaped them in turn. As John Sutton has argued, in a Cartesian view "our memories shape who we are even in the most literal sense of curving folds in brain fibers."[14] In this way, Christians were made as faith was enfolded viscerally into their flesh. And this bodily-spiritual constitution of memory was relevant to musical activities too. As Georg Falck asserted in a music instruction book of 1688, "music is not everyone's thing; for people's complexions are so varied that they cause one to incline towards this, the other towards that." Those people with certain intrinsic predilections could not help but make music, to "bring to the ear, with various modulations and ornaments, that which they have grasped in their memory through devoted learning."[15] Some decades later, Johann Mattheson mused: "We bring nothing with us into this world except a good or poor arrangement of the brain and the animal spirits in the blood. . . . Various souls are like wax, others like stone. Although that which is engraved in stone does last longest, we still prefer in the art of music a brain that is waxy, so to speak, to one that is stone-hard."[16]

The hymn tunes learned by Catholic and Protestant congregations across early modern Europe and beyond were stored, then, in the fibers of such softer or harder brains or hearts, with the effect that, as Raupach related, listeners would be impelled to recall the words of a particular hymn when the organist struck up the tune in a prelude. Absorbed by the spirits coursing through their ears and bodies, that tune would flow through the specific channels carved into their inner organs as a result of repeated prior listening or singing. This scenario lends a striking tangibility to Stephen Rose's observation that "by memorizing a piece, performers made it part of themselves."[17] Any concomitant activation of the associated words did not constitute an exclusively mental process either, but engaged the bodily memory of producing those syllables and sounds in their throats and mouths. Musical skill, as many writers at the time acknowledged, operated largely on such a corporeal level. Urban Gottfried Bucher used music as a key example for the non-volitional nature of many human pursuits: "Someone who is learning instrumental music can want as much as they want, yet he cannot force his clumsy fingers to produce that which his Master must not even think of."[18] While a fully materialist position such as Bucher's lent itself particularly well to articulating this agency of the body, more mainstream writers equally acknowledged that agency in attaining musical expertise. Georg Heuermann affirmed that, although such bodily agency could not be regarded as "purely mechanical," it still appeared to be operative when a dancing master "has trained his feet through practice so that without the soul taking note they can move artfully to the beat of the music; or in a musician, where a comparable skill is produced through practice"; or indeed in speaking, where the muscles of the tongue perform the correct motions to produce words without conscious mental effort.[19]

Another source of activation of that embodied knowledge of the hymn repertoire, alongside an organist's preluding, were the innumerable copies of hymnals printed over the long seventeenth century, offering a different sort of material imprint or trace of the bodily-spiritual practice of communal singing. In this sense, hymn books acted as a form of "extended" memory that offered a repository for these traces beyond the brain or heart.[20] An introduction to the art of psalm singing by the Boston-based writer Thomas Walter of 1721 recommended that learning to read notation could help the "uncertain and doubtful conveyance of Oral Tradition," since singing tunes that one had learned "by heart" meant that these melodies were "left to the Mercy of every unskilful Throat to chop and alter, twist and change, according to their infinitely divers and no less odd Humours and Fancies."[21] This corporeal memory could go wrong, in other words, deformed over time by the whims of humoral flows, while an external memory store such as an engraved hymn book could help avoid such distortion. More than preserving a collection of discrete musical objects, then, these hymnals presented a set of scripts that their users often already knew from memory, and which guided them toward the requisite sequence of bodily-spiritual motions for executing a particular tune. The printed melody and words of, say, the popular hymn *Nun dancket alle Gott*, from Johann Crüger's collection *Praxis pietatis melica* (first published 1647), served as a trigger for congregants forming certain sounds

Lob- und Dancklieder. 445

NUn dancket alle Gott mit herzen/ mund
und händen/ Der groſſe dinge thut an
uns und allen enden, Der uns von mutter-
leib und kindesbeinen an Unzählich viel zu
gut und itzo noch gethan.

2. Der ewigreiche GOTT woll uns bey
unſerm leben Ein immerfrölich hertz und
edlen frieden geben/ Und uns in ſeiner gnad
erhalten fort und fort/ Und uns aus aller
noht erlöſen hier und dort.

3. Lob/ ehr und preis ſey Gott dem Vater
und dem Sohne / Und dem / der beyden
gleich im höchſten himmelsthrone / Dem
dreyeinigen Gott/ als er urſprünglich war/
Und iſt/ und bleiben wird itzund und im-
merdar.

FIGURE 20.1. Hymn *Nun dancket alle Gott*, from Johann Crüger, *Praxis pietatis melica* (Frankfurt: Wust, 1662), 445. © British Library Board, Music Collections 4400.i.27. Courtesy of the British Library, digitized by the Google Books project.

in their heads and mouths that were already there in the body, ready to be sounded (fig. 20.1).

That same activation of pre-existent bodily know-how underpinned practices of musical improvisation. As Christian Wolff affirmed, "the imagination does not produce anything but what we have previously felt or thought; and therefore imaginations are nothing but representations of a past state of the world."[22] The importance of formulas and commonplaces in early modern musical improvisation has been widely recognized in recent scholarship. Rebecca Herissone has shown not only that early modern improvisation relied on combining memorized material and formulaic filling passages, but also that it may have played a part in the written transmission of musical repertories.[23] In current neuroscientific research on improvisation and creativity, too, the central role of the body has been widely documented. As David Bashwiner outlines, "the vast majority of this 'extraordinary machine' [of musical improvisation] is subcutaneous, subcogitative, subliminal. Its system is not that of the explicit, consciously accessible, verbally scrutable apparatus, but rather that of the implicit, unverbalizable, procedural memory apparatus."[24] In 1734, Johann Wilhelm Albrecht proposed a similarly embodied model of "the formation of ideas": "Thoughts and dreams arise when a series of ideas previously received from external objects . . . is stimulated anew through internal causes. These internal causes, alongside many others, can be primarily 1) the rush of the blood directed towards the whole brain or one of its parts, 2) the quality of the blood, 3) the movement and quality of the nerve fluids, 4) the disposition of the viscera, etc."[25] Like memory, the human imagination constituted a faculty of the soul, but was likewise closely tied to the fluctuations of one's internal fluids. In Albrecht's model, a musician's choices of where to go next in an improvised performance would have been grounded less in cognitive volition than where the flows (or the fingers on a keyboard) took them. Roger North described how a musician's memory will be

> filled with numberless passages of approved ayre, and have *ad unguem* all the cursory graces of cadences and semi-cadences, and comon descants, and breakings, as well as the ordinary ornaments of accord, or touch. And all these in a manner that may be termed memoritèr, in like manner as persons that deal in tunes and lessons have them by heart and can performe without thinking, and even sometimes comon fidlers will play when fast asleep; which I mention to shew what exactness and perfection of memoriall habit a master ought to be armed with, to enable him to be a perfect voluntier.[26]

For North, an accomplished improviser knew those ayres, lessons, cadences, and ornaments "by heart," but also had absorbed them "ad unguem," a telling phrase that could simply mean "to perfection," but at root related to the manual practice of sculptors using their fingernail ("unguis") to add the finishing touches to their artwork. Keyboardists, too, held the intricacies of their art at their fingertips. As Carl Philipp Emanuel Bach stated, "through diligent practice the use of the fingers eventually will become so automatic" that a performer no longer had to expend conscious mental effort to guide them.[27] Such descriptions corroborate David Yearsley's account of early modern organists more or less thinking with their feet. Musical touch, Yearsley argues, constituted a "way of seeing sounds with the body," and not just for those practitioners with visual impairments, but as a foundation for any organist "to grasp intangible music—especially abstract counterpoint—with his limbs. . . . The organ allowed the organist, blind or sighted, to hold polyphony in his body."[28] Note, too, the agency ascribed to bodily extremities in the following description by Raupach, charting how the inner joy of a faithful musician could spill out onto the keys and pedals of the organ: "The hands and feet of Christians, who are used to playing the organ artfully and with their own good imagination in a skilled way, powerfully demonstrate the soul's joy in God and his gifts on that instrument, incited by the words of the song, with joyful-sounding harmonies, leaps, and modulations."[29] These pre-formed musical materials, stored away in the performer's bodily fibers or limbs and activated in the moment of extemporized performance, thus also had immediate affective potential—whether they were notated or not.

A consideration of these mnemonic and improvisatory practices urges us, then, to adjust our view of (early modern) musical notation, from regarding it as an abstract system for recording musical works, toward recognizing these notated texts as somatic scripts that offer insights into the bodily habits and dispositions that (re)produced these repertories. In some ways, musical notation could certainly be seen as getting in the way of the creative impulses at work in improvisation, by interposing a representational gimmick of the mind. As John McKean has claimed, the abstraction of notational conventions "subjugates the keyboardist's body to the dictates of the mind," whereas the partial or complete absence of notation, for instance in figured bass or improvised playing, "leaves a poietic space for the body to directly influence the nature and substance of the music it produces."[30] Such a view, however, not only reifies the dualist mind-body conception that early modern musical practices so consistently challenged, but also overlooks the bodily substrate of these notational conventions, which reproduced in ink those mnemonic traces held within the body and afforded their bodily reactivation in performance. This bodily substrate, I think, suggests a greater degree of convergence between improvisatory practices and playing from notation than implied by McKean. A similarly oppositional conception of improvisation as cut loose from the constraints of literacy shines through in Martha Feldman's assertion that "only beyond the reach of script" could early modern song attain its "ineffable sensual power endowed with neoplatonic force."[31]

There is no doubt, of course, that different technologies of musical notation, whether tablature or stave, distanced the content they conveyed from its corporeal moorings to varying degrees. However, as Bruce Smith has argued, most written documents in Western history can in fact be understood to encode physical or performative acts to some extent; and, in relating directly to an embodied practice, musical scores arguably occupied a position closer to the corporeal end of this spectrum.[32] While Sally Sanford is surely right to point out that the appropriate "mental 'software'" is essential to reading notation of the period, any meaningful engagement with these notated scores also required a habituated bodily disposition that allowed the mnemonic traces of musical skill stored in musicians' brains and limbs to be reanimated in the moment of turning notation into sensible sounds.[33]

21

Partien auf das Clavier

Christoph Graupner's *Partien auf das Clavier,* a set of eight partitas for keyboard published in 1718, are about as fully notated as one could hope for at the time. The edition provides various kinds of ornaments and even the odd indication of articulation, tempo, and dynamics. Looking at the beautifully engraved score today, one might easily sustain the illusion that it preserves a series of immaculate, disembodied artefacts. As the art historian Pamela Smith has pointed out, viewing an artwork in the pristine setting of a museum invites us to overlook the bodily labor that went into making it.[1] In Graupner's publication, which the composer himself prepared, we get a glimpse of that bodily labor not only in some visible slips of the hand or tool, such as the wavy or choppy staff lines in the first Partita's Prelude and Allemande; but also in the artist's particular turn of the hand in the curvaceous movement titles and clefs (fig. 21.1). Graupner thematized this manual effort in his preface: "The notes themselves are the first ones of my own engraving—take them as good as they have turned out," he stated, promising that in a potential second volume, they would hopefully come out "more diligent and accurate."[2] The musical scripts contained in the volume, meanwhile, also come with Graupner's flesh and blood enclosed. As Jonathan De Souza has explored, composition "is not just about putting together notes"; it integrates sonic and semiotic features with sensory and motoric aspects.[3] An early eighteenth-century keyboard composer needed to fuse their (mental and/as embodied) knowledge of harmonic and voice-leading precepts with the physical constraints of their ten digits as well as the affordances of their instrument. The bodily memory store that enabled their facility at improvisation or figured bass realization would also have underpinned their compositional endeavors. The dividing line between these practices, as much recent scholarship has shown, was not clear cut at all, given their shared reliance on preconceived patterns of diminution, cadencing, and sequencing.[4] The hands and

FIGURE 21.1. Christoph Graupner, *Partien auf das Clavier* (Darmstadt: Author, 1718), 1. Nasjonalbiblioteket Oslo, Seksjon for Musikk, Tb 243.

fingers, in kinesthetic interaction with the keyboard, knew and shaped a range of such musical formulations that could become building blocks for compositional invention; playing those compositions then further consolidated the bodily inscription of those gestures.[5] As Friedrich Erhard Niedt affirmed in his keyboard primer of 1706, musical invention was grounded in knowing the correct hand positions ("Griffe"), which provided ("an die Hand geben") musicians with "all that on which previously one might have had to expend lots of effort."[6]

Consistent fingering, which budding keyboardists learned from an early age, aided the development of this tactile memory. This helped performers "think in patterns or groups of notes rather than individual notes," thereby eliminating the need for perpetual conscious decision-making about where to go next with the fingers.[7] Phrases such as "in die Faust bringen" appear pervasively in Johann David Heinichen's keyboard treatises, which stipulated that all the chords and keys needed to "be in the fist in such a manner that one does not need to search or cogitate, but can find everything on the keyboard as if blind and instantaneously."[8] The Italian organist Girolamo Diruta, too, regarded the procedural memory acquired through repeated fingering and diminution practice as foundational to the keyboardist's art.[9] Through continual drill, the muscles gained the capacity to move independently, guided by the soul-full fluids that animated them. The standard sets of melodic, chordal, and decorative figures in early eighteenth-century keyboard practice thereby served as an array of "maximally economical improvisational tools," as Michael Callahan has argued, but also underpinned both performative skill and compositional invention at the keyboard, with the knowing hand facilitating all these pursuits.[10] Similar procedures can be posited with respect to other instruments, as in Elisabeth Le Guin's exploration of Luigi Boccherini's compositional practice on the cello, in which she imagines certain passages having "rushed into the composer's fingers" and points to "gestural ingrainments" that the hand gratefully executes. As Le Guin observes, "a hand, even a virtuosic hand, makes music rather differently than a conscious intellect."[11]

The keyboard offers a particularly intriguing case with regard to this embodied creativity, as its layout of keys visualizes the musical as well as physical space of action. Johann Mattheson linked these distinctive properties of the keyboard directly to compositional invention: "[The clavier] is the preeminent tool of the composer . . . . This should not be taken to mean that all one's pieces should be derived from this instrument . . . but only that it can give a much clearer concept of the harmonic structure than the others, even if the actual box or machine is not at hand but is only imagined in the mind: for the position, order, and sequence of sounds is nowhere as clear and visible as in the keys of a clavier."[12] The multiple feedback loops afforded by the instrument—aural, visual, haptic, kinesthetic, cognitive—rendered a musical invention not solely a notated shape on the page, but a potential bodily disposition. Take the very first gesture of Graupner's collection, the opening of the Prelude that heads the first Partita in C major (see fig. 21.1). The left hand starts off with that most basic shape of eighteenth-century tonal harmony and elementary keyboard instruction: an ascending C-major scale. We do not know what fingering Graupner used or imagined for this phrase, but if we take Johann Sebastian Bach's instructions for his son Wilhelm Friedemann as indicative (fig. 21.2), it would have involved some kind of paired fingering (1–2-1–2). Note, however, that Graupner's phrase starts off the beat, whereas Bach's starts on the beat, which would have affected the placement of stronger and weaker fingers. Moreover, fingering practices at the time were very much in flux, only gradually moving away from traditional restrictions over using the thumb and expanding the range of patterns to include thumb-under fingering, chordal fingering inspired by figured bass practice, and so on.[13] Graupner's preface warned that players not accustomed to using their thumbs would find those passages difficult in which

FIGURE 21.2. Johann Sebastian Bach, "Applicatio," from *Clavier-Büchlein vor Wilhelm Friedemann Bach* (1720), f. 4r. Beinecke Rare Book and Manuscript Library, Yale University, Music Deposit 31.

the thumb was "indispensable." But whatever way a budding keyboardist would have been drilled to tackle this scalar ascent, for those who had acquired a certain level of skill this opening would have allowed them to let their fingers take charge in executing it.

The right hand then imitates the left, though at twice the speed, once again intoning a gesture so commonplace that we also find it opening Johann Sebastian Bach's first keyboard invention in C major (BWV 772), where the upward run from middle C also breaks off at the fourth: one of those pre-existent patterns activated in the fingers and the imagination through the spiritous operations of memory. If Graupner's bodily-spiritual faculty of invention hit upon his particular version of that figure at the outset of the piece, it then kept coming back to him as the movement unfolded, starting on g in measure 6, and then on e in measure 11, a transposition that introduced a palpable shift to a bumpier topography involving two black keys. Finally, in measure 14, the gesture made its way into the bass part, as the two hands switched their roles—a classic instance of an embodied kind of contrapuntal thinking that derived its inversions from the corresponding physical arrangement of the executing limbs.[14] If my analysis seems to be ascribing a degree of agency to the musical motive as it moved up and down the keyboard and between the hands, this is not to imply that Graupner did not consciously plan these repetitions and their structural implications.[15] Once again, I would suggest that an oppositional construction of mind versus matter might hinder rather than enhance our understanding of the inventive process here; and that this kind of embodied knowledge may more profitably be seen as occupying a continuum, one extreme of which would be constituted by the knowing body acting of its own volition, the other by the conscious mind dealing in disembodied abstractions.[16] We may tentatively identify different moments and conceits within the same piece as located in different places on this continuum: while the chromatically rising progression in the left hand from measure 7, in conjunction with the broken-chord elaboration in the right, may have formed quite an "engrained" way of moving toward a new key area on the keyboard, the mirror-image descent that follows from measure 11 to get the hands back to G likely constituted a more premeditated strategy in the context of the broader tonal trajectory of the piece.[17] But overall, the movement bears out Marko Aho's insight that musical style is often less an abstract conceptual space than a "physiological resource" based on tacit rather than (or at least in conjunction with) propositional knowledge.[18]

The subsequent movements of this first Partita explore numerous aspects of tactile knowledge and kinesthetic fancy in ways that exploited the full range of diminution techniques found in contemporary improvisation manuals. Collectively, these pieces lead me to concur with John Butt's observation, with reference to Bach's music, that the notated diminutions contained therein were not only "indispensable" but formed "the very substance of the invention."[19] In the second half of the Allemande, the notation instructs its reader to abandon the prevailing contrapuntal texture in favor of a sweeping scalar descent and ascent over three and a half octaves, covering close to the full registral span of a smaller-sized harpsichord: a true "Durchgriff" or "Begreiffung" of the instrument, as Michael Praetorius formulated it.[20] This unanticipated display of hand-crossing dexterity could give the impression of the composer-performer's hands embarking on an impromptu flight of fancy, especially in a performance that rushed through these sixteenth notes unmoored from the strictures of meter, as in an exquisite 2002 recording by Geneviève Soly.[21] Aho's commentary, that it is "hard to imagine any Cartesian puppeteer who could 'pull the strings' swiftly enough, commanding 'now play G, not so fast, gently, gently . . . GO,'" seems eminently applicable here.[22] The surge of physical energy is reined in by the turn to a flattened b in the penultimate measure, arresting the fingers' unimpeded passage up and down the "naturales" (white) keys. The Courante, meanwhile, turns to another staple of keyboardists' finger skills, the arpeggio, again involving both hands in an even more sweeping exploration of the instrument's registral limits (C-c"). In place of the settled pulse of the Prelude, the first half of this movement juxtaposes different types of musical flow (eighth notes, triplets, sixteenth notes) that continually keep a player (and listener) on their toes. Once again, we might ascribe at least a degree of agency to Graupner's savvy hands in devising this freewheeling sequence of figurations; and once more it depended on an individual player's approach as to how improvisatory and guided by the whims of the fingers these passages could sound.

Finally, the closing Rigaudon en Rondeau instantiates the shift identified by McKean toward a "more chordal, Griff-based style of playing" in the years around 1700, and by extension "a more somatic basis for conceiving keyboard music."[23] In the movement's second section, any contrapuntal aspirations are put aside in favor of a chord-based texture over a running bass line, of the sort that a continuo player may have devised on the spot. The figurations gradually speed up in subsequent sections, moving through a variety of diminution patterns outlined in Niedt's *Handleitung*.[24] As a result, by the end of the movement, a performer and any putative audience would likely have found themselves in a state of heightened arousal, of expansive, fast-flowing spirits that carried with them the potential for "plaisir" that constituted Graupner's stated aim of the publication. The fairly fixed succession of dances in the early eighteenth-century keyboard suite led performers (and listeners) through a sequence of bodily-spiritual motions that could exercise, in carefully circumscribed fashion, the full gamut of human affective states, from the easygoing flow of the Allemande, via the languid turns of the Sarabande and the poised elegance of the Minuet or Gavotte, to culminate in the joyous effusions of a Gigue. As Kate van Orden has put it, "setting the soul in motion with steps, leaps and turns, dance inspired knowledge of first causes and virtue"; and this was the case whether a piece was actually danced to or not.[25] In Robert South's poetic vision, harmonious sound could stir the inner organs of the body into dance-like kinesis:

> But the Youth's trembling Heart within him strove,
> With tunelike Pulses to compose a Dance,
> As if its Fibres felt th' affecting Strains. . . .
> His sparkling Blood within his glowing Veins
> Strives to ferment into a Circ'lar Dance.[26]

The particular affect- and virtue-inducing profile of any individual movement in Graupner's partitas would have taken shape in and through an individual player's bodily engagement, composure, breath, arms, hands and, vitally, fingertips, the locus of touch. The spirituous flows that animated a keyboardist's body-soul in the act of performance emanated outward as those spirits, in Richard Sugg's words, "vibrated down the nerves and arteries, pulsing in the blood, and occasionally throbbing out to the tips of one's fingers, the fiery light of the eyes, or the ends of the hair." As Matthew Hall has argued, the overriding aim of François Couperin's treatise *L'art de toucher le clavecin* (1716) was to teach the art of "cultivating a keyboard touch as responsive to the movements of the player's soul as the voice would be." Such a "vocal" touch, claims Hall, was "tantamount to giving the instrument a soul."[27] If the prospect of communicating soul in this haptic fashion appears improbable now, we might look to the Dutch anatomist Steven Blankaart, who regarded the human soul as extending through the whole body in its liquid parts and therefore present right there in the fingertips: "The locus of sensation . . . is the soul itself, and it instantly receives or grasps the motions arising from a subtle matter (such as light, sound, and so on) in the very place where they occur."[28] A model of ensouled touch underpins the advice in Tomás de Santa María's keyboard treatise of 1565, to play "with the pads of the fingers . . . that way the notes sound completely, sweetly, softly. The reason for this is that, since flesh is a soft thing, it touches with sweetness and softness. . . . Otherwise, when you play with the nails . . . [the notes are] faint and without spirit."[29]

"Soft flesh," according to the English cleric Thomas Walkington, rendered "the sense of feeling most exact" and indicated an "abundance of spirits, not turbulent and drossy, but pure and refined."[30] As those vital spirits rushed to a player's fingertips to move the muscles that pressed down on the keys, that player's inner disposition flowed outward with the touch of their hands, to be transferred to the keyboard and from there to any listening ears and bodies. In this way, keyboard playing—whether improvised or from notation—could be as contagious as hymn singing, in mobilizing music's capacity to effect a corporeal-spiritual exchange between performer, instrument, sound, and (performer-as-)listener.

This bodily-spiritual transmission via touch might be the source, then, of the "kinaesthetic alchemy" that McKean detects between the material affordances of an early modern keyboard instrument and the physical proclivities of a player's body. In moments when that alchemy was challenged, meanwhile, when a musical gesture did not fall too easily under the fingers, this disruption could bring about its own contagious effects, of strain, tension, or contraction. I am thinking, for instance, of the third section of Graupner's Rigaudon, which starts out with suitably hand-friendly figurations. These gestures become increasingly unergonomic, however, with more black keys getting in the way, culminating in a leap of a tenth in measure 15. From there, the player's right hand can tumble down, relieved, toward the cadence as a place of physical-mental repose, and on to the subsequent sections, which return to more comfortable diminution patterns, their free-flowing ease enhanced by the preceding sense of performative tension. As Yonit Lea Kosovske has written, "tension inhibits the proper flow of oxygen and blood throughout the body, both of which are vital to clarity of thought and to obtaining a fluid, graceful technique."[31] Of course, an accomplished player may simply smooth over any of these more taxing moments and create the impression of uninterrupted, graceful flow. But Graupner clearly imagined amateurs reaching for his collection, too; and for them, those instances where their limbs struggled to execute what the notation required offered a palpable reminder that any notion of bodily ability or dis-ability necessarily remained a fluid one in relation to musical performance. Graupner's notated scripts did in many ways construct a "normal performance body," not only by requiring sight as well as functioning hands and arms, but also by presuming a habituated physiological disposition necessary for appreciating and executing its style.[32] Yet while certain sorts of bodily impairment would have prevented individuals from accessing his collection tout court, any performers who did end up playing his pieces would still have done so within the limitations of their own physical skill and constitution. These limitations would have been determined not only by their bodily-spiritual idiosyncrasies, but also by the broader exigencies of age, gender, social class, and so on. The Spanish organist Pablo Nassare cautioned in 1723 that when young students were occupied in menial labor, this could make their tendons "hard and inflexible"; therefore, those who wished to learn the art of keyboard playing should "not occupy themselves in other disciplines which might make their hands calloused or impede the mobility of their fingers, because anything that involves hard or heavy objects, or touching impure or excessively cold or hot waters, [can] inflict the humors upon the extremities, and this impedes the docility of the tendons."[33] Older students, meanwhile, were advised by Couperin to "pull their fingers" before playing, in order to get the spirits moving into the fingertips.[34] With progressive age, a person's fibers were said to dry up and become less capable of feeling and sensation; or else "their eyes, ears, and other limbs are tormented with stagnant moisture."[35] Whether tackled by aged hands, or those of a manual laborer, or those afflicted by gout, in each case Graupner's *Partien* would have taken on a distinct sonic-affective profile—perhaps a wetter, drier, or achier version of that overriding sweep of "plaisir."[36]

In this sense, Graupner's music emphatically did not constitute an abstract figment of the mind, but could only come into being as a result of multiple processes of bodily and material mediation. The clavichord, as McKean notes, was the most delicate and complex of early modern keyboard instruments in terms of transmitting a player's bodily-spiritual energy, by responding "most effectively to an articulate touch whereby the natural weight of the hand and arm is transferred directly into the key through the fingertips."[37] But even with the most touch-sensitive of instruments, any such sonic-affective transmission would have been multiply mediated by the physical interfaces of the instrument, from fingers on keys to the levers that operated the hammers or plectra that made the strings vibrate, to the air that propagated those vibrations. In this sense, a musical instrument indeed functioned as a "transducer" that converted patterns of bodily-spiritual movement into patterns of sound.[38] A view of musical instruments as external mechanical devices or "prostheses" has been pervasive in studies on the origins of music since Jean-Jacques Rousseau, allowing writers to position vocality as the older, purer, unmediated version of human musical expression.[39] Yet we might temper this view in relation to early modern practices in light of the belief, for instance, that clothes took on their wearer's disposition because of the spirits that their body continually exhaled. "Therefore take heed," wrote the Scottish physician Christopher Irvine, not to "touch the sheets" that are "impregnate" with the "exhalations of an unsound body." He continued that "it is good also for a weak body, to use the company and garments of strong and sound men, for from hence he may draw such spirits as will fortifie weak nature."[40] Perhaps, with Bernhard Stiegler, we might regard these material implements—clothes, instruments, musical scores—not as a "mere extension of the human body"; but rather as "the constitution of this body qua 'human.'"[41] It was on this basis that organists could use their hands and feet to "en-spirit" ("begeistern") their instruments; and that a musician's "hand and breath" could "animate wood, metal, and gut."[42]

III

Ensoulment

✷ 22 ✷
Souls

It would be impossible to write a physiology of early modern music without reference to soul. In most of its manifold formulations, this physiology was fundamentally a psycho-physiology, in which the operations of body, soul, and spirit(s) were densely intertwined and often inextricable. The nature of the interactions between these key components of human nature was heavily contested across the period and construed along different—sometimes intersecting, sometimes radically diverging—lines by different individuals. Yet the general consensus held not only that humans had a soul but that this soul was what made them both alive and human. In Monique Scheer's summary, at least prior to the Cartesian turn, "the soul was what distinguished a living creature from a lifeless object." The soul was "responsible for everything lifelike," encompassing, in the Aristotelian tradition, growth and nutrition (vegetative soul), perception and movement (sensitive soul), and thought (rational soul).[1] The Lutheran reformer Philipp Melanchthon's influential anthropology was built on this classic tripartite model of the soul, overlaid with the Platonic-Galenic division of the soul into rational, passionate, and appetitive functions, lodged in the brain, heart, and liver, respectively.[2] The appeal of the Aristotelian model reached well into the eighteenth century, with the lexicographer Johann Heinrich Zedler still reporting it in his 1730s encyclopedia.[3] The variety of options for construing "soul" covered in Zedler's lengthy entry on the topic illustrates the enduring multiplicity of philosophical and theological opinions on the subject. My aim here, however, is not to delineate these different models and their complex genealogies: a task that could easily demand a book-length study in itself, and which by the end would still leave unanswered the question of which of these ideas may have been most relevant for particular musicking communities or experiences at different times.[4] I only propose to outline here some of the broader assumptions that shaped contemporary experiences of being "en-souled" in acts of music-making; as well as clarify some of the ways in which musicking put persistent pressure on a dualist body-soul conception of human nature.

In a medical dictionary of 1682, the Altdorf physician Jacob Pancratius Bruno distinguished between two primary definitions of "anima": a "philosophical" one, which defined soul as an "incorporeal and immortal substance that is considered separate from the body"; and a "medical" one, going back to Galen, which defined it as "heat, spiritus, air, fire, vital flame, biolychnium [fire in the heart], nature, or whatever other name you want to call it."[5] In its initial version (Messina, 1598), as well as in several later editions published across Europe, the dictionary had only cited the latter, Galenic reading of the term, equating "amina" with "calor nativus" (innate heat). Yet Bruno's added "philosophical" (Cartesian) definition in fact appears to chime better with certain longstanding Christian tendencies of denigrating the body as a flawed material container reluctantly inhabited by the soul. As the Protestant physician Christian Friedrich Richter put it, the body "is the least and mortal part of a human, which is not even to be regarded as a property"; he advised that people should only look after their bodies because it enabled them to serve God. In any other respect, he wrote, "you should be ashamed of it, for it accords poorly with the nature and subtleness of the soul." Viewed from a bodily perspective, a person was merely "earth or muck tempered and mixed with water, which artfully and subtly coalesces into a certain form, with lots of tubes and threads, like a spider's web, and is shaped into certain limbs." This material shape had to be cleaned daily or a person would "drown in excrement."[6] It was only by the power of the soul that this pile of matter received and maintained its shape, for the soul could separate out the liquid and solid parts and send the nutritive juices into the appropriate places, "choosing those atoms or particles from which flesh, skin, cartilage, or blood could be made." Otherwise, Richter surmised, "cartilage might grow where there is meant to be flesh, etc., so that in a few weeks a human would be transformed into a monster and a completely unusable machine."[7] It is no wonder that, in this scenario, a soul would be only too happy to part from this bodily container with its monstrous potential for liquids, vapors, or passions to rise and contaminate its ruling agent. At the point of death, the soul gladly left that container behind to rot.

Yet I would note two caveats here with regard to this antagonistic conception of body and soul. The first concerns the way in which the biblical concepts of spirit and flesh, which formed the "beginning point of early modern anthropology," sat awkwardly against the newer Cartesian notions of mind and body.[8] As the theologian N. T. Wright has noted, "when [the Apostle] Paul speaks of the conflict between the spirit and the flesh, the *pneuma* and the *sarx*, he certainly isn't referring to a conflict between the non-material element of the person and the material element." Instead, Wright argues, each of these key terms of spirit, flesh, and soul "*denotes* the entire human being, while *connoting* some angle of vision on who that human is and what he or she is called to be." Flesh, for instance, "refers to the entire human being but connotes corruptibility, failure, rebellion, and then sin and death," whereas psyche "denotes the entire human being, and connotes that human as possessed of ordinary mortal life, with breath and blood sustained by food and drink."[9] This aspective conception of human nature also underpinned the early modern anthropology pursued here, where, for instance, "spirit" spanned the material and immaterial dimensions of human nature; and "flesh" referred to the sinful earthbound state of postlapsarian humanity—"human nature spoilt through sin," as a homiletic dictionary of 1734 put it.[10] When Sigismund Scherertz claimed that "a Christian must engage in a daily struggle with its inner enemy, their own flesh and blood," such a formulation confounds the familiar modern categories of an "outer" material body housing an "inner" immaterial self.[11] Scherertz's formulation perhaps owes rather more to Martin Luther's doctrine of the twofold existence of Christian believers under the Law and under the Gospel, in which "flesh is otherwise called the old Adam or the old human, the external human: spirit, the new and interior human."[12]

This invocation of the "new" human brings me to my second caveat, concerning the early modern Christian belief that while at the point of death the earthly body decayed, it was not only the soul that was promised a continued existence past the Day of Judgment: the body, too, or rather the human being *in toto*, would be resurrected in glory, liberated from Law and sin. Erin Lambert has explored how communal singing in the Lutheran tradition could serve as a means of prefiguring that glorious future state of the resurrected body.[13] In the early eighteenth century, debates raged over whether that new body would be immaterial or not, and whether the musical instruments that this body would be operating in heaven to the praise of God would be made of actual wood and metal.[14] But regardless of the precise nature of this transfigured state, clearly a Christian's physical body as it existed in earthly time and beyond could not easily be written off as a lifeless and worthless mechanism. The Dutch physician Levinus Lemnius ascertained: "The Body for a time is transitory and mortall; but since it is the vessel and receptacle of the Soul and useth its Ministery, God hath also design'd that for eternity; and by the Mystery of the Resurrection, it shall be made partaker of the same Gift, that is, of immortality."[15] Music, in its capacity to anticipate the joys of eternal life, brought out these complexities in an especially palpable way. According to the German scholar Adam Erdmann Mirus, music's potential for offering a foretaste of heaven did not merely appeal to the soul as an abstract entity but to earthly human existence as a whole: "Pythagoras and the Platonic philosophers taught that the soul takes pleasure in music because it makes it recall the heavenly music that it heard before it was pushed into the body. . . . But we say, as Christians, . . . that music is pleasurable because God has given it for the recreation of human life."[16] As Martin Heinrich Fuhrmann put it, "among all the liberal arts invented by humans through the inspiration of the Holy Spirit, none is as powerful as music and none can so powerfully govern our affections, direct our morals, and affect our souls."[17] This holistic appreciation of music's effects on a human body-soul is pushed further in Fuhrmann's remark that a well-formed discant voice could sound like "an incarnated angel" that "bewitches" its listeners and simultaneously "melts their ear wax."[18] Music's prefiguring of the soundscape of paradise thus had a significant material dimension, potentially generating a felt sensation of mellowing in a believer's body-soul, who lived in the expectation of rising again after death as an integrated whole.

Early modern experiences of music-making thus raised the problem of the soul in the body, the world, and the afterlife in pressing ways that challenged both dualist and materialist accounts of (Christian) human nature. Time and again, music's effects seemed to confirm Friedrich Hoffmann's declaration that we cannot "amputate" the soul and its motions from the tabernacle of the body, an insight that troubled both somatically oriented medicine and post-Cartesian philosophy in different ways.[19] Early modern medical writers did often push the soul explicitly to the margins of their accounts. In a 1701 medical textbook, Johann Helffrich Jüngken asserted that human bodies consisted of two basic types of substances, solid and liquid. He continued: "Alongside these two substances a human being does consist of another substance, namely the soul; but this is not considered in our medicine, since the movements of the body and its parts can take place without its direction."[20] Such a strategy of separating the body as object of medical attention from any notion of soul aligned closely with Descartes's philosophical splitting of thinking self from unconscious body. Indeed, it was the Cartesian proposition that the rational soul was housed in the pineal gland at the back of the brain that promoted the gradual conflation of "mind" with "brain" that came to underpin our modern-day cranio-centrism. As a "cerebral subject," Fernando Vidal has written, the human of Western modernity is defined by the property of "brainhood"; a conception that is prefigured, for instance, in the German philosopher Friedrich Wilhelm Stosch's assertion in 1692 that "the mind is the better part of man, by which he thinks. It consists of the brain and its infinite organs, modified by the influx and circulation of the subtle matter."[21] Once soul is identified with mind and mind with brain, one may safely dispense with the notion of soul altogether, a process that reveals the very Cartesian foundations of both modern-day scientific materialism and the associated paradigm of cognition as computational data processing. As the media scholar Daniel Black has put it, in this paradigm "the brain becomes the house for an informatic mind that is ironically no less immaterial or disconnected from the body than Descartes' soul."[22]

Yet early modern music's ability to resonate across these domains of body, soul, and spirit continued to advocate for an alternative, more integrated anthropology. And those alternatives kept cropping up in the decades after Descartes. Many religious writers upheld the biblical tradition of locating the soul in the heart, with Johann Jacob Schmidt's *Biblischer Medicus* (1743) not only designating "the heart and innards" as the seat of the soul, but also calling the heart "the primary workshop of thoughts."[23] Meanwhile, already Descartes's contemporary Pierre Gassendi had famously ridiculed his colleague for insisting on the complete detachment of his thinking self from his bodily functions; a claim which Bernard Williams later described as "the scandal of Cartesian interactionalism."[24] Gassendi instead imagined a soul distributed throughout the body: "So why is it not possible that you are a wind, or rather a very thin vapor, given off when the heart heats up the purest type of blood, or produced by some other source, which is diffused through the parts of the body and gives them life? May it not be this vapor which sees with the eyes and hears with the ears and thinks with the brain and performs all the other functions which are commonly ascribed to you? If this is so, why should you not have the same shape as your whole body has?"[25] If subsequent intellectual history proved Gassendi's position to be the "losing" alternative, variants of this model nonetheless remained current in different discursive spheres into the eighteenth century (including Schmidt's treatise). The self declared Cartesian Steven Blankaart, for instance, held that perception happened immediately in the place where an external stimulus met the sense organ, thus offering a model of direct sensory comprehension that cut out any detour through the pineal gland.[26] In proposing "soul" to be present in each body part at the moment of sensation, Blankaart instead projected an Epicurean body ensouled and sensible in all its parts. The German medic Günther Christoph Schelhammer equally asserted that the soul was not to be found in the brain, but in the brain fluids that circulated throughout the body.[27] Such "off-Cartesian" models of human identity emerged, too, in the vitalist theories of Claude Perrault or later Georg Ernst Stahl.[28] Although suspicious of the theory of animal spirits,

Stahl saw the sensitive soul as an "immediate and active protagonist in every volitional, reflexive, and vegetative aspect of the body."[29] In a similar vein, Stahl's contemporary Hoffmann posited that the animal spirits have "a power impressed by God, not only of moving themselves mechanically, but also by choice, determinedly, and toward a definite purpose. This power is called the sensitive soul, and it basically exists in the most subtle fluid of the brain."[30] Even the more committed dualists often questioned whether the (soul-inhabited) brain could perform all the functions ascribed to it by Descartes. "This laxe pithe or marrow in a man's head," the rationalist theologian Henry More famously wrote, could no more pretend to "such noble operations as free Imagination and the sagacious collections of Reason, then we can discern in a Cake of Sewet or a Bowl of Curds."[31]

Early modern debates about the location of the soul, then, were not merely a matter of philosophical nit-picking; they pertained to the very fundamentals of what constituted human beings, their interactions with the material world, and their relation to the divine. Urban Gottfried Bucher's glib review of the numerous scenarios proposed by his contemporaries not only hints at the complexities of this conundrum but also confirms that the Cartesian solution merely formed one among several ultimately unverifiable alternatives.

> Some put [the soul] in the cerebrum, and many agree with this. Others put it in the pineal gland, and not a few agree with this. Yet others find this seat too small, and rightly so. . . . Therefore they place it in every part of the body (and in the whole body); and even though reason easily grasps that this means there would need to be as many souls in a human being as it had points, there are nevertheless many that ape this . . . . Still others put it in the heart, and let it swim around in the blood; for others it has to retreat into the ventricle [of the brain].[32]

Disagreements with the Cartesian position, in other words, were plentiful. Where Descartes more or less identified soul with mind, other early modern writers retained a much broader vision of the nature and functions of the soul, and ascribed to the ensouled body a range of cognitive abilities from perception to judgment and memory. And most forms of early modern musicking appeared to endorse some version of this latter, Aquinian notion of "toto in toto," of soul suffusing body. Producing and listening to musical sounds cut across any proposed body/brain or body/mind division by engaging the whole human in their flesh and spirit, thoughts and bodily fibers. Early modern musicians may well have agreed, therefore, with neuropsychologist Chris Frith's assertion that "understanding the brain is necessary but not sufficient for understanding the human person"; as well as with Bevil Conway and Alexander Rehding's recent critique of a neuroaesthetics that attempts to isolate the neural correlates of the experience of beauty.[33]

From a current secularized perspective, "soul" could perhaps be regarded simply as a useful name for something that is still hard to get at in present-day scientific discourse. Yet in an early modern context, it was experienced as both real and vital in physiological and theological as well as musical terms; found, for instance, in the manner that singing "by a delectable way, and full of plaintive sweetness" could "move and penetrate the soul, gently imprinting in it a delightful passion," as Baldassare Castiglione put it back in 1528;[34] or in Meinrad Spiess's conclusion that "nothing stirs human hearts more and nothing penetrates so deeply into their souls than a pleasant melody."[35] Neither Descartes's theory of musical rhythm as something wholly physical, felt by animals as much as humans, nor Leibniz's disembodied notion of music as "unconscious arithmetic" could quite explain how an act of music-making, by "exhilarating the animal spirits," "moderateth gratefully the affections, and thus penetrateth the interiors of the mind, which it most pleasantly doth affect."[36] When the German theologian Gottfried Ephraim Scheibel found that dissonant music "splendidly suits a melancholy nature, which accords well with the most adverse ideas such as fear, sorrow, and so on, which I can fairly call the dissonances of the spirit, as does an adagio with the slow movement of the blood," he identified the cause of these effects simply as "sympathetic matters," that is, that fundamental affinity of music with the blood and spirits of the human body-soul.[37] Imposing a Cartesian anthropology onto these experiences and explanations of musicking would arguably risk tuning out modes of composing, performing, and listening that continued to operate outside or alongside any emerging dualist certainties. Early modern acts of musicking not only posed an inconvenient challenge to such certainties, but could instantiate lived experiences of more holistic alternatives. In most of these musical endeavors, I would suggest, the soul never fully departed its bodily moorings to become a disembodied mind.

✷ 23 ✷
Liquefaction

A squirt of slippery delight, That with a Moment takes its Flight.

JOHN OLDHAM[1]

"In his setting of 'Anima mea liquefacta est,' [Heinrich] Schütz works hard to simulate 'feminine waters' and the longing for 'flow,'" wrote Susan McClary of a vocal concerto first published in Schütz's *Symphoniae Sacrae I* of 1629.[2] Her characterization stands in a line of feminist scholarship that over the past decades has transformed our appreciation of certain kinds of early modern musicking. In reintroducing (female) bodies, desire, sex, flesh, and blood to our critical purview, these writings have productively enriched or even displaced the inherited analytical emphasis on structure, rhetoric, or text painting—all those dimensions of musical works that serve to keep their wet-hot physicality at arm's length. And yet, McClary's turn of phrase continues to propose for this music a primarily mimetic function—it "simulates" rather than enacts, transmits, or induces. Richard Taruskin, too, in describing another vocal concerto from the same collection by Schütz, *O quam tu pulchra es*, reaches for the time-worn representational paradigm: "quite obviously a musical representation of a sensual climax," he writes of the final section of the piece.[3] The association of this musical idiom with sexual desire and gratification has become such a standard trope in musicological criticism that the question of what it was about early modern human physiology and/or the nature of music that enabled this conjunction has rarely been asked. When McClary finds that at the end of Jacques Arcadelt's madrigal *Il bianco e dolce cigno* the composer offers "an extended musical simulation of orgasm" by exploiting the conventional association of sexual release with death captured in the French phrase "la petite mort," her certainty seems to derive more from the assumed obviousness of the cliché than from any more sustained historical investigation.[4] To point to just one potential facet of such a more historicized approach, I could not trace the phrase "la petite mort" in any of the standard French reference volumes of the period, notwithstanding Antoine Furetière's 1690 dictionary entry for "mort" as "also a poetic and romanesque term for expressing an amorous passion."[5] For Taruskin, too, reading the baritone's ascent in *O quam to pulchra es* as a simile for sexual climax appears so intuitive as to require no further probing. Yet his blunt pictorialism not only skips over the potential layers of spiritual as well as erotic significance of such a passage for Schütz's auditors; it also locates the phenomenon squarely in the notes, sidestepping consideration of either the performative production of such sonic stimulation or its effects on listeners. What kind of orgasm is Taruskin imagining here—male or female, simulated or experienced by performers, seen in the mind's eye or co-suffered by their audiences? Such readings, in short, once again eclipse music's role as a catalyst for processes of bodily-spiritual transformation through sonorous impact.

What, then, did sexual flows have to do with musical flows? We might start with that early modern commonplace that described listening to music as a form of rape or ravishment. "The Lydian Moode," wrote Charles Butler in his 1636 music treatise, "ravisheth the minde with a kinde of ecstasi, lifting it up from the regarde of earthly things, unto the desire of celestiall joyz."[6] Simon Smith has offered a nuanced reading of this trope of musical/sexual ravishment, showing that it could be used either in a "kidnapping" sense (removing to another place) or in a "penetrative" sense. On this basis, Smith argues that the notion of musical ravishment "does not make a primary association between sexual and musical *pleasure*, but rather draws an analogy between the physiological *processes* of hearing and sex."[7] Yet in either case, this process could induce a particular state of "ecstasi"—a "trance, swooning, or astonishment, a ravishment or transportation of the spirit by passion," as the English lexicographer Thomas Blount defined the term.[8] Here is a poetic invocation by Barthold Heinrich Brockes of this ecstasy as triggered by the sounds of a lute:

> So bald ihr Ton durchs Ohr uns sanfft die Hertzen schläget:
> Kocht gleich das Blut und wall't; die Seele wird beweget
> Und steigt, Verwund'rungs-voll, aus unser engen Brust,
> Auf Leitern der Music, ins Paradis der Lust.

[As soon as its sound gently strikes our hearts through the ear, the blood immediately boils and surges; the soul is moved and rises, full of wonder, from the narrow breast, up music's ladders, into the paradise of pleasure.][9]

Both the penetrative and the kidnapping aspects of the experience are present here, as music infiltrates the ear and removes the soul out of the body to another place. Music in this way could "verzucken" (in the sense of elate or rape) someone's heart, as the linguist Matthias Kramer noted in his German-Italian dictionary of 1724; and in this moment of "Entzückung" (ecstasy), wrote Johann Heinrich Zedler, the soul entered a state "in which external sensation ceases."[10] Martin Heinrich Fuhrmann, too, described the imagined effects of hearing the angels sing in terms of such a loss of external sensation, since in the presence of this "heart-pressing song" and "soul-piercing sound" one would surely "lose the power of hearing and sight, a thousand times more than an ignorant peasant who hears a 32-foot organ played in a city church for the first time."[11] Or, as Giovanni Battista Guarini put it in his poem in praise of a female singer's throat, "Mentre vaga Angioletta":

> Così cantando e ricantando, il core,
> O miracol d'amore
> è fatto un usignolo,
> e spiega già per non star meco il volo.

[Thus singing and singing again, my heart—O miracle of love—is made a nightingale, and now takes flight so as not to stay within me.][12]

Such musically induced ecstasy, then, could "sever soul from body," in Linda Phyllis Austern's words, leaving the physical body and its sensory capacities behind as the soul soared yonder.[13]

These metaphors seem to position musical ecstasy far away from the corporeal pleasures associated with sexual gratification. Yet such out-of-body experiences were not in fact necessarily de-sensualized. In Pontus de Tyard's famous mid-sixteenth-century description of a performance by the Italian lutenist Francesco da Milano, the "ecstatic transport of some divine frenzy" he recalls in fact entailed an escalation of sensory pleasure, "as if the soul, having abandoned all other senses, had been drawn to the surface of the ears."[14] This concentration of soul or spirit in a single body part also characterized moments of sexual climax, in which "heart and brain pour out the largest portion of their heat and spirits" and "send them quickly" into the sexual organs.[15] In female orgasm, those spirits rushed to the clitoris, that "romping ground of pleasure," as Zedler called it.[16] As the French writer Nicolai Venette outlined, "in sexual intercourse this clitoris is filled up and enraptured with the fiercest spirits and consequently makes itself hard and stiff like the man's penis."[17] This concentrated spirit influx could produce a degree of sensory stupefaction akin to a "mild fainting fit."[18] The physician Johann Nicolaus Pfitzer's description of male sexual arousal affirmed that "his hotter, thicker, and more plentiful semen [compared to the female] is ejected with much greater bodily motion; by this ejaculation . . . sometimes the body's powers are affected, as if sense and wit retreated, which stems from nothing but the lustful sensitivity and sensual stimulation [Kützel]."[19] The structural homologies between musical and sexual ecstasy that emerge here extended, as well, to the metaphor of "Kützel" or "itch," which was used in both contexts to capture the distinctive kind of pleasure at play. For Pfitzer, it was the very matter of semen—made of "the pure concocted and windy superfluity of blood," according to Galen—that was "itchy, aggravating, tickly" because of the "many hot spirits trapped within"; their release engendered that "sweetest pleasure" of orgasm.[20] Musical pleasure, too, as we have heard, presented itself as an "itching of the ears" and could bring about a "pleasant tickle" in the heart and soul.[21]

Needless to say, within an early modern Christian framework, none of these terms were neutral entities. That sexual or musical itch carried immediate connotations of wanton sinfulness: itches want scratching, but the wrong kind of sensory indulgence could divert believers from the narrow path toward salvation. And yet the intense pleasures afforded by both sexual and musical immersion also carried a certain redemptive potential. Not only did both experiences potentially leave body and spirits refreshed and energized, but they could each offer a glimpse of that highest bliss of eternity that otherwise eluded mortal humans. If music's capacity for affording a foretaste of divine pleasure was widely appreciated at the time, Venette claimed that sexual pleasure, too, had been given by God in order to indicate "those pleasures which we may hope for in the afterlife."[22] That anticipatory delight was often described in terms of an intense sensory experience of sweetness. As Heinrich Müller put it, "God tastes sweet," a sweetness tasted inwardly in the heart, and "the pleasantness of song" could help sweeten the pill of his Word.[23] Pfitzer likewise asserted that those "sweetest pleasures" of coitus "make intercourse sugary and sweet, so to speak."[24] And that sweet intensity then caused a physical-spiritual outflow: "Often sacred songs bring a metaphysical sweetness from God into the heart," wrote Müller; "often the sweet taste of God's mercy enraptures us, so to speak, so that we do not know what is happening to us, and often tears of joy flow in heaps."[25] In sexual rapture, too, according to Venette, "we are as if enraptured by joy, when the semen, all inflated by spirits, makes its way through our entangled vessels. The hot and itchy vapors that arise and the extremely fast movement of the spirits as they penetrate our membranes contribute not insignificantly to our great pleasure."[26] In this ecstatic state, "our body and soul pour themselves out from joy."[27]

In all these ways, sexual, spiritual, and musical rapture could overlap or even merge, each "dissolving Passion in a Flood of Pleasure."[28] These overlapping processes of bodily-spiritual liquefaction enabled those "dark powers of audible music to dissolve the bonds between sensation and spirituality, leading through the rape of the ear to the ecstasies of divine or earthly love," as Austern has written.[29] The Song of Songs text "Anima mea liquefacta est" epitomized this nexus of music, spirit, and eros. As an entity with quasi-material dimensions that could be imprinted or penetrated, soul could indeed be liquefied, to run in one's veins as spiritous blood—hence the capacity of music to figure as an ensouled outflow of spirit. Semen likewise constituted "a foamy moisture full of vital spirits" that was "ensouled" through those spirits.[30] This ensouled liquidity formed the basis for achieving an ecstatic union with Christ no less than the generation of new life through sexual intercourse. As Lindsay Johnson has discussed, such liquified souls could merge—actually, substantively—with other sacred fluids such as Christ's blood, a process enacted materially in the Eucharist.[31] One of the hymns in Johann Freylinghausen's Pietist hymnal expressed this merging as an urgent desire: "Dissolve, my spirit, in Jesus' blood and wounds."[32] And as the human soul and Jesus's blood joined in spiritual union, so in procreation the male and female semen conjoined to similarly ecstatic and life-giving effects. McClary has described this convergence of spiritual and sexual domains as "a stark violation of our modern frame of reference, which tends to relegate the sacred and the sexual to opposite ends of the experiential spectrum."[33] In certain acts of early modern music-making, that convergence could manifest itself as an intensely felt reality.

Early modern conceptions of orgasm elucidate the homologous experiences of rapture occasioned by these processes of liquefaction. Unlike the standard narrow definition of the term today as sexual climax, in early modern writings "orgasm" often referred to a wider range of phenomena related to surging liquids or humors in the body; and on this basis, the powers of music to induce a state of arousal comparable to coitus become more plausible and tangible. Zedler's encyclopedia defined the term "Orgasmus" as "strong motions of the blood or semen," covering not just ejaculation but "surging" experiences (Aufwallung) in fevers, rage, dancing, or horse riding.[34] We may recall here that Brockes framed his own ecstatic listening experience in terms of such a "surge" as well. Ephraim Chambers's *Cyclopaedia* of 1738 did identify orgasm as an "impetuous desire of coition, occasioned by a turgescency of the seminal vessels," but pointed out that the term could refer to any "impetuous, or too quick motion of the blood, or spirits, whereby the muscles are distended with uncommon force."[35] In 1762, the dictionary of the Académie Française still explained the term broadly as an "agitation, a movement of the humors which seek to evacuate themselves."[36] These definitions suggest that the various "surges" of bodily-spiritual liquids referenced here were more similar in their felt reality than our neat separating out of sexual pleasure now suggests. When Müller discussed hymn singing as an experience of being "filled up with the joy-wine of the Holy Spirit," where "the joy of the spirit is like a stream" that "drenches us in pleasure" and "swells and breaks forth" from the heart, which "boils and wells up [wallen] and overflows from joy," would this "Wallung" have been of a musical, spiritual, or erotic nature?[37]

These convergences open up the potential for rehearing certain musical utterances that have tended to be subsumed under a representational paradigm. Instead of reading their notated gestures as depicting explicit sexual acts, we might become more attuned to the ambiguous intensities of the bodily-spiritual motions that such utterances could elicit. If during coitus the sexual organs were "dampened" with a "sharp" or "biting" moisture that then had to be purged through an outflow of semen, could the sharpness of a dissonance like the clashing f-sharp–b-flat in measure 13 of Alba Tressina's setting of "Anima mea" have had a comparable effect of liquefaction? Zedler affirmed that strong affective motions in the human body could be stilled through expelling either tears or semen, attesting to the shared cathartic effects of these outflows. Lindsay Johnson's sensitive reading of Tressina's piece does suggest that music could both represent and engender experiences of divine ecstasy, but her "humoral analysis" still repeatedly retreats to pictorialism: the piece's opening descending lines "mimic moving water," thereby "depicting the first line of text," while the subsequent section "depict[s] black bile."[38] My own sense is that if we take seriously the countless contemporary descriptions of music as inducing feelings of gushing ecstasy, we must push beyond the notion that Tressina's musical outpouring functioned as a sonic depiction of souls melting, and instead assume that souls indeed melted in the act of singing or listening to it. Most likely Tressina's piece would have been intoned by its three female vocalists in a private devotional setting, enabling an intimate contagious experience of bodily-spiritual liquefaction, of the sort that Johnson explores in her closing "speculative recreation" of a historical performance moment, with the nuns "gasping for air," their throats "tense in pain." I deeply sympathize with Johnson's account here and would only wish to remove the air of fabrication that surrounds it in her article. On the basis of the sources explored here, Johnson's compassionate reading

EXAMPLE 23.1. Heinrich Schütz, *Anima mea liquefacta est* (SWV 263), from *Symphoniae Sacrae* I (Venice: Magni, 1629), mm. 18–36.

strikes me as no more fabricated than a narrative that insists on a primary process of representational encoding and decoding.

A performance of Schütz's setting of "Anima mea," I would propose, could have afforded similarly powerful experiences of liquefaction. The sonic imprint of the wind playing that opens the piece—Schütz prescribed either cornettini or fiffari (transverse flutes)—could have had an immediate mellowing effect through its distinctive muted/airy timbral qualities, especially if the players chose to accentuate those qualities through soft attacks and legato articulation. When the two tenors subsequently entered, one after the other, a feel of liquidity may have been palpable in numerous ways outside of inherited notions of Baroque text painting: in their mode of vocal production, their timbre, intonation, and sonic interplay, features perhaps made more potent if the singers had cared to fine-tune the viscosity of their own bodily fluids through appropriate food intake and vocal exercise.[39] Given appropriate training as well as adequate moisture and temperature levels in the singers' vocal tracts, their opening stream of "a" vowels, initially declaimed on the same repeated pitch, could have been delivered with a soft, open throat, allowing for a smooth passage of spiritous air that in turn mellowed the bodily-spiritual flows of any attendant listeners (ex. 23.1). Since the two instrumental parts had moved in parallel thirds and sixths for most of the introduction, the entrance of the second tenor, with its close suspension against the first voice in measure 23, would have offered a first moment of palpable friction, of a "Kützel" in the ear, heart, or groin region. Dissonances, like the liquid that stoked sexual desire, could be "scharff," too.[40] Those frictions then gradually reached their apex in the second part of Schütz's composition, *Adjuro vos* (SWV 264), to the extent that the singers' sonic-spiritual surges ended up overpowering the basic proprieties of musical syntax.[41] But my point is not that these syntactical transgressions would therefore have symbolized sexual transgression, or that this passage of heightened harmonic frisson offered a legible depiction of sexual gratification. Rather, these contagious sonic-spiritual surges emanating from the musicians' body-souls would have had the potential to immerse listeners in their own experiences of surging liquids, whose intensities would have remained multivalent but no less tangible and transformative as a result. It may of course be the case that this kind of music functioned mainly as a straightforward "mechanism of sublimation" in a sexually repressed environment that we now find easy to unmask.[42] But my materials here seem to suggest differently: they indicate that music's rapacious force could indeed induce experiences of ecstatic bliss that liquefied the boundaries between flesh and soul.

24
Softness

> [The body] has always known, without needing it explained in language, that language is soft and hard.
>
> MICHEL SERRES[1]

In her analysis of Alba Tressina's *Anima mea liquefacta est*, Lindsay Johnson identifies the dominant humoral-affective character of the piece as "pleasurable melancholy," grounded in the lovesickness articulated in the text that "Renaissance doctors would have labeled as melancholy."[2] In musical terms, one might suggest that the low register of the vocal parts (three female voices singing in alto/tenor range) could have helped generate this humoral profile. As Girolamo Mei affirmed, it was "very well known that pitches intermediate between the extremely high and the extremely low are appropriate for showing a quiet and moderate disposition of the affections, while the very high are signs of a very excited and uplifted spirit, and the very low of abject and humble thoughts."[3] The "abject and humble" was unequivocally the domain of melancholy, that illness which reportedly afflicted such a significant proportion of the early modern populace, especially of the higher social classes.[4] And yet, there is a fundamental contradiction here. The underlying text deals primarily in liquids, and those liquids, according to Johnson, shaped many of the piece's "watery" or "bubbling" motives. But melancholy, in an early modern humoral physiology, was chiefly characterized by dryness (and coldness), putting it fundamentally at odds with the liquidity of these words and gestures. The term "melancholy" referred both to an actual bodily fluid, black bile, and to the diseases caused by its excess, whose numerous symptoms included ulcers, tumors, lethargy, and noxious vapors that clouded the brain and hence also afflicted the mind.[5] Robert Burton, that foremost seventeenth-century authority on the subject, described black bile as "'cold and dry, thicke, blacke, sowre, begotten of the more faeculent part of nourishment, and purged from the Spleene."[6] In a medical handbook of 1744, the German physician Lorenz Heister outlined how "in melancholy, because the vital spirits are too lethargic and dampened, they need to be re-awoken," initially through purging or bleeding, and then "the thick, heavy and immobile juices need to be thinned and distributed."[7] Black bile impeded the body's flows, causing them to dry up and coagulate, and bringing about hardness and roughness in the voice. As Athanasius Kircher stated: "In sad and sorrowful people, the heat draws in from the circumference toward the center of the heart, together with the animal spirits, so that the upper body parts are deprived of heat, and are gripped by coldness; since in this place coldness now dominates, the voice tends to be slow and rough."[8] Concerning the condition's overall psychosomatic effects, the Lutheran writer Sigismund Scherertz presented melancholy as "the most detrimental affliction of the soul, through which the body is emaciated and weakened; and as a woodworm eats through a tree or plank and a weed suffocates and smothers the good wheat: thus melancholy weakens the heart and robs it of its strength." Moreover, it could "extinguish in the heart all devotion for prayer, hope, and patience, indeed almost all exercises of your Christian faith; it pushes the blessedness within you to the ground, and the Holy Spirit, which is a joyful spirit, is prevented thereby from unfolding its blessed effects in you."[9] In its more severe manifestations, a melancholic disposition could wreak havoc with a Christian faith and lifestyle.

So where does this leave the supposed melancholy expressed or engendered in Tressina's piece? If the women intoning it were filled with melancholic longing, would there have been a notable lack of mellifluousness in their voices? Or could these liquid musical lines have helped to re-moisten their innards, to melt what had become hard and dry through unfulfilled desire? The web of metaphors that is emerging here points to certain fundamental contradictions in a psycho-physiology that emphatically did not present a closed system. While aging, for instance, had since antiquity been understood as a process of wilting or drying out, the equally prevalent doctrine of the four ages of man associated senescence with winter, the cold and moist season, and hence with phlegm.[10] Similarly, the wombs of women who had multiple sexual partners were considered hungry, hot, and craving the cooling male seed; and yet the male constitution and hence its outflows were otherwise held to be hotter than their female counterparts.[11] As for melancholy, the condition was remarkably diverse, as black bile could mix with other humors to produce a range of melancholic dispositions.[12] Burton found that a "confused mixture of symptoms" made it hard to disentangle the malady's different types, but he identified, among others, a "head melancholy," stemming from a "hot and dry distemperature"; and a "windy hypochondriacall" type, which caused "Feare & Sorrow, sharpe belchings, and fulsome crudities, heat in the bowels, winde and rumbling in the guts," and so on.[13] Love melancholy, meanwhile, "makes the blood hot, thicke and blacke, and if the inflammation gets into the braine, with continuall meditation and waking, it so dries it up, that madnesse followes, or else they make away themselves."[14] Here we seem to be straying into the hot/dry domain of the choleric. More recently, Peter Holman characterized early modern lovesickness as the opposite of moist and warm love, as the lover "became cold, dry and melancholic if his love was thwarted."[15] We must conclude, I think, that any attempt to get to the bottom of these discrepancies would eventually find that anything or nothing could be humorally determined by black bile, an insight that might throw the validity of the whole system into serious question.

Music's capacity to act as a protean emotional catalyst does not offer much help in disentangling these issues. Music was frequently embraced as a vehicle of melancholy, offering a means for those afflicted to give voice to their distemper, but it could also serve as an antidote, and perhaps do both at the same time. As Holman finds with regard to John Dowland's iconic *Lachrimae* collection (1604), "one of the functions of his seven pavans, presumably, was to cure the melancholy they so powerfully evoke."[16] Heister listed music as a potential remedy for melancholy alongside wine, exercise, thin tea, pleasant recreation, travel, and walking in gardens.[17] Burton similarly called music a "roaring-meg" against melancholy, claiming it could "ereare and revive the languishing soule, affecting not only the eares, but the very arteries, the vitall & animall spirits, it erects the mind, & makes it nimble."[18] But while a certain way of singing a piece like Tressina's may have made the musicians feel nimble and sprightly, it might just as powerfully have drawn them into the affective maelstrom of languishing desire and left them there. And this, of course, was the danger of indulging in musical pursuits more generally: they could render their participants soft and liquid in a way that, especially for men, threatened to deprive them of their hot and hard vitality. If sleeping in a soft bed was considered bad for you because it made you soft, already Plato had cautioned that too much music enfeebled a warrior as it "melts and liquefies till he completely dissolves away his spirit."[19] As Thomas Lacqueur's seminal work has shown, most early moderns did assume that men and women were fundamentally made of the same stuff, but tended to map sociopolitical differences and gender hierarchies directly onto the body and its properties; so a male melancholic's inability to regulate his humoral fluids pushed him worryingly close to a feminine state, characterized by a lack of control over bodily outflows and diminished rational capacities.[20] Music, in "alluring the auditorie to effeminacie . . . muche like unto Honey" and making the mind "queasie," as Philip Stubbs put it, carried the exact same dangers.[21] Within the confines of Tressina's convent, the problem of men turning into women presumably did not arise. Yet more generally, the idea of music as a soft and softening power not only remained at odds with its capacity to "ravish" or "penetrate" her listeners, but in that paradox pinpointed some of the broader contradictions that pervaded this flow-based anthropology.

Crucially, those musical qualities of softness/hardness were not simply associated with certain sounds or gestures, but were woven into the very fabric of the Western musical universe. The etymology of the two basic modes of being in music—"durus" and "mollis" (plus, in medieval hexachord theory, the neutral "naturalis")—created a system that entrenched certain sonic-moral qualities from the outset. A typical definition by Wolfgang Mylius stated that "mollis" indicated a "soft or melancholy, sad song" and "durus" a "hard or joyful" song.[22] Carl Dahlhaus has explored the complex history of these terms in some detail, showing how they encompassed "the mathematical foundation and perceptibility of intervals, their mode of intonation, their expressive content, and their moral or aesthetic value."[23] "Durus" and "mollis" could be applied at different levels of abstraction, referring to the shape of their notational signs, to scales, intervals, pitches, or accidentals; but initially the distinction between the two was grounded in the physical reality of a string tightening for sharper pitches and slackening for flatter ones. As Mattheson noted, the term "durus" "stems from the harder or stiffer tension of a string," and the meaning of "mollis" from "its slackness or loosening."[24] And if, for at least some of Mattheson's contemporaries, a human body was permeated by nerve fibers that resembled taut strings, then that physical reality extended to the response of those bodies to sonic stimulation: as their nerves resonated with incoming sound waves, they would have tightened or relaxed sympathetically.[25] Still, many writers from Ptolemy to the eighteenth century did not consider the relative tension of a string but the interval of the semitone itself to harbor soft, sweet, or effeminate properties. Thomas Morley prescribed that "when you would expresse a lamentable passion, then must you use motions proceeding by halfe notes . . . those accidentall cords which are marked with these signes sharp and flat . . . make the song as it were more effeminate & languishing."[26] Mauritius Vogt likewise asserted that the "chromatic genus," whose semitone saturation caused

EXAMPLE 24.1. Andreas Hammerschmidt, *Anima mea liquefacta est*, from *Motettae, unius et duarium vocum* (Dresden: Bergen, 1649), mm. 1–7.

"sweeter pleasure," "softens" souls and "enervates" lofty spirits.[27] The opening of Andreas Hammerschmidt's *Anima mea liquefacta est*—notably devoid of any "flowing" eighth notes—presumably afforded easy activation of that softening potential of chromaticism (ex. 24.1). But these characterizations applied to cadence types and other interval classes, too: Vincenzo Galilei attested that Phrygian cadences were "effeminate and lascivious" due to their "many softenings and the quantity of semitones in the outer voices";[28] and Giovanni Battista Doni found that "motion by step or small intervals" made a melody "soft and somber," whereas moving by leap or remote intervals rendered the song "virile and sustained."[29]

Such ambiguities around the locus and value of musical softness extended to the human condition more generally. If hard virility was prized as superior, nonetheless it was softness that enabled the basic lineaments of humanity to emerge, as Ovid's tale of stones softened by music affirmed:

> The stones (who would believe the thing, but that the time of old
> Reports it for a steadfast truth?), of nature tough and hard,
> Began to wax both soft and smooth and shortly afterward
> To win therewith a better shape; and, as they did increase,
> A milder nature in them grew and rudeness gan to cease.[30]

Francis Bacon described the differing conditions of material bodies as follows: "Some (we see) are hard, and some soft: The hardness is caused (chiefly) by the Jejuneness of the Spirits; and their imparity with the Tangible parts: Both which, if they be in a greater degree, maketh them not onely hard, but fragile, and less enduring of pressures . . . . Softness cometh (contrariwise) by the greater quantity of Spirits, (which ever helpeth to induce yielding and cession;) and by the more equal spreding of the Tangible parts, which thereby are more sliding, and following."[31] If hardness in the material world had its drawbacks, making bodies more brittle, in a human body-soul its detrimental effects included the inability to receive the word and grace of God. A dedicatory poem introducing Samuel Michael's collection *Psalmodia regia* described how "the finger of God, when it brings us pious oracles by way of coarse and even stubborn things, has mixed with them the most sweet pleasure of music, so that, our ears thus being lined, the mysteries flow into our hearts in a hidden way and barely sensed. O divine Music! You are wholly the image of divine sweetness; with your strength you soften pagan hearts immediately and straightaway purge them."[32]

Perhaps we can locate such a capacity for grace-bestowing mollification in Schütz's *Anima mea,* specifically in a passage just before the end of the opening section. The unexpected introduction of a-flats in the two vocal parts in measure 33, foreign to the prevailing D-Aeolian mode, would have drawn performers and listeners into an audibly slacker or softer region of the musical gamut (see ex. 23.1). Although from a structural perspective one might dismiss these a-flats as insignificant inflections in a broader move toward the median F, this would not diminish their potential aural-bodily effect as this passage unfolded in the performative moment. If we believe Michael, such a device did not merely look "rounded" on the page, or signified softening hearts, but could exert a tangible pull toward corporeal-spiritual mellowing in a well-disposed recipient—especially tangible, perhaps, in a 2008 rendering by Les Voix Baroques, who linger achingly on that "mollis" sonority.[33] If music could "line" listeners' ears, if it could be a material-spiritual entity that impacted human bodies in a haptic way, it becomes more plausible to imagine feeling musical sound to be hard or soft to the touch. In that sense, Schütz's and Hammerschmidt's chromatic antics may have produced not only an aural effect of distortion or slipping, but also a physical effect of wrenching or drenching your insides.

But, again, any such musical-humoral referents were not consistent. Many musicians affirmed that "chroma" could in fact engender sharp and harsh musical effects; hence those "sowrest sharps" in William Byrd's song *Come woeful Orpheus,* published in 1611.[34] It was widely agreed that sharp and sour things could do terrible things to human bodies: not just the sourness of black bile, but the "miasma" of venereal disease, for instance, which "insinuates itself into the body and the blood through transpiration, and then permeates the whole body, sours and spoils it and impregnates it with the venereal poison."[35] So when Andreas Herbst described the Phrygian mode as "saurzapffig," we may assume that encountering such a sonic mode potentially brought detrimental bodily-spiritual effects.[36] The classification of musical modes according to their affective-humoral characteristics, meanwhile, was another domain rife with inconsistencies. Especially over the course of the seventeenth century, as the mode system had to be continually adapted to musical practices that increasingly outstripped it, these modal-affective schemes became more variable and contested. But already in Gioseffo Zarlino's seminal taxonomy, the possible expressive functions of the authentic mixolydian mode stretched all the way from "lascivious" and "cheerful" to "threat, perturbation and anger."[37] Though continuing well into the eighteenth century, such attempts at tying specific affects to specific modes or keys ultimately failed to capture those affective qualities that not only remained slippery and hard to pin down, but that, especially in an increasingly well-tempered musical environment, were produced in performative action as much as contained in the notes. Is the potential harshness in the opening of Johann Sebastian Bach's sin-drenched aria "O Menschen" from Cantata 122 primarily a function of its C-minor key signature, or of its chromatic alterations, looking jagged and angular on the page and sounding "sour" in performance (fig. 24.1)? Or is it at least as much a matter of a cellist's bow scraping against string to generate a harsh, grating timbre as she activates these jagged gestures? The unapologetically hoarse rasping in John Eliot Gardiner's version from

FIGURE 24.1. Johann Sebastian Bach, aria "O Menschen," from *Das neugeborne Kindelein* (BWV 122), excerpt. Staatsbibliothek zu Berlin—Preußischer Kulturbesitz, Musikabteilung mit Mendelssohn-Archiv, Mus.ms. Bach P 868.

his 2000 Cantata Pilgrimage to me does not simply depict the ugliness of human sin, but can leave me feeling pierced and soured within myself.[38]

Many writers at the time sensed these discrepancies in their musical systems. Kircher tried to explain, unconvincingly, that a "plangent" affect differed from a "dolorous" one in that the former had rough, hard, and syncopated intervals, whereas the latter had broken, soft, and foreign ones.[39] The German organist Andreas Werckmeister lamented the inadequacy of the terms "durus" and "mollis," pointing out that "durus" "does not accord with the harmony, so that when something sad is played, one instantly says 'that is very dur'"; although he did find that the word "mollis" "does still accord fairly well with the harmony that is now in use."[40] If, in humoral-spiritual terms, softness was an ambiguous but ultimately desirable and often pleasurable experience, in musical terms it likewise constituted an alluring yet elusive and ambivalent property. What seems clear, however, is that this ambivalence in no way erased the powerful experiences of softening, mellowing, or melting that an encounter with particular musical sounds could induce; even if that "magnetic pull," as Kircher called it, remained perilous and unaccountable.[41]

25

Liebe, sag', was fängst du an?

> Living Persons, with reall Eyes burning with Love, or soft Glances sunk and overwhelmed with Passions; with real Tears in the Actors which likewise draw Tears from the Spectators. In short, with such true motions and gestures, as kindle and Scatter the same Sentiments all around, and set the Pit and Boxes on fire.
>
> JACQUES-BÉNIGNE BOSSUET[1]

Early modern staged spectacle in the Western tradition was fundamentally about bodies: theater, writes Simon Shepherd, "consciously exhibits the body."[2] Across the long history of Western theater and opera, those bodies ostensibly shared certain basic properties, such as eyes and tears, lungs and sexual organs; they had to contend with "sweat, phlegm, and dirty feet," as the twentieth-century soprano Elisabeth Söderström put it.[3] But if these bodies, with their tears and phlegm, were never simply natural givens, this is doubly the case in the context of (musical) theater. First, these performing bodies, like all the bodies considered in this book, were particular to and shaped by the time, place, and situation in which they stepped onto the stage to speak or sing. They not only signified differently, but felt differently, were constituted differently. And second, as these bodies stepped on stage, they did so in order to embody another, to inhabit the voice, gestures, gender, and self of a character in a story. They set out to do what another body would do. As Linda and Michael Hutcheon assert, "the living body of the singing actor on the operatic stage both *has* and *performs* a body," and—in both those senses—"that body is more than a biological entity."[4]

What does this consideration of bodies as theatrical entities, of make-believe as a basic mode of embodiment, do to the corporeal-spiritual processes of affect transmission we have been tracing so far? What happens to the interpersonal flows of affect when the affects projected by a singer belonged not to them but to the character they were acting out? One answer might be that operatic musicking was indeed a different kind of experience from some of the other musical encounters explored here. By the early eighteenth century, opera had grown into an art form that rendered emotions consumable; the operatic aria, in this model, offered a form of "voyeuristic gratification."[5] Bonnie Gordon accordingly tells a narrative of disenchantment as opera left behind the affective immediacy of its early seventeenth-century beginnings (in works such as Monteverdi's *Arianna*): "The stage was a contained and fictional space which might not invade the very pores of the audiences who now clapped at the end of a performance but did not cry or feel their blood boil. They watched stories but did not experience them in the manner of the ladies at the 1608 festivities."[6] Yet Tim Carter has rightly cautioned against the tendency to imagine a utopian moment of oneness with the world prior to the disruptive arrival of modernity.[7] On this basis, another answer to the question of how early modern opera impinged upon its participating body-souls might be that, like in most other musicking situations, these experiences were multivalent, dependent on the shape of individual performances and their participants. Certain effects of musical matter penetrating these body-souls may have unfolded regardless of an individual's humoral disposition or attention levels, eliciting habitual responses from habituated bodies; and beyond this a variety of different modes of engagement were available and—presumably—practiced. These may have reached from wholesale immersion in the affective transaction on stage to detached aesthetic judgment and being dazzled or aroused by the vocal brilliance of the star singers.

A closer look at an aria by the Hamburg opera composer Reinhard Keiser, "Liebe, sag', was fängst du an?," can help delineate some of these modes of engagement more closely. What might have happened to, within, and between the body-souls involved in a performance of this piece? Keiser's opera *Croesus*, from which the aria is drawn, premiered in 1711 at the Gänsemarkt in Hamburg, and re-joined the business of selling emotion in 1730, when it was revived in a heavily redacted form at the same venue. Much of the opera's initial emotional content was repackaged for this revival, as Keiser wrote no fewer than 37 new arias for it (including "Liebe, sag'"). He also changed the voice parts of two of the main protagonists: the Lydian king Croesus, who had been a tenor in 1711, became a bass, and his son, the mute prince Atis, turned from bass to soprano. Exchanging arias and tailoring parts to particular singers was common operatic practice at the time, of course. But subsequently the most popular of these arias often became detached from the specific bodies/voices that initially produced them and circulated as disembodied objects in domestic or concert settings. The seemingly autonomous existence of these musical-affective artefacts no doubt contributed to the later musicological perception of an operatic aria as an objectification of both music and affect: it seemed to render them both "out there" as reproduceable entities, uncoupled from their embodied realization on stage, and seemingly of greater permanence than those fleeting mortal bodies that enacted them in the theater. The fact that Keiser fashioned quite so many of these reproduceable objects (according to Johann Gottfried Walther, he wrote arias for over 107 operas) certainly invites a reading of his oeuvre as an instantiation of that Baroque typology of affects that the *Affektenlehre* of twentieth-century musicology so determinedly hoped to pin down.[8] There was love, joy, wonder, triumph, fury, envy, fear, despair, and so on, and a distinct musical mode for encapsulating each of these.

"Liebe, sag'" yields readily to a taxonomic reading of musical affect. Its first part is all soft love, a mode for which, according to Johann Adolph Scheibe, Keiser had a particular penchant: "Keiser's pieces are galant, enamored, and show all those sentiments whose force the human heart suffers most." His melodies, Scheibe asserted, "are fiery, without coercion"; they are "love itself."[9] The aria's opening ritornello spins a lilting diatonic melody, played in unison by violins and oboes, over a stepwise descending bass in A major (ex. 25.1). According to Mattheson, the key of A major, although it "sparkled" ("brilliret"), "strongly affected" a listener and "tended more toward plangent and sad passions than to divertissements."[10] Mattheson rejected the claim that "when a piece had a flat signature, it inevitably had to sound soft and tender, but when it had a signature of one or more sharps, its nature had to be hard, fresh, and cheerful."[11] Certainly the Akademie for Alte Musik Berlin, in a 2008 recording with soprano Sandrine Piau, did not read the three-sharp signature in this aria as an indication for harshness or liveliness, opting instead for a smoothly flowing rendition that projects softness of larynx and tenderness of heart. From measure 17, meanwhile, present-day devotees of the *Affektenlehre* will find an archetypal instantiation of pain in the chromatic melisma on the word "Schmerz" (ex. 25.2); followed by an equally conventional representation of joy in the ensuing B section, marked "Vivace," with its diatonic vocal effusions over simple repeated chords in the instruments (ex. 25.3). The protagonist's uncertainty over her emotional state—she is asking, "shall I feel pain or joy?"—is pressed into concrete sonic-gestural shapes that seem to leave no doubt about their respective affective meaning. We might conclude here, as Rolf Dammann did, that in this kind of aria, "it is not

EXAMPLE 25.1. Reinhard Keiser, "Liebe, sag', was fängst du an," from *Croesus* (1730), mm. 1–8.

an individually shaped inner life that is expressed"; instead, such a piece seems to portray a generalized affective state that signified beyond the particular individual and situation.[12]

And yet. My discerning readers will have noticed that my descriptions of these moments of pain and joy very much focused on aspects easily legible

EXAMPLE 25.2. Keiser, "Liebe, sag', was fängst du an," mm. 17–20.

from a score—harmonic and melodic features as well as some aspects of rhythm and tempo. But of course any palpable emotive impact would only have emerged when the affective potential afforded by those features was activated in performance, by living, breathing bodies that had to mold and stretch their corporeal-spiritual state in order to give persuasive expression to those sentiments. Granted, these were performing bodies who entangled their audience in layers of simulation and disguise. Elmira, who sang the aria "Liebe, sag'," was a Persian princess, most likely embodied on stage by a white Christian female soprano singer. Elmira's object of love, meanwhile, the Lydian prince Atis, was another foreign non-Christian character who, in this part of the narrative, would have been standing in front of her in disguise, dressed up as a Persian soldier. Since castratos did not appear on the eighteenth-century Hamburg stage, his soprano register suggests that he would likewise have been played by a (white European) female singer, further complicating the layers of pretense in terms of gender and racial identities. The audience, of course, would have known that this was a woman disguised as a man, a Christian disguised as a heathen,

EXAMPLE 25.3. Keiser, "Liebe, sag', was fängst du an," mm. 21–33.

and Atis disguised as another character in the play. They would have been able to appreciate the spectacle of mixed-up identities and feelings from a knowing distance and be entertained by the narrative and emotional turmoil. None of this, however, would have ruled out the possibility for affective contagion. As the German poet Barthold Feind found, it often happened that wicked people came back from the opera enlightened by its "natural presentation of vice with a horrific ending." This, Feind claimed, "sinks foremost into hardened souls and leaves behind a strong imprint, especially when music joins in, which in any case has an almost superhuman power to move the heart."[13] In this theory of theatrical spectatorship, even if audience members knew that Elmira was merely acting a role, dressed up in borrowed costume and emotion, her musical utterances still had the potential to penetrate their innards to effect palpable transformations there.

Keiser's heading for Elmira's aria proves instructive in this regard: he marked it "alla siciliana." Most commentators at the time had little to say about that term "siciliana" (or "siciliano"), which we now tend to associate with a specific sonic-affective profile, characterized by compound meter, dotted rhythms, and an overall gentle, "pastoral" feel. In light of this seeming familiarity, it is easy to overlook that for early eighteenth-century Northern European listeners, the idea of the siciliana would still have carried resonances of Sicilian lands and people as "quite-other," drawing on the "Orientalist fantasy of the southern Italian peasant as a dark African or Asiatic other."[14] As Mauritius Vogt outlined, whereas Bohemians liked rough dissonances and Spaniards liked gravity, "the Sicilians like at least the appearance of simplicity: hence an Italian who wants to produce an aria of simplest sweetness writes the heading 'Siciliano.'"[15] In inhabiting this borderland of musical expression, then, the white Christian body of the singer who took Elmira's part would indeed have come to function as "the most intimate of contact zones."[16] For that "siciliana" mode of musical femininity—"languissant," according to Johann David Heinichen—did not merely afford a representation of otherness for audience consumption.[17] The sonic suavity that this body emitted in singing this aria made the threat of seduction by (female-oriental) alterity directly audible and transmissible, producing an instance of what Jennifer Linhart Wood has called the "sonic uncanny," that is, the odd experience of being sounded through by something alien yet strangely familiar.[18] In order to produce the soft sound waves of Sicilian otherness, a singer would have had to direct her inner flows and disposition toward that softness, amplified by the multiple feedback loops of her own vocal production, the sounds of the accompanying ensemble, and her audience's affective responses. As Michael Ettmüller affirmed, "music leaves people effeminate, not only in listening but in executing it."[19] The outspoken detractor of the "unnatural" art form of opera, Johann Christoph Gottsched, put it as follows: "The tenderest sounds, the most beguiling poetry, and the obscenest gestures of the operatic heroes and their enamored goddesses bewitch careless souls and infiltrate them with a poison .... In this way softness is implanted in the souls of people from their youth, and we become similar to effeminate Italians, before we have realized that we should be masculine Germans."[20]

Music's othering potential is here bent into explicitly chauvinist sentiments, rooted in those same beliefs about softness and hardness as physical markers of difference, with hardness allegedly written into the innate disposition of Northern Europeans. Elmira's aria could thereby certainly function as a representation of the other, consolidating notions of the superior European male white body and the attendant commodification of other bodies on the operatic stage or in the slave trade. But it simultaneously had the power to infiltrate and reshape the bodies of those in attendance. These experiences of infiltration, as Simon Smith has pointed out, gendered performers and auditors not by anatomy but by role, with both men and women equally susceptible to sonic-affective penetration. Hence Andreas Ornithoparchus could claim that the power of music to delight "is so great, that it refuseth neither any sexe, nor any age."[21] Elmira's effeminate siciliana in this way might have ravished, softened, and imperiled even its most hardened or detached listeners, who had only come to enjoy a good story and/or some vocal pyrotechnics. For even when they went not to church but to the opera house to be entertained, those listeners' bodies still brimmed with sinfulness and seduceability.[22] Although Feind claimed that an opera was "only a shadow play, so to speak, where one sees something but no flesh or bone is touched," his contemporary Meinrad Spiess affirmed that a well-composed aria could cause that "after the musical piece is finished, the melody stays behind in the imagination, the moral sentence or verdict is presented clearly to the mind and may be well imprinted in the memory. Thereby it attains all the more certainly the true purpose of music, which is to move the hearts of listeners by means of good and pleasant sounds to all good virtues and deter them from sinful desires, in order to further the honor of God thereby."[23]

Going to the opera and absorbing its melodies, then, could change a listener's bodily habitus and their leanings toward virtue or vice, even if the affective intensities of those melodies belonged to a fictional character. And even if, as Brockes proposed, hearing an operatic lament would primarily have caused listeners an affective experience of pleasure, that pleasure still engendered a bodily motion that brought about corporeal-spiritual change.[24] This insight chimes with Mark Franko's claim that performativity does not erase the "body natural," but "underscores the active exercise of continuity through persistent yet unstable actions" of that body natural.[25] It might also shed some light on the sustained appeal of the da capo aria, that perennial challenge for present-day stage directors of Baroque opera. For early modern listeners, those musical-affective motions needed time to be imprinted in the body-soul and unfold their (hopefully) virtue-inducing effects. In a music treatise of 1624, the Italian doctor and music theorist Cesare Crivellati pointed out that a brief piece of music which only repeated three or four words could not arouse any affect, "since action requires time."[26] Aria lengths duly increased in the decades around 1700, from around 3–4 minutes in 1680 to 7–8 minutes by 1720.[27] And while some early eighteenth-century commentators openly complained about the "boring repetition" in da capo arias, others, like Pier Francesco Tosi, affirmed that these pieces moved listeners so strongly that "they could not help but feel tender or cry."[28] Music, arguably, was unique among the arts in offering this kind of prolonged affective battering, allowing ample time for listening body-souls to become attuned to the spiritual-affective motions it carried.

Crucially, in enabling such sonic forms of affective flow, an operatic aria could simultaneously help discipline these flows. As Silke Leopold has explored, music was indeed "janus-like" in giving voice to passionate motions but also providing a means for bringing those motions under control.[29] Leopold considers the da capo aria to have functioned as a tool of social disciplining in line with contemporary conduct books: an opening instrumental ritornello, for instance, gave the character on stage the chance to recognize their own emotions, in order that they may have them sufficiently under control when they started to sing. Ultimately, however, such rationalization strategies only worked so far. Not only did the repetitive circularity of the da capo design counteract the linear operations of reason, but the switching between different emotional states required in a piece like "Liebe, sag'" remained difficult to accomplish in the heat of the musicking moment. As Descartes pointed out, "there is one reason why the soul cannot readily alter or check its passions . . . . This reason is that they are almost all accompanied by some excitation taking place in the heart, and consequently also throughout the blood and the spirits, so that until this excitation has ceased they remain present to our thought."[30] These emotional residues meant that Elmira's aria offered not simply a clear-cut succession of neatly packaged affects to be decoded and mastered. Instead, it could effect a layering or blending of these contrasting affective strands, and thereby instantiate a complex emotional reality that eluded capture under one definitive emotion label. Reading the love, pain, and joy enacted in "Liebe, sag'" as representations of discrete affective states would certainly have presented one possible mode of listening engagement. But all these states in themselves already constituted complex and multivalent phenomena, which in a moment of performance would then have mutually inflected each other in unquantifiable and individually varied ways.

The musical gestures that encapsulated these affective states were complex and multilayered phenomena, too. In looking at a score of "Liebe, sag'," the combinations of notes that Keiser put together to inspire this particular affective utterance might seem easily identifiable as entirely conventional. And yet, each instantiation of these musical formulas for love or joy, as imagined by a composer and activated by a performer, would have been unique and different in nuanced and meaningful ways. In that 2008 recording, the dramatic plunge down a ninth by the violinists and oboists at the end of the opening measure, for instance, introduces a sudden cragginess and depth of timbre that subtly colors the prevailing sense of soft melodiousness. Moreover, the clear representational qualities of some of these gestures (e.g., those lively major-key turns and arpeggios for depicting joyfulness) in no way erased their potential for inflecting their listeners' bodily-spiritual flows, alongside any cognitive process of decoding their meaning.[31] Indeed, I would argue that any such meaning-making processes would have been closely tied to or emergent upon the associated bodily-spiritual flows. By Keiser's time, certainly, many of these musical conventions had become "naturalized," that is, sunk deep into the hearts and bones of operatic composers, performers, and listeners in a way that rendered any engagement with these gestures and sounds ineluctably corporeal. For singers, as Tosi affirmed, that "overflow of unexpected decorations" that they were meant to produce in their aria performances was impossible to achieve with a "dry head"; only an appropriate bodily disposition and pre-conditioning enabled these customary roulades to emerge.[32] For listeners, those sounds would then have meaningfully enveloped their habituated body-souls, whether they cultivated a fully empathetic attitude to an operatic character's predicament or directed their attention primarily to a singer's vocal prowess. These eighteenth-century aria performances thereby lend support to Daniel Stevens's view that musical expression is developed through bodily gesture in the act of performance, rather than performance merely offering "the realization of an abstract concept."[33] *Pace* Leopold, who concludes that it was "the music itself" that took on the "depiction of individual characters" in these operas, it was performative action carried out by individual bodies that made those affective intensities resonate meaningfully through these theatrical communities.[34] In that sense, opera simply emerges as a heightened form of "travestimento," of the corporeally based performative engagement that musicking required of all its participating body-souls.[35]

26

Hearts

"When he came thither, this griefe so wrought upon his high spirit, as it apparantly brake his brave and formerly undaunted heart."[1] Thus runs an account of the death of Lord General Sir John Norreys in Münster in 1597, as recorded by the English travel writer Fynes Moryson. This is by no means an isolated case of early modern people dying of a broken heart. But what did that phrase mean as an actual cause of death? "Heartbreak" constitutes a particularly enduring early modern metaphor that is still widely in use today. Like those notions of softness or flow explored in earlier chapters, there is an inherent figural dimension to the term, in that those broken hearts were not usually imagined to have literally split into pieces. And yet "Hertzbrechen" formed an accepted medical diagnosis; according to Steven Blankaart, it was "nothing else than that the usual mechanical motion is at times arrested or delayed. . . . in such a case there must be some object or hinderance in the fibers of the heart, whereby the nerve juice is continually obstructed in its normal, orderly, and even flow."[2] Medical professionals today offer a differently calibrated explanation for that same image of heartbreak: researchers have recently identified certain biomarkers that increase the likelihood of takotsubo syndrome, a severe acute heart failure colloquially known as broken heart syndrome.[3] As Barbara Duden has wisely counseled, "if I only understand the heart metaphorically, then I assume a physical reality of the organ that is always already there, a priori, which seems more 'actual' than the metaphors attached to it. But in all epochs physis and psyche of the heart are inseparably made of the same stuff."[4]

Duden advises that, in order to come to grips with the constitution of pre-modern hearts, historians need to develop both "methodological doubt about their own hearts" and "courage to informed intuition when entering into the heart of another world."[5] And that courage, I would submit, needs to be directed at least in part toward taking more literally those formulations that might in hindsight be too easily dismissed as "merely" metaphorical. If the pioneering work of George Lakoff and Mark Johnson has taught us that key metaphors in Western discourse have a physical basis, I suggest taking this a step further by challenging any strict dichotomy between the literal and the metaphorical; or between an empirically verifiable "external" reality that can be described in plain declarative language and a subjectively experienced "inner" reality that can only be captured metaphorically.[6] Instead we might recognize the two as inevitably enmeshed and co-constitutive. Already in the 1980s, John Christie encouraged scholars to question "the validity of the literal/figural dichotomies and their unproblematised role in the history of modern Western thought."[7] More recently, Gail Kern Paster has argued that early modern ways of experiencing the passions "would seem to collapse our modern distinction between the literal and metaphorical."[8] It may appear straightforwardly literal, for instance, to say that the body has an inside, which cannot be seen or touched, and an outside, which is perceptually accessible. But complications quickly arise not only in determining where the outside stops and the inside begins (most obviously in liminal regions such as the mouth or vagina), but also with regard to the numerous more figural strands of meaning (e.g., inside as soul, outside as flesh) that are woven into the Western conception of the physical body as an inside/outside kind of entity.[9] In an early modern context, the close contiguity between these "literal" and "figural" domains becomes strikingly evident in an engraving from an illustrated Bible by Johann Jakob Scheuchzer, where Psalm verse 33:15 ("He who forms the hearts of all") is accompanied by an anatomically precise drawing of a heart, rendered down to its smallest blood vessels, and embedded in an allegory of God as the omniscient seer into human hearts (fig. 26.1). In Carsten-Peter Warncke's reading, if the image can seem jarring or "ridiculous" to readers today, this is because the tight conjunction of the literal and the metaphorical that it assumes no longer holds.[10]

The early modern Christian heart was a biblical heart.[11] Unlike the brain, which hardly figures in the Bible, the heart is frequently referenced, and its early modern capabilities were rooted in the qualities ascribed to it in Scripture. As Robert Erickson has argued, the term "heart" in the Bible served as the "single most important word referring both to the body and to the mind. No other word performed what 'heart' did, and no other word today quite replaces it."[12] The early modern heart formed the central human organ in terms of both physiology and faith. It was the source of vitality and personhood. It could sense, feel, love, sigh, think, remember, plot murder, believe, pray, sing, crave, transgress. It could bleed, harden, melt, and break. It had eyes, ear lobes, doors, and wings.[13] In taking these

FIGURE 26.1. Illustration for Psalm 33:15. Johann Jacob Scheuchzer, *Kupfer-Bibel* (Augsburg and Ulm: Wagner, 1731–1735), Tabula DXLIV. ETH Zürich, Rar 5864.

notions seriously, I propose to quell any sense of impatience we may now feel toward the "careless thinking in analogies of the time with respect to externally equivalent terms."[14] I propose to question, with Christie, the assumption that (only) scientific language could describe the "hard" facts and that theological or poetic writing necessarily obscured those facts with layers of figuration that require stripping away. I am less concerned, then, with the veracity of these descriptions in terms of modern scientific standards, and more with the felt experiences that they attempted to capture; experiences that were, once more, co-constituted through an interplay of the literal and the figurative. Considering early modern hearts thereby becomes an exercise in thinking together the two terms of this dichotomy, in the manner of Gina Bloom finding that "in the theatre, breath is not only a metaphor, but, indeed simultaneously, the physical substance that enables the actors to convey to audiences the language of the script."[15] When blood, spirits, music, or grace flowed in and out of hearts in early modern acts of musicking, they all, in different ways, flowed "for real"—tangibly, and with the power to transform those hearts, bodies, and souls.

Perhaps there is, then, not quite as much distance as we might assume between early modern anatomical and devotional discourses of the heart. William Harvey's scientific descriptions of the organ in his landmark 1628 treatise on blood circulation, for instance, turn out to be fundamentally metaphorical in nature, in that they imagine the heart as an ejaculatory organ, a powerful virile figure invigorating the colder, feminized outer parts.[16] Meanwhile, the Lutheran theologian Johann Quirsfeld described how the faithful would "taste spiritual joy not with their tongues but with their hearts," and that this sweetness "can turn even the bitterest gall to sugar and the greatest torment of the heart into joy."[17] While clearly figurative on numerous levels, his account was grounded in, and attempted to find words for, a felt experience of having faith, namely that sensation of heavenly sweetness that music was so often said to provide with particular intensity. Quirsfeld's account chimes, moreover, with Johann Helffrich Jüngken's prescription that a patient suffering from an obstruction of the heart vessels by "thickened" and "sour" blood would need to ingest certain remedies that "sweetened" that acid.[18] The humoral qualities of hot and cold, the liquidity and acidity of the body's flows, were ultimately inseparable from a person's emotions, faith, and virtue. Hence the German theologian Johann Benedict Carpzov advised in a funeral sermon of 1693 that "everyone should take note of their heart, that it may not grow cold from unmercifulness, nor heat up from rage and lust." "Barmhertzig" (merciful), he pointed out, meant as much as "warmhertzig" (warmhearted).[19] A cold or hardened heart constituted both a dangerous medical condition and a fundamental obstacle to salvation. Where Georg Heuermann described how the heart sac could become hardened when its blood vessels received too little fluid, the librettist for Johann Sebastian Bach's Cantata 181 admonished that "hearts of rock, which resist evilly, will squander their own salvation and perish."[20]

So what did these different medical-moral conditions of the heart feel like? Figure 26.2, from a book of emblems by the German poet Georg Philipp Harsdörffer (aka Fabian Athyrus), depicts a "pressed" or "compressed" heart, another trope commonly shared between scientific and theological writings. Jüngken described this sensation as an aberrant pulse, "when the heart beats very fast so that there is almost no gap in between, and often moves so strongly that one can see and hear it. The patient feels as if their heart is being compressed by someone." This, Jüngken stated, could cause "slow breathing, trepidation, and so on."[21] Harsdörffer's explanation of his image, meanwhile, confirmed the ambiguous status of the heart as belonging to both body and soul: "Just as a person has two essential parts, body and soul, so he is subjected to two types of tribulation, depicted here by the two screws with which the heart is pressed."[22] His contemporary Heinrich Müller elaborated further: "From these and other inner tribulations of the soul a great and intense fear arises in the

FIGURE 26.2. The heart in a press. Fabian Athyrus, *Das erneuerte Stamm- und Stechbüchlein* (Nuremberg: Gerhard, 1654), 240. Herzog August Bibliothek Wolfenbüttel: A: 165.19 Eth. (1).

soul. In describing this fear, the Bible uses a little word that means a compression of the heart, for the heart is depressed, so to speak, since it is being pressed from fear like the grapes in the winepress."[23] According to Georg Heuermann, melancholic people and women tended to suffer more frequently from such feelings of heart compression, caused by their excessive moisture levels; and if the heart sac and the heart inside it became too squeezed, this could cause a "suffocation of the movement of the blood and thereby death."[24] Theologians, too, identified stagnant liquids as a cause for a constricted heart, as in Sigismund Scherertz's description: "When a person grows properly sad, frequent sighing is usually accompanied by the shedding of tears. For the fearful and pressed heart almost swims in water from the sighs and tears, and this inner sweat of fear rises up to the brain, which drives out the internal droplets and lets them spring through the eyes onto the cheeks."[25]

Accordingly, in Harsdörffer's image, the pressure of the tightening screws indeed leads to droplets being squeezed from the suffering heart into a receptacle below. Many contemporary writers concurred that sighing, crying, or music-making all offered means of relieving this unhealthy pressure on the heart, since sighs, tears, and music were all substances that flowed out of the body and thereby helped adjust its fluid economy. As Christoph Frick put it, referencing the Lutheran reformer Johannes Mathesius: "When someone's soul is sad, full of fear and misery, heavy from sin and dullness, and the heart is all clamped and compressed and so dull that no consolation can enter and no word or sigh can emerge, quickly think of or sing a psalm . . . . It is certain that a Christian music will be a consolation for us against all heaviness and tribulation, even against the devil himself."[26] For another "ridiculous" illustration of this capacity of the heart to relieve physical-spiritual pressure through singing or praying, we might look at the frontispiece to a devotional volume by Christian Gottlieb Kern (fig. 26.3), where the "prayer-juice" squirts out of the afflicted heart like a fountain. In a Christian body-soul, this cleansing could then make room for the indwelling of Jesus in the heart, another metaphor that gained experiential veracity in the commingling of the bodily juices of the faithful with the blood of Christ in the Eucharist.[27] Anatomical knowledge informed many of these theological accounts of indwelling, as in Christoph Frick's description: "The heart of man shall be the dwelling of God. Not far from the heart God positioned the lung, the main artery, the windpipe, the mouth, and the tongue, which make the voice and song, so that a human upon regarding themselves shall remember to use their organs around the heart in such a manner that God, who wants to dwell in the temple of our heart, is praised and sung to from true gratitude."[28] Like

FIGURE 26.3. The praying heart. Christian Gottlieb Kern, *Geistliche Safft- und Andachts-Quelle* (Nuremberg: Otto, 1700), frontispiece. Württembergische Landesbibliothek, Stuttgart, Theol.oct.9521.

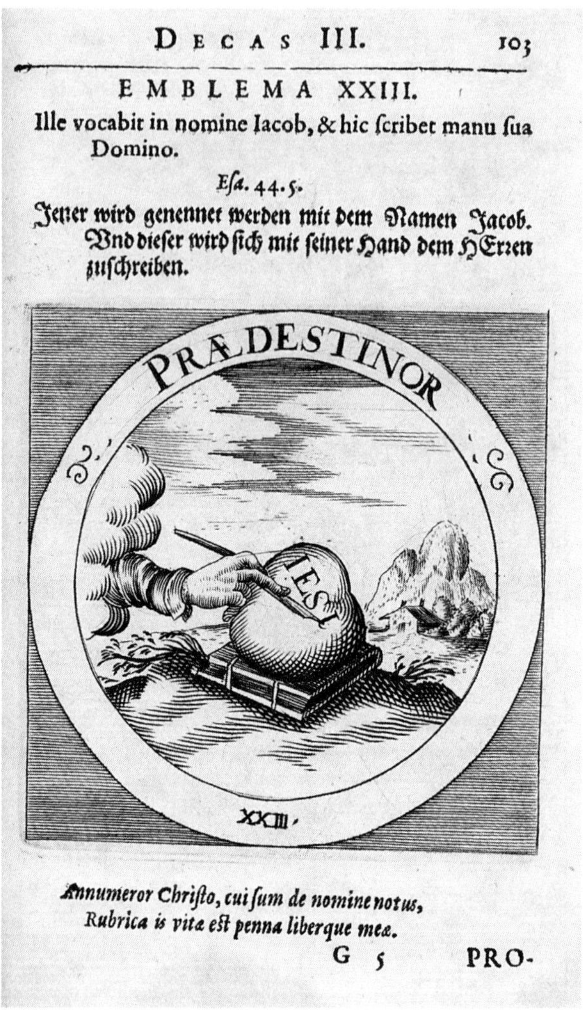

DECAS III. 103

EMBLEMA XXIII.

Ille vocabit in nomine Iacob, & hic ſcribet manu ſua Domino.

Eſa. 44.5.

Jener wird genennet werden mit dem Namen Jacob. Vnd dieſer wird ſich mit ſeiner Hand dem HErren zuſchreiben.

Annumeror Chriſto, cui ſum de nomine notus,
Rubrica is vita eſt penna liberque meæ.

G 5 PRO-

FIGURE 26.4. The heart inscribed. Daniel Cramer, *Emblemata Sacra* (Frankfurt: Jennis, 1624), 103. Herzog August Bibliothek Wolfenbüttel: A: 87.1 Poet. (3).

most of the quotes offered here, Frick's explanation teems with metaphor; but taken together, these accounts nonetheless support Peter Harrison's challenge to "the insistence that science sets the standards for what counts as genuine knowledge," which, Harrison claims, "remains a characteristic feature of modern Western epistemological discourse."[29] The early modern heart presents a locus where that convergence of the scientific and the devotional, or the literal and the metaphorical, becomes all but unavoidable.

These insights offer opportunities, I think, for reimagining various early modern heart-related discourses and musical practices. They might inspire us, for instance, to appreciate the fleshliness of the devotional language of someone like Müller or Quirsfeld, beyond a general appeal to the tropes of Pietism. As Peter Damrau has shown, Pietist writers indeed foregrounded the heart as the organ which acted as the guarantor of true faith and virtue.[30] But the wholly embodied nature of that faith experience arguably became obscured by the related Pietist emphasis on an "inner" sphere, which took on increasingly disembodied qualities as modernity progressed. I might even suggest that the intensely heart-focused discourses of Pietism to some extent helped preserve in the popular imagination an older medical-scientific paradigm where many of the vital, emotional, and even rational human functions were still located in the heart, prolonging it into a period where scientific discourses became more determinedly cranio-centric. Or they might invite us to return to a piece like Giulio Caccini's *Amarilli, mia bella,* in particular that striking moment when the singer exclaimed, "Open my chest and find inscribed on my heart" the name of their beloved, Amarillis. Lucia d'Errico has identified this musical passage as a gesture of "incredible violence," based on Susan McClary's reading of the phrase as "the body opened up for a moment of profound erotic surrender."[31] McClary grounds her reading in a modal transgression effected by the singer, who in measure 10 eschews the expected F-sharp for an F-natural, thereby dragging their listeners into an imagined realm of interiority. Yet beyond evoking a concrete image of skin cut open, of the human dissection practices of Renaissance anatomists, this poetic-musical moment instantiates the power of music to imprint itself onto the heart as the physical seat of memory. In line with contemporary devotional images showing the name of Jesus inscribed on a Christian heart (fig. 26.4), we might again read such a process of imprinting as above all metaphorical. But the addition of music in particular meant that the repeated exclamations of "Amarilli" could engender an actual sensation of (painful) inscription, of melodic gesture engraved in memory by means of the vital spirits carving channels in the flesh.[32] It can be surprisingly difficult to imagine inhabiting a bodily disposition where committing something to memory is not exclusively experienced as a mental process, immediately felt to take place in the head. But I would suggest that, for an early modern body-soul, listening to Caccini's piece with a sufficiently soft and receptive heart could afford an experience of the very sensation articulated by the singer, of being opened up, penetrated by sound, and left with a tangible mark on the heart.

27
Chills

Musicking could make you unwell. It could corrupt your body-soul in ways that were neither entirely metaphorical nor exclusively moral: it could warp your organs' material fibers and adulterate the substances that animated them. While in 2005 Elisabeth Le Guin found that "we simply can no longer believe that too fine an attention to a melancholic piece of music might result in physical illness," more recent explorations of the uses of music in/as torture have reaffirmed the early modern conviction that sonic impact could have harmful psychosomatic effects.[1] This association of music with illness did not exhaust itself in the age-old allegory of the human body as a harmonious entity or well-tuned instrument that could be forced out of tune. The German scholar Christoph Lehmann captured this vision succinctly: "Illness is nothing other than a destruction of the natural order of the body. The harmony of the strings in the body is destroyed, and often times one has to retune them for a long time until they are brought into concord again."[2] This resonance-based conception of illness indeed persisted throughout the early modern period and beyond, transformed in the later eighteenth century into notions of "Stimmung."[3] But actual experiences of musical sound waves entering and wreaking havoc with a human body-soul were in fact more often understood in terms of a disturbance of flow. The German physician Friedrich Hoffmann outlined the common view that "the health of our body consists in a constant, placid, free, and unencumbered motion, circulation, and evacuation of the spirits, blood, and fluids throughout the vessels of the whole body. . . . Conversely, all disease or diseased motion basically consists in a too slow or fast motion of a part of the fluids, spirits, or blood, corrupted by irregular circulation and secretion of the execrable parts."[4]

Michael Stolberg has rightly pointed out that the term "flow" in these medical discourses no longer pertained exclusively to the four ancient humors and their hot/cold and wet/dry admixtures; such a view, he claims, would underestimate the complexity of early modern conceptions of ill health and its causes.[5] Instead, it was a more broadly conceived notion of "Geblüt" or "humors" as a multitude of bodily fluids, whose qualities and circulation could deteriorate in a variety of ways, that underpinned conceptions of illness in most medical writings and patient reports. These flows could become obstructed through thickening, stagnation, or fermentation, they could become putrid, acidic, or gelatinous, causing unhealthy moistures, vapors, and plethoras, or a "hardening and stickiness that clog the vessels and obstruct the orderly motion of nerve juice in a particular way."[6] Often those obstructions were caused by specific but hard-to-pin-down agents originating either inside or outside the body, characterized in vaguely threatening terms as that "encroaching, invading mortiferous matter that instrumentally aims at the cutting of the thread of life."[7] As specified in the numerous health and diet guides published across the period, disturbances in the body's "non-naturals," such as polluted air, excessive or wrong food and drink, lack of exercise and sleep, or sexual debauchery, could produce adverse flows. Given the complexities of an early modern body's operations, the causes and effects of these obstructions were often difficult to disentangle: according to Philip Barrough, a headache could be due to "a simple distemper without any humours," or "the evill quality" or "great abundance" of the humors; it could be caused by "humours that stop the passage of the vapours and moisture in the head, sometime through windinesse engendred in some part of the head" or "some disease in the stomacke"; or by "an outward cause, as of heate of the Sunne, of great cold, of drunkennesse, or of some stripe or wound."[8]

Another of the non-naturals that could cause disease was affect; since the affections brought the bodily flows out of balance, an excess of affective motions could engender serious bodily-spiritual disturbances. Peter Friedrich Detry defined illness as an "obstacle" of the soul or body, and found that the soul is "perturbed in its orderly motion, either through hot affects, rage, anger, revenge, whereby the blood and the other bodily fluids come into a fermentation and surge," or through "cold and constricting" affects of sadness, fear, and so on, which thicken and slow the juices.[9] Once again, the intertwined nature of body, soul, and spirit in this early modern anthropology made it difficult to separate symptoms from causes: when the body had an obstruction, Detry stated, the soul "immediately feels this destruction of its housekeeping," which then caused physical symptoms such as "fevers, vomiting, diarrhea," and so on.[10] Conversely, affective motions might cure certain ailments, such as infertility in obese women, sometimes treated by inducing rage or sadness in the patient in order to bring about weight loss.[11] Such notions bear out Barbara Duden's observation that in much early modern medical practice the soul was hardly considered a carrier of personality in the modern sense, but rather treated as almost another body part. They also underline her insight that "in all these illnesses, the somatic reality is not separable from the experiential world."[12]

For the majority of early modern Europeans, this experiential world of illness was couched in the beliefs and lived experience of the Christian faith. Illness, in that world, was ultimately a result of original sin, that "contagious leprosie," the "natural illness and contagion innate in all humans."[13] Postlapsarian humanity was inherently blighted by corruption, as the capacities of mortal body-souls had become despoiled through sinfulness. Christian Friedrich Richter identified sin as the prime immaterial cause of illness, for "it lives in the body [and] as a sting of death unquestionably injures the body."[14] This sin, according to the Jena lexicographer Christian Stock, has "crawled through our flesh and blood in such a manner that from the soles of the foot up to the head nothing healthy is found within us."[15] The Lutheran theologian Johann Rittmeyer offered a striking visual representation of that infestation of the body with ill-making agents, some in the shape of snakes, others like little bugs that have taken up residence in the heart (fig. 27.1).[16] As the Anglican clergyman Andrew Burnet put it, once more in liquid terms, "the natural man is so cloyed with the liquorish relish of carnal things that he cannot raise his affections to the true contemplation of the things of God."[17]

Music, as a powerful kind of non-natural, could do exactly that to a person's ears and insides: cloy them with the liquorish relish of carnal things. Profane songs, wrote the French historian Jean Lebeuf, "carry corruption into the heart," echoing Jean Calvin's sentiment from two centuries earlier that "the venom and corruption" of bad words is "distilled to the depths of the heart by the melody."[18] If Printz's claim that the shouting of novice singers "could easily cause a bout of colic" was perhaps no more than a rhetorical flourish, there was little doubt among early modern theological writers that music could not just heal a body-soul but make it ill; and the medical literature provided a basis for explaining those effects physiologically.[19] The Spanish physician Juan Lazaro Gutierrez's assertion that human beings could be "infected and poisoned" by dissonant voices and that "the voice is to be classified among the causes of pestilence" certainly presented an extreme view.[20] Steven Blankaart reported the more widely shared opinion that an obstruction or thickening of the "Geblüt" usually stemmed from either excessive acidity or excessive cold; and music had the capacity to induce both of these conditions, either with those "sour" modes discussed above, or by causing the body to cool down.[21] Music's potential to inspire or advance the cold condition of melancholy was of course

FIGURE 27.1. The heart infested. Johann Rittmeyer, *Himmlisches Freuden-Mahl der Kinder Gottes auf Erden* (Lüneburg: Stern, 1743), 56. Universitäts- und Landesbibliothek Düsseldorf, urn:nbn:de:hbz:061:1–535206.

widely recognized. And excessive coldness was seen as a prime driver of illness more generally, with the ultimate threat of the body growing cold in death. The English physician Richard Lower described how people who overconsumed cold food and drink in the evening would be accosted by a coldness that "starts on the inside, extends outward into the skin, and causes not only suffocation but also windy-watery swellings and boils."[22] In the Aristotelian tradition, coldness was considered not merely an absence of warmth, but a primal substance or power that could interfere with the inherent warmth of living creatures: external cold could, for instance, turn the blood in the uterus grainy.[23] As this cold power entered the body, "if the warmth does not immediately cede, but resists and fights in the sweat pores that it occupies, this fight is called a chill or trembling."[24] Music, wrote the German medic Ernst Anton Nicolai, could produce exactly such feelings of chill: "Often we feel a strong chill in the skin when we hear music. The hairs stand on end, the blood moves from outside to inside, the external parts begin to grow cold, the heart beats faster and we breathe a bit more slowly and deeply."[25] His colleague Michael Ettmüller claimed similarly that everyday experiences of music included feelings of "horror or stiffness through the skin" as well as "erection of the hairs."[26] The Lutheran preacher Johann Ludwig Hartmann explained in 1673: "In singing there are sometimes tremolos, triplets, and notes that are so hard that they can only be sung with difficulty. These can be related to the manifold tribulations of the devil with which he torments people and brings them to trembling and terror, so that sometimes they almost cannot stand and overcome it anymore."[27]

So, might Henry Purcell's famous frost scene in his semi-opera *King Arthur* have given its performers or auditors the shivers? The initial aria sung by the cold genius, "What power art thou?," includes both the tremolos and the hard dissonances mentioned by Hartmann, devices that are easily decoded by knowing listeners today as part of a conventional musical representation of coldness. But in the context of early modern music's potential for sonic-affective contagion, those tremors produced by a quivering finger or larynx may well have yielded actual chills and their associated affective flows in a well-disposed listener. As Carl Philipp Emanuel Bach found, a performer who suffered from too cold a temperament might end up transferring that quality to their listeners: their "hypochondriac nature" announced itself in their "flabby fingers" so plainly as to cause (cold) sensations of disgust in a listener.[28] Purcell's trudging repeated eighth-note chords (marked "slow" in the vocal part) offered the opposite of the fast and furious chord repetitions of Claudio Monteverdi's "stile concitato," that hot, loud, angry battle music that could make a listener's blood boil. Here that idiom seems decelerated to just above the freezing point. At that temperature, fear, horror, and stiffness reigned supreme. Performers today have experimented with vastly differing approaches to instantiating the frosty effect afforded by the notation and theatrical context: one need only compare the light-touch quivering bow strokes of the Deller Consort with the callous ponticello attacks of a 2014 recording by VOCES8 to be reminded that there is very little that is essentially "cold" in those notes on the page, unless their chilling potential is activated in a suitably tremulous performance.[29]

Trembling was, of course, a sign not just of cold but of fear, as the philosopher Friedrich Gladov pointed out when noting that "Tremuliren" in its original Italian "actually means trembling, teeth gnashing from fear"; in music, it is a "sharp trembling of the voice on a long note, which touches the next note."[30] Fear and cold went hand in hand, then: on beholding a "horrific object," wrote Athanasius Kircher, "cold vapors rise from the black gall," causing feelings of sadness, pain, fear, and compassion. Musical sounds, Kircher claimed, could "agitate the vapors" in exactly that way, thereby pulling a listener's affections in the same direction.[31] Whether the cold genius rising from the depths would have seemed a "horrific object" in any early modern staging of Purcell's piece is, of course, impossible to ascertain. There may have been a sense of fearful anticipation among the audience at a 2017 staging of this frost scene from Berlin, followed by a degree of terror or revulsion at the slow-moving mummy-like creature that emerges from its enclosure—though much would have depended on the affective dynamics in the theater to determine whether a chilling or comedic effect prevailed.[32] Heightening the potentially terrifying effect for early modern listeners would have been the association of cold music with notions of sin and hell. Congregational music-making in church was "cold" and "dead" if produced by people with cold, unfaithful hearts.[33] Sin made your blood freeze: "See how the blood is frozen in my veins! The poison of sin makes me so cold and hard"; and its most effective remedy was God's warming grace, "when you penetrate my rigid sinner-blood with your hot flood of mercy."[34] Music could provide such curative warmth, too, to soften cold and unbelieving hearts. Conversely, cold sounds such as teeth gnashing formed part of the soundscape of (both Protestant and Catholic) hell: "This weeping, howling and roaring of the damned, as it were of brute beasts, wil proceed from their mighty and grieuous paines, which shal constraine the most stony harts to breake forth into desperate lamentations. With these Odes and warbling tune shal the eares of these miserable creatures be daily vexed. The burden of this musick shal be *stridor dentium* gnashing of teeth through exceeding great cold."[35]

As Purcell's slow-moving harmonies crept under a listener's skin, they may have felt their pulse rate and blood flow beginning to stagnate, while their skin curled up in goose bumps as excessive black gall flooded outward from their inner organs and their soul stiffened with the fear of hell. In this way, hearing this aria could have afforded a more pronounced version of the cooling effects of melancholy music: as Thomas Wright explained, "although the hearte hath more excesse of heate than colde, yet a little melancholly blood may quickly change the temperature, and render it more apt for a melancholly Passion."[36] Present-day research into the phenomenon of musical chills or "frisson" has shown, however, that these days such music-induced shivers down the spine are not primarily caused by features that conventionally occur in "cold" Baroque music, but tend to come about in moments of unexpected change, whether in dynamics, texture or tempo, or the entry of a voice.[37] Also, crucially, they are usually experienced as pleasant: in David Huron and Elizabeth Margulis's definition, musical frisson is "a pleasant tingling feeling associated with the flexing of hair follicles, resulting in gooseflesh (technically called piloerection) accompanied by a cold sensation, and sometimes producing a shiver."[38] In evolutionary terms, biologists believe that piloerection served both to keep mammals warmer in cold temperatures and to make them seem bigger in moments of danger, in the manner of porcupines raising their quills when threatened—a bodily defense mechanism, in other words. But in humans, chill experiences are now also associated with feelings of euphoria and sexual arousal; hence Gunther Bernatsky's term "skin orgasm."[39] There are a few instances in early eighteenth-century writings that articulate this pleasurable version of musical chills.[40] Johann Mattheson found that "when I hear a solemn symphony in church, I am overcome by a pious shudder."[41] We may also recall Johann Adolph Scheibe's commentary on Telemann's Passion oratorio "freezing" his blood, an experience that for him culminated in sensations of wonder and awe.[42] These same bodily-affective motions often occurred, too, in contemplating eternity, as encapsulated in this Pietist hymn verse: "Lord God, whenever I consider [eternity] at length, fear and dread cut through my veins and joints, my skin shudders, my ears ring and chime, my mouth and heart tremble and lift up."[43] What Mattheson or Scheibe seem to be describing, then, is a kind of pleasurable, aestheticized version of the fear of hell and eternity, a transposition that points to the theological roots of the eighteenth-century notion of the aesthetic sublime. It may be that this capacity for experiencing musical chills as pleasant rather than ill-making is one of the factors that set later listeners distinctly apart from their early modern counterparts.

28
Pain

Thus, wondring at the strange and powerful Skill·
With *trembling*, like the Strings, he seems to *feel*
Each Stroke the Artist plays; and every Sound,
As by some Magick, seems t' inflict a Wound:
And yet so pleasant all appear, that still
His *sooth'd* tho' *suff'ring* Mind, at once they *wound* and *heal*.

ROBERT SOUTH[1]

The powers of early modern music were fundamentally dialectical. If musicking could make you ill, it could also be curative. The Jena-based medic Werner Rolfinck advised a patient that after a bout of vomiting blood he should cleanse himself with the suavity of song.[2] The French physician Pierre Desault prescribed music as a cure for rabies.[3] Harmonious sound waves could restore order to discombobulated spirits in a variety of health conditions. They could act as a prophylaxis for the plague.[4] Music served as an analgesic, able to "mitigate the harshness of pain."[5] Yet these widely acknowledged therapeutic effects existed side by side with music's well-known harmful potential. Music could unfold either negative or positive (physiological and/or moral) effects in the body-souls it touched. It could cause acute pain as well as lessen it. It could be simultaneously pleasurable and poisonous; it could drive people to murder or to divine ecstasy; it could line the path to heaven or hell. Or it might offer benefits to its participants only through hurting them, a bit like those exceedingly painful early modern treatments for various bodily afflictions, such as the hot iron some doctors applied to the ear in order to alleviate a toothache.

One musical phenomenon known for its potential to cause acute pain was dissonance. "Dissonances," the German theorist Andreas Herbst observed, "arise when one puts the sounds or tones together in such a way that by nature they hurt one's ears."[6] If an inept organist tried to tackle a figured bass with some missing figures, the resulting sounds could "make your ears ring and your teeth hurt."[7] Toothache was a frequently attested side effect: "Certain sounds are so incongruous and difficult that one's teeth grind and ache from them," wrote Athanasius Kircher.[8] Elsewhere he explained: "When the sounds are disproportionate, they have an adverse effect on human bodies: because of their vehemence they either injure them, or give rise to great pain within them."[9] The English philosopher Thomas Hobbes concurred that harsh sounds sometimes affected a body with "a Kind of Horror beginning at the Teeth."[10] A botched organ improvisation could make listeners feel like "the hairs in their ears are being pulled out with tweezers."[11] Andreas Werckmeister complained about the disgust caused by a "shifting, pulled" kind of music, "oversalted with too many dissonances" and "confused in its harmony"; such music he defined as "illness itself."[12] Of course, plenty more anodyne descriptions of dissonance existed, too; Johann Gottfried Walther, for instance, outlined that dissonances were useful because they allowed composers to "move more comfortably from one interval to the next" or to "vary and decorate a composition."[13] Many commentators emphasized the function of dissonance to enhance the pleasant effects of consonance. But this experience of displeasure followed by pleasure was often described in bodily or sensory terms, too. As Martin Heinrich Fuhrmann attested, a piece of music that consisted only of consonances would be too sweet and had to be tempered by the "vinegar" of dissonance; a "sharp-sour" kind of vinegar that could "constrict the throat."[14] As a phenomenon that contravened the natural proclivities of the human body, dissonant sounds could engender tangible physical discomfort.

Once again, we might dismiss such reports as hyperbolic or metaphorical. But it is not only their widespread occurrence that suggests otherwise. Pain is a puzzling phenomenon. It may seem to constitute one of the most universally shared human experiences, in the sense that "people in pain generally want the pain to 'go away.'"[15] Yet one of the most problematic aspects of pain concerns its subjective nature: its experience is fundamentally unshareable, to the extent that an outsider's primary mode of approaching another person's pain might be to have doubt.[16] Present-day medical technologies are able to capture certain "objective" traces of pain by detecting some of its neural substrates in the brain; but an MRI scan does not reveal anything of an actual pain experience.[17] Early modern commentators instead tried to capture pain by means of language, often by describing it in terms of disturbances of flow. Toothache, according to Philip Barrough, was caused by a "hote or cold distemper"; by the "flowing of humours out of the head unto the roots of the teeth, which with their sharpnesse either do gnaw about them, or else with their abundance they engender like griefe in the teeth, as if inflammation were about the fleshy parts." This, Barrough confirmed, was "the most cruel & grievous" of all pain experiences.[18] According to Christian Stock, pain meant "a close pressing together, or a great fear and most intimate suffering," like someone who has a cutting feeling in their gut or is giving birth.[19] Johann Helffrich Jüngken also named pressure or compression a defining feature of pain: "In painful illnesses . . . when the nerve juice is too thick, too sharp, and of that kind of quality and thereby clogs the subtle pores of the nerves and cannot yield to the particles that are pressing in behind, from this feeling of pressure a very strange painful sensation must be felt by the soul."[20] The intermingled agencies of body and soul assumed by Jüngken challenge the modern "myth" of two pains, physical and mental: these early modern medics rarely drew a clear-cut distinction between, say, toothache and heartache, both of which were potentially caused by worms and associated with feelings of grief.[21] Their notions of pain seem more in line with Donald Price's recent insight that the unpleasantness of pain reflects "the contribution of several sources, including pain sensation, arousal, autonomic, and somatomotor responses, all in relation to meanings of the pain and to the context in which pain presents itself."[22] In its multimodal nature, pain has posed a continual challenge to a Cartesian anthropology.

In a certain way, all music constituted a version of the painful "pressing in" described by Jüngken. As Descartes himself had put it, music "doth concusse, or shake all circumjacent bodies."[23] Dissonance could be a particularly potent form of violent assault. The Italian composer Agostino Steffani explained that when the proportions of dissonance entered a listening body-soul, this caused the "vital spirits to contract; and the smaller the intervals get, the more the disgust that is felt by the ear increases."[24] His contemporary Christoph Raupach expanded on this proportional model of dissonance causing bodily contortion: "The two consonances, namely the octave and fifth, cause a certain expansion of the vital spirits, more pronounced in the case of the former than the latter; which stems from the size of their proportions, which take the form of 1–2 and 2–3. . . . The smaller the proportions get, the less expansion occurs. . . . The smallest intervals with proportions 8–9, 9–10, 15–16, 24–25, etc., cause the ear to feel disgust and the vital spirits to contract ever more."[25] From this perspective, the clustered dissonances encountered, for instance, in the "Crucifixus" of Johann Sebastian Bach's *Mass in B Minor* did not only "depict the death and suffering of Jesus Christ in a moving way."[26] They certainly could be heard to do so very effectively; but in the process, they could affect a congregant's internal flows directly and injuriously. Moreover, like illness and pain, musical dissonance was frequently framed as a burden placed on mankind after the Fall: this corrupted human nature, claimed Nucius, produced nothing but roughness, "like an organ whose pipes have got bent and out of tune."[27] Just as the pain caused by the "poison" of venereal disease—associated with fleshly desire and illicit sexual contact—was "felt on the skull and the bones" as it "eats through, pricks, and tears apart the sensitive skin around the bones," so some dissonances "go so hard together" that "they pierce one's heart and brain."[28] As Anna Sophia of Hesse-Darmstadt put it, referring to Job 14:22, "Because humans carry the flesh about them, they must have pain."[29] Her theologically grounded understanding of pain works against the modern Western conception that pain constitutes an exclusively medical problem, and instead takes us back to the Latin root of the term as "poena," punishment.[30]

This early modern Christian constellation of pain, dissonance, original sin, and the postlapsarian human condition might inspire us to fundamentally reimagine Elaine Scarry's striking claim that pain forms the first condition for any act of human imagining or creating.[31] Why, if musical dissonances caused actual pain experiences, would composers of the period persist in employing them so regularly and pervasively? The increase in pleasure afforded after a dissonant disturbance resolved to a consonance served as one explanation. Yet dissonant music could do more than that. It could function as an agent in a Christian faith experience that required believers to actively live through Christ's suffering on the cross within their own body-souls, thereby generating heartfelt remorse and penitence that could then lead to a purging of the heart in readiness for receiving grace. As Johann Quirsfeld explained, "just as Christ is woefully tortured in body and soul for our sinfulness, so we likewise need to be tortured in our conscience by our sins."[32] In this context, being penetrated by the dissonant sonorities of Bach's "Crucifixus" could not only help actualize this co-suffering, but, like a bitter medicine, serve as a catalyst for driving out the morbid, sinful matter that permeated the flesh. The Nuremberg writer Erasmus Finx stated: "Just as deep wounds cause great pain, thus heavy sins have to be followed by painful remorse. Penitence does not just consist in bending your knees, but in turning away from evil, as well as in great heart-work, in tears and prayers to God."[33] "Brich, mein Herz, zerfließ in Tränen" (Break my heart, flow out in tears), as Barthold Heinrich Brockes's widely distributed Passion libretto intoned.

Purging was, of course, the go-to medical cure for most human ailments at the time, achieved through bloodletting or by administering emetics, laxatives, or sweat-inducing drugs. Any liquid that exited the body—tears, sweat, blood, phlegm, urine, and so on—could be curative, by relieving an overabundance of fluids, restoring their balance and liquidity, or expelling morbid matter. But the benefits of these outflows were not exclusively medical; they also extended to a person's spiritual-moral condition. If, as Jean Jackson points out, "biologically speaking, pain is indispensable" despite its aversive quality, then for an early modern Christian believer this was also the case in terms of their salvation.[34] True penitence felt like having "all bones broken, the heart crunched up, and the spirit made fearful."[35] Release from this suffering could likewise be found through purgation: "True tears of penitence have a very driving and cleansing power and effect . . . and there is no impurity too big that it could not be ground down and driven out by this sharp penitential acid."[36] As Sigismund Scherertz affirmed, tears "relieve the soul, cool the heart, and alleviate the mind of the woeful; they drive out many evil vapors, so that the person feels lighter and easier. Many make themselves calmer with crying and pour out the pain together with it."[37] Sighs and prayers constituted alternative forms of this beneficial outflow. If evolutionary scientists today still puzzle over how the shedding of tears came to seem advantageous to the human species, for an early modern Christian their usefulness resided largely in this potential for bodily-spiritual cleansing.[38] These beliefs and practices not only underline, once again, the fundamentally embodied nature of early modern Christian faith, but also support David Morris's insight that often "preanesthetic cultures responded to pain not with denial but with curious forms of affirmation."[39]

When Georg Philipp Telemann claimed that dissonant musical figurations could replace any other kind of "Schwitz-Pulver" (sweating powder), this further confirmed music's role in a faith-driven process of fluid regulation.[40] Although it will remain impossible to ascertain whether during a performance of his *Brockes-Passion*, in Frankfurt in April 1716, any of those in attendance broke out in sweat or tears, his description might at least encourage us to listen for certain registers of this music to which we have become less attuned. The aria "Heul, du Schaum der Menschenkinder," which comes after Peter's threefold denial of Jesus, gives voice to a powerful sense of despair and remorse: "Wail, you scum of humankind, whine, wild menial of sin! Watery tears are not enough; weep blood, you obstinate sinner!" The opening sigh motives and grating chromatic contortions would not simply have served to depict or represent these distressed sentiments, but could have caused a listener's own spirits and fluids to contract violently, constricting the heart and blood flow and thereby instilling an anxious, sorrowful state (ex. 28.1). Telemann's listeners may have found themselves inescapably caught in what Arnie Cox has called a "first-person

EXAMPLE 28.1. Georg Philipp Telemann, "Heul, du Schaum der Menschenkinder," from *Brockes-Passion* (TWV 5:1), mm. 1–10.

subject position," with their body-souls suffused by the contagious affective sounds produced by the performers.[41] Overall, listening to a Passion narrative like this *Brockes-Passion* thereby entailed more than the mental appreciation of an unfolding narrative. It could initiate a visceral process of bodily-spiritual catharsis that led listeners to experience a sense of abject sinfulness and subsequent joy about God's promised salvation within their own selves. For "true penitence consists in the conversion and transformation of the whole human . . . so that through heartfelt insight and painful remorse he turns away from sin."[42]

One of the foremost purposes of such musical dissonance, then, may have been to cleanse people's bodies of sinful affects and matter to restore a sense of equilibrium that enabled true faith and moral conduct. This affective trajectory, which Eric Chafe has summarized under the heading "tears into wine," structured numerous sacred cantata compositions of the time, from Telemann's own "Zerknirsche du mein blödes Herze" from his *Harmonischer Gottesdienst* to Johann Sebastian Bach's *Mein Herze schwimmt im Blut*.[43] Many such cantatas ended in a chorale arrangement, an idiom that, after the preceding arduous musical-affective journey, returned congregants to that ideal state of moderate cheerfulness advocated by writers on music as much as medical practitioners at the time. In bringing about this "sabbath of the heart," these cantatas acted as a form of biopower, producing a community of serene, docile, well-behaving Christians, as "through a

Christian music the hearts of people are stricken, moved, and . . . inclined to virtue."[44] Although these early modern discourses and metaphors about music as painful can often appear inconsistent or contradictory—music could spike ears but soften hearts—they may be best understood as different attempts to capture this broader intersubjective experience of bodily-spiritual torment followed by release. Modern research has shown both that the experiential world of a pain sufferer will be significantly shaped by the other persons participating in that world, and that persistent pain can produce lasting changes in their nervous system pathways, thereby affecting future responses to pain. As musical dissonances entered congregants to leave their imprints in their innards and redirect the liquids that animated them, it aided in the production of faithful, virtuous body-souls. In this sense, it was the pain of original sin that formed the foundation for these acts of musical creation.

✷ 29 ✷

Beastliness

The body-souls of early modern Europeans were volatile and in flux, only gradually taking on the defining characteristics of the modern Western—white, male, autonomous, rational, exceptional—human. The fears, desires, and domination strategies that enabled the eventual consolidation of modernity's racialized, sexualized conception of the human body are more or less easily legible from many of the sources I have considered so far. Acts of music-making, I would argue, were particularly potent in delineating and strengthening, but also troubling or transcending, the limits of what it meant and felt like to be an embodied human being across the long seventeenth century. Mortal and sinful by way of their basic condition of embodiment, these early modern Christian subjects entertained uneasy relationships with those animate non-human others that surrounded and, in their otherness, defined them: angels, demons, animals. And music could make those human/non-human boundaries seem promisingly or perilously porous. Acts of musicking could transport their participants into the realm of the angelic; they could drive out demons, but they also shared some of the devil's sinister powers of corruption. I experience that peculiar capacity of musicking to make you feel the other as part of yourself in Youri Egorov's 1975 performance of Johann Sebastian Bach's Fugue in B Minor from the *Well-Tempered Clavier* I.[1] Here the fugue subject's chromatic contortions seem to stretch the out-of-tuneness of human existence to demonic proportions, even when this pianist chose not to lean into the sighing potential of the opening semitone descents, which Bach's autograph slurs seems to invite (fig. 29.1). But Egorov's understated rendering also works to normalize that condition of dissonance, to the extent that by the time the first softly intoned interlude arrives in measure 17, this consonant sonic profile seems to hail from another place (fig. 29.2). In Bach's environment, that other place may well have been experienced as a glimpse of the heavenly or the angelic. Yet arguably any such potential

FIGURE 29.1. Johann Sebastian Bach, Fugue in B Minor (BWV 869), from *Well-Tempered Clavier* I, excerpt. Staatsbibliothek zu Berlin—Preußischer Kulturbesitz, Musikabteilung mit Mendelssohn-Archiv, Mus.ms. Bach P 415, f. 45v.

FIGURE 29.2. Johann Sebastian Bach, Fugue in B Minor (BWV 869), from *Well-Tempered Clavier* I, excerpt. Staatsbibliothek zu Berlin—Preußischer Kulturbesitz, Musikabteilung mit Mendelssohn-Archiv, Mus.ms. Bach P 415, f. 45v.

meaningfulness initially emerged from the flesh, as ears and body were invited to relax into the predictable and relatively discord-free sound-world of the descending sequence (though even here there is "mild" dissonance in the suspensions that drive that sequence forward; as well as the threat of the chromatic subject intruding again halfway through). Egorov's muted evocation of this angelic other as the place where the body wants to find repose rarely fails to give me the chills, especially in its third instantiation, which occurs toward the end of the fugue after a seemingly unending stretch of dissonant meandering. Perhaps such musical experiences could indeed drive out the devil, as in the biblical story of the conversion of Saul, that frequently invoked test case for the claim that the Holy Spirit could act on human body-souls through music.[2]

If music could invoke or make tangible humanity's demonic and angelic others, it also posed a perennial challenge to a Cartesian cosmology that positioned human beings as categorically distinct from animals, by virtue of human rationality. As Erica Fudge has explored, the sixteenth- and seventeenth-century discourse of reason in fact rarely upheld such a strict distinction; in many ways, the picture was more complicated and those complications are vital in any attempt at reconstructing an early modern anthropology.[3] Humans had a fundamental kinship with beasts in their shared bodily capacities of movement and sensation. And indeed, not least for Descartes, these shared capacities explained the appeal of music, and its metrical properties in particular, to both animals and humans. The sound heard on the first beat of a measure, he wrote, "doth more smartly and violently concusse or agitate our Spirits, by which we are excited to motion; as also by consequence, that Beasts may dance to number, or keep time with their feet, if they be taught and accustomed thereto; because to this, nothing more is required, then only a mere natural Impetus, or pleasant violence."[4] If you could hear, if you had a body that could be concussed by musical beats, you could learn to dance. Consonance and dissonance, too, for Descartes, were entities principally apprehended by the sense of hearing, which both humans and animals possessed. Reason does not seem to figure in his assertion that when a perfect consonance is played, "the hearing is therewith fully satisfied," or that a fifth "possesses and exercises the Hearing more fully" than an octave.[5] The sense of delectation that music could inspire in its hearers, as well as its power to move the affections, in Descartes's view relied on basic material processes of spirits moving rhythmically-harmonically around animate bodies.

Sitting uncomfortably alongside this ontology of music as based in the capacities of the animal body was the notion of music as a humanizing force: the ancient Orphic tale of wild beasts tamed and its early modern reenactment in the form of savages civilized by Christian hymns. Yet, as Vanessa Agnew has pointed out, these early colonial encounters with non-European others also had the potential to upset the power relations inscribed in the Orpheus myth, as in encountering indigenous musics and dance, the ancient classical enchanter turned into a "listener captive to wild, violent and uncontrollable sounds."[6] Even more troublingly, it was not just non-European body-souls that allegedly held that potential for wildness within them. Christian bodies, too, could turn bestial, for instance in the delirium caused by the bite of a rabid dog, or in the condition of lycanthropy described by Bernard Lamy, where a "black and burnt choler," if it passed from body to mind, "does in a manner turn a man into a beast."[7] As Gail Kern Paster has found, the animal likenesses so often invoked in the period in describing human character traits were grounded in the assumption of a basic shared corporeality, from vocal timbres to body odor.[8] Athanasius Kircher built his "phonognomia" of the human voice firmly on this assumption: "Those who speak with a high and intense voice are wrathful, wanton, impudent, and prurient, like the billy-goat, whose nature they share, for the goat is an animal whose temperament leans toward dryness, and melancholy mixed with phlegm, which, since they do not go together well, is a sign of the moist corrupting the dry; which is what gives rise to their stench as well."[9] For many writers, animals certainly served as a necessary foil for reifying a rational human self; yet the more they tried to explain human nature and behaviors physiologically, the harder it became to discern much of a difference.[10]

In acts of musicking, any such difference could easily become blurred. Sometimes that blurring was instrumental in delineating early modern Christian humans against their non-Christian (less fully human) others, as when the Lutheran pastor Johann Meißner repeated the longstanding slur that "the songs of the Jews, heretics, and infidels sound like pigs snorting and donkeys braying."[11] Sometimes it served to differentiate bad from good music, for instance in Martin Heinrich Fuhrmann's comparison of poor discant singing with the squeaking of moles and bad alto singing with the sounds of an ill sheep.[12] But the potential for the bestial resided in even the most virtuous and well-tuned, as evident in the curious effects of being bitten by the so-called tarantula. A bite from this arachnid, found in the Italian region of Apulia, initially caused "violent sickness, difficulty of breathing, universal faintness, and sometimes trembling" (symptoms now summarized under a diagnosis of latrodectism); it could also transfer the spider's innate color preferences to the patient.[13] Historical reports suggest that the "tarantati"—sufficiently altered by the experience to warrant their own nomenclature—came from all walks of life, from peasants to nobles. In women, the poison could draw out a dangerous brand of feral femininity: when bitten, "Maids and Women, otherwise chaste enough, without any Regard to Modesty, fall a sighing, howling, and into very indecent Motions, discovering their Nakedness."[14] Other transgressions into the bestial domain included patients "rolling themselves in the dirt like Swine," evoking that classic Homeric tale of the natural order coming under threat when Odysseus's men turned into pigs. As Kircher explained:

> There are various kinds of poison that have an effect on the imagination in strange ways. Through these poisons the humors that are awoken in the whole body rise to the brain, take in the spirits and finally the imagination: via the spirits, however, the liquids of the whole body are agitated and disquieted according to the forms conceived in the imagination and according to the different temperaments of the people. It is therefore no wonder that people, when they are infected by these spirits, think they are that which their imagination shows them.... Aconitum [a poisonous species of flowering plant] transforms people in their imagination and their external appearance into fish, goose, duck, etc.... It is no different with

> tarantism, for because the spiders differ, they have different poisons and can agitate different humors.[15]

For Kircher, then, an actual change of material substance took place through an alteration of bodily fluids. A "tarantata" effectively became spider-y—if not in external shape, then in her internal humoral makeup that determined her physical-spiritual constitution and outward behavior.

As was widely known, the only effective cure for the condition was playing a certain kind of music that drove the patient to perform a frenzied dance until the illness abated and their humanity was restored. Kircher attested that the spider's poison "lies hidden in the innermost fibers of the blood vessels like a sharp, biting, and slimy fluid"; yet, when the right tune started up, the spirits suffusing the patient's muscles and veins "are woken up, heated up, and agitated together with the poison, and affect all the muscles with an itch," inducing the patient to dance.[16] As the medical consensus had it, the virulent dancing made the patient sweat profusely, thereby driving out the poisonous particles; and, with them, the "violent impressions are quite extirpated from the Blood and the Fluid of the Nerves."[17] Yet this description could not account for the most surprising aspect of the cure, namely the fact that any usual sweat-inducing remedies seemed to fail in the case of tarantula poisoning. "Those that are stung by the Tarantula die in a little time, without the present Assistance of Music, all other Remedies giving no Relief," wrote Giorgio Baglivi, a key authority on the topic whose 1696 tract continued to be cited throughout the following century.[18] Richard Mead's attempt at an explanation ran as follows: "The benefit of music arises not only from their dancing to it, and so evacuating, by sweat, a great part of the poison, but the repeated percussions and vibrations of the air break the cohesion of the parts of the blood, and prevent coagulation. So that the heat being removed by sweating, and the coagulation by the contraction of the muscular *Fibrillae*, the wounded person is restored to his former condition."[19] If a musician struck up the right tune, music developed an uncanny capacity not just to move but to reanimate matter, in a process that seemed to hover somewhere between the demonic and the divine. As Mead outlined: "As soon as the patient has lost his sense and motion, a musician is sent for, who tries several tunes on an instrument, till he hits on that which is most agreeable to the disordered person. This is known by his first moving his fingers, then his arms, then his legs, and by degrees, his whole body, till at length he rises on his feet and begins to dance, which he continues for several hours."[20]

Yet although this form of musicking clearly acted as a healing and rehumanizing agent, the dance ritual itself threw the rational humanness of those afflicted into serious question. As Mead reported: "While the tarantati, or affected, are dancing, they lose in a manner the use of all their senses, like so many drunkards, do many ridiculous and foolish tricks, talk and act obscenely and rudely."[21] If music offered a cure, or exorcism, for the incursion of a non-human substance into a human body-soul, it only did so by making those affected pass wholesale through the portal of bestiality in the course of the dance. A classic Derridean *pharmakon,* in other words, constituting "the medium in which opposites are opposed, the movement and the play that links them among themselves, reverses them or makes one side cross over into the other."[22] In the case of tarantism, those opposites encompassed not only the human/animal divide, but the exoticized other of the Mediterranean South as much as an ancient Bacchanalian other. As Kélina Gotman has noted, the fascination with frenzied dancing rites across Western modernity has been "saturated with Orientalist prejudices against obscurity, unintelligibility, primitiveness, and Eastern-inflected Dionysianism."[23] Early modern dance could discipline the body to control or suppress its bestial impulses, but it could also expose and accentuate those impulses. In enabling or enforcing such transgressions into humanity's others, dance music could threaten the very foundations of what Giorgio Agamben has called anthropogenesis, the process of separating human from animal life. But it was not just tarantic dancing that threw a spanner in the works of the "anthropological machine," the making of humans by humans.[24] If tarantism presented an extreme case of the body- and soul-bending qualities of musical sound, music's transformative powers more generally betrayed the inadequacy of a fully mechanistic conception of the human body controlled by a disembodied rational mind. As Marcel Knaup has argued, certain manifestations of human life, such as dance or songs of jubilation, cannot be classified "bureaucratically as either 'purely physical' or 'purely mental.'" They are "not just connected with something inside you, but quite concretely with you as a living whole."[25] If gavottes and minuets had the power to "move the human mind and foot," as Mauritius Vogt asserted, this power affirmed a holistic notion of being human, in which body, soul, and spirit remained inextricably entangled.[26]

✷ 30 ✷
Mensa sonora

And so we arrive at *Tafelmusik*, the kind of music heard at early modern aristocratic or urban feasts and festivities that has traditionally occupied the lowest rung on the musicological ladder of aesthetic value—a "pleasant noise," as Immanuel Kant flatteringly put it.[1] It may have aided the flow of conversation and spread an atmosphere of jolly conviviality, but that is where, for Kant, its appeal ended. In asserting that such forms of musicking only engaged the body's sensory faculties without affording supposedly higher-order modes of reflection, Kant's evaluation attests to the severing of body from mind in late eighteenth-century aesthetic discourse. Yet in the context of a more integrated body-soul-spirit anthropology, we may find the early modern practice of *Tafelmusik* sitting not so much at the bottom of the pile, but rather at the very nexus of the corporeal, affective, and spiritual processes that enabled those historical acts of musicking and shaped their felt experiences. In grappling with forms of music-making that do not readily lend themselves to the structural-hermeneutic modes of listening habitually practiced in the modern academy, we may instead be compelled to adopt Bruce Smith's paradigm of "hearing green"; to embrace "a physiology of knowing in which the passions 'hear' sensations before reason does."[2] In other words, *Tafelmusik* may be particularly well placed to help us access some of the ways in which the early modern body-souls we have tried to reimagine in these pages could attend and respond to musical stimuli. Rather than dismissing this music's appeal as "merely" sensual, then, I would propose that, while these early modern listening responses were indeed fundamentally based in the body, we may find soul and mind enfolded in those corporeal-spiritual processes.

Heinrich Ignaz Biber's collection of instrumental sonatas titled *Mensa sonora* was published in 1680, "for the table" of his Salzburg employer Archbishop Maximilian Gandolf. According to the Italian music theorist Angelo Berardi, alongside reviving the spirits and increasing the body's warmth, music indeed held the power to "promote digestion";[3] and perhaps this would have been considered one of the primary functions of such a publication. But of course the body's digestive processes were not easily separable from an early modern consumer's overall corporeal-spiritual disposition. As food entered the body, it progressed along that material-immaterial scale that encompassed the stuff of human body-souls: through successive processes of rarefaction, chyle (the nutritive liquid produced in the digestive system) was turned into blood, which itself generated spirit, which in turn shaped a person's inner state, the moistness of their brain, the agility of their mental faculties, the kind of music they might write, and the kind of music they might like. For when "the free passage through the abdomen is obstructed, these congestions sometimes rise toward the head and brain, and confound the natural actions there."[4] In current research into the association of the human gut microbiota with neuropsychiatric conditions such as schizophrenia or autism spectrum disorders, this interconnection has been termed the "gut-brain axis."[5] In early modern parlance, "food is transformed into the substance and nature of those that eat it."[6] And, like food, the intake of music as a material-spiritual substance could produce comparable effects on receiving body-souls. In Andreas Herbst's formulation, "just as different foods cause and precipitate various flows in the human body . . . so human hearts and souls are miraculously transformed, taken in, and moved by such songs that are embellished with various alterations of the voices."[7] Herbst's analogy suggests that these shared effects were both bodily and spiritual, affecting humors, hearts, and souls. As Charles Brewer has pointed out, Biber's preface emphasized not the physical benefits of his music, but their impact on the spirit or soul, since "the foretaste of the supreme delight does not penetrate our spirits by another means more completely than by the consonant harmony of faithful strings."[8] This broader aim of spiritual uplift or recreation alongside any digestive or entertainment function becomes even more evident in those numerous seventeenth-century compilations of *Tafelmusik* that included hymns or sacred songs, not least Biber's own collection from a few years earlier, "for the altar or the court" (tam aris quam aulis servientes).[9] And, lest we forget, the ultimate feasting scenario in the early modern Christian imagination was of course the heavenly wedding meal with Christ, accompanied by the eternal harmonies of the angels, or, in its earthly instantiation in the Eucharist, by the worldly sounds of communion music.[10]

Such worldly music, like the material or spiritual food it accompanied, could taste sweet, a sweetness that could be sensed by ears or heart or spirit. Herbst asserted that the more varied and contrapuntally skillful a piece was, "the more pleasant and, so to speak, sweet as honey the song will seem to the ears."[11] Theodor Christlieb Reinholdt's paean to music affirmed that the art form "knows to feed with sweet power the tired mind with pleasant tunes if they are mobile; it pours the drink of nectar which penetrates to the deep ground of the tender spirit; it shows the heart what sweetness is found in those tones."[12] As I have explored above, that sweetness was both theologically and physiologically desirable: in John Floyer's formulation, "we must preserve a due Heat and Rarifaction, and sweetness in our Humours, by a Diet moderate as to Heat, and of a sweet Taste which will breed an oily, sweet and viscid Nutriment."[13] Hence, a German medical primer of 1748 advised, "all sulfurous medicines are known to sweeten the blood, by keeping the sour particles within their limits, which cause the blood to coagulate unnaturally and become full of clumps."[14] Barthold Heinrich Brockes was not alone in assuming that these qualities arose from the actual shape of the particles ingested: sweet foods, he wrote, have round, soft, light particles, whereas in sour foods the particles are sharp like little arrows that sting the tongue and taste buds.[15] In devotional terms, Heinrich Müller affirmed that "through tasting, feeling, and sensing we come to the true knowledge of Christ."[16] Godly song smelled good, he found, whereas worldly song "stinks before God."[17] These sensory conjunctions urge us, I think, to take seriously, at least for the early modern period, Steven Connor's assertion that "we would be wrong to see synesthesia as always exceptional, revolutionary or transcendent."[18] Running through these accounts is the assumption of a fundamental convergence of sensory modalities that allowed people to taste joy and smell salvation.

Perhaps, then, "hearing sweet" rather than "green" might be a plausible stance to adopt toward these early modern *Tafelmusik* repertories, in a way that can begin to reverse what Lydia Goehr has termed the "disenfranchisement of the culinary from the tradition of aesthetic theory."[19] Such a stance reveals the category of aesthetic taste as it took shape over the eighteenth century to have indeed been grounded in the gut—a gut that, according to recent scientific insight, is lined with a network of neurons so extensive that it has been dubbed a "second brain."[20] As the eighteenth-century theorist Meinrad Spiess affirmed, the capacity to appreciate tasteful music was determined by bodily pre-conditioning: "Just as those who have a too sour stomach have an aberrant appetite for other too sour foods, thus those whose hearing has been pampered, altered, and spoiled [by too much dissonance] can find more pleasure in the wailing generated by the most horrific dissonances than in the true taste of a pure, well-sounding music."[21] In such a scenario, the later Kantian notion of a pure judgment of taste independent of the sensory stimulus would have to appear chimerical. Of course, my own attempt at a "sweet" hearing of the first of Biber's sonatas does not assume an ability on my part to slip back easily into such a pre-Kantian disposition. Following Roseen Giles's assertion that listening to Biber's *Mystery Sonatas* could indeed "physically alter the body," my hearing only extends some feelers in that direction, in order to try to imagine what it might have felt like to have these sounds suffuse one's intestines, heart, and soul.[22]

To "hear sweet" in this way, I return to a "concatenationist" mode of listening, focusing on the experiential quality of musical sounds and gestures as they emerge and evolve over time in the act of performance—in this case, a recording of 1988 by Musica Antiqua Köln under the direction of Reinhard Goebel.[23] The opening chord, rich and resonant, strikes my attentive ears and body as not a stable entity but something more like an animated substance, internally bubbling with that flourish in the harpsichord, and spreading outward to penetrate auditors or diners, doing what Kant called "imposing itself" (sich aufdringen) on its surroundings and any adjacent body-souls regardless of their desire to be sounded through.[24] The sound of this string ensemble, harmonious and in a comfortable register, feels a good place to be, inviting listeners to sink back into a piece of plush upholstery; though at the same time the brightness of the major third and the timbral profile of D major produced on this combination of instruments renders the sonority more alerting and vibrant than slack and soft. And there is in the timbre that material resistance of bow on string—a necessary friction, unlike in the brass ensemble of Schütz's *Fili mi, Absalon*, of animal hair rubbing against animal gut in order to make the sound happen. With the fifth on top, the sonority feels open and full of potential, and it is opened up further by the violinist's subsequent upward leap, which then cajoles the other players into motion as well. Material friction is joined by sonic friction as the lower parts ascend to create a dissonant suspension, thereby propelling the players into further bodily action to move the sound toward resolution. It is not a memorable melody that emerges here, but a swell of sonorities that offers to transport you somewhere if you care to be swept along. The sonic flow of these opening measures, as realized by Goebel's ensemble, to my ears produces an enveloping sense of spacious anticipation, heightened further rather than quelled when the players come to pause on that half cadence on A major in measure 6, with its subtly altered timbral profile of open strings and chromatic inflections—a slightly different flavor of sweet, one might say, resonating in subtly different locations in the ear and body. The inscription in the score for this opening section reads "grave," which, although an aristocratic Salzburg diner would not have been aware of it, might have

EXAMPLE 30.1. Heinrich Ignaz Biber, Sonata I, from *Mensa sonora seu musica instrumentalis* (Salzburg: Mayr, 1680), mm. 1–14.

inspired the Archbishop's performers to adopt a stately pace and rounded, solemn tone quality similar to Goebel's performance, with bows on the heavy side and spirits raised just above the sluggish (ex. 30.1).

My attempt to articulate some of the sonic-affective impact of these opening moments has taken much longer to write or read than the actual musical phrase lasts. The resulting description has not only ended up replete with metaphors; more generally, in translating that impact into words, it necessarily jettisons the immediacy of the experience and distorts it for lack of just the right adjectives to capture just those particular degrees of sweetness. But I would want to resist the temptation once again to fall back on a binary model of head versus body, or affect versus meaning. In the more permeable and integrated body-soul I am trying to assume, a reasoned assessment such as "the violin part leaps up a fourth" would not be fully separable from the felt experience of such a leap; and neither would that rational version of interval recognition appear necessarily superior or that felt experience of expansion necessarily prior. Clearly, in any endeavor to talk or write about "hearing sweet," words will still need to be used—which in themselves, of course, have bodily dimensions, too. When I note that the imitative "Allegro" section that follows the opening passage impresses my ears as dense yet light, the relationship of those words "dense" and "light" to the felt experience is oblique in some ways, but not completely unmoored from past physical experiences of density or lightness that a body-soul might recall. This sonic density is by no means an excessive one, just the expected kind of sensory overload produced by a four-part imitative texture that cannot be fully disentangled in the listening moment.[25] The individual entries as each player joins in successively are clearly audible, but subsequently the voices blend into the texture as it expands and buzzes, generating that "honey-sweet" sensation in the ears that an artful musical imitation could engender.[26] If this passage can boggle the mind, it nonetheless affords an overall sense of ease and delight. Its light-touch rendering in Goebel's performance, as the upward-directed subject encounters its downward-running counterpart in various configurations, could incite a listener's spirits to surge and bound along as the players coast toward the concluding cadential moment of relaxation.

Later on in Goebel's recording, the perpetual motion of the Gavotte to my ears exudes a joie de vivre that approaches that tarantic power of music to incite limbs usually trained to hold still to begin to wiggle or dance. The ensuing Gigue, meanwhile, runs counter to such straightforward metric-rhythmic contagion, in that despite its regular pulse it keeps its listeners guessing as to where the downbeat is. The swift tempo at which Goebel's performers take it, and their play with the inherent metric ambiguities of the 6/4 time signature, hinders any conclusive reasoned assessment of the piece's metric properties. In throwing a listening body-soul off kilter in this way, such music could potentially draw more of the attention of its distracted consumers to itself, in a manner not unrelated to the metrical humor David Yearsley has detected in Johann Sebastian Bach's first Brandenburg Concerto.[27] The return of the opening movement at the end of Biber's sonata strikes me as such an attention-raising moment, too. The peculiar sense of altered sameness it generates may in part register in cognitive terms (i.e., understanding the structure as cyclical), but it also affords that strange bodily-spiritual sensation of finding oneself in a familiar yet somehow different, richer place. When the opening aria sounds again at the end of Bach's Goldberg Variations, that reprise can, in a similar way, seem so profoundly comforting and yet so utterly transformed after what a performer and/as listener has gone through in the meantime.[28]

If it might appear unwarranted to some readers to compare Biber's modest sonata with that acclaimed work by Bach, I would note that by drawing out these potential similarities in effect, I am not suggesting that one could simply stand in for the other. If we considered the modes of musicking explored in this book as wholly based in a pre-conscious body, or wholly reducible to the vibration of material particles, then presumably any suitably ordered noise would do. As the French physician Pierre-Jean Burette affirmed, if the impact of music's vibrational force on nerves, fibers, and animal spirits could cure certain diseases, a "very coarse and vulgar" music was as likely to achieve those effects as any more refined kind.[29] But this would leave one hard pressed to explain why these early modern musicians insisted on producing ever new and different versions of musical joy, love, sadness, or rage. This, then, might be where the unique powers of this music to "move the affections"—to incite, shape, or give voice to particular bodily-spiritual motions—primarily resided: to allow people to live through just *that* kind of joie de vivre, as it took shape in any given performance of Biber's Gavotte, offering a singular experience that engaged the visceral, spiritual, and intellectual aspects of human nature in unquantifiable admixtures. Not incidentally, this capacity for virtually inexhaustible variety and particularity was a key characteristic of the imagined music of heaven, too, which, we are told, sounded "without end, yet without boredom; without end, yet without repetition."[30] It was in providing this seemingly infinite multiplicity of ways to modulate the human spirit that music's capacity for the recreation of bodies and souls emerged—re-creating or making whole, at least temporarily, that body-soul-spirit entity otherwise so often under serious threat of being pulled apart.

Envoi

There are many body parts that have remained untouched in these pages; and many wise words about bodies, sounds, music, affects, and their histories that did not come to be acknowledged in my narrative. The peculiar constellation of black letters on white ground that ended up becoming this book therefore constitutes merely one partial attempt to fathom something of that irrepressible human drive to make things: to compose music, craft and play instruments, sing songs, make meaning. For my early modern European subjects, this urge to generate (dis)harmonious sound was felt to pour out of their body-souls as a vital power that could corporeally and spiritually transform themselves and those around them. That power acted efficaciously in multiple ways that revealed "music" to be not a monolithic object but a gathering of constituent features—sounding matter, material-spiritual flow, embodied experience, evanescent performative act, flight of fancy, affective catalyst, carrier of contagion, agent of social cohesion or coercion, maker of faith, hermeneutic invitation. One could perhaps imagine redrawing Gioseffo Zarlino's wise and beautiful illustration of music's compound nature along these lines (fig. 31.1).[1] This multiplicity meant that there was no single way in which musicking impinged upon an early modern body-soul, just as there were multiple modes of experiencing and describing the body-souls that coexisted across the period. But if there was no single unified early modern musical physiology, what has become apparent here is that acts of music-making enriched, challenged, or complicated most contemporaneous attempts at delineating human nature in its physical and spiritual dimensions.

And this capacity of music-making to enrich, challenge, and complicate may well be worthwhile attending to today. Not only does my exploration of these early modern ideas and experiences invite us to start listening to their musics in different ways that augment or outstrip modern musicology's traditional concerns with representation, text-painting,

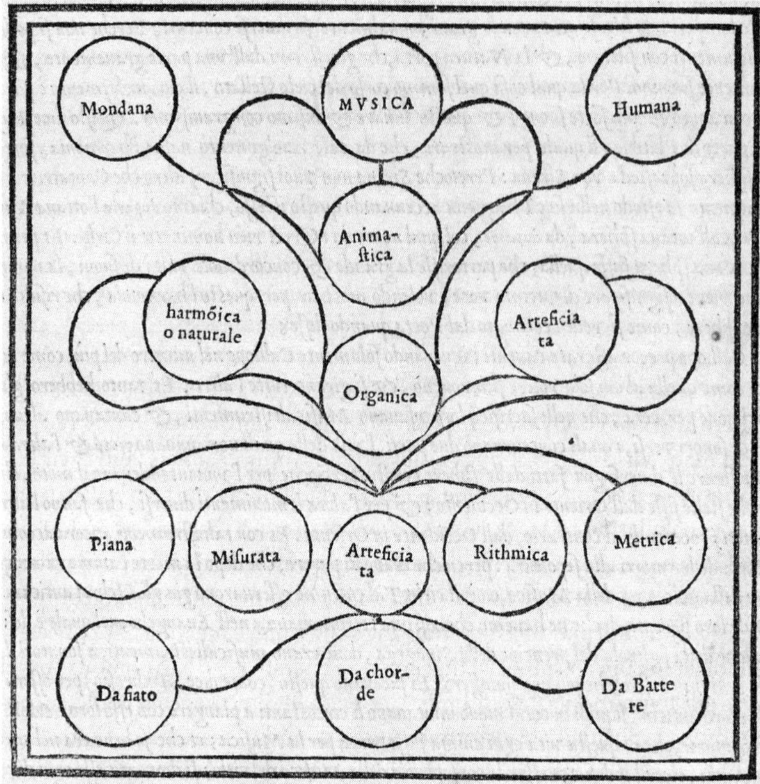

FIGURE 31.1. The constituent parts of music. Gioseffo Zarlino, *Le istitutioni harmoniche* (Venice: Senese, 1562), 11. © British Library Board, General Reference Collection 786.l.22. Courtesy of the British Library, digitized by the Google Books project.

and semantic meaning. More fundamentally, music's potential to disrupt early modern debates about human nature still raises pressing questions now, about those persistent dualisms on which Western modernity was founded and which have ultimately failed to provide a fully satisfactory explanation of humanity's music-making capacities. I might point here only to Gary Tomlinson's sweeping evolutionary account of the emergence of music, which concludes with the insight that "musicking should occupy a special place in the effort that has recently coalesced from various disciplines to analyze and describe the embodied aspects of all our modes of consciousness."[2] In its irrepressible tendency to cut across the domains of body and mind, human musicking very often does not sit well with a dualist anthropology that regards the physical body as detached from and governed by an immaterial, computational mind. These early modern musical activities urge us to reconsider, as well, the assumed foundational binary between literal and metaphorical ways of engaging with the world; and to rethink the very mechanisms through which meaning might emerge in interpersonal affective communication. They ask puzzling questions of the operations of human emotion and cognition that are set to keep present-day scientific communities occupied for some time yet; and quite a few of the answers that have recently emerged (concerning thinking guts, for instance, or breaking hearts) resonate tellingly with early modern explanatory models that might otherwise be dismissed as outlandish. Some aspects of what these early modern musical subjects were attempting to articulate, then, might hold considerable promise as a starting point, at least, for imagining alternative, historically and critically alert answers to the lasting conundrums of what human beings are and might be capable of.

In the early modern contexts I have explored here, music could be heard and felt to bring together what some contemporary philosophers were busy splitting apart. Few other earthly pursuits could activate and conjoin quite so many facets of early modern human nature as musicking did, and in the process it revealed that nature as a complex, volatile, entangled body-soul-spirit formation. In the capacious, if still incomplete, summation of the Catholic preacher Ignatius Ertl: "Music refreshes the blood flow, rouses the spirit, stirs the feet, moves the hands, loosens the tongues, tickles the ears, opens the eyes, pulls the whole human heart toward itself; music enflames love, soothes rage, alleviates pain, dispels, and chases away all melancholy follies from the head; music appeases God in the high heavens, delights the angels in their nine choirs, amuses us people on earth, charms the animals, vanquishes the devils; music quells the tears of children in their cradles, invigorates laborers in their work, rouses soldiers to battle, uplifts believers in their prayers."[3] If we embrace the possibility that early modern acts of musicking could indeed accomplish even some of these feats, we might begin to find our own musical modes of being-in-the-world peculiarly altered.

Notes

Preamble

1. "Musica laetitia est in corde, in mente voluptas: Musica in ore mel est; Musica in aure melos." Hieronymus Ammon, in Herbst, *Musica poetica* (1643), n.p.

2. "Weil die natürliche Geister unsers gemühtes und Geblütes dem lieblichen Gesange / und klange der Musicken so verwand / und zugethan," Silber, *Encomion musices* (1621), 15.

3. "eine Hertz-Glocke / welche . . . alle Hertzenäderlein durchdringet / und desselben Affectus . . . erwecket." Frick, *Music-Büchlein* (1631), 90.

4. "wann iemand die Proportion wissen solte / welche der sonus eines Instruments zu den Geistern / Muscheln und Adern des Menschlichen Leibes hat / würde er alles bei ihm erwecken und würcken können / was er nur wolte." Kircher, *Musurgia universalis* (1662), 192.

5. "La Musique & le son des Instrumens, contribuent à la santé du corps & de l'esprit, aident la circulation des humeurs, purifient le sang, dissipent les vapeurs, & dilatent les vaisseaux & les pores." Vigneul-Marville, *Mélange d'histoire et de littérature* (1713), 189. This passage is also cited in Raupach, *Veritophili Deutliche Beweis-Gründe* (1717), 36.

6. "eben als mit einem scharff-sauren Eßig / der einem die Kähle zusammen zeucht." Fuhrmann, *Musicalischer Trichter* (1706), 55.

7. I borrow the coinage "body-soul" from James, *Passion and Action*, 42.

8. The idea of the musical score as a script is developed in Cook, *Beyond the Score*, esp. 249–287.

9. On historical phenomenology, see especially Smith, *Phenomenal Shakespeare*, 24–37.

10. For a thoughtful reflection on some of these recent endeavors, see Smith, "Producing Sense, Consuming Sense, Making Sense."

11. Newton, "A Letter of Mr. Isaac Newton" (1671/72), 3085.

12. Chalmers, "Facing Up to the Problem of Consciousness."

13. Sevush, *The Single-Neuron Theory*, 2.

14. Kowalik, *Theology and Dehumanization*, 35.

15. "Structures of feeling" is Raymond Williams's phrase; see his *Marxism and Literature*, 131–132. See McClary, "Introduction: On Bodies, Affects, and Cultural Identities," 15.

16. Le Guin, *Boccherini's Body*.

17. Grosz, *Volatile Bodies*, 23.

18. See Cunningham, "The Pen and the Sword."

19. Riskin, *The Restless Clock*, 22.

Chapter 1

1. "L'oratione sia padrona del armonia e non serva," Monteverdi, *Scherzi musicali* (1607), "Dichiaratione," n.p.

2. Palisca, "The Artusi-Monteverdi Controversy," 152.

3. "L'harmonia, & il Numero debbeno seguitare la Oratione," Zarlino, *Le istitutioni harmoniche* (1558), 339.

4. Carter, "Two Monteverdi Problems," 419–420.

5. See especially Ossi, *Divining the Oracle.*

6. Though Silke Leopold has noted that "oratio" may have referred to the delivery of the words; see her *Monteverdi: Music in Transition*, 50.

7. Tomlinson, *Monteverdi and the End of the Renaissance*, 120–131.

8. Tomlinson, *Monteverdi and the End of the Renaissance*, 127.

9. Cusick, "'There Was Not One Lady'"; Gordon, *Monteverdi's Unruly Women.*

10. Gordon, *Monteverdi's Unruly Women*, 59.

11. Wilbourne, *Seventeenth-Century Opera*, 52–71.

12. Cusick, "'There Was Not One Lady,'" 25–26.

13. Gordon, *Monteverdi's Unruly Women*, 31.

14. Codice Morbio 1, c. 29r, cited and translation in Wilbourne, *Seventeenth-Century Opera*, 56.

15. Abbate, "Music: Drastic or Gnostic?," 505.

16. Kivy, *Sound Sentiment*, 21.

Chapter 2

1. Buelow, "Johann Mattheson and the Invention of the *Affektenlehre.*"

2. Schulze, *Die Bach-Kantaten*, 445.

3. Chafe, *Tonal Allegory in the Vocal Music of J. S. Bach*, 407.

4. Ringer, *Bach's Operas of the Soul*, 142.

5. Ringer, *Bach's Operas of the Soul*, 143.

6. Schulenberg, *Music of the Baroque*, 95.

7. Anderson, *The Arts of Persuasion*, 54.

8. Taruskin, *The Oxford History of Western Music*, vol. 2, 321.

9. Heller, *Music in the Baroque*, 215.

10. Elferen, *Mystical Love in the German Baroque*, 98.

11. Eidsheim, *Sensing Sound*, 21.

12. Burmeister, *Musica poetica* (1606).

13. See my article "'Mutato semper habitu.'" See also Isabella van Elferen's recent rethinking of Baroque affect in her "Rethinking Affect."

14. "Illud ornamentum, quo textus significatio ita deumbratur, ut ea, quae textui subsunt et animam vitamque non habent, vita esse praedita, videantur." Burmeister, *Musical Poetics*, 62.

15. Cited in Bartel, *Musica Poetica*, 8.

16. "Welche alle mit dem Sono oder Klang / durch veränderung und abwe-

chßlung der Noten zu exprimiren und außzudrucken seyn." Herbst, *Musica poetica* (1643), 111.

17. See Carter, "The Search for Musical Meaning," 165.

18. "Wenn aber eine Gemüths-Regung zu exprimiren ist, soll der Componist mehr auf dieselbe, als auf die eintzeln Worte sehen." Walther, *Praecepta*, 158.

19. Burmeister, *Musica poetica*, 61.

20. *J. S. Bach: Christmas Cantatas*, Emmanuel Music, dir. Craig Smith, Koch International Classics 3-7462-2H1 (1999).

Chapter 3

1. Cited in Fabbri, *Monteverdi*, 297. "Zolfa" refers to the (nonsensical) solmization syllables used in singing teaching throughout the period.

2. Stocker, *De musica verbali libri duo* (ca. 1570), 236.

3. Vicentino, *L'Antica musica* (1555), 80v. See Harrán, "Vicentino and His Rules of Text Underlay," 624.

4. Millet, *La belle méthode* (1666), viii.

5. "Melismaticus stylus, dulcis, ariosus, rhytmicus, maximè opera & arte canentis expressivus." Vogt, *Conclave thesauri* (1717), 5.

6. "Con intentione di significare alcuna cosa, cioè, per inferire il sentimento delle parole." Maffei, *Delle lettere . . . libri due* (1562), 30.

7. Caccini, *Le nuove musiche* (1601), "A I Lettori," n.p.

8. Rathey, *Bach's Major Vocal Works*, 31.

9. Pirrotta, "Monteverdi's Poetic Choices," 39.

10. *Reinhard Keiser: Der geliebte Adonis*, Capella Orlandi Bremen, dir. Thomas Ihlenfeldt, cpo 999 636-2 (2001).

11. "Sensum litterae non evacuet, sed faecundet." Vogt, *Conclave thesauri*, 95. Vogt is citing Bernard of Clairvaux here.

12. Quitschreiber, *Musicbüchlein* (1607), chapter 9, n.p. His prescription draws on Ornithoparcus, *Musicae activae Micrologus*, of which John Dowland published an English translation in 1609.

13. "Erstlich muß er lernen denselben ohne Text singen und clavisiren. Darnach den Text fein artlich unterlegen / und alle Syllaben desselben recht aussprechen." Ahle, *Kurze / doch deutliche Anleitung* (1690), 4.

14. Christine M. Neufeld discusses the "unruly voice that issues from the abjected female body" in her *Avid Ears*, 44.

15. Cusick, *Francesca Caccini*, 157.

16. McClary, *Desire and Pleasure*, 28. On orgasm, see pp. 173–180.

17. Maffei, *Delle lettere . . . libri due*, 59–60.

18. Smith, *The Acoustic World of Early Modern England*, 12, 14.

19. On meaningfulness, see Butt, *Bach's Dialogue with Modernity*, 181–184.

20. "Qui iubilat, non verba dicit, sed sonus quidam est laetitiae sine verbis: vox est enim animi diffusi laetitia." Augustine, in *Patrologiae cursus completus*, vol. 37, 1272. Translation in McKinnon, *Music in Early Christian Literature*, 158.

21. Cusick, *Francesca Caccini*, 160.

22. See Braun, "Die evangelische Kontrafaktur," 107.

23. Primaudaye, *The French Academie* (1618), 380.

24. *J. S. Bach—"In Dir ist Freude" BWV 615*, Ulf Norberg (organ), live recording, September 2015, https://www.youtube.com/watch?v=MS-8J9-2qaU.

25. "Et quia laudes aeternae vitae humanis verbis non resonabunt, quaedam ecclesiae mystice pneumatizant sequentiam sine verbis." Anon., *Speculum ecclesiae*, cited in Fassler, *Gothic Song*, 62.

Chapter 4

1. Gordon, *Monteverdi's Unruly Women*, 12. See also Fisher and Lochhead, "Analyzing from the Body."

2. Glüxam, *"Aus der Seele muß man spielen . . . ,"* 20.

3. Leech-Wilkinson, *The Changing Sound of Music*, chapter 2.1. This paragraph draws on my article "Musical Expression," 63. Reused with permission.

4. Diamond and Bronfen, review of Carolyn Abbate, *In Search of Opera*, 215.

5. Robinson, *Deeper Than Reason*, 412.

6. Johnson, *After Debussy*, 206. My approach as a whole here resonates with Johnson's evocative exploration of Claude Debussy's keyboard music in these terms; see 201–212.

7. *Like as the Hart: Music For the Templars Garden*, The Choir of New College Oxford, dir. Robert Quinney, novum NCR1392 (2017).

8. *Dietrich Buxtehude: Quemadmodum desiderat cervus*, Marc Mauillon (tenor), Ground Floor, live recording, Paradyz, 22 August 2015, https://www.youtube.com/watch?v=8nqPQ6v7a7Q.

9. "Damit die Sänger respiriren / und die Instrumentisten in specie die Blasiasten per Intervalla sich wieder refrischiren können / denn das continuirliche Singen / Streichen und Blasen würde die Musicanten zu sehr exhauriren." Fuhrmann, *Musicalischer Trichter* (1706), 49.

10. "per dar maggiore spirito al crescere, e scemare della voce, alle esclamazioni, e tutti gli altri affetti," Caccini, *Le nuove musiche* (1601), "A I Lettori," n.p. See Sanford, "A Comparison of French and Italian Singing," 2.4.

11. Everett, "Languages in Drier Climates."

12. Melrose, *A Semiotics of the Dramatic Text*, 218. Bacilly, *Remarques curieuses* (1668), 258. On Bacilly, see Gordon-Seifert, *Music and the Language of Love*, 208–210.

13. Erlmann, "Refiguring the Early Modern Voice," 94.

14. Winkler, "'Our Friend Venus Performed to a Miracle,'" 278.

15. Heller, *Emblems of Eloquence*, 169.

16. Zuckerkandl, *Man the Musician*, 40.

17. Koelsch, *Brain & Music*, xi.

Chapter 5

1. Nussbaum, *The Musical Representation*, 4.

2. Calcagno, "Signifying Nothing," 473. Calcagno's analysis is carefully circumscribed, however; he ventures that "only momentarily" might the singer's vocal prowess efface the sense of the words (488).

3. Tomlinson, *Metaphysical Song*, 40. On modernity as a series of schisms, see also Chua, *Absolute Music*, esp. 23–28. I would like to acknowledge here the inspiration I took from Chua's imaginative chapter organization in designing the layout of my book.

4. Cox, *Sonic Flux*, 3. Jane Bennett positions her vision of "thing-power" as "detached or radically free from representation"; see her *Vibrant Matter*, 3.

5. Carter, "The Search for Musical Meaning," 191.

6. "eine Kraft . . . sich die Welt vorzustellen," Wolff, *Vernünfftige Gedancken von Gott* (1720), 426.

7. Maisano, "Infinite Gesture," 66.

8. Descartes, *Excellent Compendium* (1653), 50; van Orden, "Descartes on Musical Training and the Body," 17.

9. This paragraph draws on my chapter "Early Modern Voices," 250–251. Reused with permission of Oxford University Press.

10. Cottingham, "Cartesian Dualism," 252. See also Jolley, "The Reception of Descartes' Philosophy."

11. Smart, review of Gary Tomlinson, *Metaphysical Song*, 105.

12. For one attempt at such a dialogue, see Anderson, *The Renaissance Extended Mind.*

13. Clarke, *Ways of Listening*, 15, 18, 43.

14. Scheibe, *Critischer Musikus* (1745), 554.

15. Aristotle, *Poetics*, 47. On "locus descriptionis," see Mattheson, *Der vollkommene Capellmeister* (1739), 127.

16. For a detailed reading of this letter in its correspondence context, see Carter, "Winds, Cupids, Little Zephyrs and Sirens."

17. Wilson, *Roger North on Music*, 110, 128.

18. Mattheson, *Das forschende Orchestre* (1721), 271.

19. Sullivan, "The Role of the Arts in the History of the Emotions," 120.

20. Watkins, *Musical Vitalities*, 142.

21. Carter, "Resemblance and Representation," 129.

22. See pp. 127–137.

23. Taussig, *Mimesis and Alterity*, xvii.

Chapter 6

1. "singekunst, die kunst auf musicalischen instrumenten zu singen oder zu spielen." Ludovici, *A Dictionary* (1706), 456.

2. "Musica ist eine kunst, recht zu modulieren." Altenburg, *De Musica*, 177; Butler, *The Principles of Musik* (1636), 1.

3. See Small, *Musicking.*

4. Werckmeister, *Musicae mathematicae hodegus curiosus* (1687), 9–10.

5. "La Musique est la Science des Sons; par conséquent le Son est le principal objet de la Musique." Rameau, *Traité de l'harmonie* (1722), 1. Translation in Rameau, *Treatise on Harmony*, 3.

6. "Todas aquellas cosas, que pertenecen à la especulacion del entendimiento"; "todo aquello que se executa con alguno, ò algunos de los miembros corporales." Nassare, *Fragmentos músicos* (1700), 2.

7. Austern, "Introduction," 6. For a more expansive exposition of early modern debates over music as act or object, see also her *Both from the Ears and Mind*, 19–24.

8. "welcher blos mit der Vernunft / alles was in der Harmonischen Music vorlauffen kan / judiciret und urtheilet: ein practicus ist dagegen / der sich allein auf seinen Gehör-sinn verläst." Kircher, *Musurgia universalis* (1662), 72.

9. Austern, "Introduction," 5–6; she is quoting David L. Burrows here.

10. Abbate, "Music—Drastic or Gnostic?," 510–511.

11. Berger, "Musicology According to Don Giovanni," 497.

12. Hamilton, *Music, Madness, and the Undoing of Language*, 103.

13. Eagleton, "The Ideology of the Aesthetic," 327.

14. Mascia-Lees, "Aesthetic Embodiment," 3.

15. See Devereaux, "Feminist Aesthetics."

16. https://www.camerata-musica.org/attending-concert.

17. Holsinger, *Music, Body, and Desire*; Davies, *Romantic Anatomies of Performance*.

18. Peters, "Introduction," 4.

19. Calvör, "Vorrede" (1717), n.p.

20. In a letter to Carl Heinrich Graun, Georg Philipp Telemann asserted that in French recitative, "everything flows continuously like champagne." Cited in *Georg Philipp Telemann: Briefwechsel*, 282. For Augustine's comment, see Harrison, *On Music, Sense, Affect and Voice*, 80. For Mattheson's comments on melody, see his *Kern melodischer Wissenschaft* (1737), 36.

21. Playford, *An Introduction to the Skill of Musick* (1674), vol. 1, n.p.

Chapter 7

1. Pascal, *Pensées*, no. 65.

2. Cusick, "Feminist Theory, Music Theory," 16. See various contributions in Lock and Farquhar, eds., *Beyond the Body Proper*.

3. See Schoenfeldt, "The Unbearable Permeability," 105.

4. Paster, *The Body Embarrassed*, 10; Sawday, *The Body Emblazoned*. See also Craik, *Reading Sensations*; Klemm, *Bildphysiologie*; Waldron, *Reformations of the Body*. See also Charalampous, *Rethinking the Mind-Body Relationship*.

5. Kuriyama, *The Expressiveness of the Body*, 14.

6. Paster, *Humoring the Body*, 20.

7. Coakley, "Introduction: Religion and the Body," 3–4.

8. Fischer-Lichte, "Verkörperung/Embodiment," 13.

9. Yearsley, *Bach's Feet*.

10. Cusick, "Feminist Theory, Music Theory," 18–19.

11. Raupach, *Veritophili Deutliche Beweis-Gründe* (1717), 28. The story is retold in many other early modern sources, for instance Brookbank, *The Well-Tuned Organ* (1660), 28–29.

12. Le Guin, *Boccherini's Body*, 6–7.

13. See Cox, *Music and Embodied Cognition*, 36–57.

14. "diejenigen Nerven / so innerhalb des Leibes sind / wodurch die Natur von dem / was in den Leib gekommen ist / Kundschafft erlanget," Richter, *Kurtzer und deutlicher Unterricht* (1705), 102.

15. Cited in Hogg, "Enactive Consciousness," 83.

16. See, for instance, Tomlinson, *The Singing of the New World*; or Bloechl, *Native American Song*.

17. "Habent hymni suam singularem dulcedinem, ex concinna numerorum harmonia atque melodia, ut non solum summa cum voluptate et delectatione canantur, sed etiam mirifice in animos & corda audientium penetrent, et affectus verae pietatis,

laetitiae & gaudii ardentis in pectoribus inflamment." Ettmüller, *Disputatio effectus musicae* (1714), 6. On hymn singing, see also pp. 139–144.

18. See Austern, *Both from the Ears and Mind*, 155–216; and Gouk, "Music and Spirit," 221–240.

19. Csordas, "Embodiment as a Paradigm for Anthropology."

20. See Klemm, *Bildphysiologie*, 25–94.

21. "ein Temperament eines lebendigen Leibes und nicht bloß hin eine Complexion eines aus leblosen materien gemischten Cörpers." Stahl, *Observationes clinico-practicae* (1726), "Vorrede," n.p.

22. "Geblüt, Haut, Körperöffnungen lassen sich . . . nicht auf anatomische Organe reduzieren." Duden, "Anmerkungen zur Kulturgeschichte des Herzens," 131.

23. On Wright, see Robinson, "Thinking Feeling," 114–119. On Perrault, see Erlmann, "The Physiologist at the Opera."

24. Cunningham, "The End of the Sacred Ritual of Anatomy."

Chapter 8

1. Crooke, *Mikrokosmographia* (1615), 174.

2. "tout perspirable, & euaporable pour sa rareté, & ouvertures des pores qui percent sa peau & son cuir." Binet, *Essay des merveilles* (1622), 553.

3. See Paster, *The Body Embarrassed*; Rublack, "Fluxes."

4. Keil, *Handbüchlein* (1730), 5.

5. "tous ensemblément coulent dans les veines, & dans la masse sanguinaire." Binet, *Essay des merveilles* (1622), 553.

6. Richter, *Kurtzer und deutlicher Unterricht* (1705), 42–44.

7. Fuhrmann, *Musica vocalis*, 54.

8. Detry, *Betrachtung des Menschen*, 50.

9. See pp. 231–235.

10. Reiss, *Mirages of the Selfe*, 97.

11. See Caughie, "Let it Pass."

12. "Le corps est donc ouvert de toutes parts aux matières qui l'environnent." Sénac, *Traité de la structure du coeur* (1749), vol. 2, 65. Cited in Koschorke, *Körperströme und Schriftverkehr*, 49.

13. Boorde, *A Compendyous Regyment* (1547), n.p. Later editions appeared in 1552, 1557, 1575, 1587, and 1598.

14. Burton, *The Anatomy of Melancholy*, 5.

15. Melanchthon, *Initia doctrinae physicae* (1550), 136. See Wels, *Manifestationen des Geistes*, 102.

16. "denn das Astralische Firmament zuvorn seine gifftige Stralen . . . auff den Erdboden / oder in das Wasser / oder in die Lufft ergiesse / alsdann werden nicht allein die Früchte auff dem Erdboden vergifftet . . . das Wasser und die Fische werden vergifftet und sterben / die Luft wird corrumpirt. Wie nun die Erde / das Wasser und die Lufft corrumpirt wird / also auch die kleine Welt: . . . das Hertz / Leber / Hirn / empfahen auch durch an sich ziehender Lufft eine enderung und mutation der innerlichen Kräfften / des Spiritus Vitalis." Popp, *Thesaurus medicinae* (1628), 429.

17. See Sugg, *The Smoke of the Soul*, 14.

18. "durch ihre unaufhörliche Bewegung / Tages und Nacht seine anmuthige

Himmels-Music und Tripudium, ohn daß es unsere taube und dicke Menschen-Ohren hören." Calvör, "Vorrede" (1717), n.p.

19. "Und wie die klingende Harmonie in unsere Ohren fällt; Und die Fluctus, so von einem Sono erreget werden, ein ander corpus oder Seyte, so mit selbigem sono überein gestimmet, und in gleicher Proportion stehen, anregen und klingend machen: Also fället die Harmonie des Gestirnes in unser Gemüthe, regieret und treibet dasselbe. . . . Und wie die Constellationes sich von Zeit zu Zeiten verwechseln; also werden die Gemüther durch solchen Sterngeist und Harmonie verändert, daß von einer Zeit zu der andern die humores und mores der Menschen verändert werden." Steffani, *Sendschreiben* (1760), 31–32.

20. Printz, *Musica modulatoria* (1678), 17–18.

21. Jüngken, *Leib-Artzt* (1699), 4.

22. Blankaart, *Reformirte Anatomie* (1691), 281.

23. Detry, *Betrachtung des Menschen* (1726), 121.

24. "Die Art und weis zu singen sei eines ieden Lands und Volcks eigen / iedes hab seinen sonderbaren stylum, so nach der natürlichen Complexion der Menschen und deß Lands Beschaffenheit sich richtet. . . . Die Teutschen haben ein kaltes Land / also ein kalte Complexion und grobe Stimm. Die Frantzosen sind frölicher leichter Natur / daher lieben sie auch am meisten den stylum hyporchematicum im Tantzen / Springen / Galliarden / Courente. . . . Die Italiäner aber haben den Vorzug in der Music / weil sie das allertemperirteste Land haben / also auch den allervollkommensten und temperirtesten stylum, so ihrer Natur gemäs ist." Kircher, *Musurgia universalis* (1662), 131–132.

25. Doni, *Compendio del trattato* (1635), 88.

26. "Das Feuer der Teutschen ist mehrentheils so beschaffen, daß es eine beständige gleiche Hitz von sich gibt, und nicht zu stark, noch zu schwach ist, und dahero weder verlöschet, noch verflattert," Spiess, *Tractatus musicus* (1745), 216.

27. Albrecht, *Tractatus physicus* (1734), 72.

28. Le Gallois, *Lettre de Mr Le Gallois* (1680), 40–44.

29. Earle, "'If You Eat Their Food . . . ,'" 688, 689. See also Bloechl, "Race, Empire, and Early Music."

30. Kircher, *Musurgia universalis* (1662), 259–260.

31. Smith, *Nature, Human Nature, and Human Difference*, 59. See also Jean Feerick's enlightening account of the "sanguinary nature" of early modern conceptions of race, in his *Strangers in Blood*, 10 and passim.

32. "Die Haut des Menschen wird schwarz, theils von der Sonne . . . , wie also bey den Mohren, Indianern und andern unter dem heißen Gürtel-Strich wohnenden Völkern, ihr hitziges Clima dergleichen Veränderung der Farbe und äußerlichen Gestalt verursachet, welche auch ihre schwarze Haut nicht verwandeln können . . . theils von Melancholie und Traurigkeit, wenn das zähe, dicke Geblüt gleichsam coagulirt, oder in den äußersten Aederlein stecken bleibt, und der äußern durchscheinenden Haut eine Schwärze mittheilet . . . theils von einer innern Ursache der Krankheit, da wegen der scharfen, die Haut durchfressenden Geschwüre, die einfallenden Licht-Stralen nicht . . . zurücke prallen, sondern eindringen und verschlucket werden." Schmidt, *Biblischer Medicus* (1743), 111–112.

33. Riskin, *The Restless Clock*, 79.

34. "Ferner hat auch unser unbegreiflicher Schöpffer einem jedem Dinge eine gewisse Krafft sich selbst zu bewegen und zu würcken anerschaffen. . . . Wie aber in einer

künstlichen Machine etwas seyn muß das alle Bewegungen derselben anhebet und verursachet . . . also ist auch in dem menschlichen Cörper / so lange er sein Leben hat / dergleichen anzutreffen / und zwar gedoppelt / nehmlich eine geistliche in Ansehung der Seelen und ihrer Kräffte und eine leibliche in Ansehung des Leibes und desselben Zubereitung." Hoffmann, *Gründliche Anweisung* (1716), vol. 2, 317–318.

35. See Merricks, "The Word Made Flesh," 281–300.

36. Rublack, "Fluxes," 2 (emphasis in original).

Chapter 9

1. Taussig, *Mimesis and Alterity*, xvii.

2. See various contributions in Kennaway, ed., *Music and the Nerves*.

3. Trippett, "Music and the Transhuman Ear," 200.

4. Hoffmann, *Dissertationes physico-medicae* (1708), 249.

5. Scheuchzer, *Kupfer-Bibel* (1735), 770.

6. On electrification in experiment and metaphor around 1800, see Lockhart, *Animation, Plasticity, and Music*, 133–150.

7. Alberti, *Matters of the Heart*, 39.

8. Wetherell, *Affect and Emotion*, 27.

9. DeLanda, *A Thousand Years of Nonlinear History*.

10. Cox, *Sonic Flux*, 2, 119.

11. Cox, *Sonic Flux*, 118.

12. See Kane, "Sound Studies without Auditory Culture," 9.

13. Cox, *Sonic Flux*, 7.

14. See Thompson, "Whiteness and the Ontological Turn."

15. Taussig, *Mimesis and Alterity*, xvii.

16. "Also werden auch alle Ding mit einem beständigen motu beweget: aus dieser immerwärenden Bewegung entstehet die Zusammen-stossung der Leiber: aus diser collision, nach dem die corpora sonora beschaffen sind / entstehen die unendliche Varietäten sonorum, welche zwar nicht allezeit / aber wohl köndten vernommen werden / wann das Gehör entweder durch höhere Göttliche Kraft / oder vermittelst eines sonderbahren Ohr-Instruments / corroborirt und gestärcket würde." Kircher, *Musurgia universalis* (1662), 12–13.

17. "Dann wann gantz keine Bewegung wäre in diser sichtbaren Welt / so wäre auch gantz keine Zusammenstossung der Leiber / wäre gantz keine Bewegung deß Lufts / gantz kein sonus noch schall / wäre alles unbeweglich / alles müste mit einem ewigen / der Natur gantz widrigen Stillschweigen versitzen und verdammet seyn." Kircher, *Musurgia universalis* (1662), 1.

18. "ein flüßiges und überaus bewegliches Wesen." Hoffmann, *Gründliche Anweisung* (1716), 342.

19. "dass unser gantzer Leib durch-wehend oder duchlufftet seye / und daß die Spaan- und Sehn-Ader / wie auch die so genannte Fleisch-Mäuse oder Musculi von dem äusserlichen Thon oder Hall / eben die impression und Fühlung haben / welche die auff leichtem und resonirendem Holtz auffgespannte Saitten empfinden." Kircher, *Neue Hall- und Thon-Kunst* (1684), 138.

20. "Sed non solum auditus organum Musica in homine afficitur, sed perquam probabile videtur, velocissimum motum a Musicis instrumentis concitatum cuti ac mox fluido nerveo sanguinique communicari, a quo fibrae crispantur, membranae,

nervi & musculi subsultant, et humores alterantur, aliquosque in motus adiguntur." Ettmüller, *Disputatio effectus musicae* (1714), 18.

21. Mead, *A Mechanical Account of Poisons* (1702), 71. For more on tarantism, see pp. 228–230.

22. Curzon, *The Universal Library* (1712), vol. 2, 121.

23. "dass der Klang nicht in der Lufft stecke / wie wir meynen; vielweniger, daß die klingende Corpora selbigen in sich halten . . . daß er sich nirgend / als in uns selbst ereigne / nachdem das Ohr gerühret und erschüttert wird." Mattheson, *Das forschende Orchestre* (1721), 7. We should note that his view may have been shaped in part by Mattheson's own encroaching deafness; see Cannon, *Johann Mattheson*, 59.

24. "Nein, sage mir doch / was ist den der Sonus oder Schall / der hier gleichsam aus dem Tode lebendig wird / für ein Ding? Ist es etwa ein Geist / der da in der Lufft liegt und schläfft / und dahero / wenn die Lufft durch die äusserliche Instrumenta beweget und beunruhiget wird / aufwachet / und auf das / was der Musicant ihn gleichsahm durch die Rührung seiner Stimme oder Instruments fraget / antwortet? Oder / ists ewa / wie kurz zuvor erwehnet / eine blosse Touchir-Berühr- und Pulsirung des Nervi acustici, oder auch der von der Natur eingeschaffenen Ohrlufft / welche Instrumenta Auditoria, wann Sie von der außwendigen Lufft gerühret und in die Bewegung gebracht sind / ferner den Sensum communem, oder auch den inwendig-residirenden Geist erwecken / welcher dann in dem Gehirn durch den inwendigen Schall auf das auswendig-gemachte Getümmel antwortet . . . und solcher massen der Geist des Musici mit dem Geist des Zuhörers communication pflege? . . . Oder endlich was ists? Du sprichst / Ich weiß es nicht; Und ich weiß es auch nicht: Ecce! Arcanum Soni et Musices." Calvör, "Vorrede" (1717), n.p.

25. Bacon, *Sylva Sylvarum* (1670), 45–46.

26. Bacon, *Sylva Sylvarum* (1670), 53.

27. "Wer hätte . . . wol anders als der unendlich weise Gott ein so herrliches und schönes Medium erfinden, angeben und machen können, welches alle und iede Eindrückungen und Bewegungen anzunehmen fähig wäre. . . . und die Melodey einer ieglichen gerührten Sayte, die harmonischen Schläge einer ieden lebendigen Stimme oder Pfeiffe und andern musicalischen Instruments dem Gehöre wieder zuführet? . . . daß vermittelst der curieusen Lage der Gehörnerven die Lebensgeister in geschwinde Bewegung gesetzet, und die Affecten grossen theils beweget oder wieder gestillet werden können . . . daß die Music nicht nur die Phantasie ergetzet, sondern auch unser Hertz von Kummer und Betrübniß entledigen, ja alle ungestümme und tobende Passiones des Gemüths beruhigen kann, die durch eine unmässige Gierung und Wallung im Geblüte in uns erreget worden?" Hecker, *Betrachtung des menschlichen Cörpers* (1734), 408–409. He is referencing the English theologian and scientist William Derham here.

28. "Das Gethöne oder der Schall beweget innerlich den Menschen / und führet ihn mit sich zu solchen Dingen, welche nicht vom Gehör herkommen können / als zur Erbarmung / zum Todtschlage / zur Unzucht / zur Faulheit / zur Raserey / zur Stilligkeit. . . . Daher / daß die Lebens-Geisterlein / so im Hertzen arbeiten / die zitternde und hüpffende Lufft in die Brust führen / und / weil sie ihres gleichen ist / sich mit derselben vereinigen. Dene folgen die andern Gemüths-Geisterlein in den übrigen Theilen des Leibes / und bewegen die Musculen / oder halten sie an sich / nachdem das Gethöne gemässiget wird . . . Gleich wie / wann auff der Geige oder anderm Seyten-Spiel die eine Seyte gerühret wird." Großgebauer, *Drey geistreiche*

Schrifften (1667), 192–193. The same passage is cited in several seventeenth-century English writers, including John Playford and Robert Burton. See Austern, *Both from the Ears and Mind*, 198–199.

29. Steffani, *Sendschreiben* (1760), 7.

Chapter 10

1. "un canal qui est touiours plain d'eau, quand elle coule." Mersenne, *Harmonie universelle* (1636), vol. 6, *L'Art de bien chanter*, 354.

2. Brockes, *Irdisches Vergnügen* (1739), vol. 2, 358.

3. Bloom, *Voice in Motion*, 6.

4. Binet, *Essay des merveilles* (1622), 520.

5. "Percioche per la dilatatione del petto si tira l'aere che raffredda, e tempra la soverchia caldezza del core, e per lo stringere si manda fuora tutto'l fumo, e tutti gli escrementi ch'ivi si trovano. Gli direi, che la materia della voce generalmente parlando . . . è l'espiratione; ma piu propriamente dicendo, è l'espiratione molto copiosa se con violenza mandata fuora." Maffei, *Delle lettere . . . libri due* (1562), 11, 17.

6. Larson, *The Matter of Song*, 5.

7. Sperling, *Principia musicae* (1705), 70; Mylius, *Rudimenta musices* (1686), n.p.

8. Fuhrmann, *Musica vocalis*, 50.

9. "Les qualitez de la voix peuvent estre reduites à trois differences, car elle est foible & forte, claire & rauque, grave & aigue: La forte se fait par le violent mouvement des muscles du thorax, la claire par l'humidité bien temperée des cartilages, des membranes, & des muscles du larynx, & la rauque par la trop grande humidité, ou secheresse des mesmes parties." Mersenne, *Harmonie universelle* (1636), vol. 5, *Traitez de la voix*, 6.

10. "Neben diesem bringt auch die Natürliche Beschaffenheit deß laryngis, welche in der Figur / Grösse / Sitz / Gang und superficie bestehet / underschied der Stimmen herfür: ist derselbe lang und rund / machts eine gleiche / helle / ungekrümte / unverkehrte Stimm; ist der meatus durch den laryngem weit und breit / so gibts eine grosse und tieffe Stimm . . . Der Luft macht auch underschiedene Stimmen: grober Luft macht ein grobe Stimm / reiner Luft ein reine Stimm; daher sind die Stimmen im Winter gröber als im Sommer." Kircher, *Musurgia universalis* (1662), 38–39.

11. Kircher, *Musurgia universalis* (1662), 156; Speer, *Unterricht* (1697), 3.

12. See Glüxam, "*Aus der Seele muß man spielen. . . ,*" 75.

13. Leppert, *The Sight of Sound*, xx. The following three paragraphs draw on my chapter "Early Modern Voices." Reused with permission of Oxford University Press.

14. "Ist das temperament feucht / ohne Zufluß anderer Feuchtigkeiten / so bringt sie herfür ein dunckele / dusele und confuse Stimm: ists aber mit andern humoribus angefüllt / so machts ein rauhe und heisere Stimm; Ist das Temperament trucken / so machts eine helle / klare / wohlerklingende Stimm." Kircher, *Musurgia universalis* (1662), 38.

15. Hast, *The Larynx, Organ of the Voice, by Julius Casserius*, 10.

16. "una voce piena, Sonora . . . per la qual buona voce si ricerca molto caldi, che allarghi le vie, e tanto humido, che le intenerisca, e mollifichi." Strozzi, *Le glorie*, 9. Cited in Rosand, *Opera in Seventeenth-Century Venice*, 232.

17. "Denn weil die Weibes Personen / sonderlich Jungfern von Natur reinere und hellere Stimmen haben / als die Männer / so können sie auch anmutiger singen /

bewegen auch das Hertze und Gemüthe vielmehr . . . Gratior est pulchro veniens e corpore cantus." Meißner, *Musica Christiana* (1664), n.p.

18. "Daher geschichts auch / daß die sich heftig förchten / keine andere / als eine geringe gebrochene Stimm von sich geben / dann in solcher Forcht gehet die Wärm under sich dem Hertzen zu / verlast die obern Theil / welche von solcher Wärm destituiret, anfangen zu erkalten / darnach zu erschwachen / letzlich eine geringe schwache Stimm von sich geben." Kircher, *Musurgia universalis* (1662), 40.

19. "Welche Menschen mit einer grossen Stimm gar grob schreyen / die werden von Aristot. under die Esel gerechnet / wird geschlossen / daß sie seyen homines injuriosi, contumeliosi, petulantes, das ist / boshaftige Leut: dann der Esel hat gar ein grosse und grobe Stimm / und ist darbey gantz indiscret, boshaftig / muthwillig. Die Ursach aber solcher starcken Stimm ist die grosse Luftröhren / dardurch viel Luft ausgeblasen wird; die Ursach der groben Stimm ist / wann der viele Luft gar langsam aus der Luftröhren ausgestossen wird: gehört also zur starcken Stimm / ein grosse / weite Brust / ein grosse arteria, dicker Hals . . . . Eine grobe tiefe Stimm aber entstehet aus Kälte und Langsame / zeiget an ein kaltes und truckenes . . . Temperament / wer damit begabet ist / der ist geitzig / forchtsam / indiscret, grob / stoltz." Kircher, *Musurgia universalis* (1662), 65.

20. "daß ein Vocalist / sonderlich Discantist und Altist / keusch und züchtig lebe / und dem Frauenzimmer durchaus nicht zu nahe komme / noch mit ihnen conversire: Weil der hohen Stimme nichts schädlichers / als die Conversation des Frauenvolckes." Printz, *Musica modulatoria* (1678), 19.

21. Duverney, *Treatise of the Organ of Hearing* (1737), 88–89.

22. Kircher, *Musurgia universalis* (1662), 185.

23. Descartes, *Excellent Compendium* (1653), 1–2.

24. Bacon, *Sylva Sylvarum* (1670), 210.

25. Chua, *Absolute Music*, 80.

26. LaMay, "Composing from the Throat," 367.

27. McClary, *Desire and Pleasure*, 89.

28. Wistreich, "'Inclosed in this Tabernacle,'" para. 1, 19.

29. "wie ein Leib / der eine blosse Machine ist / und vor sich keine Vernunfft hat / dennoch vernünfftig reden kan. . . . daß auch aus der Krafft des Leibes der Mund alle zu den Vernunffts-Schlüßen erforderte Worte vorbringen kan / ohne daß sich die Seele mit darein mischet." Wolff, *Vernünfftige Gedancken von Gott* (1720), 432, 463.

30. Brockes, *Irdisches Vergnügen* (1739), 363.

31. "daß die Lufft durch eine solche kleine und geringe Bewegung der Zungen / und darnach auch noch durch eine geringere Bewegung der Kelen oder des Halses / also auf mancherley Art und weise / nachdem wie es durch das Gemüth geregieret und gelencket wird / auch also kräfftig und gewaltig / Wort / Laut / Gesang / und Klang von sich geben könne / daß sie so fern und weit / gerings herum / von jedermann unterschiedlich / nicht allein gehöret / sondern auch verstanden und vernommen wird." Werckmeister, *Der Edlen Music-Kunst Würde* (1691), 37–38.

32. Connor, "Acousmania."

33. "der überaus gewaltige und zugleich süße Eindruck, welchen die Musik . . . auf unser Herz machet: so gar, daß wir beynahe zu glauben geneigt sind, sie werde einen Theil der Seligkeit des ewigen Lebens ausmachen." Tosi, *Anleitung zur Singkunst* (1757), xi.

34. Watkins, *Musical Vitalities*, 1.

35. "wenn wir eine künstliche Melodie singen hören, solche nothwendig von der Stimme einer lebendigen Creatur herkommen muß." Hecker, *Betrachtung des menschlichen Cörpers* (1734), 410.

Chapter 11

1. Cousser, *The Universal Applause* (1711), 3.

2. "Eine klingende Schelle oder Cymball ist ein Musicalisches Instrument / darauf ein vernünfftiger Spielmann eine so Hertz-Brennende Melodey or Reimen spielen kan / daß alle / die es hören / sich des Tantzens kaum enthalten können. Dennoch hat die Cymball kein Leben: die Music kommt nicht von ihr / sondern durch die Kunst dessen / der da spielt." Arnold, *Das Leben der Gläubigen* (1701), 919.

3. "Erstlich bedeuten sie eines wahren Christen Gott lobenden Mund und Hertz ja seinen gantzen Leib und alle Glieder desselben / welcher gleich einem Instrument durch den Heil. Geist angeblasen / geschlagen oder bewegt wird. . . . die Hertzen derselben / als so viele Harffen / Citharen / Posaunen und andere Instrumente nach ihrer besonderen Art / also anstimmt / daß alles einmüthig gerichtet ist zur Verherrlichung der Göttlichen Majestät." Ziegler, *Der Singende Christ* (1723), "Vorrede," n.p.

4. "Was bistu mit Leib und Seel / mit Augen / Ohren / Händen / Füssen / Mund / Lippen und Zunge / und derselben tausendfacher Bewegung / zuforderts / wenn du Stimm und Odem erhebest in einen Musicalischen-Gethöne anders / als ein woleingerichtetes / wolklingendes Harffen-Spiel." Calvör, "Vorrede" (1717), n.p.

5. Moser, *Heinrich Schütz*, 470.

6. *Heinrich Schütz, Great Motets*, Pro Cantione Antiqua, dir. Edgar Fleet, Alto ALC1118 (2010).

7. Levinson, *Music in the Moment*, 19. On structural listening, see Subotnik, *Deconstructive Variations*, 148–176.

8. Leonard, "The Role of the Trombone," 65.

9. Radice, *Chamber Music*, 21.

10. "Nihme die klägliche Trauer-Posaune / und blase mit betrübten Klang ein allgemeines Leyd aus." Raymundus, *Drey-tägige Trauer- und Lob-Rede* (1740), n.p.

11. Praetorius, *Syntagma musicum, tomus secundus* (1619), 14.

12. Ziegler, *Der singende Christ* (1723), "Vorrede," n.p.

13. "der Klang der Evangelischen Posaune ist biß an die äusserste Gränzen der Welt gehöret worden." Torsellini, *Apostolisches Leben* (1674), 564.

14. "wird von den Stadtpfeifern auf den Thürnen Rathhaußgänglein, in Kirchenmusiquen und bey andern Gelegenheiten gebraucht," Zedler, *Universal-Lexicon* (1731–1754), vol. 28, 1695–1696.

15. "ein recht Christliches Werck / und welches vor andern die Christlichen Hertzen zu Gottes Preiß und Ehre zu entzünden vermag! . . . Diese pflegen noch heutiges Tages alle Morgen auff hohen Thürmen einander zuzuruffen: La alla elle alla . . . Wievielmehr will uns Christen zustehen / alle Tage ja alle Stunden auff Gottes Ehre zu denken?" Pezel, *Hora decima* (1670), 4.

16. Gritten, "Resonant Listening," 116.

17. Zedler, *Universal-Lexicon* (1731–1754), vol. 28, 1696.

18. "a perito Musico ita debet inspirari, ut Tubae militaris sonos non imitetur, magisque accedat ad vocis suavitatem, ne reliquorum Instrumentorum, ipsarumque

vocum humanarum concentibus officiat, & sonum potius militarem quam pacificum edat." Mersenne, *Harmonicorum libri* (1635), vol. 2, 111.

19. "e di maniera imprime in altrui l'affetto di quelle parole, che è forza, e piangere e rallegrarsi secondo che egli vuole." Gagliano, *La Dafne* (1608), "A I Lettori," n.p. Translation in McClintock, ed., *Readings in the History of Music in Performance*, 189. See also Wistreich, "'La voce è grata assai,'" 18.

20. Scherertz, *Fuga melancholiae* (1682), 220.

21. Connor, "Edison's Teeth: Touching Hearing."

22. On "durus" and "mollis," see pp. 184–185.

23. Praetorius, *Syntagma musicum, tomus secundus* (1619), 32.

24. "So viel ist wohl gewiß / daß wenn man auf einem Instrumente in die Chromatic hinein gehet, es nicht anders seyn kan, als daß durch so eine langsame und herbe Bewegung, die Lebens-Geister eingeschläffert, und per consequenz die Circulation des Geblüthes, in seiner sonst schnellen Bewegung gleichsam ein wenig gehemmet, angehalten, und zu einer ernsthafften Aufmercksamkeit gebracht werden." Baron, *Untersuchung des Instruments der Lauten* (1727), 49.

25. Speer, *Unterricht* (1697), 276. On chromaticism and dissonance, see also pp. 217–223.

26. *Heinrich Schütz, Symphoniae Sacrae I*, dir. Hans-Christoph Rademann, Carus 83.273 (2017).

27. *Heinrich Schütz, Symphoniae Sacrae I*, Musica Fiata, dir. Roland Wilson, Deutsche HM 88697524182 (2010).

28. *Heinrich Schütz, Symphoniae Sacrae I*, Concerto Palatino, Accent ACC 30078 (2004).

Chapter 12

1. Newton, "General Scholium" (1729), 393.

2. See p. 50.

3. Rousseau, *Nervous Acts*, 18. See also Smith, *The Animal Spirit Doctrine.*

4. Gouk, "Music and Spirit," 223.

5. "1. Pro eo, quod plane immutabile est, ut Deus. 2. pro eo, quod materiae expers est, ut Angelus. 3. Pro corpore tenui et subtilissimo." Wirdig, *Nova medicina spirituum* (1673), n.p.

6. I borrow this phrase from Barbara Duden's inspiring monograph *The Woman Beneath the Skin.*

7. Paster, "Nervous Tensions," 110.

8. Sugg, *The Smoke of the Soul*, 3.

9. "Der Geist ist der dritte Theil des Menschen; dadurch der Mensch eigentlich von denen Thieren unterschieden wird. Es ist derjenige Theil / darinnen das Bilde Gottes beruhet / und wovon nach dem Fall des Menschen noch ein Zunder übrig geblieben." Detry, *Betrachtung des Menschen* (1726), 15. Explicitly trichotomist views such as his were often grounded in Paul's blessing in 1 Thessalonians 5:23.

10. Paster, "Nervous Tensions," 113.

11. Crooke, *Mikrokosmographia* (1615), 173–174.

12. "Es sollen die Lebens-Geister die geistreichen, zarten, flüchtigen und höchst beweglichen Theilgen des lebendigen Leibes seyn, welche . . . täglich durch die Speisen ersetzt, in dem Hirn und Hirnlein, wie auch einiger Massen in dem Rück-Marcke

von dem Puls-Ader-Blute abgesondert, durch die Nerven in alle Theile des Leibes geführet, und in unterschiedlichen Theilen auf mancherley Art verändert werden, und endlich der Bewegung aller Sinne, Empfindung und aller Functionen, welche nur in denen belebten Leibern vorfallen, Urheber und die würckende Ursache sind." Zedler, *Universal-Lexicon* (1731–1754), vol. 16, 650.

13. "die allerlebhafftesten u. geschwindesten Theile des Bluts, als wir die lebhaften Geister begreiffen können / steigen auf von der lincken Kammer des Hertzens durch die . . . Puls-Adern in die Hölen des Gehirns / alda sie verkehret werden in eine subtile Flamme oder Wind, der gemeiniglich der Spiritus animalis genennet wird." *Curioser Chirurgus* (1719), 33.

14. Paster, "Nervous Tensions," 117.

15. Boerhaave, *Academical Lectures* (1743), vol. 2, 297.

16. "ist leicht zu erkennen, daß im Gehirn von dem vielen zum Haupt hinauffliessenden Blut, ein nöthiger und zur Erhaltung des Lebens dienlicher Saft müsse abgesondert werden. Denn man kann sonst keine hinreichende Ursache eines so grossen Apparatus, Instrumenten und Theile angeben." Hecker, *Betrachtung des menschlichen Cörpers* (1734), 350–351.

17. Harvey, *Exercitatio anatomica* (1649), 59–60; translation in Harvey, *The Circulation of Blood*, 149.

18. Boerhaave, *Academical Lectures* (1743), vol. 2, 318.

19. On Cheyne, see Gouk, "Cosmic Vibrations," 18–24.

20. Boerhaave, *Academical Lectures* (1743), vol. 2, 310–311.

21. See Galvani, *De viribus electricitatis* (1791).

22. Park, "The Organic Soul."

23. "daß das drüsige Wesen des Gehiernes die Werckstat ist / wo die Lebens-Geister von dem subtilesten Blute der Puls-Adern abgesondert werden. Und demnach zeiget sich hier noch eine neue Ursache / warum alle Nerven aus dem Gehierne entspringen / nemlich daß sie daher die Lebens-Geister erhalten / wodurch der Leib belebt oder gleichsam beseelet wird." Wolff, *Vernünfftige Gedancken Von dem Gebrauche* (1725), 461.

24. Sugg, *The Smoke of the Soul*, 4.

25. Helmont, *The Spirit of Diseases* (1694), 26–27.

26. Varela, Thompson, and Rosch, *The Embodied Mind*, xxvii.

27. Bucher, *Brief-Wechsel* (1713), 19.

28. Crick, *The Astonishing Hypothesis*.

29. See Dennett, *Darwin's Dangerous Idea*, 82.

30. "Überdem allen hat der Leib von dem Umtriebe des Geblüthes noch diesen besondern herrlichen Nutzen / dass durch Hülffe desselben Leib und Seele aufs festeste verknüpfet und verbunden werden. . . . daß die Verrichtungen unserer Seele eben so befunden werden / als wie unser Blut durch das Gehirn seinen Lauff hat. Wenn derselbe schnell gehet / so fähret das Gemüth auch hurtig drein." Hoffmann, *Gründliche Anweisung* (1716), vol. 2, 330–331.

31. Bacon, *Sylva Sylvarum* (1670), 200.

32. "daß der Biß eines in Zorn gebrachten Menschen, den andern dergestalt in Raserey gesetzet, daß er davon sterben müssen." Hecker, *Betrachtung des menschlichen Cörpers* (1734), 360.

33. See Reardon, *Holy Concord*, 109.

34. "dann etliches ist sehr subtil, und kommet der geistlichen Natur sehr nahe, als welches mit und in der Lufft ausgetheilet . . . gleichwie ein Leib den andern inficiret

und anstecket die Geister oder Seelen der Mensch noch vielmehr in distanz die Emanation derer Seelen-Kräffte empfinden und davon angestecket gerühret." Detry, *Betrachtung des Menschen* (1726), 165, 167.

35. Democritus, *Kranckheit und Arzney* (1713), 41.

36. "ut agnitio Dei sit illustrior, et adsensio firmior et motus sint ardentiores erga Deum." Melanchthon, *Liber de anima* (1560), "De Spiritibus," n.p.

37. Wels, *Manifestationen des Geistes*, 95. See also McDonald, "Melanchthon's Theory of Spirit." The legacy of Ficino looms large in early modern accounts of spirit; see Tomlinson, *Music and Renaissance Magic*, 101–139.

38. "Wie das Wasser durchs Feur erwärmet wird / so macht der H. Geist durch den Glauben das Hertz warm / milde und fliessend zu allem Guten." Müller, *Himmlischer Liebes-Kuß* (1724), 481.

39. "der Geist Gottes ists / welcher anstimmt / damit das Gesang seinen fortgang habe / das ist / das es durch das Hertz gehe . . . . Darumb wir sinds nicht / die wir also Geistlich singen oder reden / sondern der Geist unsers himlischen Vatters ists / der in uns wohnet." Saubert, *SeelenMusic* (1624), 10.

40. Agrippa, *Three Books of Occult Philosophy* (1651), 257.

Chapter 13

1. "Marteria autem vocis est aer seu spiritus." Sennert, *Medicinae practicae tomus primus* (1641), 461.

2. Rathey, *Bach's Major Vocal Works*, 128–129; Elferen, *Mystical Love in the German Baroque*, 289.

3. Chafe, *Analyzing Bach Cantatas*, 244; Gardiner, *Music in the Castle of Heaven*, 423.

4. Heuss, *Johann Sebastian Bachs Matthäuspassion*, 129; cited in Melamed, "How Did," 5.

5. Head, "C. P. E. Bach 'In Tormentis,'" 211–234.

6. Melamed, "How Did."

7. Butt, *Bach's Dialogue with Modernity*, 136.

8. See p. 64.

9. "der Sonus und Harmonia der Violen und Geigen continuiret sich immer nach einander mit sonderbarer Liebligkeit / ohne einige respiration, deren man uff Posaunen und andern blasenden Instrumenten nicht entrathen kann." Praetorius, *Syntagmatis musici tomus tertius* (1619), 136.

10. "weil sie fürnehmlich in der Natur stekken / welche dieselben auch einem ieden Menschen an zu töhnen eingepflantzet hat." Ahle, "Anmerkungen" (1704), 22.

11. *Elin Manahan Thomas, Eternal Light*, Universal Music 4765970 (2007). Jeffrey Levenberg reflects on the out-of-tuneness of much of this music in the context of the Monteverdi-Artusi debate in his "*Seconda Pratica* Temperaments."

12. Cooper, "In a Season of Boys' Choirs."

13. *J. S. Bach—Matthäus Passion—Aus Liebe—sopran aria*, https://www.youtube.com/watch?v=Ec40c_r-5s8.

14. Mecke, "Johann Sebastian Bachs Sopranisten," 189–206.

15. "lauter Himmelsböhrlein und Hertz-friemerlein / damit ihr Gott dem Herrn könnet das Hertz durchgraben." Frick, *Music-Büchlein* (1631), 96. He is referencing the Lutheran theologian Valerius Herberger here.

16. Fuhrmann, *Musicalischer Trichter* (1706), 80.

17. Mattheson, *Der vollkommene Capellmeister* (1739), 94.

18. See for instance Mattheson, *Der vollkommene Capellmeister* (1739), 95; his explanation is based on Athanasius Kircher.

19. Mattheson, *Der vollkommene Capellmeister* (1739), 14. On cracking voices, see also Bloom, *Voice in Motion*, 21–65.

20. See Bloom, *Voice in Motion*, 40.

21. "von Natur eine schöne / lieblich / bebende und zum trillo bequeme Stimme und glatten runden Hals haben . . . einen steten langen Athem / ohne viel respiriren oder Athem holen." Mylius, *Rudimenta musices* (1686), 43–44.

22. Quirsfeld, *Breviarum Musicum* (1695), 28.

23. See Falck, *Idea boni cantoris* (1688), 91–92; Fuhrmann, *Musica vocalis*, 49–51.

24. "so stark schreyen / daß sie erschwartzen / und die Augen verkehren wie ein gestochener Bock . . . und ehe für ein Geschrey bezechter Bauren oder heulender Hunde / als eine zierliche Music gehalten werden möchte." Printz, *Musica modulatoria* (1678), 8.

25. Connor, "Strains of the Voice."

26. Printz, *Musica modulatoria* (1678), 12.

27. Heuermann, *Physiologie Zeweyter Theil* (1752), 42. See also Müller, *Seelen-Musik* (1684), 89, who describes the tongue as a bell whose rope is connected to the heart.

28. "unreiner / neblichter / sehr kalter oder hitziger Lufft / Nordwinden / Rauch und Staub / sonderlich von Flachs und Kalck." Printz, *Musica modulatoria* (1678), 17.

29. Printz, *Musica modulatoria* (1678), 20. See also Butt, *Music Education*, 77–87.

30. See for example *Vade-mecum curiosum* (1694), 33.

31. Mattheson, *Der vollkommene Capellmeister* (1739), 20. Mattheson drew his advice from the French physician Denis Dodart; see Butt, *Music Education*, 86.

32. Mattheson, *Der vollkommene Capellmeister* (1739), 98, 96–97.

33. Gildon, *The Life of Mr. Thomas Betterton* (1710), 100. Gildon is referencing the views of Plutarch here. See Roach, *The Player's Passion*, 49.

34. "daß die Kinder offt böse und sträffliche Gemüths-Bewegungen mit der Milch an sich trincken / die ihnen Lebenslang anhencken / ja auch wol schwere und unheilsame Kranckheiten auf sich erben können." Hohberg, *Georgica curiosa* (1687), 278. On the racial implications of contemporary anxieties around wet-nursing, see Feerick, *Strangers in Blood*, 55–77.

35. Floyer, *The Physician's Pulse-Watch* (1707), 179. In early modern anatomy, the term "chyle" described a variety of digestive fluids; it now refers to the milky liquid formed in the small intestine during digestion.

36. Conboy et al., "Rejuvenation of Aged Progenitor Cells."

37. "Ob zwar im Singen die Variationes notarum heutiges Tages nicht mehr in Usu, daß man auf denen Noten viel Coloraturen mache / wo sie der Componist nicht gesetzt." Beyer, *Primae lineae* (1703), 60.

38. Quirsfeld, *Breviarum Musicum* (1695), 28.

39. "Hinweg mit den neuen lächerlichen wälschen Sprüngen und Sirenen-Liedern / die nicht nach der geistlichen Herzens, sondern üppigen Welt-Freude zielen!" Johann Conrad Dannhauer, as cited in Ahle, "Anmerkungen," (1704), 81. See also Butt, *Music Education*, 121–165, for a more detailed exploration of changing attitudes to ornamentation.

40. Gibson, "Hearing the Viola da Gamba," 431–436.

41. "In der Ergötzung oder Belustigung sind die Hirnsäffte in einem angenehmen und sanfft streichelnden Fluß / als welcher gestalt sie unserer Seele eine liebliche Bewegung mittheilen . . . so daß alle Theile des Hertzens und verschiedene andere Leibes Glieder / durch solche genaue Ubereinstimmung der Sennadern anmuthig beweget werden / ingleichen auch der Umlauff aller Säffte unseres Leibes viel ordentlicher / als sonsten gehet / worvon in dem gantzen Leib eine angenehme Wärme entstehet." Blankaart, *Reformirte Anatomie* (1691), 287.

Chapter 14

1. Bourdelot, *Histoire de la musique* (1715), 150.

2. Malik et al., "Mammalian Taste Cells."

3. Li, "Taste Perception."

4. Bacon, *Sylva Sylvarum* (1670), 32.

5. See Favier and Couvreur, eds., *Le Plaisir Musical*, 20.

6. Mattheson, *Der vollkommene Capellmeister* (1739), 66.

7. Mattheson, *Das forschende Orchestre* (1721), 66.

8. Hecker, *Betrachtung des menschlichen Cörpers* (1734), 404.

9. "macht darauf eine Eindrückung in den Nerven, wodurch denn der Nerven-Saft erschüttert und zu dem Gehirn fortgeführet wird, woselbsten die Vorstellung des Schalles geschiehet." Heuermann, *Physiologie Zeweyter Theil* (1752), 807.

10. "von übel beschaffenen spiritibus, wann diesen flatus untermischt werden / oder wann sie . . . durch die gewaltsame Pressung sehr aus einander getrieben und starck beweget werden." Jüngken, *Grund-Reguln* (1701), 143.

11. "Causa est humoris, in tubulis Aurium collecti et stagnantis." Zwinger, *Compendium medicinae universae* (1724), 191. On early modern conceptions of deafness, see also Verwaal, "Fluid Deafness."

12. Barrough, *The Method of Physick* (1624), 63.

13. I borrow this phrase from Ihde, *Listening and Voice*, 115.

14. "bey Anhörung einer angenehmen Sache die Bewegung der Lebensgeister nicht nur in den Gehör-Nerven, sondern aus diesem ebenermassen auch durch den Nervum intercostalem, in die Nerven des Hertzens, Lungen etc. stärcker einfliessen müsse." Heuermann, *Physiologie Zweyter Theil* (1752), 797–798.

15. Brockes, *Irdisches Vergnügen* (1739), vol. 2, 949.

16. Wolff, *Vernünfftige Gedancken Von dem Gebrauche* (1725), 406.

17. See p. 61.

18. "Zur Andacht kan nichts mehr bereiten / Zur Freude dient nicht grössre Lust / Als wenn in beyden unsre Brust Vernimmt den Ton der süssen Sayten." Mattheson, *Exemplarische Organisten-Probe* (1719), n.p.

19. Hellwig, *Lexicon* (1713), 859.

20. "Wer die ohren des hertzens nicht aufthut / die stimme des Herrn zu hören / der ist verhärtet und vertäubt im hertzen / ist ein verdorben werckzeug auf erden / und stehet unterm urtheil der verdammnis." Arnold, *Unpartheyische Kirchen- und Ketzer-Historie* (1700), vol. 2, 513.

21. Watzel, *Der predigende Augustinus* (1756), 236.

22. "Deine Herzens-Thüren sind die Augen / Ohren / und der Mund / die stehen

am Tage weit offen / dadurch gehet offt hinein / was die innere Andacht zerstöret." Müller, *Seelen-Musik* (1684), 75–76.

23. *The Burwell Lute Tutor*, cited in Craig-McFeely, "The Signifying Serpent," 303.

24. "daß der Sinn des Fühlens, der allgemeineste ist, und die übrigen Sinne nur gleichsam unterschiedene Arten desselben sind." Heister, *Compendium anatomicum* (1721), 125. This notion goes back to Tommaso Campanella's pronouncement, "tutti li sensi esser tatto." See Heller-Roazen, *The Inner Touch*, 170.

25. Newton, *Opticks* (1730), 166–167.

26. "Berühret nun die gedrückte Lufft die Paucke des Ohrs / oder die Sonnen-Strahlen die Nerven der Augen / oder rauhe / schwere / kalte und warme Cörperchen die Haut / drücken sich in dieselbe und gelangen zum Nervensafft / so muß derselbe nothwendig von aussen bey der Berührung eingedruckt / fortgestossen / und das innerste im Gehirne . . . erhoben werden." Feind, *Deutsche Gedichte* (1708), 12–13.

27. "Ja es werden oft unsere Leiber und Herzen erzitteren von gewissem Hall / und Klang der Trompeten / oder einer grossen Orgel." Scheuchzer, *Physica* (1711), vol. 1, 84.

28. Koelsch, *Brain & Music*. For a more holistic account of hearing, see for instance Serres, *The Five Senses*, 106–111.

29. "variae et determinatae tum solidorum, tum fluidorum mutationes producerentur, atque ex his explicarentur effectus Musices in corpus animatum." Albrecht, *Tractatus physicus* (1734), 109–110, 115.

30. See, for example, Kennaway, *Bad Vibrations*.

31. Guarini, *Rime* (1598), 119r. Cited and translation in Wistreich, "Of Mars I Sing," 76.

32. Erlmann, *Reason and Resonance*, 9–27.

33. "daß die Sinnliche Geister von starkem / oder auf gewisse Weiß eingerichtetem Don gleichsam aufgewekt werden / daß sie das in dem Geblüt steckende Gift außtreiben / oder andere mit den Dönen übereinstimmende Bewegungen verursachen." Scheuchzer, *Physica* (1711), vol. 1, 90.

34. "Der Klang der Music, welcher vielmehr spirituel als materialisch ist / wird mittelbar / zugleich mit der von demselben bewegten Lufft ausgebreitet und dem Gehöre zugeführet; Er durchdringet auch die festen Cörper / aber vielmehr unsere menschliche Cörper / als welche sehr lockericht und voll von Poris sind; Er geht uns nicht nur in die Ohren / sondern auch ans Hertze selbst / welches die Werckstatt der Lebens-Geister / die im Gehirn / in und um das Hertz herum / und in den übrigen Theilen des Leibes zerstreuet sind. Die Lebens-Geister / welche aus einem sehr zarten und beweglichen Blut-Dampff / bestehen / werden auch gar leicht von der Harmonisch- oder Musicalisch-bewegten Lufft beweget; welche Bewegung / weil die Seele sie fühlet / nach unterschiedlicher solcher Geist-Bewegung / auch unterschiedene Gemüths-Bewegungen erzeiget." Raupach, *Veritophili Deutliche Beweis-Gründe* (1717), 19.

35. On immersive listening as a category of historical analysis, see also Holzmüller, "Between Things and Souls."

36. See Juslin, *Musical Emotions Explained*, 250.

37. Braithwait, *Essaies upon the Five Senses* (1620), 6.

38. "wann wir eine lieblich und anmuthige Music, Lied / oder Thon hören / Wir / so zu reden gleichsam einen Kützel oder liebliches Jucken in dem Hertzen

und Gemüthe fühlen." Kircher, *Neue Hall- und Thon-Kunst* (1684), 127. See also Thomas Wright describing music as "a certaine artificiall shaking, crispling, or tickling of the ayre" that "beateth and tickleth" the heart, in his *The Passions of the Minde* (1604), 170.

39. Schneider, "Die aisthetische Dimension der Geistwesen," 16. For a contemporary take on this mode of hearing "with our whole bodies, not just our ears," see Guck, "Analysis as Interpretation."

40. Raupach, *Veritophili Deutliche Beweis-Gründe* (1717), 54.

Chapter 15

1. Nancy, *Listening*, 12.

2. Dammann, *Der Musikbegriff*, 316.

3. South, *Musica incantans* (1700), 6; Moulinié, *Airs* (1624), cited in Favier and Couvreur *Le Plaisir musical*, 209. On ravishment, see also pp. 174–175.

4. Morley, *A Plaine and Easie Introduction* (1597), 297.

5. "Sed non ab omnibus concentibus Musicis omnes aequaliter homines efficiuntur . . . . Sunt enim, qui hoc, alii, qui alio delectantur instrumento Musico, alio hoc, alii alio modo Musico flecti se patiuntur. Causa hujus est diversa natura, textura, constitutio et temperamentum diversum corporum humanorum id est differunt spiritus volatilitate, humores fluxilitate, partes solidae tensione." Ettmüller, *Disputatio effectus musicae* (1714), 22.

6. Fuhrmann, *Musica vocalis*, 46. The reference to "thick" ears goes back to a biblical image in Isaiah 6:10, "laß ihre Ohren / dicke sein." Luther, *Die Propheten all Teutsch* (1561), 8.

7. "In dünnem Hirn können sich die Geister besser bewegen / welche / wann es dick / stecken bleiben." Beverwijck, *Schatz der Ungesundheit* (1672), 359.

8. Fuhrmann, *Musicalischer Trichter* (1706), 15.

9. Fuhrmann, *Musicalischer Trichter* (1706), 26.

10. Clarke, *Ways of Listening*, 19.

11. Bacon, *The Essays* (1696), 19. For the sixteenth-century background to these theories, see Weststeijn, "Seeing and the Transfer of Spirits."

12. "Il est certain, qu'il y a dans nos yeux une source de lumiere, & qu'elle pousse incessamment ses rayons au dehors . . . ces traits lumineux ne sont que des esprits." Chalussay, *Morale galante* (1669), vol. 2, 8–10.

13. Brockes, *Irdisches Vergnügen* (1739), 326.

14. "An die Spitzen der Finger und zähen des Fusses, wo vornehmlich das besondere Gefühl seinen Sitz hat und die Nerven-Wärtzgen sich befinden, daselbsten hält man davor, daß bey der Berührung einer Sach die Nerven-Wärtzgen jederzeit sich in etwas verlängern, und weiter heraus begeben, um desto genauer von der Beschaffenehit einer Sache sich zu erkundigen." Heuermann, *Physiologie Zweyter Theil* (1752), 494.

15. Heuermann, *Physiologie Zweyter Theil* (1752), 494.

16. Brockes, *Irdisches Vergnügen* (1739), 193–194.

17. Vogt, *Conclave thesauri* (1717), 25.

18. Hecker, *Betrachtung des menschlichen Cörpers* (1734), 404. On this etymology, see also Home-Cook, *Theatre and Aural Attention*, 2.

19. Watkins, *Musical Vitalities*, 2.

20. "denn es ist ein zärtlich Ding ums Gehör und um unsere Andacht / so bald ermüdet und ausreisset." Raupach, *Veritophili Deutliche Beweis-Gründe* (1717), 12.

21. Raupach, *Veritophili Deutliche Beweis-Gründe* (1717), 32.

22. Dell'Antonio, *Listening as Spiritual Practice.*

23. On rests, see Walther, *Praecepta*, 52; on unison writing, see for example Bach, *Versuch* (1762), 173.

24. Nicolai, *Die Verbindung der Musik* (1745), 9, 22.

25. "Weil alle Sinnen im Gefühl bestehen / und solches am ersten / von dem beständigen Betasten einerley Dinges / ermüdet und dermassen stumpff gemacht wird / daß nicht nur Mangel an Lebens-Geistern / sondern offt eine gäntzliche Fühllosigkeit daraus entstehet. . . . Es findet ja das Gehör keine grössere Belustigung / als in der Abwechslung so vieler Töne / Lieder und Melodien: in diesem Fall höret sich das Ohr nimmer satt." Niedt, *Musicalischer Handleitung Anderer Theil* (1721), 2.

26. "Le plus bel ornament des oreilles d'un Chrêtien est qu'elles soient bien disposes & toûjours prestes à écouter avec attention, & recevoir avec soûmission les instructions qui regardent la religion & les maxims du saint Evangile." De La Salle, *Les regles* (1708), 8. Translation in De La Salle, *The Spirituality of Christian Education*, 174.

27. See Seow, *Sensing Corporeality*, 37–45.

28. Wright, *A display of dutie* (1589), 34.

29. "Gottes Wort mit desto grösserer Lust und Nachdruck den Leuten mehrmals gar tieff ins Hertz gepflantzet worden." Raupach, *Veritophili Deutliche Beweis-Gründe* (1717), 31.

30. On text audibility, see my article "Distributed Listening," 214–219.

31. "Die Lieblichkeit des Gesanges dienet darzu / daß die Nutzbarkeit der schönen Worte durchs Gehör eher ergriffen werde / ehe wirs selber mercken." Müller, *Seelen-Musik* (1684), 7.

32. "Was auch die beredteste und eyffrigste Prediger mit äussersten Droh- und Versprechungen nicht können zuweg bringen . . . eißkalte Hertzen schmeltzen / harte erweichen / und endlich in der Stille die Zäher mit Gewalt hervordringen." Spiess, *Tractatus musicus* (1745), "Vorrede," n.p.

33. Tomlinson, "Fear of Singing," 119.

34. "die aufmercksamen Gemüther / gleichsam mit Gewalt und zu einem annehmlichen / verliebten oder andächtigen Trauren zwinget." Printz, *Phrynis Mitilenaeus* (1696), 91.

35. Printz, *Musica modulatoria* (1678), 12.

36. Vogt, *Conclave thesauri* (1717), 100.

37. Kevorkian, *Baroque Piety*, 29–52.

38. Niedt, *Musicalischer Handleitung Dritter und letzter Theil* (1717), 54.

39. "Das Jucken der Ohren; . . . da sie nur mit liebkosenden Reden, und solchen Predigten, welche nach eiteler menschlichen Weisheit eingerichtet sind, wollen gekrauet seyn, welches dem Fleische zwar sanft thut, aber desto mehr Schmerzen dem Geiste hinterläßt." Schmidt, *Biblischer Medicus* (1743), 217.

40. Niedt, *Musicalische Handleitung Oder Gründlicher Unterricht* (1710), chapter 2, n.p.

41. "Ihren Ohren jücket nach etwas neues / und wo man nicht mit allerhand Veränderungen einer flüchtigen und wilden Composition, welches sich besser auf dem Theatro schicket / und wornach man eher tantzen als eine Andacht zum Lobe

Gottes erwecken kan / das auditorium amusiret / rumpffet man bald die Nase / und gehet wol gar zur Kirchen hinaus." Meyer, *Unvorgreiffliche Gedancken* (1726), 55.

42. "wie die Spinnen / bey welchen der aus den süssen Blumen von ihnen gesogener schöner Safft / sich nachmals in Gifft verwandelt." Raupach, *Veritophili Deutliche Beweis-Gründe* (1717), 47.

Chapter 16

1. Dixon, *From Passions to Emotions.* On this point, see also Stolberg, "Emotions and the Body," 117.

2. For an overview, see Rosenwein and Cristiani, *What Is the History of Emotions?*

3. See Schnell, *Haben Gefühle eine Geschichte?*

4. Sullivan, "The Role of the Arts," 118.

5. Plamper, *The History of Emotions*; Boddice, *The History of Emotions*; Maddox and Davidson, "Music."

6. Scheer, "Are Emotions a Kind of Practice."

7. Mattheson, *Der vollkommene Capellmeister* (1739), 224–234.

8. Scherertz, *Fuga melancholiae* (1682), 222.

9. Wright, *The Passions of the Minde* (1604), 64.

10. Descartes, *Principia philosophiae* (1644), 18.

11. "Wenn aber das Denk-Bild von etwas angenehmen oder widrigen uns eingebracht wird, so fließen die Geister in Kraft der Vereinigung der Seele mit dem Leibe weiter fort, und überschwemmen alle Theile des Leibes, gleich als ein Regen-Bach, ie nach Verschiedenheit der erregten Paßion . . . also wird auch durch die erregten Affecten das Gleichgewicht zwischen Leib und Seele, oder zwischen dem Einfluß der sinnlichen Geister in die äußern Theile und der Bewegung des Geblüts, der Nerven und der Blut-Adern aufgehoben." Schmidt, *Biblischer Medicus* (1743), 57.

12. "daß die sinnlichen Geister in dem Gehirn aufgemuntert werden, und in den ganzen Leib, in die Augen, Ohren, und andere Werkzeuge der Sinnen ausfließen, daher man alsdenn scharf siehet, das Gehör spannet; ja so werden sie auch dem Herzen und der Brust häufig zugeleitet, damit das Herz seine Kräfte anwenden kann, zu desto stärkerer Ausprützung des Geblüts, weswegen den in der Liebe das Angesicht oft erröthet, und eine angenehme Wärme in der Brust und dem ganzen Leibe empfunden wird, wie den der Liebe Eigenschaft ist, daß sie brünstig sey. . . . Weil auch das Geblüt aus der linken Herz-Kammer mit großer Gewalt und Heftigkeit in die Puls-Adern ausgesprützet wird, so geht der Puls stark und das Herz klopft heftig. . . . Oefters ist die Liebe sehr peinlich . . . und alsdenn werden die sinnlichen Geister oder der Nerven-Saft Meister über das Herz, und treiben das Geblüt von denen äußern Theilen züruck, daß das Angesicht erblasset, der Leib in eine Ohnmacht fällt, oder sonst krank, und matt wird." Schmidt, *Biblischer Medicus* (1743), 61.

13. "eine Abzehrung, so das Mark in den Knochen verzehret, und den Leib Tag und Nacht abfrisset." Schmidt, *Biblischer Medicus* (1743), 64.

14. Mattheson, *Der vollkommene Capellmeister* (1739), 17.

15. "Denn wenn dem Menschen traurige Gedancken aufsteigen, so haben die sogenannten sinnlichen Geister das Uebergewicht über das Herz, weil dieses von dem übermäßigen Anlauf des Geblüts, gleichsam überschwemmet, gedrucket und in die Enge gezogen, mithin die Brust gleich als mit Stricken gebunden wird . . . . Der Umlauf des Geblüts gehet durch die äußersten Aederlein gar sacht und gemächlich fort,

um so vielmehr, da es sich immer mehr und mehr verdicket und verstopfet. Daher die ganze Haut sich gleichsam einziehet, als wollte sie dem bevorstehenden Uebel entfliehen und sich in Sicherheit bringen; der ganze äußere Leib erbleichet und erkaltet, schwindet und nimmt merklich ab. . . . das ganze Angesicht wird dunkel . . . . Die Haare werden steifer und leicht grau. . . . der Verstand hat keine Lebhaftigkeit in sich; die Rede bestehet in betrübten Worten; die Stimme ist kläglich und mit stetem Seufzen vermischt." Schmidt, *Biblischer Medicus* (1743), 67–68.

16. "Denn so erweitert sich [das Herz] in einer starken Ausssprützung des Geblüts in die äußern Glieder, in Ausfüllung aller äußersten holen Blut-Röhrlein, damit iedoch auch ein geschwinder Lauf der sinnlichen Geister, und folglich mehrere Hurtigkeit des ganzen Leibes verbunden ist. Daher bey frölichen Leuten alles lebet und hüpfet (Luc. 6, 23). Sie spüren eine annehmliche Wärme in dem ganzen Leibe; das Angesicht ist schön und roth von Farbe; Die Stimme ist aufgeklärt; der Mund redet mehr als sonsten, jauchzet und singet zuweilen, Es. 16, 10. Ps. 65, 14. . . . in den Gedanken schwebet nichts, als dasjenige Vergnügen, das man genießet; und alle Werke richten sich dahin, daß man seines Vergnügens recht genießen möge." Schmidt, *Biblischer Medicus* (1743), 65.

17. Myers, *Psychology*, 500.

18. Callard and Papoulias, "Affect and Embodiment," 257. Callard and Papoulias are reporting on Antonio Damasio's work.

19. Bacon, *Sylva Sylvarum* (1670),150.

20. "Denn wenn das Blut aus Verstopfung der Adern / so man Mesaraicas nennet / so wol der Miltz verderbet ist / so werden die Spiritus vitales / und das Hertz samt dem Gehirn sehr verletzet . . . . Hierauß erregen sich allerley ungesunde Humores, oder Feuchtigkeiten / die der Brust die Lufft benehmen / und wie Wolcken und Nebel in das Haupt steigen, das Organon, und Werckzeug der Vernunfft verletzen / und allerley seltzame betrübte / auch offt ungeheure Gedanken im Gemüthe formiren." Scherertz, *Fuga melancholiae* (1682), 21.

21. Albrecht, *Tractatus physicus* (1734), 59–60, 103.

22. Bacon, *Sylva Sylvarum* (1670), 32.

23. "Wer disen Consens zwischen dem spiritu animali und dem Affect / wie auch zwischen dem inner- und äusserlichen Luft vollkomlich verstehen solte / der würde einen ieglichen Menschen nur blos mit der Stimm in alle Affecten / wie er wil / bewegen können." Kircher, *Musurgia universalis* (1662), 153–154.

24. Cox, *Music and Embodied Cognition*, 5.

25. *Gasparo Zanetti: Il scolaro*, Musica Antiqua, dir. Christian Mendoze, Disques Pierre Verany PV.792012 (1992).

26. *Vivaldi, Vespri per L'Assunzione di Maria Vergine*, Concerto Italiano, Rinaldo Alessandrini, Naïve OP30475 (2008).

27. "Denn ob man gleich nicht wircklich in der Kirche mit den Füssen hüpffet und springet, so hüpffet und springet manchem Zuhörer doch offt das freudige Hertz im Leibe, wenn er eine pathetische, muntere Harmonie vernimmt, und sich dabey die ewige Glorie und Herrlichkeit nur im Schatten vorstellet . . . . Was bedeutet das in der heil. Schrifft so offt vorkommende Wort, exultare, anders, als tantzen, hüpffen, aufspringen, jauchtzen." Mattheson, *Der musicalische Patriot* (1728), 17.

28. Kircher, *Musurgia universalis* (1662), 138.

29. "Also wann ein Mensch in seiner Devotion stehet / in Betrachtung himlischer Ding / und man bringt ihm deroselben Süssigkeit und Liebligkeit in das Gedächt-

nus / durch ein schöne darzu erfundene Harmony / da wird man sehen / wie plötzlich er in äusserliche Affecten und raptus mentis, durch die harmonische Süssigkeit wird commovirt werden." Kircher, *Musurgia universalis* (1662), 137. On sweetness, see also p. **xxx**.

30. Mattheson, *Der vollkommene Capellmeister* (1739), 16.

31. Grant, "Music Lessons," 40.

32. Mattheson, *Der vollkommene Capellmeister* (1739), 17. See also the chapter "Von den Sinnen" in his *Das forschende Orchestre* (1721) for a longer exposition.

33. Mattheson, *Der vollkommene Capellmeister* (1739), 17.

34. Mithobius, *Psalmodia* (1665), 49.

Chapter 17

1. Scheibe, *Critischer Musikus* (1745), 85.

2. "comme si l'ame . . . se fut retiree au bord des oreilles." Binet, *Essay des merveilles* (1622), 503.

3. Austern, *Both from the Ears and Mind*, 186–188.

4. Descartes, *Les passions de l'âme* (1649), translated as *The Passions of the Soul*, Art. 70, 223.

5. Tomlinson, "Sign, Affect, and Musicking."

6. Steffani, *Sendschreiben* (1760), 40.

7. "ich weiß nicht, was mehr vermischtes empfinden." Steffani, *Sendschreiben* (1760), 39–40.

8. Ban, *Kort Sangh-Bericht* (1643), cited in Walker, "Joan Albert Ban," 240.

9. Raupach, *Veritophili Deutliche Beweis-Gründe* (1717), 22.

10. Caussin, *The Holy Court* (1650), 46.

11. *Barbara Strozzi, Diporti di Euterpe*, Emanuela Galli, Ensemble Galilei, dir. Paul Beier, Stradivarius STR33487 (2013).

12. "la Musique separe en quelque maniere l'esprit du corps, & le met dans un estat, où il est plus propre à la contemplation qu'à l'action . . . les mouvements tardifs des airs tristes . . . ramenent l'esprit à soy-mesme, lequel à plus de loisir de contempler la beauté de la voix . . . le ravissent dans une plus profonde speculation." Mersenne, *Harmonie universelle* (1636), vol. 2, *Des chants*, 174–175.

13. For more on this Telemann chorus, see my article "Musical Expression," 69–71.

14. "Nous ne cognoistrons pas la raison pourquoy une configuration, ou un movement donne plus de Plaisir l'un que l'autre." Mersenne, *Harmonie universelle* (1636), vol. 2, *Des chants*, 177. Cited in Favier and Couvreur, *Le plaisir musical*, 14, 15.

15. See Rosand, *Opera in Seventeenth-Century Venice*, 369–376.

16. Dammann, *Der Musikbegriff*, 364.

17. See Tomlinson, *Metaphysical Song*, 49.

18. René Descartes, letter to Marin Mersenne (1630), cited in Jorgensen, "Descartes on Music," 415.

19. Aho, *The Tangible in Music*, 17.

20. Tim Carter raises this possibility of a parodic reading in relation to the *Lamento della Ninfa*; see his "Lamento della Ninfa (1638)," 198.

21. Roach, *The Player's Passion*, 83.

22. Joubert, *Traité du ris* (1579), 93–94. See Fudge, *Brutal Reasoning*, 17.

Chapter 18

1. Koelsch and Jäncke, "Music and the Heart."

2. Mollakazemi et al., "Synchronization of Autonomic and Cerebral Rhythms."

3. Bernardi et al., "Dynamic Interactions."

4. "Ein wundersam Ding ists auch / daß solches Solo, Psalm oder blosse Melodie das Gemüthe weit anders afficiret / wann sie aus der tieffen oder mittelmässigen als hohen Octava, anders wenn sie langsam / anders wenn sie geschwinde / mit gelinder oder gedämpfter / anders mit starcker Stimme / wenn sie aus einem gleichen oder Tripel-Tact, aus mollem oder duren, aus nähern und kleinern / oder aus weiter entlegenen grössern Intervallen gehet / gesungen oder gespielet wird." Calvör, "Vorrede" (1717), n.p.

5. "auß der differenten Bewegung der äusserlichen Luft oder Aetheris, in dem dieselbe / da sie entweder starck forciret oder doucement gleichsam gestreichelt / langsam oder geschiwnde etc. in den motum gebracht wird / in gleiche Bewegung die correspondirende Lufft oder Aetherem samt dem gerührten Nervo acustico und connectirten Spiritibus und Affecten, setzet und bringet." Calvör, "Vorrede" (1717), n.p.

6. Juslin, *Musical Emotions Explained*, 126.

7. Juslin, *Musical Emotions Explained*, 251.

8. Descartes, *Excellent Compendium* (1653), 28.

9. Grimarest, *Traité du récitatif* (1707), 147.

10. Bacilly, *Remarques curieuses* (1668), 200. See Gordon-Seifert, *Music and the Language of Love*, 217.

11. Mace, *Musick's Monument* (1676), 130. See Haynes and Burgess, *The Pathetick Musician*, 128.

12. Haynes and Burgess, *The Pathetick Musician*, 213, 215.

13. Wright, *The Passions of the Minde* (1604), 174.

14. Roach, *The Player's Passion*, 24–25.

15. "Le Mouvement est . . . une certaine qualité qui donne l'ame au Chant, & qui est appellé Mouvement, parce qu'elle émeut, ie veux dire elle excite l'attention des Auditeurs, mesme de ceux qui sont les plus rebelles à l'harmonie; . . . elle inspire dans les coeurs telle passion que le Chantre voudra faire naistre, principalement celle de la Tendresse. . . . Je ne doute point que la varieté de la Mesure ou prompte, ou lente, ne contribuë beauoup à l'Expression du Chant, mais il y a sans doute encore une autre qualité plus épurée & plus spirituelle, qui tient toûjours l'Auditeur en haleine, & fait que le Chant en est moins ennuyeux." Bacilly, *Remarques curieuses* (1668), 200–201. Partial translation in Haynes and Burgess, *The Pathetick Musician*, 135.

16. Fenner, *A Treatise of the Affections* (1641).

17. Vilar, *Medicinisches und chirurgisches Wörterbuch* (1747), 450.

18. Thieme, *Haus-, Feld-, Arzney-, Koch-, Kunst- und Wunder-Buch* (1700), 1457.

19. Heuermann, *Physiologie Erster Theil* (1751), 318.

20. Spadoni, *Studium curiosum* (1695), 124.

21. Struthius, *Sphygmicae artis* (1555), vol. 1, 23; Fludd, *Utriusque cosmi* (1624), vol. 1, 167. See Kümmel, "Puls und Musik," 272–275.

22. "Der Takt . . . ist von der Beweg- und Klopfung des Hertzens erfunden worden." Ahle, "Anmerkungen" (1704), 34.

23. Grube, *De ictu tarantulae* (1679), 55.

24. Bergier, *La musique speculative*, 198–200; see van Orden, *Music, Discipline and Arms*, 85–86.

25. "illa titillatio quam in nobis ad pulsum instrumentorum sentire solemus, praesertim cum corpus vino sublevatum est, spiritibusque gaudet vividioribus ac subtilioribus . . . in praesentia Concentus Musici à saltu se vix abstinere posset." Vallerius, *Disputatio physico-musica* (1674), par. 69, n.p.

26. Beyer, *Primae lineae* (1703), 25. On changing conceptions of meter in the period, see Grant, *Beating Time and Measuring Music*.

27. Descartes, *Excellent Compendium* (1653), 6.

28. "da der tact in ungleiche Theile getheilet / und gleichsam wie auf drey Füssen hinckend daher springet / so hincken und hüpffen die Spiritus sampt denen Leibes-Füssen mit sonderbahrer Lustigkeit mit daher. . . . wenn die Geige auf ihren Mittel-chorden einen langsahmen reutirlichen Ton daher machet," Calvör, "Vorrede" (1717), n.p.

29. Duverney, *Treatise of the Organ of Hearing* (1737), 89.

30. Mattheson, *Der vollkommene Capellmeister* (1739), 212. *J. S. Bach, Matthäus-Passion*, Berliner Philharmoniker, Sir Simon Rattle, Peter Sellars, DVD recording (2014), BPHR 140021

31. Tom Huizenga, "Bach's St. Matthew Passion."

32. Downame, *Spiritual Physicke* (1600), 52.

33. "daß das Blut endlich durch Mund, Nase, Ohren, die Mutter, oder auch zu den Wunden heraus ja zuweilen gar die Seele aus dem Leibe fahre," Schmidt, *Biblischer Medicus* (1743), 82.

34. As noted by Melamed, *Hearing Bach's Passions*, 13–14.

35. *Johann Sebastian Bach, Matthew Passion*, Dunedin Consort & Players, dir. John Butt, Linn Records (2008); *Johann Sebastian Bach, Matthäus-Passion, Highlights*, Rundfunkchor Leipzig, Staatskapelle Dresden, dir. Peter Schreier, Phillips (1987).

36. *J. S. Bach, Matthäus-Passion*, Collegium Vocale Gent, dir. Philippe Herreweghe, Harmonia Mundi France (1998); *Une Passion et ils me cloueront sur le bois*, Akadêmia Ensemble, dir. Françoise Lasserre, Bayard Musique B-308435-2 (2014).

37. "Also der arme Leib mit seinen festen und flüßigen Theilen zwischen zweyen End-Puncten, so zu reden, hin und her ballotirt oder geworfen wird." Schmidt, *Biblischer Medicus* (1743), 80–81.

38. Marin Mersenne, letter to Constantijn Huygens, cited in Walker, "Joan Albert Ban," 253.

Chapter 19

1. Schaefer, *Religious Affects*, 3.

2. Seigworth and Gregg, "An Inventory of Shimmers," 1.

3. Goodman, *Sonic Warfare*, xv.

4. Kane, "Sound Studies Without Auditory Culture." See also Leys, "The Turn to Affect."

5. Thompson and Biddle, "Introduction," 14.

6. Becker, *Deep Listeners*, 73.

7. See for instance Richter, *Kurtzer und deutlicher Unterricht* (1705), 130.

8. Koschorke, *Körperströme und Schriftverkehr*, 43.

9. Fuhrmann, *Musicalischer Trichter* (1706), 92.

10. Karant-Nunn, "'Gedanken, Herz und Sinn,'" 90. For a counterargument, see Baum, *Reformation of the Senses*, 20.

11. "daher wir dann so mancherley köstliche Gesänge und Psalm haben / welche beyde mit Worten / und auch mit dem Gesang und Klang / die Hertzen der Menschen bewegen." Werckmeister, *Der Edlen Music-Kunst Würde* (1691), 39.

12. "da die Krafft des Göttlichen Worts zugleich mit anmuthigen den Geist erweckenden Melodeyen durchs Hertz dringen / und ungläubliche Veränderung bey dem Menschen zu Wege bringen kann." Olearius, *Geistliche Singe-Kunst* (1671), "Vorrede," n.p.

13. "die Christliche Lehre den Menschen beydes Alt und Jung also eingeflösset / und dermassen ins Hertz gebildet wird / dass man es draus nicht reissen kan." Frick, *Music-Büchlein* (1631), 82.

14. See for instance Goodman, *Sonic Warfare*, 135.

15. "Denn die Gesänge haben die sonderbare Art und Eigenschafft / daß sie dem Menschen ein Ding tief einbilden und anmutig machen. Dahero wenn von Hertzen gesungen wird / es geschehen kan / daß bey manchem mit einem Christlichen Gesange auch das / welches bißweil wol mit einer Predigt nicht geschicht außgerichtet wird." Frick, *Music-Büchlein* (1631), 79. For a similar argument about the powers of collective song, see Herdman, "Songs Danced in Anger," 158.

16. "Denn es ist eine Krafft des Heiligen Geistes in den Liedern / wann dieselbige den Geist deß Menschen berühret / so zündet ein Geist den andern an: da seudet und brennet denn Geist im Geist." Müller, *Seelen-Musik* (1684), 58.

17. "Es werde durch die Music beweget alles / was lebet / weil die himmlische Seele / so allen das Leben giebet ihren Ursprung aus der Music habe." Mithobius, *Psalmodia* (1665), 306.

18. Mithobius, *Psalmodia* (1665), 306. See Ahmed, "Affective Economies," passim.

19. San Antonio, *Chrónicas* (1738–1744), vol. 2, 505–506, cited in Irving, *Colonial Counterpoint*, 115.

20. See Earle, *The Body of the Conquistador*, 159–174.

21. Cited in Filippi, "Songs in Early Modern Catholic Missions," 40.

22. Wood, *Sounding Otherness*, 2.

23. "Dann weilen das Hertz die Residenz und Sitz deß Geistes ist / so empfahen und führen diese Lebens-Geister den zittrenden und springenden Lufft in die Brust / und kommen also mit dem geführten Thon überein; Diesen folgen so dann die Geisterlein in den andern Gliedmassen . . . . Dann die Geister / so in dem Hertzen sich auffhalten / werden nach der Bewegung deß äusserlichen Thons beweget . . . . Und daher ist die Ursach abzunehmen / warum die Menschen / wann sie andere singen hören / so gerne mit singen oder mit sumsen." Kircher, *Neue Hall- und Thon-Kunst* (1684), 133.

24. "alle Hertzenäderlein durchdringet / und desselben Affectus . . . erweckt. . . . Dadurch [der heilige Geist] nicht allein viel böses bey den Menschen verhindert / sondern auch zu wahrer devotion zu inbrünstiger Dancksagung / zu frewdiger verrichtung ihres Beruffes / und sonsten zu allerley Christlichen Tugenden ihre Hertzen entzündet inflammiret, unnd ermuntert." Frick, *Music-Büchlein* (1631), 90–91.

25. "Denn wenn sich Gott der Seelen offenbaret / als die höchste Süssigkeit / so durchgehet er / wie ein Feuer / Leib und Seele / alle Sinne und Kräffte / berührt ein jedes Bluts-Tröpfflein / und zündets an in heisser Gegenliebe. Wie nun unsere Liebe ist / so sind alle unsere Bewegungen: die Liebe zeucht das gantze Gemüt nach sich / mit seiner Hoffnung / Furcht / Freude / Traurigkeit / etc. und wie die Bewegungen sind / so fliessen die Psalmen." Müller, *Seelen-Musik* (1684), 66.

26. "und wil Gott der Herr / daß in dem Lobgesang / Mund und Hertz geschäfftig seyn solle; in dem Hertzen sol sich regen wahre Andacht und geistliche Freude aus Betrachtung Göttlicher Wolthaten: und dann darauff durch die Stimme / Mund und Zunge herausbrechen." Praetorius, *Vernünfftiger Gottesdienst* (1689), "Vorrede," n.p.

27. Fisher, *Music, Piety and Propaganda*, 35.

28. "weil es nicht genug ist / daß der gifftige Dunst das Fleisch berühre / sondern daß der Lebens-Geist denselben empfinde." Musitano, *Chirurgische und physicalische Waag-Schaale* (1703), 47.

29. "Wann jemand Psalmen singet/ . . . im Geiste / das kan die Gemeine nicht bauen; wann aber die gantze Gemeine im Sinne singet / und gleichsam einer zu dem andern durch Psalmen redet / das bessert und machet voll Geistes." Großgebauer, *Drey geistreiche Schrifften* (1667), 194.

30. Spitzer, *A History of Emotion*, 3.

31. "dass wir es freylich auch für Sünde und Unrecht halten / wenn man / im singen und spielen / mehr auf die Melodey und süssen Klang der Stimme / als auf den Text und Worte selber Achtung giebet / den die Harmonia und Liebligkeit des Gesanges wird nur zu dem Ende angestellet / daß uns das edle Wort Gottes desto mehr ins Hertz dringe / gleich wie man eine Artzney zu überzuckern pfleget / da es bloß und allein um die Artzney / nicht aber um den Zucker zu thun ist." Mithobius, *Psalmodia* (1665), 297.

32. "und findet man offt unter hunderten sehr wenig / die es recht practiciren / die singen zwar in der Kirchen mit / aber alieno animo, . . . flattern mit den Gedancken in der Kirche / Werckstatt / in Indien und der neuen Welt herümb." Meißner, *Musica Christiana* (1664), n.p.

33. "Viele singen zwar / aber ohne Geist und Andacht: Der Mund ist wol da / aber das Hertz fern davon: Die Worte sprechen sie zwar / aber empfinden davon keine Krafft im Hertzen: darum bleiben sie inwendig dürr und kalt; und weil sie niemahls einige Brunst und Süssigkeit im Gesang empfinden / vergehet ihnen nach gerad alle Lust zum Singen." Müller, *Seelen-Musik* (1684), "An den christlichen Leser," n.p.

34. Brown, *Singing the Gospel*, 43 and passim.

35. "darüm solten billig so wohl Musici als andere sich freuen / wenn sie den lieben Gott mit voller Stimme anzuruffen und zu loben Gelegenheit hätten / keiner solte sich dessen schämen: Aber hierinn erfahren wir auch offt das Widerspiel / ja es finden sich noch wol böse Leute / so die Frommen / wenn sie laut mitsingen / verlachen." Werckmeister, *Der Edlen Musik-Kunst Würde* (1691), 6.

36. Downame, *Spiritual Physicke* (1600), "To the Christian reader," n.p.; Shusterman, *Thinking Through the Body*, 97.

Chapter 20

1. "Corpus humanum multas pati potest mutationes et nihilominus retinere objectorum impressiones seu vestigia." Spinoza, "Ethica" (1677), Pars III, Postulatum 2; English translation at http://www.ethicadb.org/pars.php?parid=3&lanid=3&lg=en.

2. Primaudaye, *The Second Part of the French Academie* (1605), 161.

3. See for instance Hutchins, "The Embodied Descartes."

4. "Pensés donc à cet effet . . . ils passent de là par les tuyeaux . . . dans les pores ou intervalles qui sont entre les petits filets dont cette partie du cerveau B, est composée;

& qu'ils ont la force de élargir quelque peu ces intervalles, & de ploer & disposer diversement les petits filets qu'ils recontrent en leurs chemins, selon les diverses façons dont ils se meuvent, & les diverses ouvertures des tuyeaux par où ils passent . . . Ce qui est cause que ces figures ne s'effacent pas non plus si aisement, mais qu'elles s'y conservent en telle forte, que par leur moyen les idés qui ont esté autrefois sur cette glande, s'y peuvent former derechef long-temps apres. . . . Et c'est en quoy consiste la *Memoire*." Descartes, *L'Homme* (1664), 74–75. Translation in Descartes, *Treatise of Man*, 87–88. His account harks back to Bernardino Telesio; see Boenke, *Körper, Spiritus, Geist*, 159–60. See also John Sutton's detailed account in his *Philosophy and Memory Traces*, 57–66.

5. Opitz, *Buch von der deutschen Poeterey* (1624), chapter 8, n.p.

6. "Merke, mein Herze, beständig nur dies, wenn du alles sonst vergisst, dass dein Heiland lebend ist." Libretto for BWV 145.

7. Raupach, *Veritophili Deutliche Beweis-Gründe* (1717), 31.

8. "u. so der Fußstapffen der Bildnüsse durch die kleinen Pulß-Adern zu den Hertzen geführet werden / und ihre Strahlen durch das gantze Geblüt ausbreiten / so kan dahero herkommen / daß zuweilen die Leibes-Frucht mit gewissen Zeichen oder Muttermahlen gezeichnet wird." *Curioser Chirurgus* (1719), 36.

9. "Les traces de ces idées passent par les arteres vers le coeur, & ainsi rayonnent en tout le sang; Et comment mesme ells peuvent quelquefois estre determinées par certaines actions de la mere, à s'imprimer sur les membres de l'enfant qui se forme dans ses entrailles." Descartes, *L'Homme* (1664), 73; translation in *Treatise of Man*, 87.

10. Shusterman, *Thinking Through the Body*, 92.

11. Liester, "Personality Changes."

12. Primaudaye, *The French Academie* (1618), 417–418.

13. "in den übel disponirten spiritibus animalibus zu suchen / wann diese zu dick / zu träge und langsam sind / und die objecta nicht wohl annehmen und fassen." Jüngken, *Grund-Reguln* (1701), 57.

14. Sutton, *Philosophy and Memory Traces*, 16–17.

15. "Dann der Menschen Complexiones, so unterschiedlich sind / verursachen / daß einer zu diesem der ander zu jenem inclinire. . . . was sie durch getreue Information in Memoriam gefasset / kan die Phantasia nicht ruhen / biß dasselbe durch allerhand Modulos und Coloraturen dem Gehör beygebracht werde." Falck, *Idea boni cantoris* (1688), "Christliche Vorrede," n.p.

16. "Wir bringen zwar nichts mit uns auf die Welt, als eine gute oder üble Einrichtung des Gehirns und der thierischen Geister im Geblüte . . . . Etliche Gemüther sind wie ein Wachs; andre wie ein Stein. Ob nun zwar dasjenige / was in einen Stein gehauen wird, am längsten dauret; so ziehen wir doch in der Ton-Kunst ein Gehirn, das gleichsam wächsern ist, dem steinern vor." Mattheson, *Der vollkommene Capellmeister* (1739), 106–107.

17. Rose, "Memory and the Early Musician," 8.

18. "Einer, der die Instrumental-Music lernet, mag wollen, wie er will, so kan er die noch ungeschickten Finger nicht zwingen, dasjenige zu prästiren, darauf sein Meister nicht einmal dencken darf." Bucher, *Brief-Wechsel* (1713), 21.

19. "der seine Füsse durch die Uebung dazu gewöhnet, daß sie ohne Bemerckung der Seele nach dem Tact der Music sich künstlich und geschwinde bewegen können; oder auch bey einem Musico, bey wlechem eine gleiche Fertigkeit durch Uebung zuwege gebracht wird." Heuermann, *Physiologie Erster Theil* (1751), 11.

20. See Clark and Chalmers, "The Extended Mind."

21. Walter, *The Grounds and Rules of Musick* (1721), 3.

22. "Die Einbildungs-Krafft bringet nichts hervor / als was wir vor diesem empfunden oder gedacht / und also sind die Einbildungen nichts anders als Vorstellungen von vergangenem Zustande der Welt." Wolff, *Vernünfftige Gedancken von Gott* (1720), 445.

23. Herissone, *Musical Creativity*, 370.

24. Bashwiner, "The Neuroscience of Musical Creativity," 512.

25. "Cogitationes & Somnia fiunt, dum series idearum ab objectis externis . . . denuo excitatur à causis internis. Illae causae internae, praeter alias multas, forsitan esse poterunt primariae, 1) impetus sanguinis versus totum cerebrum, vel in aliquam ejus partem directus, 2) Sanguinis qualitas, 3) impetus & qualitas liquidi nervei, 4) dispositio viscerum etc." Albrecht, *Tractatus physicus* (1734), 49.

26. *Roger North on Music*, 140.

27. "dass durch fleissige Uebung der Gebrauch der Finger endlich so mechanisch wird." Bach, *Versuch* (1762), 20.

28. Yearsley, *Bach's Feet*, 105.

29. "Ja auch die Hände und Füsse der Christen / welche gewohnt sind / die Orgel nach der Kunst und mit eigener beyfallenden guten Fantasie fertig zu tractiren / geben / durch Veranlassung der Worte im Gesang / offtmahls auf bemeldtem Instrument, die Freude der Seelen über Gott und seine Gaben mit freudig-klingenden Harmonien / Sprüngen und Modulationen kräfftig zu erkennen." Raupach, *Veritophili Deutliche Beweis-Gründe* (1717), 45.

30. McKean, *Towards a Wahre Art*, 43.

31. Martha Feldman, unpublished paper, cited in LaMay, "Composing from the Throat," 369.

32. Smith, *The Acoustic World of Early Modern England*, 114.

33. Sanford, "A Comparison of French and Italian Singing," 8.1.

Chapter 21

1. Smith, *The Body of the Artisan*, 110.

2. Graupner, *Partien auf das Clavier* (1718), "Vorrede," n.p. The link between bodily constitution and handwriting was explored, for instance, in Spadoni, *Studium curiosum* (1695), 155–157.

3. De Souza, *Music at Hand*, 118.

4. See for instance Gjerdingen, *Music in the Galant Style*, and various chapters in Morabito, ed., *Musical Improvisation in the Baroque Era*.

5. See my chapter "Embodied Invention," 119–121. Some of the material in the following two paragraphs is based on excerpts from this chapter. Reused with permission of Oxford University Press.

6. Niedt, *Handleitung / zur Variation* (1706), n.p.

7. Ruiter-Feenstra, *Bach and the Art of Improvisation*, vol. 1, 20, 23.

8. "dergestalt in der Faust seyn / daß man gar nicht mehr suchen oder sich bedencken / sondern gleichsam alles blindlings und augenblicklich auf dem Clavier zu finden wisse." Heinichen, *Neu erfundene und Gründliche Anweisung* (1711), 161.

9. Diruta, *Il Transilvano*, 11–13; see Guido, "Climbing the Stairs of the Memory Palace," 42–43.

10. Callahan, *Techniques of Keyboard Improvisation*, 4.

11. Le Guin, *Boccherini's Body*, 34.

12. "Es ist das besondere Componisten-Werckzeug . . . . Doch muß es nicht so verstanden werden, als ob man alle seine Sätze von diesem Instrument herzuholen . . . sondern nur, daß es einen weit deutlichern Begriff vom harmonischen Bau geben könne, als die übrigen, wenn auch der Kasten oder die Maschine gar nicht vorhanden ist, sondern nur in blossen Gedancken vorstellig gemacht wird: den die Lage, Ordnung und Reihe der Klänge ist nirgends so deutlich und sichtbar, als in den Tasten eines Claviers." Mattheson, *Der vollkommene Capellmeister* (1739), 106.

13. See Ruiter-Feenstra's helpful summary of fingering principles in *Bach and the Art of Improvisation*, vol. 1, 25–26.

14. See Bungert, "Bach and the Patterns of Transformation," 109–110.

15. On the agency of musical materials, see also Rose, "Bach and Material Culture," 11–36.

16. See King and Waddington-Jones, "Performers' Perspectives," 256.

17. See for instance Niedt, *Musicalische Handleitung Oder Gründlicher Unterricht* (1710), chapter 11, on how to modulate.

18. Aho, *The Tangible in Music*, 5.

19. Butt, *Music Education*, 163.

20. Praetorius, *Syntagmatis musici tomus tertius* (1619), 25.

21. *Graupner, Partitas for Harpsichord, Vol. 1*, Geneviève Soly (harpsichord), Analekta FL 23109 (2002).

22. Aho, *The Tangible in Music*, 142.

23. McKean, *Towards a Wahre Art*, 221

24. Niedt, *Handleitung / zur Variation* (1706), chapter 6, n.p.

25. Orden, *Music, Discipline and Arms*, 82. See also Wald-Fuhrmann on the "psychohygenic subtext" of Froberger's improvisatory music, in "Modell Orpheus," 237.

26. South, *Musica incantans* (1700), 4–5.

27. Hall, "François Couperin," 34.

28. "daß der Ort der Sinnlichkeit . . . die Seele selber sey / auch daß selbige die Bewegungen so vermittelst einer subtilen Materie (als zum Exempel von dem Licht / einen Schall und so fortan /) vorgehen / an einer jedewederen Stelle / wo solche geschehen / sobald empfange oder begreiffe." Blankaart, *Reformirte Anatomie* (1691), 284.

29. "herir las teclas con las yemas de los dedos . . . suenan las bozes enteras, dulces, y suaves. La razon desto es, porque como la carne sea cosa blande, hiere con blandura y suavidad. . . . Y por el contrario, quando se hiere con las uñas . . . desmayadas y sin spiritu." Santa María, *Libro llamado arte de teñer fantasia* (1565), vol. 1, f. 37; translation in Kosovske, *Historical Harpsichord Technique*, 31.

30. Walkington, *The Optick Glasse of Humors* (1607), 48.

31. Kosovske, *Historical Harpsichord Technique*, 18.

32. See Blake, "Disabling Music Performance," 196–200.

33. "no se ocupen en otros que les puedan encallecer las manos, y entorpezer los dedos: porque todo lo que es manejar cosas duras, ú de peso, tocar agues impuras, sobrademente frias, ó excessivamente calientes, atraen humores á dichos miembros, los quales impiden en los nervios la docilidad." Nassare, *Esquela musica* (1723), vol. 2, 472; translation in Kosovske, *Historical Harpsichord Technique*, 6.

34. Couperin, *L'art de toucher le clavecin* (1716), 9–10.

35. "die Augen, Ohren und andere Gliedmassen mit stillstehenden Feuchtigkeiten . . . gequälet werden." Hecker, *Betrachtung des menschlichen Körpers* (1734), 285.

36. On gouty limbs playing the keyboard, see Head, "C. P. E. Bach 'In Tormentis.'"
37. McKean, *Towards a Wahre Art*, 16.
38. Baily, "Ethnomusicology, Intermusability, and Performance Practice," 123.
39. See De Souza, "Voice and Instruments," 21–36.
40. Irvine, *Medicina magnetica* (1656), 86.
41. Stiegler, *Technics and Time I*, 152–153.
42. Fuhrmann, *Musica vocalis*, 19–20; "Da Hand und Athem Holtz, Metall und Darm belebet," Reinholdt, *Poetische Gedancken* (1736), 19.

Chapter 22

1. Scheer, "Topographies of Emotion," 39.
2. See Helm, "Galen-Rezeption."
3. Zedler, *Universal-Lexicon* (1731–1754), vol. 36, 1052.
4. For an exceptionally lucid attempt at this task, see Serjeantson, "The Soul."
5. "substantiam illam incorpoream & immortalem abstractivè a corpore consideratam . . . Calor, Spiritus, Aura, Ignis, Flamma vitalis, Biolychnium, Natura, vel quocunque tandem nomine appellare libuerit." Bruno, *Castellus renovatus* (1682), 85–86.
6. "Er ist ja der schlechteste und vergängliche Theil des Menschen / so nicht einmal vor ein Eigenthum zu achten ist. . . . An sich selbst aber findet man grosse Ursach / sich desselben zu schämen: denn er hat gar eine schlechte Ubereinstimmung mit dem Wesen und der Subtilheit der Seele. . . . eine mit Wasser temperirte und vereinigte Erde oder Schleim / welcher in eine gewisse Form / in lauter Röhren und Faden / wie Spinnen-Gewebe subtil und künstlich zusammen getrieben / und in gewisse Glieder gebildet worden." Richter, *Kurtzer und deutlicher Unterricht* (1705), "Vorrede," n.p.
7. "diejenigen Atomos oder Stäublein auszusuchen / aus welchen fleischichte, hautichte oder Knorplichte Theile / oder Geblüt könne gefertigen werden. . . . daß an einem Orte / da Fleisch wachsen solte / ein Knorpel entstünde / u.s.w. wodurch denn der Mensch in wenig Wochen in ein Monstrum, und in eine gantz unbrauchbare Machine würde verwandelt werden." Richter, *Kurtzer und deutlicher Unterricht* (1705), 36.
8. Wels, *Manifestationen des Geistes*, 129.
9. Wright, "Mind, Spirit, Soul and Body." For a more extensive exploration of this biblical anthropology, see Green, *Body, Soul, and Human Life*.
10. Stock, *Homiletisches Real-Lexicon* (1734), 430.
11. "Ein Christ muß täglich mit dem innerlichen Feinde seinem eigenen Fleisch und Blut zu Feld liegen." Scherertz, *Fuga melancholiae* (1682), 143.
12. "Fleisch heißt sonst der alte Adam oder der alte Mensch / der eusserliche Mensch; Geist / der neue und innerliche Mensch." Pfeiffer, *Apostolische Christen-Schule* (1704), 739.
13. Lambert, *Singing the Resurrection*, 23–46.
14. See for instance Mattheson, *Behauptung der himmlischen Musik* (1747).
15. Lemnius, *A Discourse Touching Generation* (1664), 31. On resurrection theology as a challenge to both a fully humoralist and a fully cognitivist model of human nature, see also Gil, "What It Feels Like to Be a Body."
16. "Pythagoras und die Platonischen Philosophi haben zwar gelehret / die Seele hätte deßwegen an der Music ihr Vergnügen / weil sie gedächte an die himmlische Music / die dieselbe zuvor gehöret / ehe sie in den Leib gestossen worden. . . . Alleine

wir . . . sagen / als Christen / die Music sey deßwegen angenehm / weil sie Gott als eine Erquickung des menschlichen Lebens gegeben." Mirus, *Kurtze Fragen* (1715), 82.

17. "Unter allen freyen Künsten / so durch Eingeben des Heiligen Geistes von Menschen erfunden / ist keine so mächtig als die Music, und kan keine unter denselben unser Gemüth so kräfftig regieren / unsere Sitten dirigiren / unsere Seele afficiren." Fuhrmann, *Musica vocalis*, 17.

18. Fuhrmann, *Musicalischer Trichter* (1706), 80.

19. Hoffmann, *Dissertationes physico-medicae* (1708), 112. See Geyer-Kordesch, "Georg Ernst Stahl's Radical Pietist Medicine," 68.

20. "Beneben beyden obgedachten Substantien / bestehet zwar der Mensch noch aus einer andern Substantz / nemlich der Seelen; es wird aber diese in unserer Medicin nicht consideriret, weilen unseres Leibes und seiner Theilen bewegung auch ohne derselben direction geschehen kan." Jüngken, *Grund-Reguln* (1701), 4.

21. Vidal, "Brainhood," 6 and passim. "Mens est melior pars hominis, qua cogitat constans cerebro & infinitis ejus organis varie modificatis, affluxu & circulatio materiae subtilis." Stosch, *Concordia rationis* (1692), 11.

22. Black, *Embodiment and Mechanisation*, 8. On the shift from soul to mind as the entity-that-knows, see also Martin and Barresi, *The Rise and Fall of the Soul*, 142–170.

23. Schmidt, *Biblischer Medicus* (1743), 50–51.

24. Williams, *Descartes*, 287.

25. Gassendi, "Fifth Set of Objections," 181–182.

26. Blankaart, *Reformirte Anatomie* (1691), 283–284.

27. Schelhammer, *Dissertationem* (1710), 49.

28. See Erlmann, "The Physiologist at the Opera," 35.

29. Smith, *The Animal Spirit Doctrine*, 157.

30. "Spiritus animales . . . potentiam habent à DEO impressam non solum mechanice sese movendi, sed & electivè determinate & ad certum finem: quae potentia dicitur anima sensitiva & radicaliter inexistit subtilissimo cerebri fluido." Hoffmann, *Fundamenta medicinae* (1695), 33.

31. More, *A Collection* (1662), 34.

32. "Bald setzet sie einer in Cerebrum, da setzen sie ihm viele andere nach. Bald setzet sie einer in die Glandulam Pinealem, und dem folgen auch nicht wenige. Wieder andern scheint dieser Sitz zu enge, und gar recht. . . . Darum postiren sie sie in quamvis Corporis Partem gantz (und intote Corpore gantz) und ob gleich die Vernunfft leicht begreifft / daß so viele Seelen in einem Menschen seyn müsten / als Puncta an ihm sind / so finden sich doch viel Affen / die es auch so machen . . . . Noch andere setzen sie ins Hertze, und lassen sie sich im Blute herum schwemmen; bey andern muß sie ins Ventriculum kriechen." Bucher, *Brief-Wechsel* (1713), 8.

33. Frith, "The Brain, Consciousness and the Soul," 69; Conway and Rehding, "Neuroaesthetics."

34. Castiglione, *The Courtier* (1588), vol. 1, 37; cited in Toft, *With Passionate Voice*, 3.

35. "Nichts rühret die Hertzen der Menschen mehr, nichts dringet so tieff in die Seel, als ein anmuthige Melodey." Spiess, *Tractatus musicus* (1745), 113.

36. A. B., *Synopsis of Vocal Musick* (1680), 2. On Leibniz, see Butt, "'A Mind Unconscious,'" 60 and passim.

37. "kommt mit seiner Melancholischen Naturell, welches sich die wiedrigsten Ideen / als da ist Furcht / Traurigkeit etc. welch ich billig Dissonantien des Gemüthes nennen kan / machet / vortrefflich überein / gleichwie ein Adagio mit dem langsamen

Lauff des Geblüthes." Scheibel, *Zufällige Gedancken* (1721), 14. Translation in Scheibel, "Random Thoughts," 233.

Chapter 23

1. Oldham, *The Works of John Oldham* (1684), 114.
2. McClary, *Desire and Pleasure*, 154.
3. Taruskin, *The Oxford History of Western Music*, vol. 2, 64.
4. McClary, *Modal Subjectivities*, 61.
5. Furetière, *Dictionaire universel* (1690), vol. 1, entry "Mort."
6. Butler, *The Principles of Musik* (1636), 1.
7. Smith, *Musical Response in the Early Modern Playhouse*, 29–31.
8. Blount, *Glossographia* (1661), entry "Ecstasy."
9. Brockes, *Bethlehemitischer Kinder-Mord* (1725), 491.
10. Kramer, *Il nuovo dittionario* (1724), 979; Zedler, *Universal-Lexicon* (1731–1754), vol. 8, 1305.
11. "über dem Hertzzwingenden Gesang und Seel-durchdringenden Klang Hören und Sehen vergangen seyn / tausendmahl mehr / als einem einfältigen Bauer / so zum ersten mahl eine 32. Füßige Orgel . . . in einer Stadt-Kirchen schlagen höret." Fuhrmann, *Musicalischer Trichter* (1706), 4.
12. Guarini, *Rime* (1598), f. 131r. Cited and translation in Wistreich, "'Inclosed in This Tabernacle,'" 10–11.
13. Austern, *Both from the Ears and Mind*, 71.
14. "comme si l'ame ayant abandonné tous les sieges sensitifs, ce fust retiree au bord des oreilles." Tyard, *Solitaire second* (1555), 114.
15. "das hertz und gehirne entschüttet sich alsdenn des grösten theils ihrer hitze und geister." Venette, *Abhandlung* (1738), 206.
16. Zedler, *Universal-Lexicon* (1731–1754), vol. 6, 436.
17. "Sintemal in dem liebes-handel diese clitoris mit den heftigsten geistern erfüllet und entzücket, sich nachgehends hart und steif, wie des mannes ruthe, machet." Venette, *Abhandlung* (1738), 17.
18. Nigrinus, *Phönix* (1709), 174.
19. "darzu seinen hitzigern und vor jenem dickern / auch mehrern Saamen viel geschwinder / und mit weit grösserer Leibs-Bewegung . . . aussprützet: auf welche Auslassung . . . manchmaln die Kräfften deß Leibes leiden / ja so zu reden / Sinn und Witze vergehen; welches ja nirgends anderst her / als von der wollüstigen Empfindlichkeit / und empfindlichen Kützel / mag herrühren." Pfitzer, *Zwey sonderbare Bücher* (1673), 114.
20. Pfitzer, *Zwey sonderbare Bücher* (1673), 111. On semen as an irritant, see also Laqueur, *Making Sex*, 44.
21. See p. 103.
22. Venette, *Abhandlung* (1738), 200. Venette is referencing Augustine here.
23. Müller, *Seelen-Musik* (1684), 7.
24. Pfitzer, *Zwey sonderbare Bücher* (1673), 110.
25. "Offt bringen die geistliche Lieder eine übernatürliche Süssigkeit aus Gott ins Hertz. . . . Offt entzückt uns gleichsam der süsse Geschmack Göttlicher Güte / daß wir nicht wissen / wie uns geschiehet / offt fliessen die Freuden-Thränen mit Hauffen." Müller, *Seelen-Musik* (1684), 55–56. Comparable ecstatic outflows could occur when

reading devotional literature: according to the poet Elizabeth Singer Rowe, "we feel a strange Warmth boyling within, the Blood dances through the Veins, Joy lightens in the Countenance, and we are insensibly led into a pleasing Captivity." *Divine Hymns* (1704), preface, n.p. See Pappa, *Carnal Reading*, 51.

26. "Wir seynd vor freuden gleichsam entzücket, wenn der saamen, so gantz von geistern aufgeblasen, seinen weg quer durch unsere verwickelte gefässe nimmt. Die hitzigen und kützelnden dämpfe, die sich erheben, und die überaus geschwinde bewegung der geister, so unsere häutlein durchdringen, thun nicht wenig zu unserer grossen wollust." Venette, *Abhandlung* (1738), 206.

27. "den unsere seel und leib ergiessen sich, also zu reden, vor freude." Venette, *Abhandlung* (1738), 204.

28. Hill, *A Full and Just Account* (1709), xii; cited in Pappa, *Carnal Reading*, 53.

29. Austern, "'For Love's a Good Musician,'" 616.

30. Paré, *WundtArtzney* (1601), 955–956.

31. Johnson, "Experiencing Alba Tressina's *Anima mea*," 43.

32. Freylinghausen, *Geistreiches Gesangbuch* (1737), 813.

33. McClary, *Desire and Pleasure*, 117.

34. Zedler, *Universal-Lexicon* (1731–1754), vol. 25, 1870.

35. Chambers, *Cyclopaedia* (1738), vol. 2, entry "Orgasm."

36. "Agitation, movement des humeurs qui cherchent à s'évacuer." *Le Dictionnaire de l'Académie française* (1762), 265.

37. "wann wir mit dem Freuden-Wein des Heiligen Geistes . . . erfüllet sind . . . Die Freude des Geistes ist wie ein Strom: Du tränckest sie mit Wollust / wie mit einem Strom. . . . quillt und bricht durch liebliche Gesänge herfür: Da siedet und wallet das Hertz und laufft über für Freuden." Müller, *Seelen-Musik* (1684), 66.

38. Johnson, "Experiencing Alba Tressina's *Anima mea*," 53–54.

39. See p. 94. See also my chapter "Early Modern Voices," 259–260.

40. On dissonance, see pp. 184–185.

41. See Rifkin, "Schütz and Musical Logic," 1068.

42. Muchembled, *Orgasm and the West*, 13 and passim.

Chapter 24

1. Serres, *The Five Senses*, 116.

2. Johnson, "Experiencing Alba Tressina's *Anima mea*," 53.

3. Girolamo Mei, letter to Vincenzo Galilei, 8 May 1572, trans. in Palisca, *The Florentine Camerata*, 57–58.

4. The literature on early modern melancholy is substantial; see for instance Gowland, *The Worlds of Renaissance Melancholy*; or more recently Sullivan, *Beyond Melancholy*.

5. For a useful summary, see Gibson, "Music, Melancholy and Masculinity," 43–45.

6. Burton, *The Anatomy of Melancholy* (1621), 21.

7. "In der Melancholie, weil die Lebens-Geister gleichsam zu träge und unterdrücket, muß man sie wieder aufwecken. . . . Hernach muß man die dicke, schwere und unbewegliche Säffte verdünnen und zertheilen." Heister, *Practisches Medicinisches Handbuch* (1744), 376.

8. "daß bei den Traurigen und Leidmütigen sich die Wärme versamlet / von der Circumferentz bis an das centrum des Hertzens / sambt den Lebens-geistern / also

daß die obere Glieder von der Wärm verlassen / und mit Kält ergriffen werden: weil nun an solchem Ort die Kälte praedominiret, so pflegt die Stimm langsam und grob zu seyn." Kircher, *Musurgia universalis* (1662), 65–66.

9. "Die Traurigkeit ist das schädlichste Leyden der Seelen / dardurch der Leib außgemergelt / und geschwächet wird / Und wie ein Holtzwurm einen Baum oder Bret durchfrisset / das Unkraut den guten Weitzen ersticket und unterdrücket: Also schwächet auch die Traurigkeit das Hertz / und nimmt ihm seine Stärke. . . . Die übrige Betrübnüß leschet gar offt im Hertzen auß alle Andacht zum Gebet / Hoffnung und Gedult / ja fast alle Ubungen deines Christenthums / sie drücket die Gottseligkeit in dir zu boden / und wird der H. Geist / der ein freudiger Geist ist / dardurch verhindert / daß er seine selige Wirckungen in dir nicht verrichten kan." Scherertz, *Fuga melancholiae* (1682), 12.

10. See Schäfer, "More Than a Fading Flame," 248–249.

11. See Crawford, *European Sexualities*, 121–122.

12. See Lindemann, *Medicine and Society*, 44–45.

13. Burton, *The Anatomy of Melancholy* (1621), 257.

14. Burton, *The Anatomy of Melancholy* (1621), 624.

15. Holman, *Dowland: Lachrimae*, 58.

16. Holman, *Dowland: Lachrimae*, 52.

17. Heister, *Practisches medicinisches Handbuch* (1744), 377.

18. Burton, *The Anatomy of Melancholy* (1621), 372. He is citing Levinus Lemnius here.

19. On soft beds, see Ferrand, *De la maladie d'amour* (1623), 47, cited in Altbauer-Rudnik, "Love, Madness and Social Order," 38. For Plato, see Gibson, "Music, Melancholy and Masculinity," 53.

20. See Gibson, "Music, Melancholy and Masculinity," 50.

21. Stubbs, *The anatomie of abuses* (1583), 109v. See Austern, "'Alluring the Auditorie to Effeminacie,'" 343–354.

22. Mylius, *Rudimenta musices* (1686), chapter 3, n.p.

23. Dahlhaus, "Die Termini Dur und Moll," 282–283.

24. Mattheson, *Critica musica*, vol. 2 (1725), 156.

25. See pp. 57, 84.

26. Morley, *A Plaine and Easie Introduction* (1597), 177.

27. Vogt, *Conclave thesauri* (1717), 27.

28. Galilei, *MSS Galileiani, Anteriori a Galileo*, f. 139r. Cited in Palisca, "Vincenzo Galilei's Counterpoint Treatise," 95.

29. Doni, *Trattato della musica scenica*, published posthumously in *De' trattati di musica* (1763), 79.

30. Ovid, *Metamorphoses*, 476–480.

31. Bacon, *Sylva Sylvarum* (1670), 181.

32. "Digitus Dei, pientiora oracula, Nobis rudibus & usque refractariis Laturus, illis miscuit dulcissimam Jucunditatem Musices, ut auribus sic delinitis, pectori mysteria Latenter & vix sense penitus influant. Oh dia musica! tota mellis instar es dii: tuis pagana corda viribus lenis statim, prorsusque deles." Michael, *Psalmodia regia* (1632), 5. Translation by Derek Stauff.

33. *Canticum Canticorum*, Les Voix Baroques, Atma Classique ACD2 2503 (2008).

34. Byrd, *Psalmes, Songs, and Sonnets* (1611).

35. "Das Venerische Miasma sich per transpirationem in dessen Leib insinuiret,

und das Geblüte, welches den gantzen Leib durchströhmet, versäuret, verderbet, und mit dem Venerischen Gifft anschwängert." Oehme, *Medicinische Fama* (1749), 202.

36. Herbst, *Musica poetica* (1643), 103.

37. Zarlino, *Le istitutioni harmoniche* (1558), 327.

38. *Bach Cantatas*, vol. 16, Monteverdi Choir, English Baroque Soloists, dir. John Eliot Gardiner, SDG 137 (2000).

39. Kircher, *Musurgia universalis* (1662), 159.

40. Werckmeister, *Musicae mathematicae hodegus curiosus* (1687), 125.

41. Kircher, *Musurgia universalis* (1662), 160.

Chapter 25

1. Bossuet, *Maximes and Reflections* (1699), 14.

2. Shepherd, *Theatre, Body and Pleasure*, 5.

3. Cited in Leonardi and Pope, *The Diva's Mouth*, 8.

4. Hutcheon and Hutcheon, "Embodied Representation," 303.

5. Garavaglia and Weir, "The Time Scale of the Baroque Aria," 41.

6. Gordon, *Monteverdi's Unruly Women*, 166.

7. Carter, "Review: The Power of Song?," 699.

8. Walther, *Musicalisches Lexicon* (1732), 338. On *Affektenlehre*, see pp. 9–13.

9. "Kaisern seine Sätze sind galant, verliebt, und zeigen alle Leidenschaften, deren Gewalt das menschliche Herz am meisten unterworfen ist." Scheibe, *Critischer Musikus* (1745), 763.

10. "ist mehr zu klagenden und traurigen Passionen als zu divertissemens geneigt." Mattheson, *Das neu-eröffnete Orchestre* (1713), 250.

11. "wenn eine Pieçe mit dem b. bezeichnet sey / so müste sie unumgänglich weich und tendre klingen; wenn sie aber mit einem oder mehr Creutzen versehen / so müsse ihre Natur hart / frisch und lustig seyn." Mattheson, *Das neu-eröffnete Orchestre* (1713), 232–233.

12. Dammann, *Der Musikbegriff*, 264. *Reinhard Keiser, "Liebe, sag', was fängst du an?,"* Sandrine Piau, Akademie für Alte Musik Berlin, dir. Bernhard Forck, live recording, 20 October 2008, https://www.youtube.com/watch?v=Hbrrc3tu29g.

13. "Dieses senckt sich am allerersten in verhärtete Gemüther ein / und läst einen kräfftigen Nachdruck nach sich / zumahl wenn die Music, die ohne dem eine schier übermenschliche Krafft / das Herz zu bewegen / an sich hat / dazu kömmt." Feind, *Deutsche Gedichte* (1708), 117.

14. Gotman, *Choreomania*, 182.

15. "Siculi [gaudent] sincera, saltem ad apparentiam simplicitate: unde Italus, si suam Ariam simplicissima suavitate produci vult, suprà scribit: siciliano." Vogt, *Conclave thesauri* (1717), 98–99.

16. See Bloechl, "Listening as an Innu-French Contact Zone."

17. Heinichen, *Der General-Bass in der Composition* (1728), 62.

18. Wood, *Sounding Otherness*, 4.

19. "Effoeminati redduntur homines ex Musica, non tam audita, quam exercita." Ettmüller, *Disputatio effectus musicae* (1714), 38.

20. "Die zärtlichsten Töne, die geilesten Poesien, und die unzüchtigesten Bewegungen der Opernhelden und ihrer verliebten Göttinnen bezaubern die unvorsichtigen Gemüther, und flößen ihnen ein Gift ein . . . . So wird die Weichlichkeit von

Jugend auf in die Gemüther der Leute gepflantzet und wir werden den weibischen Italienern ähnlich, ehe wir es inne geworden, daß wir männliche Deutsche seyn sollten." Gottsched, *Versuch einer Critischen Dichtkunst* (1751), 741.

21. Ornithoparcus, *Micrologus* (1609), Dedication, n.p.

22. The theological framing of operagoing was made explicit in the Hamburg "Opernstreit" of the late seventeenth century; see Hinrichsen, "Theologie, Ästhetik, Politik."

23. "Ein Schauspiel ist / so zu sagen / nur ein Schatten-Spiel / allwo man zwar etwas siehet / aber kein Fleisch und Bein berühret." Feind, *Deutsche Gedichte* (1708), 78. "Damit nach Vollendung des Musicalischen Stücks die Melodie immer in der Phantasie zuruck bleibe, der Moralische Spruch oder Sentenz aber dem Verstand deutlich vorgestellet, und der Gedächtnus wohl möge imprimirt werden, um dadurch desto gewisser den wahren Zweck der Musique zu erreichen, welcher ist, durch geschickte und annehmliche Kläng die Hertzen der Zuhörern zu allen schönen Tugenden zu bewegen, und von allen sündlichen Leidenschafften abzuhalten, damit solchergestalt die Ehr Gottes beförderet werde." Spiess, *Tractatus musicus* (1745), 214.

24. Brockes, *Irdisches Vergnügen* (1739), 353.

25. Franko, "Majestic Drag," 72. Franko is drawing on Judith Butler here.

26. Crivellati, *Discorsi musicali* (1624), 60, cited in Garavaglia and Weir, "The Time Scale of the Baroque Aria," 44.

27. Garavaglia and Weir, "The Time Scale of the Baroque Aria," 42.

28. See for instance Mattheson, *Das neu-eröffnete Orchestre* (1713), 180; Tosi, *Anleitung zur Singkunst* (1757), 183.

29. Leopold, "Über die Inszenierung in der Musik," 12.

30. "Et il y a une raison particuliere qui empeche l'ame de pouvoir promtement changer ou arrester ses passions . . . . Cette raison est, qu'elles sont Presque toutes accompagnés de quelque émotion qui se fait dans le coeur, & par consequent aussi en tout le sang & les esprits, en forte que jusques à ce que cette émotion ait cessé, ells demeurent presentes à nostre pensée." Descartes, *Les passions de l'âme* (1649), 65–66. Translation in Descartes, *Passions of the Soul*, 44.

31. On conventional gestures fulfilling both mimetic and humoral functions, see also Carter, "The Search for Musical Meaning," 165–166.

32. Tosi, *Anleitung zur Singkunst* (1757), 172.

33. See Stevens, "Rhythm and the Performer's Body," 194.

34. Leopold, "Über die Inszenierung in der Musik," 10.

35. On "travestimento," see Wilbourne, "Travestied Sound," 2.

Chapter 26

1. Moryson, *An Itinerary* (1617), 20.

2. "welches nichts anders ist / dann daß die gewöhnliche Mechanische Bewegung zu Zeiten aufgehalten oder verträgert wird. . . . daß in sothanem Zufall einiger Gegenstand oder Verhinderniß in denen bewegenden Fäßern des Hertzens vorhanden seyn müsse / durch welche der Sennadern Safft immerfort an seinem gewöhnlichem / ordentlichen und gleichem Durchfluß verhindert wird." Blankaart, *Cartesianische Academie* (1699), 531.

3. Couch et al., "Circulating MicroRNAs."

4. Duden, "Anmerkungen zur Kulturgeschichte des Herzens," 131.

5. Duden, "Anmerkungen zur Kulturgeschichte des Herzens," 134.

6. Lakoff and Johnson, *Metaphors We Live By*.

7. Christie, "Introduction," 2.

8. Paster, "Introduction," 17.

9. The liminal status of these bodily openings is explored in several contributions to Hillman and Mazzio, eds., *The Body in Parts*.

10. Warncke, *Sprechende Bilder*, 59.

11. Sugg, *The Smoke of the Soul*, 30.

12. Erickson, *The Language of the Heart*, 11.

13. On the ear lobes of the heart, see for instance Keil, *Hanbüchlein* (1730), 69–70. See also p. 100.

14. Kümmel, "Puls und Musik," 278.

15. Bloom, *Voice in Motion*, 69.

16. See Erickson, *Language of the Heart*, xvi.

17. "die geistliche Freude . . . die ein Gläubiger nicht mit seiner Zungen / sondern nur in seinem Hertzen zu schmecken bekömmt / die kan auch die bitterste Galle zu Zucker / und das grösseste äusserliche Hertzeleid zur Freude machen." Quirsfeld, *Allersüssester Jesus-Trost* (1696), 36.

18. Jüngken, *Medicus* (1725), 330–331.

19. "Dannenhero nehme doch ein jeweder sein hertze war / daß es weder durch unbarmherzigkeit erkalte / noch durch zorn und unzucht erhitze." Carpzov, *Ein schönes Trost-Bild* (1693), 19.

20. Heuermann, *Physiologie Erster Theil* (1751), 207.

21. "wann das hertz geschwind auf einander schlägt / so daß fast kein tempo darzwischen / ja auch offt so starck sich beweget / daß man es höret und siehet. Dem Patienten dünckt als ob ihm das hertz von iemand zusammen gepreßt wäre." Jüngken, *Medicus* (1725), 329.

22. "Wie der Mensch zwey wesentliche Theile hat / Leib und Seele / als ist er auch zweyerley Drangsal unterworffen / abgebildet durch die zwo Schrauben / dardurch das Hertz gepresset wird." Athyrus, *Das erneuerte Stamm- und Stechbüchlein* (1654), 2141.

23. "Aus diesen und dergleichen inneren Seelen-Anfechtungen entstehet grosse und hefftige Angst in der Seelen. Die Schrifft braucht in Beschreibung dieser Angst eines Wörtleins / welches eine Zusammendrückung des Hertzens bedeutet / da das Hertz gleichsam beklummen ist / da es unter der Angst gepresset wird / wie die Trauben vom Keltertretter." Müller, *Himmlischer Liebes-Kuß* (1724), 546. See also Eric Chafe's commentary on this passage in his *Tears into Wine*, 209–210.

24. Heuermann, *Physiologie Erster Theil* (1751), 208.

25. "Wenn ein Mensch recht betrübet wird / so ist bey vielem Seufftzen die Vergiessung der Thränen gemeiniglich ein Gefehrte / Denn das geängstete und gepreste Hertz von dem Seufftzen und Thränen schwimmet für Angst gleich im Wasser / und steiget solcher innerlicher Angstschweiß ins Gehirn / welches die innerlichen Tröpflein heraus treibet / und durch die Augen auff die Backen springen lässet." Scherertz, *Fuga melancholiae* (1682), 69. See also my article "Heart-Felt Musicking," 43–44.

26. "Wenn eines Seele betrübt / gar voller Angst und Noth / von Sünd und Unlust beschweret / und das Hertz gar in einander geklempt / unnd gleich zusammen gepresset / unnd so unlustig ist / das kein Tröstlein hinein / kein wort oder Seufftzer heraus wil / flugs an einen Psalm gedacht oder gesungen. . . . ist es gewis / dz eine

Christliche Musica wider alle Schwermuth und Anfechtung / ja wider den Teufel selbst uns tröstlich seyn werde." Frick, *Music-Büchlein* (1631), 102–103. On sighs and/as flow, see also Marks, *Sighs of the German People*, 74 and passim.

27. These issues became especially pressing in light of Reformation disputes around the Eucharist and the presence of Christ in his pronouncement "This is my body." Judith Henderson has called the Protestant reinterpretation of this sentence the "seminal insight into the metaphoricity inherent in the verb of being." See her *Translating Investments*, 44.

28. "Denn das Hertz des Menschen sol Gottes Wohnung seyn / nicht weit vom Hertzen / hat Gott die Lunge / die arteriam, die Lufftröhre / den Mund und die Zunge gesetzt / welche die Stimm und den Gesang machen / auff daß der Mensch wenn er sich selber anschawet / sich erinnerte er solte seiner Gliedmaß um das Hertz also gebrauchen / daß Gott / der in dem Tempel unsers Hertzens wohnen wil / gelobet und aus warer Danckbarkeit angesungen werde." Frick, *Music-Büchlein* (1631), 58.

29. Harrison, *The Territories of Science and Religion*, 190.

30. Damrau, *The Reception of English Puritan Literature*, 106.

31. D'Errico, *Powers of Divergence*, 97; McClary, *Desire and Pleasure*, 32.

32. See my earlier commentary on this piece, p. 18. On bodily inscription, see also pp. 145–152; and Erin Lambert, *Singing the Resurrection*, 47–84.

Chapter 27

1. Le Guin, *Boccherini's Body*, 206; Cusick, "Towards an Acoustemology of Detention," 275–291.

2. "Kranckheit ist nichts anders / alß ein zerüttung der Natürlichen ordnung des Leibs. Die Harmony der Seiten im Leib wird zerstört / unnd hat man offt lang dran zu stimmen / biß man sie wider zur Consonans bringt." Lehmann, *Florilegium politicum* (1639), 443.

3. See for instance Herzfeld-Schild, "Resonanz und Stimmung."

4. "sanitatem corporis nostri versari in aequabili, placida, libera & expedita spirituum, sanguinis & fluorum per totius corporis tubulos motione, circulatione & excrementorum per debita evacuatoria secretione. . . . Contra vero omnis morbus & motus morbosus consistit immediatè in motu partium fluidarum spirituum & sanguinis tardiori vel celeriori, circulatione inaequali & secretione partium excrementitiarum plane depravata." Hoffmann, *Dissertationes physico-medicae* (1708), 110–111.

5. Stolberg, *Experiencing Illness*, 86.

6. "von Verhärtungen und Klebrigkeiten herrühren, welche die Gefäße verstopfen und die gehörige Bewegung des Nervensaftes auf eine besondere Art verhindern." *Kern der ganzen Medicin* (1748), 59.

7. Thomson, *The True Way of Preserving the Bloud* (1670), 40.

8. Barrough, *The Method of Physick* (1624), 2.

9. "daß die Seele in ihrer ordentlichen Bewegung turbiret wird eines theils durch hitzige Affecten / Zorn / Grimm / Rachgierde / wodurch das Blut und übrige Leibes-Säffte in einen Jast und Wallung gerathen." Detry, *Betrachtung des Menschen* (1726), 163.

10. Detry, *Betrachtung des Menschen* (1726), 12.

11. See Kümmel, *Musik und Medizin*, 136.

12. Duden, "Anmerkungen zur Kulturgeschichte des Herzens," 138.

13. Downame, *Spiritual Physicke* (1600), 1; Hutter, *Compendium locorum theologicorum* (1610), 71.

14. "da sie in dem Leibe wohnet / als ein Stachel des Todes freylich den Leib verletztet." Richter, *Kurtzer und deutlicher Unterricht* (1705), 128.

15. "Weil die Sünde unser Fleisch und Blut dergestalt durchkrochen, daß von der Fußsohlen an bis auf das Haupt nichts gesundes an uns zu finden ist." Stock, *Homiletisches Real-Lexicon* (1734), 431.

16. Rittmeyer, *Himmlisches Freuden-Mahl* (1743), 57. The numerous editions of this devotional volume across the period each fill this heart space with a slightly different array of imaginary creatures and shapes of sin. Rittmeyer's images are based on the popular Catholic image series *Cor Iesu amanti sacrum* (around 1600) by Anton II Wierix.

17. Burnet, *Anatomy Spiritualized* (1696), 231.

18. Lebeuf, *Traité historique et pratique* (1741), 10; Jean Calvin, foreword to the Geneva Psalter (1545), cited in Begbie, *Music, Modernity and God*, 16.

19. Printz, *Musica modulatoria* (1678), 9.

20. "Est ergo per auditum capax homo recipiendi etiam venenum, & inter pestis causas vox reponenda." Gutierrez, *Febrilogiae lectiones pincianae* (1668), 164.

21. Blankaart, *Neuscheinende Praxis der Medicinae* (1700), 5. See pp. 186–187.

22. "da dann die Erkältung von inwendig anfanget / sich biß in die Haut hinaus erstrecket und nicht nur obangezogne Erstickung, sondern auch Wind-wässerige Erfüllungen / und Geschwulsten verursachet." Lower, *Wassersucht* (1719), 22.

23. Zwinger, *Compendium medicinae universae* (1724), 530.

24. "wenn die Wärme nicht allemal weichet und vergeht, sondern sich in den Schweißlöchern, die sie eingenommen hat, widersetzt und streitet. Welcher Streit der Schauer und das Zittern genannt wird." "Abhandlung von dem Ursprunge der Kälte" (1747), 60.

25. "Man empfindet öfters einen starcken Schauer in der Haut, wenn man eine Musik anhöret. Die Haare richten sich in die Höhe, das Blut beweget sich von aussen nach innen, die äussern Theile fangen an kalt zu werden, das Hertze klopft geschwinder, und man hohlt etwas langsamer und tiefer Othem." Nicolai, *Die Verbindung der Musik* (1745), 21.

26. Ettmüller, *Disputatio effectus musicae* (1714), 18.

27. "In dem Gesang gibt es bisweilen Tremulanten / Tripel und solche harte Noten / die man schwerlich singen kan. Diese können gezogen werden auf die vielfältige Anfechtungen deß leidigen Satans / damit er dem Menschen zusetzet / und ihn zum Zittern und Schrecken bringet / daß ers manchmal fast nimmer ausstehen und überwinden kan." Hartmann, *Denck- und Danck-Säule* (1673), 29–30.

28. Bach, *Versuch* (1762), 86.

29. *Purcell, King Arthur,* Deller Consort & Choir, The King's Musick, Alfred Deller, Harmonia Mundi (1986); *A Purcell Collection*, VOCES8, Les Inventions, Signum Classics SIGCD375 (2014). On the history and uses of this kind of tremolo across the seventeenth century, see Carter, "The String Tremolo in the 17th Century."

30. "Tremuliren, heist eigentlich zittern, it. vor Furcht mit den Zähnen knirschen. In der Music heist es einen Triller schlagen." Gladov, *A la Mode-Sprach der Teutschen* (1728), 755.

31. Kircher, *Musurgia universalis* (1662), 138–139.

32. *Henry Purcell, King Arthur*, dir. René Jacobs, Staatsoper Berlin, Schiller Theater, 21 January 2017.

33. Sorge, *Anweisung zur Stimmung und Temperatur* (1744), 45.

34. "Sieh wie das blut in meinen adern starrt! Der Sünden gift macht mich so kalt und hart; Du, du kanst mich erweichen und erwarmen, Wenn du mit deiner heissen Gnadenfluth Durchdringest mein erstarrtes Sünden-blut." Thommen, *Erbaulicher Musicalischer Christen-Schatz* (1745), 90.

35. Drexel, *Nicetas* (1633). This popular pamphlet against sexual voluptuousness was originally published in Latin in Munich (1624).

36. Wright, *The Passions of the Minde* (1604), 35.

37. See Grewe, Nagel, Kopiez, and Altenmüller, "Listening to Music as a Re-Creative Process."

38. Huron and Margulis, "Musical Expectancy and Thrills," 591.

39. See Panksepp, "The Emotional Sources of 'Chills,'" 203.

40. See also Vanessa Agnew's evocative essay, "Gooseflesh."

41. "Vernehme ich in der Kirche eine feyerliche Symphonie, so überfält mich ein andächtiger Schauder." Mattheson, *Kern melodischer Wissenschaft* (1737), 67.

42. See above, p. 119.

43. "Herr Gott! so offt ich diß nach aller läng bedencke, so schneidet angst und furcht durch adern und gelencke, so schauert mir die haut, so gellt und klingt das ohr, so bebet mund und hertz, und hebet sich empor." Freylinghausen, *Geistreiches Gesang-Buch* (1737), 462–463.

Chapter 28

1. South, *Musica incantans* (1700), 5.

2. Rolfinck, *Ordo et methodus medicinae* (1669), 597.

3. Desault, *Dissertation sur les maladies veneriennes* (1733), 314.

4. See for instance Untzer, *Bericht Von der Pestilentz* (1607), chapter 5, n.p.

5. Albrecht, *Tractatus physicus* (1734), 127.

6. "Dissonantiae seyn / wenn man sonos, Laut oder Klang zusammen setzt / die einem von Natur in den Ohren weh thun." Herbst, *Musica poetica* (1643), 19.

7. "daß einem die Ohren gältzen / und die Zähne davon wehe thun möchten." Niedt, *Musicalische Handleitung / Oder Gründlicher Unterricht* (1710), chapter 12, n.p.

8. "Sintemalen etliche soni also ungereimt und beschwärlich fallen / daß einem die Zähn davon knirschen und wehe thun." Kircher, *Musurgia universalis* (1662), 163.

9. "Wann aber die soni disproportionirt seyn / so haben sie widrigen Effect in den menschlichen Leibern: dann wegen ihrer vehementz verletzen sie entweder dieselbe / oder erwecken grossen Schmertzen in denselben." Kircher, *Musurgia universalis* (1662), 192.

10. Hobbes, *The Moral and Political Works* (1750), 15.

11. "man ziehe ihm die Härlein mit Pincetten aus den Ohren heraus." Mattheson, *Exemplarische Organisten-Probe* (1719), 16.

12. Werckmeister, *Der Edlen Music-Kunst Würde* (1691), 28.

13. Walther, *Praecepta*, 234.

14. Fuhrmann, *Musicalischer Trichter* (1706), 55.

15. Kowalik, *Theology and Dehumanisation*, 34.

16. Scarry, *The Body in Pain*, 4.

17. Jackson, "Pain and Bodies," 375.

18. Barrough, *The Method of Physick* (1624), 69.

19. "eine enge Zusammendrückung, oder eine grosse Angst und innigstes Leiden." Stock, *Homiletisches Real-Lexicon* (1734), 978.

20. "bey schmertzhafften Kranckheiten . . . wann dieser Safft zu dick / zu scharff / und dergleichen Art beschaffen / die subtile poros der Nerven verstopfft / und den nachpressenden Theilgen nicht weichen kann / da dann aus solcher Pressung nothwendig ein gantz frembdes schmertzhafftes Gefühl die Seele empfinden muß." Jüngken, *Grund-Reguln* (1701), 23.

21. See Morris, *The Culture of Pain*, 9.

22. Price, "Psychological and Neural Mechanisms," 1769.

23. Descartes, *Excellent Compendium* (1653), 6.

24. "daß sich die Lebensgeister zusammen ziehen, und je kleiner die Intervallen werden, je mehr wächst der Eckel, so das Gehör darob empfindet." Steffani, *Sendschreiben* (1760), 40.

25. "Die zwey Consonantien, nemlich die Octava und Quinta verursachen eine gewisse Erweiterung der Lebens-Geister / und zwar geschicht eine grössere durch die erste als durch die andere. Welches herkommt von der Grösse ihrer Proportionen / die diese Form 1–2 und 2.3. haben . . . . Je kleiner aber die Proportiones werden / je mehr mangelt an der Erweiterung. . . . Die kleinere Intervallen folgender Proport. 8–9, 9–10, 15–16, 24–25 u.d.g. machen / daß das Gehör darob einen Eckel empfindet und die Lebens-Geister sich auch mehr zusammen ziehen." Raupach, *Veritophili Deutliche Beweis-Gründe* (1717), 21–22.

26. Rathey, *Bach's Major Vocal Works*, 192.

27. "quasi conturbatis & concußis organi fistulis, nil nisi raucedinem strepentis." Nucius, *Musices poeticae* (1613), chapter 2, n.p.

28. "Man fühlet sie aber immer auf der Hirn-schaale und oben auf den Knochen . . . also die sehr empfindliche Häutgen um die Knochen zerfresset, prickelt und zerreisset." Musitano, *Chirurgische und physicalische Waag-Schale* (1703), 228; "Welche durch die dissonantien hart zusammen gehen / das einem gleichsam durchs Hertz und Hirn dringen möchte." Herbst, *Musica poetica* (1643), 113.

29. "Weil ein Mensch das Fleische an sich trägt / muß er schmertzen haben." Anna Sophia of Hesse-Darmstadt, *Der Treue Seelenfreund* (1675), 93.

30. See Morris, *The Culture of Pain*, 162.

31. Scarry, *The Body in Pain*, 161–180.

32. "wie Christus an Leib und Seele jämmerlich in unsern Sünden gemartert wird / müssen wir ihm nach also gemartert werden im Gewissen / von unsern Sünden." Quirsfeld, *Geistliche Passion-Schule* (1680), "Vorrede," n.p.

33. "Gleichwie tieffe Wunden grosse Schmertzen machen: also muß / auf schwere Sünden / auch eine schmertzliche Reue folgen. Busse bestehet nicht nur im Kniebeugen; sondern auch / in dem Ablassen vom Bösen; deßgleichen / in grosser Hertzens-Arbeit / in Threnen / und Gebeten zu Gott." Finx, *Erinnerung der Morgenröthe* (1689), 573.

34. Jackson, "Pain and Bodies," 370.

35. "da uns gleichsam alle Gebeine zebrochen / das Hertz zerknirschet / und der Geist geängstiget ist." Dyke, *Nosce te ipsum* (1681), 737.

36. "Die wahre Bußthränen haben eine sehr treibende und reinigende Krafft und

Würkung . . . und ist keine Unsauberkeit so groß / welche nicht durch diese scharffe Bußlauge könne verrieben und vertrieben werden." Dyke, *Nosce te ipsum* (1681), 657–658.

37. "leichtern das Gemüht / sie kühlen das Hertze / und lindern den Wehemütigen den Sinn / sie bringen viel böser Dünste heraus / daß der Mensch sich leichter und leidlicher befindet / mit Weinen stillet sich mancher / und wird der Schmertze zugleich mit ausgeschüttet." Scherertz, *Fuga melancholiae* (1682), 72.

38. See for instance Gračanin, Bylsma, and Vingerhoets, "Why Only Humans Shed Emotional Tears."

39. Morris, *The Culture of Pain*, 48.

40. As reported in Spiess, *Tractatus musicus* (1745), 202.

41. Cox, *Music and Embodied Cognition*, 135–136 and passim.

42. "Die wahre Buße bestehet in der Umkehrung und Veränderung des gantzen Menschen . . . daß er sich durch hertzliche Erkänntniß und schmertzliche Reue von der Sünde abkehre." Pfeiffer, *Der wolbewährte Evangelische Aug-Apfel* (1685), 162.

43. See Chafe, *Tears into Wine*, passim; and my article "Heart-Felt Musicking."

44. "durch eine Christliche Musicam die Hertzen der Menschen getroffen / gerühret / und . . . zum guten beweget werden." Frick, *Music-Büchlein* (1631), 108.

Chapter 29

1. *Youri Egorov plays Bach*, Youri Egorov (piano), Pavane Records (1993).

2. See for instance Fuhrmann, *Musicalischer Trichter* (1706), 26.

3. Fudge, *Brutal Reasoning*, passim.

4. Descartes, *Excellent Compendium* (1653), 6.

5. Descartes, *Excellent Compendium* (1653), 49, 20.

6. Agnew, *Enlightenment Orpheus*, 99.

7. Lamy, *Apparatus biblicus* (1723), 465. On rabid dog bites, see also Stahl, *Praxis Stahliana* (1745), 1308–1309.

8. Paster, *Humoring the Body*, 154.

9. "Welche im reden vocem acutam & intensam von sich lassen / die sind zornmütig / muthwillig / frech und geil / wie die Böck / deren Natur sie haben / dann die Geiß ist ein solch Thier / welches solch Temperament hat / so zur Trückene declinirt / hat auch melancholiam mit Schleim vermischt / welches / weil es sich nicht wol zusammen reimet / ists ein Anzeigen einer corruption deß feuchten im Trucknen / daher dann auch ihr Gestanck komt." Kircher, *Musurgia universalis* (1662), 67. See also above, pp. 64–66.

10. See Dyck, "Materialism in the Mainstream," 900–901.

11. "der Jüden / Ketzer und ungläubigen Lob-Gesänge grunnitum suum & clamorem asinorum, ein Saugruntzen und Eselsgeschrey." Meißner, *Musica Christiana* (1664), n.p.

12. Fuhrmann, *Musicalischer Trichter* (1706), 36.

13. Mead, *The Medical Works* (1767), 49. See also Penelope Gouk's account in "Music and the Nervous System," 62–64. Some of the materials in the following three paragraphs draw on my article "Metamorphosis and the Beast Within."

14. Baglivi, *The Practice of Physick* (1723), 331.

15. "Es sind etliche Arten Gift / welche auf ein sonderbare weis ihre Würckung in die Phantasy haben / als vermittelst deren die im gantzen Leib erweckte humores in

das Hirn aufsteigen / darnach die Geister / letzlich die Phantasy einnehmen: vermittelst der Geister aber / werden alle Feuchtigkeiten deß gantzen Leibes nach den concipirten Gestalten in der Phantasy / und nach Unterschied deß Temperaments in den Menschen erreget und unruhig gemachet. Ist also kein Wunder / wann sie durch die Geister angestöckt / meynen / sie seien das / was ihnen die Phantasy vorbildet: . . . das aconitum, wans zu viel genommen wird / veränderts die Menschen / ihrer Einbildung und dem äusserlichen Schein nach in Fisch / Gäns / Endten / etc. . . . . Nicht anderster verhält sichs auch mit dem Tarantismo / dann weil die Spinnen underschiedlich sind / so haben sie auch ein underschiedliches Gift / so können sie auch underschiedene humores erregen." Kircher, *Musurgia universalis* (1662), 187.

16. "deß verborgenen Gifts / so wie ein scharpfer / beissiger und schleimichter humor in den innersten medullis der Ader-fäserlein verborgen ligt . . . dieser sinnliche Geist sambt dem Gifft erweckt / erhitzigt und erregt / gleichsam mit einem pruritu oder jucken alle musculos afficiret." Kircher, *Musurgia universalis* (1662), 179.

17. Baglivi, *The Practice of Physick* (1723), 331.

18. Baglivi, *The Practice of Physick* (1723), 343. Cited among many others in Raupach, *Veritophili Deutliche Beweis-Gründe* (1717), 38.

19. "A Description of the Tarantula" (1748), 253.

20. Mead, *The Medical Works* (1767), 253.

21. Mead, *The Medical Works* (1767), 50.

22. Derrida, "Plato's Pharmacy," 127.

23. Gotman, *Choreomania*, 5.

24. Agamben, *The Open*, 79, 33.

25. Knaup, *Unity of Body and Soul*, 142.

26. Vogt, *Conclave thesauri* (1717), 97.

Chapter 30

1. Kant, *Kritik der Urteilskraft* (1790), 239.

2. Smith, "Hearing Green," 168.

3. Berardi, *Miscellanea musicale* (1689), 48.

4. "weil die freye Passage im Abdomine gehindert ist, regurgitiren zuweilen die congestiones versus Caput und Cerebrum, und confundiren daselbst die Actiones Naturae." Stahl, *Praxis Stahliana* (1745), 1416.

5. Evrensel and Ceylan, "The Gut-Brain Axis."

6. "Die Speisen verwandeln sich in die Substanz und Wesen dessen / der sie isset." Spadoni, *Studium Curiosum* (1695), 125.

7. "gleich wie unterschiedliche Speisen in dem Menschlichen Cörper mancherley Geblüt causiren und zuwegen bringen: . . . Daß also und der gestalt / durch solche Gesänger / welche mit mancherley Verenderungen der Stimmen gezieret seyn / die Hertzen und Gemüther der Menschen wundersam verwechselt / eingenommen und bewogen werden." Herbst, *Musica poetica* (1643), 114.

8. "non aliâ re magis supernae voluptatis praegustum animis nostris insinuari, quàm consonâ, fidémq; servantium fidium harmoniâ." Biber, *Mensa sonora* (1680), Dedication, n.p. Translation adapted from Brewer, *The Instrumental Music*, 267.

9. Biber, *Sonatae tam aris quam aulis* (1676). For a comprehensive list of contemporary *Tafelmusik* publications, see Zohn, "Telemann's *Musique de table*."

10. See for instance Johann Wülfer's preface to the hymnal *Gottgeheiligter Chris-*

ten Tafel-Music (1718), or Catharina Regina von Greiffenberg's reflections in *Zwölf andächtige Betrachtungen* (1672), 623–624.

11. "je lieblicher / und gleichsam Honigsüß der Gesang den Ohren . . . fürkommen," Herbst, *Musica poetica* (1643), 114.

12. "Sie weiß den matten Sinn durch angenehme Weisen, Wenn sie beweglich sind, mit holder Krafft zu speisen; Sie schenckt den Nectar-Tranck, der bis in tieffen Grund Des zarten Geistes dringt; Sie macht dem Hertzen kund, Was sich vor Süßigkeit in denen Tonen findet." Reinholdt, *Poetische Gedancken* (1736), 18.

13. Floyer, *The Physician's Pulse-Watch* (1707), 177. See above, p. 202.

14. "Alle schwefeligte Arzeneyen versüßen bekanntermaßen das Geblüt, indem sie die säuerlichen Theilchen in den Schranken halten, die da verursachen, daß das Geblüt aussernatürlich zusammenhänget, und voller Klumpen wird." *Kern der ganzen Medicin* (1748), 30.

15. Brockes, *Irdisches Vergnügen* (1739), 357.

16. "durchs schmecken, fühlen und empfinden kommt man zu dem rechten Erkändtnüß Christi." Müller, *Evangelische SchlußKett* (1734), 1161.

17. Müller, *Seelen-Musik* (1684), 93.

18. Connor, "Edison's Teeth: Touching Hearing."

19. Goehr, "Hardboiled Disillusionment," 3.

20. Gershon, *The Second Brain*.

21. "gleichwie diejenige, so einen versäuerten Magen haben, vor anderen zu sauren Speisen einen verfälschten Appetit haben, also auch die, deren Gehör verwehnt, verkehrt, verderbt, sich an dem aus den grausamsten Dissonanzien enstandenen Heulen mehr können belustigen, als an dem wahren Gusto einer reinen, und wohlklingenden Music." Spiess, *Tractatus musicus* (1745), 182.

22. Giles, "Physicality and Devotion," 83.

23. *Biber, Mensa Sonora, Sonata Representativa*, Musica Antiqua Köln, dir. Reinhard Goebel, Archiv Production 423 701–2 (1988). See above, p. 71.

24. Kant, *Kritik der Urteilskraft* (1790), 269.

25. On the perception of individual parts in polyphonic music, see Huron, "Voice Denumerability."

26. Herbst, *Musica poetica* (1643), 114.

27. Yearsley, "Bach the Humorist," 204–210.

28. Not to mention the culinary subtext of the quodlibet that precedes the aria's return in the Goldberg Variations, as it wordlessly sings of cabbages and turnips ("Kraut und Rüben haben mich vertrieben" run the lyrics of one of the tunes Bach used here). I thank David Yearsley for tossing me this tasty morsel. See his *Bach and the Meanings of Counterpoint*, 120–122.

29. Pierre-Jean Burette, as reported in Charles Burney, "A Dissertation," 185–186. I have not been able to get hold of Burette's original dissertation from which the comment is drawn.

30. Meyfart, *Das Erste Buch von Dem Himlischen Jerusalem* (1627), 448, with reference to Revelation 14.

Envoi

1. Zarlino, *Le istitutioni harmoniche* (1558), 11.

2. Tomlinson, *A Million Years of Music*, 289.

3. "Die Music erfrischet das Geblüt / ermuntert den Geist / schwinget die Füß / beweget die Händ / löset die Zungen / kitzlet die Ohren / eröffnet die Augen / ziehet das gantze Hertz des Menschen an sich: Die Music entzündet die Liebe / löschet den Zorn / mildert die Schmertzen / treibt und verjagt alle melancholische Mucken aus dem Kopff hinweg: Die Music versöhnet Gott im hohen Himmel / erfreuet die Engel in ihren neun Chören / erlustiget uns Menschen auf Erden / ergötzet die Thier / obsieget die Teuffel: Die Music stillet die Kinder in der Wiegen / erquicket die Handwercker in ihrer Arbeit / ermuntert die Soldaten zum Streit / verzucket die Geistliche in ihrem Gebett." Ertl, *Sonn- und Feyer-Tägliches Tolle Lege* (1708), 751.

Primary Sources

BIOGRAPHICAL REGISTER AND WORKS CITED

AGRICOLA, JOHANN FRIEDRICH (1720–1774)

German composer, organist, and singing teacher, based in Leipzig and Berlin, translator of Pier Francesco Tosi's singing treatise (see below).

AGRIPPA, HEINRICH CORNELIUS (1486–1535)

German theologian, physician, and legal scholar who worked and traveled across Europe. His *De occulta philosophia libri tres*, which appeared in 1531–1533, offers a summation of Renaissance occult and magical thought.

Three Books of Occult Philosophy, trans. James Freake (London: Moule, 1651).

AHLE, JOHANN GEORG (1651–1706)

German composer, organist, music theorist, and Protestant church musician, son of Johann Rudolf Ahle (below), based in Mühlhausen, whose writings offer a comprehensive view of musical knowledge of his time.

"Johan Georg Ahlens ergetz- und nützliche / theils auch nöthige Anmerkungen," in Johann Rudolf Ahle, *Kurze / doch deutliche Anleitung zu der lieblich- und löblichen Singe-Kunst* (Mühlhausen: Brückner, 1704).

AHLE, JOHANN RUDOLF (1625–1673)

German composer, organist, educator, and Protestant church musician, based in Mühlhausen.

Kurze / doch deutliche Anleitung zu der lieblich- und löblichen Singekunst, ed. Johann Georg Ahle (Mühlhausen: Pauli, 1690).

ALBRECHT, JOHANN WILHELM (1703–1736)

Professor of anatomy, chirurgery, and botany at the University of Erfurt.

Tractatus physicus de effectibus musices in corpus animatum (Leipzig: Martin, 1734).

ALTENBURG, MICHAEL (1584–1640)

German composer, hymn writer, and Lutheran pastor, mainly based in Erfurt.

De musica, ed. Inga Mai Groote and Dietrich Hakelberg, in "Circulating Musical Knowledge in Early Seventeenth-Century Germany: *Musica Poetica* Treatises of Johann Hermann Schein and Michael Altenburg in the Library of Johann Caspar Trost," *Early Music History* 35 (2016): 177–200.

AMMON, HIERONYMUS (1591–1659)

German scholar and town lawyer in Nuremberg. He wrote a dedicatory poem to Andreas Herbst's *Musica poetica* (see below).

ANNA SOPHIA OF HESSE-DARMSTADT (1638–1683)

German Lutheran noblewoman and hymn writer. She entered the Quedlinburg Abbey in 1655 and was elected abbess in 1681.

Der Treue Seelenfreund Christus Jesus (Jena: Löfler, 1675).

ARNOLD, GOTTFRIED (1666–1714)

German Lutheran theologian, pastor, hymn writer, and historian. His Pietist-leaning two-volume history of the Christian church was widely influential if controversial among orthodox Lutherans.

Das Leben der Gläubigen (Halle: Waysenhaus, 1701).

Unpartheyische Kirchen- und Ketzer-Historie, 2 vols. (Frankfurt: Fritsch, 1700).

ATHYRUS, FABIAN

Probably a pseudonym for the German poet Georg Philipp Harsdörffer (see below).

Das erneuerte Stamm- und Stechbüchlein (Nuremberg: Gerhard, 1654).

AUGUSTINE OF HIPPO (354 CE–430 CE)

Theologian and philosopher in Roman North Africa who is regarded as one of the most important Church Fathers of the Christian church.

Patrologiae cursus completus, Series Latina, ed. Jacques Paul Migne, 221 vols. (Paris: Migne, 1844–1855).

BACH, CARL PHILIPP EMANUEL (1714–1788)

Renowned German composer, musician, and pedagogue, eldest son of Johann Sebastian Bach, employed at the court of Frederick the Great in Berlin.

Versuch über die wahre Art das Clavier zu spielen (Berlin: Winter, 1762).

BACILLY, BERTRAND BÉNIGNE DE (?1625–1690)

French composer and singing teacher mainly active in Paris. His singing treatise forms one of the most detailed sources on French vocal practice of the time.

Remarques curieuses sur l'art de bien chanter (Paris: Ballard, 1668).

BACON, FRANCIS (1561–1626)

Leading English philosopher and statesman whose work was foundational to the scientific revolution in pursuing empirical methods of observation and induction. His *Sylva Sylvarum* is more idiosyncratic in nature and most likely represents his manuscript collection of experiments and theories.

The Essays, or Councils, Civil and Moral (London: Herringman, 1696).

Sylva Sylvarum, or, A Natural History in Ten Centuries, 9th ed. (London: Lee, 1670).

BAGLIVI, GIORGIO (1668–1707)

Armenian-Italian physician and scientist who experimented widely on the physiology of animals.

The Practice of Physick (London: Midwinter, 1723).

BAN, JOAN ALBERT (1597/98–1644)

Dutch self-educated music theorist and composer who corresponded with contemporaries such as Marin Mersenne, Giovanni Battista Doni, and René Descartes.

Kort Sangh-Bericht (Amsterdam: Matthysz, 1643).

BARLEY, WILLIAM (?1565–1614)

London-based draper, bookseller, and publisher of music.

The Pathway to Musicke (London: Barley, 1596).

BARON, ERNST GOTTLIEB (1696–1760)

German lutenist, composer, and writer on music who worked at various courts across the German lands.

Historisch-Theoretisch und Practische Untersuchung des Instruments der Lauten (Nuremberg: Rüdiger, 1727).

BARROUGH, PHILIP (dates unknown)

Elizabethan surgeon and physician. He published the first book on medicine in the English language in 1587, which went into several editions.

The Method of Physick, 6th ed. (London: Field, 1624).

BERARDI, ANGELO (ca. 1636–1694)

Italian theorist, composer, and organist who worked at different institutions across Italy. His treatises offer insights into key aspects of Italian musical practice at his time.

Miscellanea musicale (Bologna: Monti, 1689).

BERGIER, NICOLAS (1567–1623)

French historian and music theorist based in Reims.

La musique speculative (manuscript), ed. and trans. Ekkehard Jost (Cologne: Arno Volk Verlag, 1970).

BEVERWIJCK, JOHAN VAN (1594–1647)

Dutch physician based in Dordrecht.

Schatz der Ungesundheit (Frankfurt: Fievet, 1672).

BEYER, JOHANN SAMUEL (1669–1744)

German composer and musical writer active in Weissenfels and Freiberg.

Primae lineae musicae vocalis (Freiberg: Kuhfus, 1703).

BIBER, HEINRICH IGNAZ FRANZ (1644–1704)

Renowned Austrian violinist and composer primarily based in Salzburg, famed for his virtuosic violin playing and composing.

Mensa sonora seu musica instrumentalis (Salzburg: Mayr, 1680).

Sonatae tam aris quam aulis servientes (Salzburg: Mayr, 1676).

BINET, ÉTIENNE (1569–1639)

Prolific French Jesuit author. His *Essay des merveilles de nature* is an eclectic volume of observations about nature and art.

Essay des merveilles de nature et des plus nobles artifices, 2nd ed. (Rouen: Beauvais, 1622).

BLANKAART, STEVEN (1650–1704)

Dutch physician, experimental scientist, and entomologist active in Amsterdam, follower of the Cartesian method, author of numerous medical treatises and dictionaries.

Cartesianische Academie Oder grund-lere Der Artzney-kunst (Leipzig: Fritsch, 1699).

Neuscheinende Praxis der Medicinae (Hanover and Wolfenbüttel: Freytag, 1700).

Reformirte Anatomie / Oder Zerlegung des Menschlichen Leibes, trans. Tobias Peucer (Leipzig: Weidmann, 1691).

BLOUNT, THOMAS (1618–1679)

English lexicographer whose *Glossographia*—a dictionary of hard or unusual words—went through several editions at his time.

Glossographia (London: Newcombe, 1661).

BOERHAAVE, HERMAN (1668–1738)

Dutch physician, chemist, and botanist active in Leiden, whose empirical work on human physiology achieved fame across Europe; he became a member of the French Academy of Sciences and the Royal Society of London.

Academical Lectures on the Theory of Physic, vol. 2 (London: Innys, 1743).

BOORDE, ANDREW (ca. 1490–1549)

English physician and writer who traveled across Europe as a student and practitioner. He published a number of popular health and dietary guides.

A Compendyous Regyment or a Dyetary of Healthe (London: Powell, 1547).

BOURDELOT, PIERRE (1610–1685)

French physician and anatomist mainly active in Paris who convened an Académie attended by some of the leading intellectuals of the day.

Histoire de la musique et de ses effects, compiled by Jacques Bonnet (Paris: Cochart, 1715).

BOSSUET, JACQUES-BÉNIGNE (1627–1704)

French Catholic bishop, preacher, orator, political philosopher, and diplomat, famed for his eloquence, who published widely on issues of theology and morals.

Maximes and Reflections upon Playes, trans. Jeremy Collier (London: Sare, 1699).

BRAITHWAIT, RICHARD (1588–1673)

English poet and writer active in various locations across England.

Essaies upon the Five Senses (London: Whittaker, 1620).

BROCKES, BARTHOLD HEINRICH (1680–1747)

German Enlightenment poet based in Hamburg, one of the first German writers to cultivate nature poetry. His passion libretto of 1712, *Der für die Sünde der Welt gemarterte und sterbende Jesus*, was set by numerous German composers at the time.

Verteutschter Bethlehemitischer Kinder-Mord des Ritters Marino (Hamburg: Kißner, 1725).

Irdisches Vergnügen in Gott, 4th ed., 2 vols. (Hamburg: Herold, 1739).

BROOKBANK, JOSEPH (1612–1668)

English clergyman and schoolmaster active in Buckinghamshire and London.

The Well-Tuned Organ (London: s.n., 1660).

BRUNO, JACOB PANCRATIUS (1629–1709)

Professor of medicine at Altdorf, studied in Jena and Padua. His medical lexicon is based on the *Lexicon medicum graeco-latinum* (1598) by the Italian humanist Bartholomeo Castelli.

Castellus renovatus, hoc est, lexicon medicum, ed. Jacob Pancratius Bruno (Nuremberg: Tauber, 1682).

BUCHER, URBAN GOTTFRIED (1679–1724)

German physician and writer who studied under the Halle physician Friedrich Hoffmann. His anonymously published *Brief-Wechsel* presents one of the earliest instances of a materialist conception of the soul in Germany.

Zweyer Guten Freunde vertrauter Brief-Wechsel vom Wesen der Seelen (Haag: Peter von der Aa, 1713).

BURETTE, PIERRE-JEAN (1665–1747)

French medic and historian of antiquity, son of the harpist Claude Burette, active in Paris, translator of Plutarch's *De musica*.

BURMEISTER, JOACHIM (1564–1629)

German music theorist, composer, and teacher based in Rostock whose *Musica poetica* offered a pioneering view of the art of musical composition.

Musica poetica (Rostock: Myliander, 1606); translated as *Musical Poetics*, trans. Benito V. Rivera (New Haven, CT: Yale University Press, 1993).

BURNET, ANDREW (1653–before 1723)

Scottish clergyman and writer, minister of St. Nicolas's, Aberdeen.

Anatomy Spiritualized (London: Marshall, 1696).

BURNEY, CHARLES (1726–1814)

English organist, composer, and significant music historian, based in London, whose European travels put him in touch with many leading musicians at the time.

"A Dissertation of the Music of the Ancients," in *A General History of Music from the Earliest Ages to the Present Period*, vol. 1 (London: Author, 1776), 1–194.

BURTON, ROBERT (1577–1640)

English scholar, writer, and Anglican clergyman, fellow of Oxford University, famed for his treatise on melancholy, which was reprinted five times over the seventeenth century.

The Anatomy of Melancholy (Oxford: Cripps, 1621).

BURWELL, MARY (dates unknown)

English amateur musician whose manuscript copy of a lute tutor (ca. 1670) offers insights into contemporary teaching and performance practice on the lute.

The Burwell Lute Tutor, ed. Leslie Hewitt (Leeds: Boethius Press, 1974).

BUTLER, CHARLES (ca. 1560–1647)

English writer, Anglican clergyman, and amateur musician employed at Magdalen College, Oxford, and later vicar at Wootton St. Lawrence.

The Principles of Musik in Singing and Setting (London: Haviland, 1636).

BYRD, WILLIAM (ca. 1540–1623)

Leading composer of the English late Renaissance, active in Lincoln and London, who made seminal contributions to all the major musical genres of the age.

Psalmes, Songs, and Sonnets (London: Snodham, 1611).

CACCINI, GIULIO (1551–1618)

Italian composer, singer, and singing teacher based in Florence who pioneered the new monodic and recitative styles.

Le nuove musiche (Florence: Marescotti, 1601).

CALVIN, JEAN (1509–1564)

Renowned French theologian active in Geneva who was a principal figure in the Protestant Reformations; founder of Calvinism.

CALVÖR, CASPAR (1650–1725)

German Lutheran theologian and polymath who corresponded with leading intellectual figures at the time. He published a substantial introduction to a treatise on musical temperature by Christoph Albert Sinn (see below).

"Vorrede," in *Musicalische Temperatura Practica* (Wernigerode: Struck, 1717).

CAMPANELLA, TOMMASO (1568–1639)

Italian Catholic theologian and Dominican friar, one of the most important philosophers of the late Renaissance with a keen interest in natural philosophy and natural magic.

CARPZOV, JOHANN BENEDICT (1639–1699)

German Lutheran theologian and Hebraist, pastor, and university professor at Leipzig.

Ein schönes Trost-Bild (Leipzig: Scholvien, 1693).

CASSERIUS, JULIUS (ca. 1552–1616)

Italian teacher of anatomy, physics, and surgery whose treatise on the voice was a pioneering contribution to the study of the human vocal apparatus.

The Larynx, Organ of the Voice, by Julius Casserius, Translated from the Latin with Preface and Anatomical Notes, ed. and trans. Malcolm H. Hast (Uppsala: Almquist & Wiksells, 1969).

CASTIGLIONE, BALDASSARE (1478–1529)

Italian writer and diplomat whose fame rests on his treatise *Il cortegiano* (first published 1528), a guide to the social etiquette of gentlemen and ladies.

The Courtier (London: Wolfe, 1588).

CAUSSIN, NICOLAS (1583–1651)

French Jesuit and orator, for a brief time confessor to King Louis XIII of France, who published an influential guide for courtiers in living a Christian life.

The Holy Court, The Command of Reason over the Passions, trans. Thomas Hawkins (London: Bentley, 1650).

CHALUSSAY, LE BOULANGER DE (dates unknown)

French author and playwright.

Morale galante, ou l'art de bien aimer (Paris: s.n., 1669).

CHAMBERS, EPHRAIM (ca. 1680–1740)

English encyclopedist based in London whose work laid the foundation for the famous French encyclopedists of the later eighteenth century.

Cyclopaedia: Or, An Universal Dictionary, 2 vols, 2nd ed. (London: Midwinter, 1738).

CHEYNE, GEORGE (1672–1743)

Scottish physician and philosopher whose interests spanned natural philosophy, medicine, astronomy, mathematics, and hygiene.

COUPERIN, FRANÇOIS (1668–1733)

Renowned French keyboardist and composer based in Paris, employed at the court of Louis XIV. His treatise on harpsichord playing is a valuable record of his own pedagogy and practice.

L'art de toucher le clavecin (Paris: Foucaut, 1716).

COUSSER, JOHANN SIGISMUND (1660–1727)

Hungarian-born composer and music director who worked in Germany, England, and Ireland.

The Universal Applause of Mount Parnassus (Dublin: Sandy, 1711).

CRAMER, DANIEL (1568–1637)

German Lutheran theologian and writer, professor, and archdeacon in Stettin. His emblem book was widely influential and imitated (e.g., in a 1649 volume by Hieronymus Ammon).

Emblemata sacra (Frankfurt: Jennis, 1624).

CRIVELLATI, CESARE (1553–1640)

Italian doctor and music theorist based in Viterbo, whose *Discorsi musicali* offers a compilation of traditional teachings on music.

Discorsi musicali (Viterbo: Discepoli, 1624).

CROOKE, HELKIAH (1576–1648)

Court physician to King James I of England. His *Mikrokosmographia*, a textbook on anatomy, gained widespread popular success.

Mikrokosmographia a Description of the Body of Man (London: Iaggard, 1615).

CRÜGER, JOHANN (1598–1662)

German Protestant musician and hymn writer, based in Berlin, who edited the most influential Lutheran hymn book of the seventeenth century.

Praxis pietatis melica (Frankfurt: Wust, 1662).

CURZON, HENRY (dates unknown)

Curzon's two-volume publication *The Universal Library* covers a range of subjects from theology to ethics and chirurgery.

The Universal Library: Or, Compleat Summary of Science, 2 vols. (London: Sawbridge, 1712).

DANNHAUER, JOHANN CONRAD (1603–1666)

Orthodox Lutheran theologian and preacher active in Strasburg.

DEMOCRITUS, CHRISTIAN (1673/74–1734)

Pen name of Johann Conrad Dippel, a German Pietist theologian, physician, alchemist, and occultist whose work attracted controversy in theological and scientific circles.

Kranckheit und Arzney Des Thierisch-Sinnlichen Lebens (Frankfurt and Leipzig: n.p., 1713).

DESAULT, PIERRE (1675–1737)

French physician.

Dissertation sur les maladies veneriennes (Bordeaux: Calamy, 1733).

DESCARTES, RENÉ (1596–1650)

French philosopher, mathematician, and scientist widely regarded as one of the founders of modern Western philosophy.

Excellent Compendium of Musick, trans. William Brouncker (London: Harper, 1653).

L'Homme (Paris: Angot, 1664); translated as *Treatise of Man,* trans. Thomas Steele Hall (Cambridge, MA: Harvard University Press, 1972).

Les passions de l'âme (Paris: Le Gras, 1649), translated as *The Passions of the Soul,* trans. Michael Moriarty (Oxford: Oxford University Press, 2015).

Principia philosophiae (Amsterdam: Elzevir, 1644).

DETRY, PETER FRIEDRICH (1685–1750)

Controversial Lutheran theologian and preacher active in Bremen.

Betrachtung des Menschen nach Geist / Seel und Leib (Frankfurt and Amsterdam: Author, 1726).

DIRUTA, GIROLAMO (ca. 1554–1610)

Italian organist and music theorist, author of the first comprehensive treatise on organ playing.

Il Transilvano, Part I (Venice: Vincenti, 1597).

DONI, GIOVANNI BATTISTA (1595–1647)

Italian philologist and music theorist who worked in Florence and France. He devoted much of his scholarship to the rediscovery of ancient Greek music.

Compendio del trattato (Rome: Fei, 1635).

Trattato della musica scenica, published posthumously in *De' trattati di musica,* ed. Anton Francesco Gori (Florence: Caesar, 1763).

DOWNAME, JOHN (1571–1652)

London-based Puritan clergyman and theologian who wrote on moral and devotional subjects.

Spiritual Physicke to Cure the Diseases of the Soul, Arising from Superfluitie of Choller (London: Simson, 1600).

DRESSLER, GALLUS (1533–ca. 1580–1589)

German music theorist and composer based in Madgeburg. His *Praecepta musicae poeticae* (manuscript, 1563) offers a pioneering description of compositional process in relation to the Renaissance motet.

DREXEL, HIEREMIAS (1581–1638)

Jesuit preacher and author of devotional literature who served as court preacher to Maximilian I, Elector of Bavaria, in Munich. His writings on virtue and the Christian life were widely distributed.

Nicetas Or The Triumph Over Incontinence, trans. Robert Samber (n.p., 1633).

DUVERNEY, GUICHARD JOSEPH (1648–1730)

French anatomist and member of the Academy of Sciences in Paris, considered the founder of scientific otology with his treatise on hearing (first published 1683).

Treatise of the Organ of Hearing, trans. John Marshall (London: Baker, 1737).

DYKE, DANIEL (THE ELDER) (d. 1614)

English theologian whose treatise *The Mystery of Selfe-Deceiving* (1614) became highly influential in Lutheran devotional practice. Its translator, Theodor Haak (1605–1690), was a German diplomat and writer who also produced a German translation of John Milton's *Paradise Lost.*

Nosce te ipsum Oder Selb-Betrug Sampt der Wahren Bueß, trans. Theodor Haak (Frankfurt: Seyler, 1681).

ERTL, IGNATIUS (1645–1713)

Augustinian hermit and preacher active in various convents and monasteries in Bavaria. His published sermon collections went through numerous editions.

Sonn- und Feyer-Tägliches Tolle Lege (Nuremberg: Bleul, 1708).

ETTMÜLLER, MICHAEL ERNST (1673–1732)

German physician and professor of anatomy and botany in Leipzig. His reputation as a teacher attracted numerous students of medicine to Leipzig.

Disputatio effectus musicae in hominem (Leipzig: Bauch, 1714).

FALCK, GEORG (1630–1689)

German composer, organist, and writer on music active in Rothenburg ob der Tauber, where he was responsible for church and school music.

Idea boni cantoris (Nuremberg: Endter, 1688).

FEIND, BARTHOLD (1678–1721)

German poet based in Hamburg who wrote numerous libretti for the Hamburg opera stage. His *Gedancken von der Opera* (1708) represents one of the key German contributions to a theory of opera at the time.

Deutsche Gedichte (Stade: Brummer, 1708).

FENNER, WILLIAM (1600–1640)

English Puritan preacher and writer on theology.

A Treatise of the Affections; Or The Soules Pulse (London: Rothwell, 1641).

FERRAND, JACQUES (ca. 1575–ca. 1620)

French physician famed for his controversial treatise on the physiology of lovesickness.

De la maladie d'amour ou mélancholie erotique (Paris: Moreau, 1623).

FICINO, MARSILIO (1433–1499)

Italian scholar, Catholic priest, astrologer, and Neoplatonist, one of the most influential philosophers of the Italian Renaissance.

FINX, ERASMUS (1627–1694)

German Lutheran author, translator, and hymn writer who worked for the Nuremberg publisher Endter.

Erinnerung der Morgenröthe / Oder: Geistliches Hanen-Geschrey (Nuremberg: Endter, 1689).

FLOYER, JOHN (1649–1734)

English physician and writer active in Lichfield, best known for his contribution to the practice of pulse rate measurement through his invention of the pulse watch.

The Physician's Pulse-Watch (London: Smith and Walford, 1707).

FLUDD, ROBERT (1574–1637)

English Paracelsian physician, astrologer, and mathematician with scientific and occult interests. He proposed a platonic view of the cosmos as a musical instrument set playing by the soul or spirit of the world. His ideas were widely debated among European intellectuals at the time.

Utriusque cosmi . . . metaphysica, physica atque technica historia, 2 vols., 2nd ed. (Frankfurt: Rotelius, 1624).

FURETIÈRE, ANTOINE (1619–1688)

French writer and lexicographer who was expelled from the Académie Française for planning to publish his own French language dictionary, which eventually appeared posthumously in the Netherlands.

Dictionaire universel, 3 vols. (La Haye and Rotterdam: Arnout, 1690).

FREYLINGHAUSEN, JOHANN ANASTASIUS (1670–1739)

German Pietist theologian and poet working in Halle. He edited the most influential of the Pietist hymnals, *Geistreiches Gesangbuch*, which went through numerous editions in the first half of the eighteenth century.

Geistreiches Gesangbuch, 2nd ed. (Halle: Waisenhaus, 1737).

FRICK, CHRISTOPH (1577–1640)

German Lutheran theologian, pastor, and writer on music.

Music-Büchlein (Lüneburg: Stern, 1631).

FUHRMANN, MARTIN HEINRICH (1669–1745)

German organist, cantor, and writer on music active in Berlin who wrote widely on aspects of contemporary music theory, practical musicianship, and music education.

Musicalischer Trichter (Frankfurt an der Spree: Autor, 1706).

Musica vocalis in nuce, Das ist: Richtige und völlige Unterweisung Zur Singe-Kunst (Berlin: Lorenz, n.d.).

GAGLIANO, MARCO DA (1582–1643)

Italian composer based in Florence who made important contributions to the early history of opera.

La Dafne (Florence: Marescotti, 1608).

GALILEI, VINCENZO (1520–1591)

Italian theorist, lutenist, singer, and music theorist who played a crucial role in the movement to revive ancient Greek musical ideals.

MSS Galileiani, Anteriori a Galileo, Biblioteca Nazionale, Florence (1588–1591).

GALLOIS, FRANÇOIS LE (1633–1693)

French writer and bibliographer.

Lettre de Mr Le Gallois à Mademoiselle Regnault de Solier touchant la musique (Paris: Michallet, 1680).

GALVANI, LUIGI (1737–1798)

Italian physician and physicist whose pathbreaking research investigated the nature and effects of electricity in animal tissue.

De viribus electricitatis in motu musculari (Bologna: Typographia Instituti Scientiarium, 1791).

GASSENDI, PIERRE (1592–1655)

French philosopher, experimentalist, scholar, and active participant in intellectual debates of his time, including his famous disputes with Descartes.

"Fifth Set of Objections," in *The Philosophical Writings of Descartes*, trans. John Cottingham, Robert Stoothoff, and Dugald Murdoch, vol. 2 (Cambridge: Cambridge University Press, 1984), 179–240.

GILDON, CHARLES (1665–1724)

English writer, critic, and dramatist who was active in the London literary scene, publishing books, pamphlets, and newspaper articles on contemporary poets and literature.

The Life of Mr. Thomas Betterton, The Late Eminent Tragedian (London: Gosling, 1710).

GLADOV, FRIEDRICH (d. 1715)

German writer and lexicographer who published on history, geography, and jurisprudence.

A la Mode-Sprach der Teutschen / Oder Compendieuses Hand-Lexicon (Nuremberg: Buggel and Seitz, 1728).

GOTTSCHED, JOHANN CHRISTOPH (1700–1766)

German literary theorist, critic, poet, and dramatist; professor of poetry, logic, and metaphysics at the University of Leipzig. He was a leading figure in the early eighteenth-century literary reform movement in Germany and a fierce critic of the art form of opera.

Versuch einer Critischen Dichtkunst, 4th ed. (Leipzig: Breitkopf, 1751).

GRAUPNER, CHRISTOPH (1683–1760)

Prolific German composer who initially worked at the Gänsemarkt opera in Hamburg and later as Kapellmeister at the Darmstadt Hofkapelle.

Partien auf das Clavier (Darmstadt: Author, 1718).

GREIFFENBERG, CATHARINA REGINA VON (1633–1694)

Austrian poet. One of the most important German-language female writers of the early modern period; member of the Nuremberg literary society *Pegnesischer Blumenorden*.

Des Allerheiligst- und Allerheilsamsten Leidens und Sterbens Jesu Christi Zwölf andächtige Betrachtungen (Nuremberg: Hofmann, 1672).

GRIMAREST, JEAN-LÉONOR LE GALLOIS DE (1659–1713)

French writer and scholar based in Paris.

Traité du récitatif (Paris: Le Fevre, 1707).

GROßGEBAUER, THEOPHIL (1627–1661)

German Lutheran theologian based in Rostock who made a significant contribution to the pre-Pietist reform literature at the time.

Drey geistreiche Schrifften (Frankfurt and Leipzig: Bild, 1667).

GRUBE, HERMANN (1637–1698)

German medic and scholar who published on the therapeutic effects of music.

De ictu tarantulae (Frankfurt: Pauli, 1679).

GUARINI, GIOVANNI BATTISTA (1538–1612)

Italian poet and dramatist based at Ferrara whose poetry was used extensively by Italian madrigal composers and opera librettists across the seventeenth century.

Rime (Venice: Giotti, 1598).

GUTIERREZ, JUAN LAZARO (dates unknown)

Spanish physician and professor of medicine in Valladolid.

Febrilogiae lectiones pincianae (Leiden: Anisson, 1668).

HALLER, ALBRECHT VON (1708–1777)

Swiss biologist, anatomist, and poet, active in Bern and Göttingen, pupil of Herman Boerhaave, considered one of the founders of experimental physiology.

HARSDÖRFFER, GEORG PHILIPP (1607–1658)

German lawyer, poet, and writer based in Nuremberg, founder of the literary society *Pegnesischer Blumenorden.*

HARTMANN, JOHANN LUDWIG (1640–1684)

German Lutheran theologian, preacher, and prolific popular writer based in Rothenburg ob der Tauber.

Denck- und Danck-Säule Von der Orgel und Instrumental-Music Ursprung und Fortpflantzung (Rothenburg: Beer, 1673).

HARVEY, WILLIAM (1578–1657)

English royal physician and physiologist based in London. He is renowned as the first Western scholar to describe in detail the process of blood circulation around the human body.

Exercitatio anatomica de circulatione sanguinis (Cambridge: Daniels, 1649); translated as *The Circulation of the Blood and Other Writings*, trans. Kenneth J. Franklin (London: Dent, 1963).

HECKER, JOHANN JULIUS (1707–1768)

German educator and theologian active in Halle and Berlin who published textbooks on anatomy and physiology.

Betrachtung des menschlichen Cörpers Nach der Anatomie und Physiologie (Halle: Waysen-Haus, 1734).

HEINICHEN, JOHANN DAVID (1683–1729)

German composer and music theorist who served as Kapellmeister at the Dresden court. His treatises on figured bass are important documents regarding the compositional and keyboard practice of his time.

Der General-Bass in der Composition (Dresden: Author, 1728).

Neu erfundene und Gründliche Anweisung Wie Ein Music-liebender auff gewisse vortheilhafftige Arth könne Zu vollkommener Erlernung des General-Basses (Hamburg: Schiller, 1711).

HEISTER, LORENZ (1683–1758)

German anatomist, surgeon, and botanist who studied in locations across Northern Europe. His publications on anatomy and surgery went through numerous editions.

Compendium anatomicum (Breslau: Hubert, 1721).

Practisches Medicinisches Handbuch (Leipzig: Blochberger, 1744).

HELLWIG, CHRISTOPH (1663–1721)

German doctor and physician active in Erfurt who published a number of popular medicine textbooks.

Vollkommenes Teutsch- und Lateinisches Physicalisch- und Medicinisches Lexicon (Hanover: Förster, 1713).

HELMONT, FRANCISCUS MERCURIUS VAN (1614–1699)

Flemish physician and alchemist who gained an international reputation working across the Netherlands, Germany, and England.

The Spirit of Diseases (London: Hawkins, 1694).

HERBERGER, VALERIUS (1562–1627)

German Lutheran theologian and renowned preacher based in Silesia.

HERBST, ANDREAS (1588–1666)

German music theorist and composer active in Darmstadt and Frankfurt who published practical treatises on signing and composition.

Musica poetica, sive compendium melopoeticum (Nuremberg: Dümler, 1643).

HEUERMANN, GEORG (1722–1768)

Dutch-German physiologist, surgeon, and university professor in Copenhagen.

Physiologie Erster Theil (Copenhagen and Leipzig: Pelt, 1751).

Physiologie Zweyter Theil (Copenhagen and Leipzig: Pelt, 1752).

HILL, AARON (1685–1750)

London-based English dramatist, essayist, and travel writer, producer of Georg Frederic Handel's opera *Rinaldo* at the Haymarket Theatre.

A Full and Just Account of the Present State of the Ottoman Empire (London, 1709).

HOBBES, THOMAS (1588–1679)

Leading English philosopher with wide-ranging interests whose materialist and empiricist views opposed aspects of Cartesianism. Widely considered the founder of modern political philosophy in the West.

The Moral and Political Works (London: n.p., 1750).

HOEFFT, GEORG JACOB (dates unkown)

Hamburg-based writer, colleague of Barthold Heinrich Brockes and Johann Mattheson.

HOFFMANN, FRIEDRICH (1660–1742)

German physician and university professor in Halle who attracted numerous medical students.

Dissertationes physico-medicae curiosae (Leiden: Haak, 1708).

Fundamenta medicinae (Halle: Hübner, 1695).

Gründliche Anweisung Wie ein Mensch Seine Gesundheit erhalten / und vor allerhand Kranckheiten / Durch ordentliche Lebens-Art / sich verwahren könne, 2 vols. (Halle: Renger, 1716).

HOHBERG, WOLF HELMHARD VON (1612–1688)

Austrian soldier, writer, and poet based in Lower Austria and Regensburg. His *Georgica curiosa* offered an encyclopedic overview of all aspects of housekeeping, child-rearing, and agriculture.

Georgica curiosa aucta (Nuremberg: Endtner, 1687).

HUTTER, LEONHARD (1563–1616)

German orthodox Lutheran theologian who taught at the University of Wittenberg. His *Compendium locorum theologicorum* served as a textbook for generations of theology students.

Compendium locorum theologicorum (Wittenberg: Helwig, 1610).

IRVINE, CHRISTOPHER (ca. 1620–1693)

Scottish physician, surgeon, and writer.

Medicina magnetica (Edinburgh: Higgins, 1656).

JOUBERT, LAURENT (1529–1582)

French physician and author of numerous medical texts in Latin and French.

Traité du ris (Paris: Chesneau, 1579).

JÜNGKEN, JOHANN HELFFRICH (1648–1726)

German physician employed as city physician in Frankfurt am Main who published a range of medical textbooks and primers.

Grund-Reguln Der Medicin (Frankfurt and Leipzig: Andreae, 1701).

Vernünfftiger und erfarner Leib-Artzt (Leipzig: Fritsch, 1699).

Wohlunterrichtender Sorgfältiger Medicus (Nuremberg: Rüdiger, 1725).

KEIL, CHRISTOPH HEINRICH (1680–1751)

German doctor who studied under Friedrich Hoffmann in Halle.

Compendiöses doch vollkommenes Anatomisches Handbüchlein (Leipzig and Hof: Martin, 1730).

KERN, CHRISTIAN GOTTLIEB (dates unknown)

German Lutheran writer.

Geistliche Safft- und Andachts-Quelle Jesum-liebender Seelen (Nuremberg: Otto, 1700).

KIRCHER, ATHANASIUS (1602–1680)

Acclaimed German Jesuit scholar, linguist, and polymath mainly active in Rome. His *Musurgia universalis* (1650) was one of the most comprehensive and influential music treatises of the time.

Musurgia universalis, trans. and ed. Andreas Hirsch as *Philosophischer Extract und Auszug / aus deß Welt-berühmten Teutschen Jesuiten Athanasii Kircheri von Fulda Musurgia Universalis* (Schwäbisch Hall: Laidig, 1662).

Neue Hall- und Thon-Kunst (Nördlingen: Schulte, 1684).

KRAMER, MATTHIAS (ca. 1640–after 1729)

German Catholic linguist and lexicographer who published a number of significant dictionaries and grammar books of the major European languages.

Il nuovo dittionario reale italiano-tedesco (Nuremberg: Endtner, 1724).

LAMY, BERNARD (1640–1715)

French mathematician, rhetorician, and theologian active at various locations across France who wrote an influential treatise on the art of oratory.

Apparatus biblicus: or; an Introduction to the Holy Scriptures, trans. Thomas Cartwright (London: Palmer, 1723).

LEBEUF, JEAN (1687–1760)

French historian and clergyman based in Auxerre who published on church history, archaeology, and music in the liturgy.

Traité historique et pratique sur le chant ecclesiastique (Paris: Herissant, 1741).

LEHMANN, CHRISTOPH (1568–1638)

German historian and archivist active in Speyer.

Florilegium politicum (Lübeck: Jung, 1639).

LEIBNIZ, GOTTFRIED WILHELM (1646–1716)

German rationalist philosopher, mathematician, and scientist who made major contributions to a range of early modern scientific and philosophical fields; detractor of Cartesian mind/body dualism.

LEMNIUS, LEVINUS (1505–1568)

Celebrated Dutch physician and writer who studied in Louvain and Padua. His medical writings enjoyed great popularity across Europe.

A Discourse Touching Generation (London: Streater, 1664).

LISTENIUS, NIKOLAUS (b. ca. 1510)

German music theorist and composer whose *Rudimenta musicae* (1533) was one of the most notable music primers of his time.

LOWER, RICHARD (ca. 1631–1691)

English physician active in Oxford and London, renowned for his work on blood transfusion and circulation.

Die Nach ihrem Ursprung, Unterschied und Wachsthum, Glücklich curirte Wassersucht (Hamburg: Liebezeit, 1719).

LUDOVICI, CHRISTIAN (1660–1728)

German doctor, teacher, and translator who translated some of Richard Lower's works into German.

A Dictionary English, German, French (Leipzig: Fritsch, 1706).

LUTHER, MARTIN (1483–1546)

Seminal figure in the Protestant Reformations, founder of Lutheranism. Professor of theology, priest, composer, hymn writer, translator of the Bible into German vernacular.

Die Propheten all Teutsch (Frankfurt: Feierabend, 1561).

MACE, THOMAS (1612/13–?1706)

English lutenist, singer, composer, and writer mainly based in Cambridge, known principally for his publication *Musick's Monument*, which offers plentiful information on contemporary English musical practice.

Musick's Monument (London: Ratcliffe, 1676).

MAFFEI, GIOVANNI CAMILLO (fl. 1562–1573)

Italian doctor, philosopher, and musician active in Naples. He combined his expertise in physiology and music in his writings on contemporary Italian singing practices.

Delle lettere del S. Gio. Camillo Maffei Da Solofra libri due (Naples: Amato, 1562).

MATTHESON, JOHANN (1681–1764)

German music theorist, journalist, critic, and composer based in Hamburg, one of the most prolific commentators on music of his time. His publications offer valuable information on contemporary German musical thought and practice.

Behauptung der himmlischen Musik aus den Gründen der Vernunft (Hamburg: Herold, 1747).

Critica musica, vol. 2 (Hamburg: Wiering, 1725).

Exemplarische Organisten-Probe (Hamburg: Schiller, 1719).

Das forschende Orchestre (Hamburg: Schiller, 1721).

Kern melodischer Wissenschaft (Hamburg: Herold, 1737).

Der musicalische Patriot (Hamburg: s.n., 1728).

Das neu-eröffnete Orchestre (Hamburg: Schiller, 1713).

Der vollkommene Capellmeister (Hamburg: Herold, 1739).

MEAD, RICHARD (1673–1754)

English medic active in London, studied in Leiden and Padua, physician to George II. He carried out seminal work on the transmission of diseases.

A Mechanical Account of Poisons (London: South, 1702).

The Medical Works of Richard Mead (London: Hitch and Millar, 1767).

MEI, GIROLAMO (1519–1594)

Italian humanist and scholar of ancient Greek music who worked in Florence, Rome, and France; correspondent of Vincenzo Galilei. His pioneering research laid the foundation for the emergence of monody and music drama.

Letter to Vincenzo Galilei, 8 May 1572, trans. in Claude Palisca, *The Florentine Camerata: Documentary Studies and Translations* (New Haven, CT: Yale University Press, 1989), 45–77.

MEISSNER, JOHANN (1615–1681)

German Lutheran theologian, preacher, and professor of theology at Wittenberg.

Musica Christiana, Das ist / Der Christen Singe-Kunst (Wittenberg: Borckgardten, 1664).

MELANCHTHON, PHILIPP (1497–1560)

First systematic theologian and intellectual leader of the Protestant Reformation, collaborator of Martin Luther, professor at the University of Wittenberg.

Initia doctrinae physicae (Wittenberg: Lufft, 1550).

Liber de anima (Leipzig: Rhambau, 1560).

MERSENNE, MARIN (1588–1648)

French mathematician, philosopher, and music theorist based in Paris. One of the leading French thinkers of the seventeenth century who corresponded widely with contemporary scientists and philosophers.

Harmonicorum libri (Paris: Baudry, 1635).

Harmonie universelle (Paris: Cramoisy, 1636).

MEYER, JOACHIM (1661–1732)

German lawyer and scholar active in Göttingen, detractor of Johann Mattheson.

Unvorgreiffliche Gedancken über die Neulich eingerissene Theatralische Kirchen-Music (n.p., 1726).

MEYFART, JOHANN MATTHÄUS (1590–1642)

German Lutheran theologian, hymn writer, and educator, professor of theology at the University of Erfurt.

Das Erste Buch von Dem Himlischen Jerusalem (Coburg: Gruner, 1627).

MICHAEL, SAMUEL (ca. 1597–1632)

German composer and organist in Leipzig.

Psalmodia regia (Leipzig: Francke, 1632).

MILANO, FRANCESCO DA (1497–1543)

Italian lutenist and composer active in Rome, famed for his virtuosic performances on the lute.

MILLET, JEAN (1618–1684)

French musician and churchman based in Besançon.

La belle méthode, ou, l'art de bien chanter (Lyon: Gregorie, 1666).

MIRUS, ADAM ERDMANN (1656–1728)

German educator, writer, and lexicographer who published popular primers on a wide range of topics.

Kurtze Fragen aus der Musica sacra (Dresden: Zimmermann, 1715).

MITHOBIUS, HECTOR (1600–1655)
German Lutheran theologian and pastor based in Rostock.
Psalmodia christiana (Jena: Berger, 1665).

MONTEVERDI, CLAUDIO (1567–1643)
Pioneering Italian composer who contributed substantially to the history of madrigal and opera. His proclamation of a "seconda prattica" of composition had a significant impact on twentieth-century music historiography.
Scherzi musicali a tre voci (Venice: Amadino, 1607).

MORE, HENRY (1614–1687)
English rationalist theologian, philosopher, and prolific writer, member of the so-called Cambridge Platonists.
A Collection of Several Philosophical Writings, 2nd ed. (London: Flesher, 1662).

MORLEY, THOMAS (ca. 1558–1602)
English music theorist, composer, publisher, and organist. His music treatise, perhaps the most famous in the English language, covers many aspects of musical practice at the time.
A Plaine and Easie Introduction to Practiall Musicke (London: Short, 1597).

MORYSON, FYNES (1566–1630)
English writer who traveled extensively across Europe and the eastern Mediterranean in the 1590s.
An Itinerary: Containing His Ten Years Travel Through the Twelve Dominions of Germany, Bohemia, Switzerland, Netherland, Denmark, Poland, Italy, Turkey, France, England, Scotland and Ireland (London: Beale, 1617).

MOULINIÉ, ETIENNE (1599–1676)
French composer mainly based at the court in Paris, famed for his *airs de court*.
Airs avec la tablature de luth (Paris: Ballard, 1624).

MÜLLER, HEINRICH (1631–1675)
German Lutheran theologian, hymn writer, and minister based in Rostock. He authored a range of devotional works that remained influential into the eighteenth century.
Evangelische SchlußKett Und Krafft-Kern (Frankfurt: Hort, 1734).
Geistliche Seelen-Musik Bestehend In Zehen Betrachtungen, 3rd ed. (Frankfurt: Wust, 1684).
Himmlischer Liebes-Kuß oder Göttliche Liebes-Flamme (Nuremberg: Endter, 1724).

MUSITANO, CARLO (1635–1714)
Italian doctor known for his study of venereal diseases.
Chirurgische und physicalische Waag-Schale der Venus-Seuche (Hamburg: Pauli, 1703).

MYLIUS, WOLFGANG MICHAEL (1636–ca. 1713)
German music theorist, teacher, and composer who worked across the German lands.
Rudimenta musices, Das ist: Eine kurtze und Grund-richtige Anweisung zur Singe-Kunst (Gotha: Author, 1686).

NASSARE, PABLO (1654–1730)
Spanish Franciscan cleric based in Zaragossa.

Esquela musica, vol. 2 (Zaragoza: Roman, 1723).
Fragmentos músicos, 2nd ed. (Madrid: Imprenta de Musica, 1700).

NEWTON, ISAAC (1642–1727)

English mathematician, physicist, astronomer, and philosopher based in Cambridge, one of the most influential thinkers in the Western tradition, with foundational contributions to the scientific revolution, mechanics, and optics.

"A letter of Mr. Isaac Newton, Mathematick Professor in the University of Cambridge, containing his new theory about light and colors," *Philosophical Transactions of the Royal Society* 80 (1671/2): 3075–3087, http://www.newtonproject.ox.ac.uk/view/texts/normalized/NATP00006.

"General Scholium," in *The Mathematical Principles of Natural Philosophy*, trans. Andrew Motte, vol. 2 (London: Motte, 1729) 387–393, https://newtonprojectca.files.wordpress.com/2013/06/newton-general-scholium-1729-english-text-by-motte-letter-size.pdf.

Opticks, 4th ed. (London: Innys, 1730).

NICOLAI, ERNST ANTON (1722–1802)

German physician, student of Friedrich Hoffmann in Halle, who published widely on medical topics.

Die Verbindung der Musik mit der Artzneygelahrtheit (Halle: Hemmerde, 1745).

NIEDT, FRIEDRICH ERHARD (1674–1708)

German music theorist and composer who worked in Jena and Copenhagen. His teaching manuals achieved wide circulation due in part to being promoted by Johann Mattheson.

Handleitung / zur Variation (Hamburg: Schiller, 1706).
Musicalische Handleitung Oder Gründlicher Unterricht (Hamburg: Schiller, 1710).
Musicalischer Handleitung Anderer Theil (Hamburg: Schiller, 1721).
Musicalischer Handleitung Dritter und letzter Theil (Hamburg: Schiller, 1717).

NIGRINUS, CASPAR (dates unknown)

His 1709 treatise on the physiology of reproduction is based on the work of the thirteenth-century Dominican friar Albertus Magnus (Saint Albert of Cologne).

Der Aus seiner Asche Sich wieder schön verjüngende Phönix (Frankfurt and Leipzig: Buggel, 1709).

NORTH, ROGER (1651–1734)

English lawyer, writer, historian of music, and amateur musician based in London. His commentaries on his musical activities offer valuable insights into contemporary musical practice. Most of his musical writings, including his notes for a theory of musical cognition, remained unpublished.

Roger North on Music: Being a Selection from his Essays Written During the Years c. 1695–1728, ed. John Wilson (London: Novello, 1959).

NUCIUS, JOHANNES (ca. 1556–1620)

German music theorist and composer from Silesia. His *Musices poeticae* is a key source on early seventeenth-century compositional practice.

Musices poeticae sive de compositione cantus (Neisse: Scharffenberg, 1613).

OEHME, JOHANN AUGUST (1693–1754)

Dresden-based medic and surgeon.

Medicinische Fama, 7th ed. (Dresden: Author, 1749).

OLDHAM, JOHN (1653–1683)
English poet and translator, based in Surrey, acquaintance of Richard Lower.
The Works of John Oldham (London: Hindmarsh, 1684).

OLEARIUS, JOHANNES (1611–1684)
German Lutheran hymn writer, preacher, and scholar. His *Geistliche Singe-Kunst* is one of the largest and most important seventeenth-century German hymnals.
Geistliche Singe-Kunst (Leipzig: Lunitz, 1671).

OPITZ, MARTIN (1597–1639)
German poet and literary theorist who introduced French and Italian literary models into German poetry. His *Buch von der deutschen Poeterey* laid the foundation for a national German literary style.
Buch von der deutschen Poeterey (Breslau: Müller, 1624).

ORNITHOPARCUS, ANDREAS (dates unknown)
Author of a Latin treatise on music, *Musicae activae micrologus* (1519), which was translated into English by John Dowland in 1609.
Micrologus, trans. John Dowland (London: Adams, 1609).

OVID (PUBLIUS OVIDIUS NASO) (43 BCE–17/18 CE)
Roman poet during the reign of Augustus. His *Metamorphoses* loomed large in the mythological imagination of European early modernity.
Metamorphoses, trans. Arthur Golding, ed. Madeleine Forey (London: Penguin, 2002).

PARÉ, AMBROISE (ca. 1510–1590)
Celebrated French physician active in Paris, surgeon to the royal household, who introduced many new medical treatments and instruments.
WundtArtzney / oder Artzney spiegell, trans. Peter Uffenbach (Frankfurt: Fischer, 1601).

PASCAL, BLAISE (1623–1662)
French mathematician, philosopher, writer, and Catholic theologian; a leading thinker of the scientific revolution who made important contributions to the study of mathematics and physics. His *Pensées* is renowned for its literary style and philosophical insight; it remained incomplete at his death.
Pensées, trans. A. J. Krailsheimer (London: Penguin, 1995).

PERRAULT, CLAUDE (1613–1688)
French architect, physician, and experimentalist based in Paris whose treatise *Du bruit* in his *Essais de physique* (1680–1688) made a valuable contribution to the study of sound vibration and acoustics.

PEZEL, JOHANN CHRISTOPH (1639–1694)
German violinist and trumpeter who spent his career as a Stadtpfeiffer (town musician) in Leipzig and elsewhere. His published collections of *Turmmusik* offer important insights into the Stadtpfeiffer tradition.
Hora decima musicorum Lipsiensium (Leipzig: Frommann, 1670).

PFEIFFER, AUGUST (1640–1698)
German Lutheran theologian, philologist, preacher, and devotional writer who took an orthodox stance against the Pietist trends of his time.
Apostolische Christen-Schule (Lübeck: Krüger, 1704).
Der wolbewährte Evangelische Aug-Apfel (Leipzig: Kloß, 1685).

PFITZER, JOHANN NICOLAUS (1634–1674)
German physician and medical writer based in Nuremberg.
Zwey sonderbare Bücher / von der Weiber Natur (Nuremberg: Endter, 1673).

PLAYFORD, JOHN (1623–1686/87)
London-based publisher, writer, and vicar-choral of St. Paul's Cathedral. He authored musical primers for various instruments; his *Introduction to the Skill of Musick* was highly popular over the following decades.
An Introduction to the Skill of Musick, 2 vols. (London: Godbid, 1674).

POPP, JOHANN (b. 1577)
German physician, alchemist, and apothecary.
Thesaurus medicinae, oder Chymischer Artzney Schatz (Leipzig: Schürer, 1628).

PORTA, GIAMBATTISTA DELLA (1535–1615)
Italian polymath, occult scientist, and playwright based in Naples. His 1586 treatise *De humana physiognomia libri IIII* was a pioneering contribution to the pseudo-science of physiognomy.

PRAETORIUS, MICHAEL (1571–1621)
German music theorist, composer, and organist based in Wolfenbüttel. His collection of treatises *Syntagma musicum* offers an encyclopedic account of contemporary theory and practice of music.
Syntagma musicum, tomus secundus de organographia (Wolfenbüttel: Holwein, 1619).
Syntagmatis musici tomus tertius (Wolfenbüttel: Holwein, 1619).

PRAETORIUS, PAUL GOTTFRIED (d. 1703)
German Lutheran preacher.
Vernünfftiger Gottesdienst im Singen (Danzig: Stollen, 1689).

PRIMAUDAYE, PIERRE DE LA (1546–1619)
French writer particularly known for his *L'Académie Française* (1577), which went through numerous editions in its original French version as well as in English translation.
The French Academie Fully Discoursed and Finished in Foure Books, trans. Thomas Bowes (London: Adams, 1618).
The Second Part of the French Academie (London: Bishop, 1605).

PRINTZ, WOLFGANG CASPAR (1641–1717)
German music theorist, historian, and composer, whose publications offer ample documentation of the theory and practice of music during his time.
Musica modulatoria vocalis, Oder Manierliche und zierliche Sing-Kunst (Schweidnitz: Okel, 1678).
Phrynis Mitilenaeus (Dresden and Leipzig: Zimmermann, 1696).

QUIRSFELD, JOHANN (1642–1686)
German Lutheran theologian and cantor active in Pirna, who authored a range of devotional books as well as a musical primer that went through a number of later editions.
Allersüssester Jesus-Trost Einer Weltverdrossenen Seelen (Leipzig: Hesse, 1696).
Breviarum Musicum, Oder Kurtzer Begriff Wie ein Knabe leicht und bald Zur Singe-Kunst gelangen (Dresden: Hübner, 1695).
Geistliche Passion-Schule (Leipzig: Köhler, 1680).

QUITSCHREIBER, GEORG (1569–1638)
German Protestant composer, pastor, cantor, and teacher.
Musicbüchlein für die Jugend, 2nd ed. (Jena: Weidner, 1607).

RAMEAU, JEAN-PHILIPPE (1683–1764)
Leading French composer and music theorist whose influential *Traité de l'harmonie* set out to offer a comprehensive theory of harmony based on the Cartesian deductive method.
Traité de l'harmonie (Paris: Ballard, 1722); translated as *Treatise on Harmony*, trans. Philip Gossett (New York: Dover, 1971).

RAUPACH, CHRISTOPH (1686–1744)
German organist, composer, and writer on music based in Stralsund.
Veritophili Deutliche Beweis-Gründe / Worauf der rechte Gebrauch der Music, beydes in den Kirchen / als ausser denselben / beruhe, ed. Johann Mattheson (Hamburg: Schiller, 1717).

RAYMUNDUS, P. À NATIVITATE B. M. V. (dates unknown)
Austrian preacher based in Vienna.
Drey-tägige Trauer- und Lob-Rede (Vienna: Kurzböck, 1740).

REINHOLDT, THEODOR CHRISTLIEB (1682–1755)
German organist, church musician, and writer active in Dresden.
Einige Zur Music gehörige Poetische Gedancken (Dresden: Hilscher, 1736).

RICHTER, CHRISTIAN FRIEDRICH (1676–1711)
German physician, theologian, and Pietist hymn writer based in Halle.
Kurtzer und deutlicher Unterricht Von Dem Leibe und natürlichen Leben des Menschen (Halle: Waysenhaus, 1705).

RITTMEYER, JOHANN (1636–1698)
German Lutheran pastor, whose devotional publications went through several editions.
Himmlisches Freuden-Mahl der Kinder Gottes auf Erden (Lüneburg: Stern, 1743).

ROLFINCK, WERNER (1599–1673)
German doctor, anatomist, and botanist, professor at the University of Jena, proponent of William Harvey's theory of blood circulation.
Ordo et methodus medicinae (Jena: Spaltholtz, 1669).

ROWE, ELIZABETH SINGER (1674–1737)
English religious poet and fiction writer based in Frome, Somerset, one of the most widely read female authors in eighteenth-century England.
Divine Hymns and Poems on Several Occasions (London: Burrough, 1704).

SALLE, JEAN-BAPTISTE DE LA (1651–1719)
French priest and influential educational reformer.
Les regles de la bien-séance et de la civilité Chrêtienne (Paris: Riviere, 1708); translation in *The Spirituality of Christian Education*, ed. Carl Koch, Jeffrey Calligan, and Jeffrey Gros (New York: Paulist Press, 2004), 168–181.

SAN ANTONIO, JUAN FRANCISCO DE (1682–1744)
Franciscan priest, historian, and missionary based in the Philippines, who published a three-volume chronicle of local life and events.
Chrónicas de la apostólica Provincia de S. Gregorio (Sampaloc: Sotillo, 1738–1744).

SANTA MARÍA, TOMÁS DE (ca. 1510–1570)
Spanish composer, organist, and theorist active at various Dominican monasteries in Castilla.
Libro llamado arte de teñer fantasia (Valladolid: n.p., 1565).

SAUBERT, JOHANNES (1592–1646)
German Lutheran theologian and librarian in Nuremberg, author of a number of devotional books and sermon collections.
SeelenMusic, wie dieselbe am Sontag Cantate . . . gehört worden (Nuremberg: Halbmayer, 1624).

SCHEIBE, JOHANN ADOLPH (1708–1776)
German composer, music theorist, and influential music critic, active in Hamburg and Copenhagen, student of Johann Christoph Gottsched in Leipzig.
Critischer Musikus (Leipzig: Breitkopf, 1745).

SCHEIBEL, GOTTFRIED EPHRAIM (1696–1759)
German theologian and teacher based in Breslau who defended the value of music in the Protestant church service.
Zufällige Gedancken von der Kirchen-Music (Frankfurt and Leipzig: Author, 1721); translated as "Random Thoughts About Church Music in Our Day," trans. Joyce Irwin, in *Bach's Changing World: Voices in the Community*, ed. Carol Baron (Rochester, NY: University of Rochester Press, 2006), 227–250.

SCHELHAMMER, GÜNTHER CHRISTOPH (1649–1716)
German medic who taught at various universities in Northern Germany.
Dissertationem de humani animi affectibus (Kiel: Peuther, 1710).

SCHERERTZ, SIGISMUND (1584–1639)
German Lutheran cleric, hymn writer, and author.
Fuga melancholiae cum speculo tentationum spiritualium (Lüneburg: Stern, 1682).

SCHEUCHZER, JOHANN JACOB (1672–1733)
Swiss physician, naturalist, and paleontologist based in Zurich whose publications combined scientific and theological fields of inquiry.
Kupfer-Bibel, In welcher Die Physica Sacra, Oder Geheiligte Natur-Wissenschafft (Augsburg and Ulm: Wagner, 1735).
Physica Oder Natur-Wissenschafft, 2 vols., 2nd ed. (Zurich: Bodmer, 1711).

SCHMIDT, JOHANN JACOB (1690–1762)
German Lutheran preacher and naturalist.
Biblischer Medicus (Züllichau: Dendeler, 1743).

SÉNAC, JEAN-BAPTISTE DE (1693–1770)
French medic and chemist active in Paris, physician to Louis XV. Renowned as a cardiologist, proponent of the theories of William Harvey and Georg Ernst Stahl.
Traité de la structure du coeur, de son action, et de ses maladies, 2 vols. (Paris: Vincent, 1749).

SENNERT, DANIEL (1572–1637)
Renowned German physician and author on alchemy and chemistry who taught at the University of Wittenberg.
Medicinae practicae tomus primus (Venice: Baba, 1641).

SILBER, WOLFGANG (1569–1639)

German Lutheran theologian and court preacher in Silesia.

Encomion musices (Leipzig: Elliger, 1621).

SINN, CHRISTOPH ALBERT (1680/81–1729)

German music theorist with interests in musical instruments and tuning. His treatise on organ tuning contains an extensive preface by his contemporary Caspar Calvör.

Musicalische Temperatura Practica (Wernigerode: Struck, 1717).

SORGE, GEORG ANDREAS (1703–1778)

German organist, composer, and music theorist active in Thuringia, renowned as an authority on organ building and tuning as well as a prolific writer of music treatises.

Anweisung zur Stimmung und Temperatur sowohl der Orgelwerke, als auch anderer Instrumente (Hamburg: Piscator, 1744).

SOUTH, ROBERT (1634–1716)

English churchman, orator, and author of a large number of sermons as well as a well-known poem about the powers of music.

Musica incantans (London: Turner, 1700).

SPADONI, NICOLA (dates unknown)

Augustinian monk and natural scientist; his *Studium curiosum* ended up on the Index of the Catholic Church but went to a second edition and was translated into German.

Studium curiosum . . . Von der Physiognomia, Chiromantia und Metoposcopia (1662), in *Höchstfürtreflichstes Chiromantisch- und Physiognomisches Klee-Blat* (Nuremberg: Zieger, 1695).

SPEER, DANIEL (1636–1707)

German music theorist, composer, and author of autobiographical novels describing his wandering life and musical experiences in southeast Europe. His *Unterricht* is an informative textbook on practical music-making.

Grund-richtiger / Kurtz- Leicht- und Nöthiger / jetzt Wol-vermehrter Unterricht der Musicalischen Kunst (Ulm: Kühne, 1697).

SPERLING, JOHANN PETER (1671–1720)

German music theorist and composer based in Bautzen who published one of the most comprehensive singing treatises of its time.

Principia musicae, das ist: Gründliche Anweisung zur Music (Budißin: Richter, 1705).

SPIESS, MEINRAD (1683–1761)

German music theorist, composer, and Benedictine priest based in Bavaria, corresponding member of Johann Mizler's illustrious music society in Leipzig, whose music treatises circulated widely.

Tractatus musicus compositorio-practicus (Augsburg: Lotter, 1745).

SPINOZA, BARUCH (1632–1677)

Dutch rationalist philosopher, one of the most important thinkers of the early modern age, pioneered modern biblical criticism as well as modern conceptions of selfhood and the universe. His writings appeared on the Index of the

Catholic Church. His *Ethics*, published posthumously, developed an alternative to Cartesian mind-body dualism.

"Ethica," in *Opera posthuma* (Amsterdam: Rieuwertsz, 1677).

STAHL, GEORG ERNST (1659–1734)

Esteemed German medical theorist and practitioner, chemist, and educator, university professor in Halle, later royal physician in Berlin. Proponent of a vitalist conception of living organisms.

Observationes clinico-practicae, 3rd ed. (Leipzig: Eyssel, 1726).

Praxis Stahliana, 3rd ed., ed. Johann Storch (Leipzig: Schönemark, 1745).

STEFFANI, AGOSTINO (1654–1728)

Italian composer, singer, clergyman, and diplomat mainly active in Munich and Hanover as court composer; as a diplomat he was involved in contemporary European political affairs in a variety of roles.

Sendschreiben, darinnen enthalten, wie große Gewißheit die Musik aus ihren Principiis habe, trans. Andreas Werckmeister, ed. Johann Lorenz Albrecht (Mühlhausen: Brückner, 1760).

STOCK, CHRISTIAN (1672–1733)

German Lutheran theologian, orientalist, and linguist, university professor in Jena.

Homiletisches Real-Lexicon, 3rd ed. (Jena: Hartung, 1734).

STOCKER, GASPAR (dates unknown)

German music theorist active in Italy and Spain. He wrote the only known treatise devoted exclusively to text underlay in the period.

De musica verbali libri duo (manuscript, ca. 1570).

STOSCH, FRIEDRICH WILHELM (1648–1704)

German Lutheran theologian and philosopher employed in Brandenburg, whose controversial treatise *Concordia rationis & fidei* drew on Baruch Spinoza in proposing a materialist account of the soul; it was banned almost immediately.

Concordia rationis & fidei (Amsterdam: Gruber, 1692).

STROZZI, GIULIO (1583–1652)

Italian poet, librettist, and dramatist who worked mainly in Rome and Venice. He was active in musical and literary circles, collaborator of Claudio Monteverdi, instrumental in the creation of Venetian opera.

Le glorie della signora Anna Renzi Romana (Venice: Surian, 1644).

STRUTHIUS, JOSEPH (1510–1568)

Polish physician, professor of medicine in Padua, and personal doctor to several Polish kings, who made seminal contributions to the study of the human pulse.

Sphymicae artis jam mille ducentos annos perditae et desideratae Libri V (Basel: Oporinus, 1555).

STUBBS, PHILIP (ca. 1555–ca. 1610)

English writer and pamphleteer, known for his *The anatomie of abuses*, a critical account of contemporary morals and customs.

The anatomie of abuses (London: Iones, 1583).

SWAMMERDAM, JAN (1637–1680)

Dutch naturalist, entomologist, and microscopist based in Amsterdam, whose work on nerve stimulation helped supersede the doctrine of the animal spirits.

TELEMANN, GEORG PHILIPP (1681–1767)

Leading German composer who worked in various locations across the German lands. Also contributed to contemporary concert life, music publishing, and music education.

Georg Philipp Telemann: Briefwechsel, ed. Hans Grosse and Hans Rudolf Jung (Leipzig: VEB Deutscher Verlag für Musik, 1972).

TELESIO, BERNARDINO (1509–1588)

Renaissance Italian philosopher whose empiricist approach to natural philosophy shaped the empiricism of Francis Bacon, Pierre Gassendi, Thomas Hobbes, and others.

THIEME, JOHANN CHRISTOPH (dates unknown)

German writer whose 1682 guide to housekeeping, nutrition, and home remedies went through several editions.

Haus-, Feld-, Arzney-, Koch-, Kunst- und Wunder-Buch (Nuremberg: Hofmann, 1700).

THOMMEN, JOHANN (1711–1783)

Swiss cantor and hymn writer based in Basel.

Erbaulicher Musicalischer Christen-Schatz (Basel: Eckenstein, 1745).

THOMSON, GEORGE (ca. 1619–1677)

English physician and medical writer based in London who followed a Helmontian approach in his critique of humoral medicine and contemporary practices of bloodletting.

Αἱματιασις; or, The True Way of Preserving the Bloud in its Integrity (London: Crouch, 1670).

TORSELLINI, ORAZIO (1545–1599)

Italian Jesuit, humanist, and writer who published a number of theological and historical treatises that enjoyed lasting popularity in reprints and translations.

Apostolisches Leben und Thaten deß heilgen Francisci Xaverii, trans. Martin Hueber (Munich: Rauch, 1674).

TOSI, PIER FRANCESCO (1654–1732)

Italian castrato, singing teacher, composer, and diplomat who worked across Northern Italy, London and the German lands; author of an influential singing treatise that was translated into English and German.

Anleitung zur Singkunst, ed. and trans. Johann Friedrich Agricola (Berlin: Winter, 1757).

TYARD, PONTUS DE (ca. 1522–1605)

Burgundian poet, priest, and writer who expounded a Neoplatonic view of music.

Solitaire second, ou prose de la musique (Lyon: Tournes, 1555).

UNTZER, MATTHIAS (1581–1624)

German physician and iatrochemist active in Halle.

Kurtzer und einfältiger doch nützlicher und nothwendiger Bericht Von der Pestilentz (Halle: Hynitzsch, 1607).

VALLERIUS, HARALD (1646–1716)
Swedish mathematician, composer, organist, and writer on music based in Uppsala.
Disputatio physico-musica de sono (Stockholm: Wankijff, 1674).

VENETTE, NICOLAS (1633–1698)
French physician who traveled across Europe before working as a doctor in La Rochelle. He published what is considered the first treatise on sexology in the West, which went through numerous editions and was translated into several European languages.
Abhandlung von Erzeugung der Menschen (Königsberg and Leipzig: Eckart, 1738).

VICENTINO, NICOLA (1511–ca. 1576)
Italian music theorist and composer active in Ferrara and Rome who made seminal contributions to sixteenth-century modal and harmonic theory.
L'Antica musica ridotta alla moderna prattica (Rome: Barre, 1555).

VIGNEUL-MARVILLE, M. DE (ca. 1634–1704)
Pseudonym for Father Bonaventure d'Argonne, French writer and Carthusian monk in Normandy.
Mélange d'histoire et de littérature, 2nd ed. (Paris: Prudhomme, 1713).

VILAR, ELIAS COL VON (1675–1747)
French physician and surgeon, member of the Faculty of Medicine at Paris. He published a surgical manual that was widely used in French medical schools, as well as a dictionary of medicine.
Medicinisches und chirurgisches Wörterbuch, trans. Hinrich Friderich Petersen (Altona: Korte, 1747).

VOGT, MAURITIUS (1669–1730)
German composer, organist, and writer on music, Cistercian monk based in Bohemia.
Conclave thesauri magnae artis musicae (Prague: Labaun, 1717).

WALKINGTON, THOMAS (ca. 1575–1621)
English clergyman and author whose treatise on the humors went through several editions and anticipated many of the themes in Robert Burton's celebrated book on melancholy.
The Optick Glasse of Humors (London: Clerke, 1607).

WALTER, THOMAS (1696–1725)
American preacher and hymnal compiler based around Boston, devoted to improving congregational singing.
The Grounds and Rules of Musick Explained (Boston: Franklin, 1721).

WALTHER, JOHANN GOTTFRIED (1684–1748)
German organist, music theorist, composer, and lexicographer based in Weimar, whose *Lexicon* serves as a fount of information about musical practices, concepts, and key figures at the time.
Musicalisches Lexicon Oder Musicalische Bibliothec (Leipzig: Deer, 1732).
Praecepta der Musicalischen Composition, ed. Peter Benary (Leipzig: Breitkopf & Härtel, 1955).

WATZEL, SIMPLICIANUS (dates unknown)
Augustinian hermit and Catholic theologian based in Prague.
Der predigende Augustinus (Augsburg: Bart, 1756).

WERCKMEISTER, ANDREAS (1645–1706)

German music theorist, organist, and composer based in Thuringia whose treatises present the culmination of Lutheran seventeenth-century views of music as a God-given mathematical science.

Der Edlen Music-Kunst Würde / Gebrauch und Mißbrauch (Frankfurt and Leipzig: Calvisius, 1691).

Musicae mathematicae hodegus curiosus (Frankfurt and Leipzig: Calvisius, 1687).

WIRDIG, SEBASTIAN (1613–1687)

German physician and university professor in Dorpat and Rostock. His medical treatise was reprinted several times and translated into German.

Nova medicina spirituum (Hamburg: Schulz, 1673).

WOLFF, CHRISTIAN (1679–1754)

Enlightenment German philosopher, mathematician, and scientist, pupil of Gottfried Wilhelm Leibniz, rigorous rationalist thinker, mainly based in Halle. A prolific and influential writer on philosophy, theology, psychology, botany, and physics.

Vernünfftige Gedancken von Gott / der Welt und der Seele des Menschen (Halle: Renger, 1720).

Vernünfftige Gedancken Von dem Gebrauche Der Theile In Menschen / Thieren Und Pflantzen (Frankfurt and Leipzig: Renger, 1725).

WRIGHT, LEONARD (1555/56–after 1591)

English writer, controversialist, and moralist, educated at Cambridge. His *Display of dutie* contains moralistic essays, advice on diet, exercise, and marriage; it went through several editions.

A Display of Dutie Dect with Sage Sayings, Pythie Sentences, and Proper Similes (London: Wolfe, 1589).

WRIGHT, THOMAS (ca. 1561–1623)

English writer, controversialist, and Roman Catholic priest active in France, Italy, Spain, the Netherlands, and England. His *Passions of the Minde*, a wide-ranging volume on psychology, physiology, and moral philosophy, went through several editions.

The Passions of the Minde in Generall (London: Simmes, 1604).

WÜLFER, JOHANN (1651–1724)

German Lutheran theologian, geographer, preacher, and educator based in Nuremberg. His *Tafel-Music* volume is a collection of hymns.

Gottgeheiligter Christen Tafel-Music (Nuremberg: Felßecker, 1718).

ZARLINO, GIOSEFFO (1517–1590)

Italian music theorist and composer, a leading figure in sixteenth-century music theory. His *Le istitutioni harmoniche* is one of the most important works of music theory and remained influential over several generations.

Le istitutioni harmoniche (Venice: Senese, 1558).

ZEDLER, JOHANN HEINRICH (1706–1751)

German publisher based in Leipzig whose *Lexicon* presents a comprehensive survey of contemporary thought and knowledge.

Grosses vollständiges Universal-Lexicon aller Wissenschafften und Künste, 64 vols. (Halle and Leipzig: Zedler, 1731–1754).

ZIEGLER, JOHANN RUDOLF (1695–1762)
Swiss theologian, preacher, and hymnal compiler based in Zurich.
Der Singende Christ, Welcher zum Lobe seines Gottes Uebereinstimmet (Zurich: n.p., 1723).

ZWINGER, THEODOR (1658–1724)
Swiss physician and botanist based in Basel. His medical compendium was compiled from writings by Michael Ettmüller, Daniel Sennert, Herman Boerhaave, and others.
Compendium medicinae universae (Basel: Thurnisios, 1724).

Unattributed Sources

A. B., *Synopsis of Vocal Musick* (London: Newman, 1680).
"Abhandlung von dem Ursprunge der Kälte," *Hamburgisches Magazin*, vol. 2 (Hamburg: Grund, 1747), 55–67.
Codice Morbio 1, Milan, Biblioteca Nazionale Braidense.
Curioser Chirurgus oder Sonderbahrer Begriff der Wund-Artzney (Dresden and Leipzig: Mieth, 1719).
"A Description of the Tarantula, and how those that are bitten by it are cured with Music," *The Universal Magazine of Knowledge and Pleasure* 2 (1748): 252–253.
Le Dictionnaire de l'Académie française, 4th ed. (Paris: Brunet, 1762).
Kern der ganzen Medicin (Hamburg: Geißler, 1748).
Vade-mecum curiosum medicum et chirurgicum, oder Sonderbahre Curiose Anleitung zur Medicin (Dresden: Mieth, 1694).

Secondary Sources

WORKS CITED

Abbate, Carolyn. "Music: Drastic or Gnostic?" *Critical Inquiry* 30/3 (2004): 505–536.

Agamben, Giorgio. *The Open: Man and Animal* (Stanford, CA: Stanford University Press, 2004).

Agnew, Vanessa. *Enlightenment Orpheus: The Power of Music in Other Worlds* (New York: Oxford University Press, 2008).

———. "Gooseflesh: Music, Somatosensation, and the Making of Historical Experience." In *The Varieties of Historical Experience*, ed. Stephan Palmie and Charles Stewart (London and New York: Routledge, 2019), 77–94.

Ahmed, Sara. "Affective Economies." *Social Text* 22 (2004): 117–139.

Aho, Marko. *The Tangible in Music: The Tactile Learning of a Musical Instrument* (London: Routledge, 2016).

Alberti, Fay Bound. *Matters of the Heart: History, Medicine, and Emotion* (Oxford: Oxford University Press, 2010).

Altbauer-Rudnik, Michal. "Love, Madness and Social Order: Love Melancholy in France and England in the Late Sixteenth and Early Seventeenth Centuries." *Gesnerus* 63 (2006): 33–45.

Anderson, Miranda. *The Renaissance Extended Mind* (Basingstoke: Palgrave Macmillan, 2015).

Anderson, Ron James. *The Arts of Persuasion: Musical Rhetoric in the Keyboard Genres of Dietrich Buxtehude* (DMA diss., University of Arizona, 2012).

Austern, Linda Phyllis. "'Alluring the Auditorie to Effeminacie': Music and the Idea of the Feminine in Early Modern England." *Music & Letters* 74 (1993): 343–354.

———. *Both from the Ears and Mind: Thinking About Music in Early Modern England* (Chicago: University of Chicago Press, 2020).

———. "'For Love's a Good Musician': Performance, Audition, and Erotic Disorders in Early Modern Europe." *Musical Quarterly* 82 (1998): 614–653.

———. "Introduction." In *Music, Sensation and Sensuality*, ed. Linda Phyllis Austern (New York: Routledge, 2002), 1–14.

Baily, John. "Ethnomusicology, Intermusability, and Performance Practice." In *The New (Ethno)musicologies*, ed. Henry Stobart (Lanham, MD: Scarecrow, 2008), 117–134.

Bartel, Dietrich. *Musica Poetica: Musical-Rhetorical Figures in German Baroque Music* (Lincoln: University of Nebraska Press, 1997).

Bashwiner, David. "The Neuroscience of Musical Creativity." In *The Cambridge Handbook of the Neuroscience of Creativity*, ed. Rex E. Jung and Oshin Vartanian (Cambridge: Cambridge University Press, 2018), 495–516.

Baum, Jacob M. *Reformation of the Senses: The Paradox of Religious Belief and Practice in Germany* (Urbana: University of Illinois Press, 2018).

Becker, Judith. *Deep Listeners: Music, Emotion, and Trancing* (Bloomington: Indiana University Press, 2004).

Begbie, Jeremy. *Music, Modernity and God: Essays in Listening* (New York: Oxford University Press, 2013).

Bennett, Jane. *Vibrant Matter: A Political Ecology of Things* (Durham, NC: Duke University Press, 2010).

Berger, Karol. "Musicology According to Don Giovanni, or: Should We Get Drastic?" *Journal of Musicology* 22 (2005): 490–501.

Bernardi, Luciano, Cesare Porta, Gaia Casucci, Rossella Balsamo, Nicolò F. Bernardi, Roberto Fogari, et al. "Dynamic Interactions Between Musical, Cardiovascular, and Cerebral Rhythms in Humans." *Circulation* 119/25 (2009): 3171–3180.

Black, Daniel. *Embodiment and Mechanisation: Reciprocal Understandings of Body and Machine from the Renaissance to the Present* (Farnham: Ashgate, 2014).

Blake, Howe. "Disabling Music Performance." In *The Oxford Handbook of Music and Disability Studies*, ed. Blake Howe, Stephanie Jensen-Moulton, Neil Lerner, and Joseph Straus (Oxford: Oxford University Press), 191–209.

Bloechl, Olivia A. "Listening as an Innu-French Contact Zone in the Jesuit *Relations*." In *Acoustemologies in Contact: Sounding Subjects and Modes of Listening in Early Modernity*, ed. Emily Wilbourne and Suzanne G. Cusick (Cambridge: Open Book Publishers, 2021), 13–36.

———. *Native American Song at the Frontiers of Early Modern Music* (Cambridge: Cambridge University Press, 2008).

———. "Race, Empire, and Early Music." In *Rethinking Difference in Music Scholarship*, ed. Olivia Bloechl, Melanie Lowe, and Jeffrey Kallberg (Cambridge: Cambridge University Press, 2015), 77–107.

Bloom, Gina. *Voice in Motion: Staging Gender, Shaping Sound in Early Modern England* (Philadelphia: University of Pennsylvania Press, 2007).

Boddice, Rob. *The History of Emotions* (Manchester: Manchester University Press, 2018).

Boenke, Michaela. *Körper, Spiritus, Geist: Psychologie vor Descartes* (Munich: Fink, 2005).

Braun, Werner. "Die evangelische Kontrafaktur: Bemerkungen zum Stand ihrer Erforschung." *Jahrbuch für Liturgik und Hymnologie* 11 (1966): 89–113.

Brewer, Charles E. *The Instrumental Music of Schmeltzer, Biber, Muffat and their Contemporaries* (London: Routledge, 2016).

Brown, Christopher. *Singing the Gospel: Lutheran Hymns and the Success of the Reformation* (Cambridge, MA: Harvard University Press, 2005).

Buelow, George J. "Johann Mattheson and the Invention of the *Affektenlehre*." In *New Mattheson Studies*, ed. George J. Buelow and Hans Joachim Marx (Cambridge: Cambridge University Press, 1983), 393–408.

Bungert, James. "Bach and the Patterns of Transformation." *Music Theory Spectrum* 37 (2015): 98–119.

Butt, John. *Bach's Dialogue with Modernity: Perspectives on the Passions* (Cambridge: Cambridge University Press, 2009).

———. "'A Mind Unconscious That Is Calculating'? Bach and the Rationalist Philosophy of Wolff, Leibniz and Spinoza." In *The Cambridge Companion to Johann Sebastian Bach*, ed. John Butt (Cambridge: Cambridge University Press, 1997), 60–71.

———. *Music Education and the Art of Performance in the German Baroque* (Cambridge: Cambridge University Press, 1994).

Calcagno, Mauro. "Signifying Nothing: On the Aesthetics of Pure Voice in Early Venetian Opera." *Journal of Musicology* 20/4 (2003): 461–497.

Callahan, Michael R. *Techniques of Keyboard Improvisation in the German Baroque and Their Implications for Today's Pedagogy* (PhD diss., Eastman School of Music, 2010).

Callard, Felicity, and Constantina Papoulias. "Affect and Embodiment." In *Memory: Histories, Theories, Debates*, ed. Susannah Radstone and Bill Schwarz (New York: Fordham University Press, 2010), 246–262.

Cannon, Beekman C. *Johann Mattheson: Spectator in Music* (New Haven, CT: Yale University Press, 1947).

Carter, Stewart. "The String Tremolo in the 17th Century." *Early Music* 19 (1991): 42–59.

Carter, Tim. "Lamento della Ninfa (1638)." In *The Cambridge Companion to Monteverdi*, ed. John Whenham and Richard Wistreich (Cambridge: Cambridge University Press, 2007).

———. "Resemblance and Representation: Towards a New Aesthetic in the Music of Monteverdi." In *Con Che Soavità: Studies in Italian Opera, Song and Dance, 1580–1740*, ed. Iain Fenlon and Tim Carter (Oxford: Clarendon, 1995), 118–134.

———. "Review: The Power of Song?" *Early Music* 33 (2005): 696–700.

———. "The Search for Musical Meaning." In *The Cambridge History of Seventeenth-Century Music*, ed. John Butt and Tim Carter (Cambridge: Cambridge University Press, 2005), 158–196.

———. "Two Monteverdi Problems, and Why They Matter." *Journal of Musicology* 19/3 (2002): 417–433.

———. "Winds, Cupids, Little Zephyrs and Sirens: Monteverdi and *Le Nozze di Tetide* (1616–1617)." *Early Music* 39/4 (2011): 489–502.

Caughie, Pamela L. "Let It Pass: Changing the Subject, Once Again." *PMLA* 112/1 (1997): 26–39.

Chafe, Eric. *Analyzing Bach Cantatas* (New York: Oxford University Press, 2000).

———. *Tears into Wine: J. S. Bach's Cantata 21 in Its Musical and Theological Contexts* (New York: Oxford University Press, 2015).

———. *Tonal Allegory in the Vocal Music of J. S. Bach* (Berkeley: University of California Press, 1991).

Chalmers, David. "Facing Up to the Problem of Consciousness." *Journal of Consciousness Studies* 2/3 (1995): 200–219.

Charalampous, Charis. *Rethinking the Mind-Body Relationship in Early Modern Literature, Philosophy and Medicine* (London: Routledge, 2015).

Christie, John R. R. "Introduction: Rhetoric and Writing in Early Modern Philosophy and Science." In *The Figural and the Literal: Problems of Language in the His-*

tory of Science and Philosophy, ed. Andrew E. Benjamin, Geoffrey N. Cantor, and John R. R. Christie (Manchester: Manchester University Press, 1987), 1–9.

Chua, Daniel. *Absolute Music and the Construction of Meaning* (Cambridge: Cambridge University Press, 1999).

Clark, Andy, and David J. Chalmers. "The Extended Mind." In *The Extended Mind*, ed. Richard Menary (Cambridge, MA: MIT Press, 2010), 27–42.

Clarke, Eric F. *Ways of Listening: An Ecological Approach to the Perception of Musical Meaning* (Oxford: Oxford University Press, 2005).

Coakley, Sarah. "Introduction: Religion and the Body." In *Religion and the Body*, ed. Sarah Coakley (Cambridge: Cambridge University Press, 1997), 1–14.

Conboy, Irina M., Michael J. Conboy, Amy J. Wagers, Eric R. Girma, Irving L. Weissman, and Thomas A. Rando. "Rejuvenation of Aged Progenitor Cells by Exposure to a Young Systemic Environment." *Nature* 433 (2005): 760–764.

Connor, Steven. "Acousmania." http://stevenconnor.com/acousmania.html.

———. "Edison's Teeth: Touching Hearing." http://www.stevenconnor.com/edsteeth.

———. "Strains of the Voice." http://stevenconnor.com/strains.html.

Conway, Bevil R., and Alexander Rehding. "Neuroaesthetics and the Trouble with Beauty." *PLoS Biology* 11(3) (2013), doi:10.1371/journal.pbio.1001504.

Cook, Nicholas. *Beyond the Score: Music as Performance* (New York: Oxford University Press, 2013).

Cooper, Michael. "In a Season of Boys' Choirs, a Question: Why No Girls?" *New York Times*, 26 December 2018, https://www.nytimes.com/2018/12/26/arts/music/boys-choir-vienna-st-thomas-kings-college-cambridge.html.

Cottingham, John. "Cartesian Dualism." In *The Cambridge Companion to Descartes*, ed. John Cottingham (Cambridge: Cambridge University Press, 1992), 236–257.

Couch, Liam S., Jan Fiedler, Giles Chick, Rory Clayton, Eef Dries, Laura M. Wienecke, et al. "Circulating MicroRNAs Predispose to Takotsubo Syndrome Following High-Dose Adrenaline Exposure." *Cardiovascular Research* (2021): 1–13.

Cox, Arnie. *Music and Embodied Cognition: Listening, Moving, Feeling, and Thinking* (Bloomington: Indiana University Press, 2016).

Cox, Christoph. *Sonic Flux: Sound, Art, and Metaphysics* (Chicago: University of Chicago Press, 2018).

Craig-McFeely, Julia. "The Signifying Serpent: Seduction by Cultural Stereotype in Seventeenth-Century England." In *Music, Sensation and Sensuality*, ed. Linda Phyllis Austern (New York: Routledge, 2002), 299–317.

Craik, Katharine A. *Reading Sensations in Early Modern England* (Basingstoke: Palgrave, 2007).

Crawford, Katharine. *European Sexualities, 1400–1800* (Cambridge: Cambridge University Press, 2007).

Crick, Francis. *The Astonishing Hypothesis: The Scientific Search for the Soul* (New York: Touchstone, 1995).

Csordas, Thomas. "Embodiment as a Paradigm for Anthropology." *Ethos* 18/1 (1990): 5–47.

Cumming, Naomi. "The Subjectivities of 'Erbarme Dich.'" *Music Analysis* 16 (1997): 5–44.

Cunningham, Andrew. "The End of the Sacred Ritual of Anatomy." *Canadian Journal of Medical History* 18 (2001): 187–204.

———. "The Pen and the Sword: Recovering the Disciplinary Identity of Physiology and Anatomy Before 1800: I: Old Physiology—the Pen." *Studies in History and Philosophy of Biological and Biomedical Sciences* 33/4 (2002): 631–655.

Cusick, Suzanne G. "Feminist Theory, Music Theory, and the Mind/Body Problem." *Perspectives of New Music* 32/1 (1994): 8–27.

———. *Francesca Caccini at the Medici Court: Music and the Circulation of Power* (Chicago: University of Chicago Press, 2009).

———. "'There Was Not One Lady Who Failed to Shed a Tear': Arianna's Lament and the Construction of Modern Womanhood." *Early Music* 22/1 (1994): 21–43.

———. "Towards an Acoustemology of Detention in the 'Global War on Terror.'" In *Music, Sound and Space*, ed. Georgina Born (Cambridge: Cambridge University Press, 2013), 275–291.

Dahlhaus, Carl. "Die Termini Dur und Moll." *Archiv für Musikwissenschaft* 12 (1955): 280–296.

Dammann, Rolf. *Der Musikbegriff im deutschen Barock*, 3rd ed. (Laaber: Laaber, 1995).

Damrau, Peter. *The Reception of English Puritan Literature in Germany* (London: Maney, 2006).

Davies, James Q. *Romantic Anatomies of Performance* (Berkeley: University of California Press, 2014).

DeLanda, Manuel. *A Thousand Years of Nonlinear History* (New York: Zone Books, 1997).

Dell'Antonio, Andrew. *Listening as Spiritual Practice in Early Modern Italy* (Berkeley: University of California Press, 2011).

Dennett, Daniel. *Darwin's Dangerous Idea: Evolution and the Meanings of Life* (New York: Simon & Schuster, 1995).

D'Errico, Lucia. *Powers of Divergence: An Experimental Approach to Music Performance* (Leuven: Leuven University Press, 2018).

Derrida, Jacques. "Plato's Pharmacy." In *Dissemination*, ed. Barbara Johnson (Chicago: University of Chicago Press, 1981), 61–171.

Devereaux, Mary. "Feminist Aesthetics." In *The Oxford Handbook of Aesthetics*, ed. Jerrold Levinson (New York: Oxford University Press, 2005), 647–666.

Diamond, Elin, and Elizabeth Bronfen. Review of Carolyn Abbate, *In Search of Opera*. *Cambridge Opera Journal* 17/2 (2005): 215–223.

Dixon, Thomas. *From Passions to Emotions: The Creation of a Secular Psychological Category* (Cambridge: Cambridge University Press, 2003).

Duden, Barbara. "Anmerkungen zur Kulturgeschichte des Herzens." In *Von der Auffälligkeit des Leibes*, ed. Farideh Akashe-Böhme (Frankfurt: Suhrkamp, 1995), 130–145.

———. *The Woman Beneath the Skin: A Doctor's Patients in Eighteenth-Century Germany*, trans. Thomas Dunlap (Cambridge, MA: Harvard University Press, 1991).

Dyck, Corey. "Materialism in the Mainstream of Early German Philosophy." *British Journal for the History of Philosophy* 24 (2016): 897–916.

Eagleton, Terry. "The Ideology of the Aesthetic." *Poetics Today* 9/2 (1988): 327–338.

Earle, Rebecca. *The Body of the Conquistador: Food, Race, and the Colonial Experience in Spanish America, 1492–1700* (Cambridge: Cambridge University Press, 2012).

———. "'If You Eat Their Food . . .': Diets and Bodies in Early Colonial Spanish America." *The American Historical Review* 115/3 (2010): 688–713.

Eidsheim, Nina Sun. *Sensing Sound: Singing and Listening as Vibrational Practice* (Durham, NC: Duke University Press, 2015).

Elferen, Isabella van. *Mystical Love in the German Baroque: Theology, Poetry, Music* (Lanham, MD: Scarecrow, 2009).

———. "Rethinking Affect." In *Rethinking Bach*, ed. Bettina Varwig (New York: Oxford University Press, 2021), 141–166.

Erickson, Robert. *The Language of the Heart, 1600–1750* (Philadelphia: University of Pennsylvania Press, 1997).

Erlmann, Veit. "The Physiologist at the Opera: Claude Perrault's *Du bruit* (1680) and the Politics of Pleasure in the *Ancien Régime*." In *Cultural Histories of Noise, Sound and Listening in Europe, 1300–1918*, ed. Kirsten Gibson and Ian Biddle (London: Routledge, 2016), 32–52.

———. *Reason and Resonance: A History of Modern Aurality* (New York: Zone, 2010).

———. "Refiguring the Early Modern Voice." *Qui Parle* 21/1 (2012): 85–105.

Everett, Caleb. "Languages in Drier Climates Use Fewer Vowels." *Frontiers in Psychology* 8/1285 (2017), https://doi.org/10.3389/fpsyg.2017.01285.

Evrensel, Alper, and Mehmet Emin Ceylan. "The Gut-Brain Axis: The Missing Link in Depression." *Clinical Psychopharmacology and Neuroscience* 13 (2015): 239–244.

Fabbri, Paolo. *Monteverdi* (Turin: EDT/Musica, 1986).

Fassler, Margot. *Gothic Song: Victorine Sequences and Augustinian Reform in Twelfth-Century Paris* (Cambridge: Cambridge University Press, 1996).

Favier, Thierry, and Manuel Couvreur (eds.). *Le Plaisir Musical en France au XVIIe siècle* (Sprimont: Mardaga, 2006).

Feerick, Jean. *Strangers in Blood* (Toronto: University of Toronto Press, 2010).

Filippi, Daniele. "Songs in Early Modern Catholic Missions: Between Europe, the Indies, and the 'Indies of Europe.'" In *Vokalpolyphonie zwischen Alter und Neuer Welt: Musikalische Austauschprozesse zwischen Europa und Latein-Amerika im 16. und 17. Jahrhundert*, ed. Klaus Pietschmann (Kassel: Bärenreiter, 2018), 39–67.

Fischer-Lichte, Erika. "Verkörperung/Embodiment. Zum Wandel einer alten theaterwissenschaftlichen in eine neue kulturwissenschaftliche Kategorie." In *Verkörperung*, ed. Erika Fischer-Lichte, Christian Horn, und Matthias Warstat (Tübingen: Francke, 2001), 11–27.

Fisher, Alexander J. *Music, Piety and Propaganda: The Soundscapes of Counter-Reformation Bavaria* (New York: Oxford University Press, 2014).

Fisher, George, and Judy Lochhead. "Analyzing from the Body." *Theory and Practice* 27 (2002): 37–67.

Franko, Mark. "Majestic Drag: Monarchical Performativity and the King's Body Theatrical." *TDR* 47 (2003): 71–87.

Frith, Chris. "The Brain, Consciousness and the Soul: Is the Brain All There Is?" In *The Concept of the Soul: Scientific and Religious Perspectives*, ed. Michael Fuller (Newcastle: Cambridge Scholars, 2014), 55–74.

Fudge, Erica. *Brutal Reasoning: Animals, Rationality, and Humanity in Early Modern England* (Ithaca, NY: Cornell University Press, 2006).

Garavaglia, Andrea, and Mark Weir. "'La brevità non può mover l'affetto': The Time Scale of the Baroque Aria." *Recercare* 24 (2021): 35–61.

Gardiner, John Eliot. *Music in the Castle of Heaven: A Portrait of Johann Sebastian Bach* (London: Allen Lane, 2013).

Gershon, Michael D. *The Second Brain: The Scientific Basis of Gut Instinct and a*

Groundbreaking New Understanding of Nervous Diseases of the Stomach and Intestines (New York: Quill, 1998).

Geyer-Kordesch, Johanna. "Georg Ernst Stahl's Radical Pietist Medicine and Its Influence on the German Enlightenment." In *The Medical Enlightenment of the Eighteenth Century*, ed. Andrew Cunningham and Roger French (Cambridge: Cambridge University Press, 1990), 67–87.

Gibson, Jonathan. "Hearing the Viola da Gamba in 'Komm, süßes Kreuz.'" In *Fiori Musicali: liber amicorum Alexander Silbiger*, ed. Claire Fontijn (Sterling Heights, MI: Harmonie Park Press, 2010), 419–450.

Gibson, Kirsten. "Music, Melancholy and Masculinity in Early Modern England." In *Masculinity and Western Musical Practice*, ed. Ian Biddle and Kirsten Gibson (London: Routledge, 2019), 41–66.

Gil, Daniel Juan. "What It Feels Like to Be a Body: Humoralism, Cognitivism, and the Sociological Horizon of Early Modern Religion." In *This Distracted Globe: Worldmaking in Early Modern Literature*, ed. Marcie Frank (New York: Fordham University Press, 2016), 163–189.

Giles, Roseen. "Physicality and Devotion in Heinrich Ignaz Biber's Rosary Sonatas." *Yale Journal of Music and Religion* 4 (2018): 68–104.

Gjerdingen, Robert. *Music in the Galant Style* (New York: Oxford University Press, 2007).

Goehr, Lydia. "Hardboiled Disillusionment: *Mahagonny* as the Last Culinary Opera." *Cultural Critique* 68 (2008): 3–37.

Goodman, Steve. *Sonic Warfare: Sound, Affect, and the Ecology of Fear* (Boston: MIT Press, 2010).

Gordon, Bonnie. *Monteverdi's Unruly Women: The Power of Song in Early Modern Italy* (Cambridge: Cambridge University Press, 2004).

Gordon-Seifert, Catherine. *Music and the Language of Love: Seventeenth-Century French Airs* (Bloomington: Indiana University Press, 2011).

Gotman, Kélina. *Choreomania: Dance and Disorder* (New York: Oxford University Press, 2017).

Gouk, Penelope. "Cosmic Vibrations: Echoes of Universal Harmony at the Time of the British Enlightenment." *Terrain* 68, October 2017, https://doi.org/10.4000/terrain.16424.

———. "Music and the Nervous System in Eighteenth-Century British Medical Thought." In *Music and the Nerves, 1700–1900*, ed. James Kennaway (Basingstoke: Palgrave Macmillan, 2014), 44–71.

———. "Music and Spirit in Early Modern Thought." In *Emotions and Health, 1200–1700*, ed. Elena Carrera (Leiden: Brill, 2013), 221–240.

Gowland, Angus. *The Worlds of Renaissance Melancholy: Robert Burton in Context* (Cambridge: Cambridge University Press, 2006).

Glüxam, Dagmar. *"Aus der Seele muß man spielen . . .": Über die Affekttheorie in der Musik des 17. und 18. Jahrhunderts und ihre Auswirkung auf die Interpretation* (Vienna: Hollitzer, 2020).

Gračanin, Asmir, Lauren M. Bylsma, and Ad J. J. M. Vingerhoets. "Why Only Humans Shed Emotional Tears: Evolutionary and Cultural Perspectives." *Hum Nat* 29 (2018): 104–133.

Grant, Roger M. *Beating Time and Measuring Music in the Early Modern Period* (New York: Oxford University Press, 2014).

———. "Music Lessons on Affect and Its Objects." *representations* 144 (2018): 34–60.

Green, Joel B. *Body, Soul, and Human Life: The Nature of Humanity in the Bible* (Grand Rapids, MI: Baker Academic, 2012).

Grewe, Oliver, Frederik Nagel, Reinhard Kopiez, and Eckart Altenmüller. "Listening to Music as a Re-Creative Process: Physiological, Psychological and Psychoacoustical Correlates of Chills and Strong Emotions." *Music Perception* 24 (2007): 297–314.

Gritten, Anthony. "Resonant Listening." *Performance Research* 15 (2010): 115–122.

Groote, Inga Mai, and Dietrich Hakelberg. "Circulating Musical Knowledge in Early Seventeenth-Century Germany: *Musica Poetica* Treatises of Johann Hermann Schein and Michael Altenburg in the Library of Johann Caspar Trost." *Early Music History* 35 (2016): 131–201.

Grosz, Elizabeth. *Volatile Bodies: Towards a Corporeal Feminism* (London: Routledge, 1994).

Guck, Marion. "Analysis as Interpretation: Interaction, Intentionality, Invention." *Music Theory Spectrum* 28 (2006): 191–209.

Guido, Massimiliano. "Climbing the Stairs of the Memory Palace." In *Studies in Historical Improvisation from Cantare super Librum to Partimenti*, ed. Massimiliano Guido (Abingdon: Routledge, 2017), 41–52.

Hall, Matthew J. "François Couperin on Touch, Movement, and the Soul." *Keyboard Perspectives* 10 (2017): 19–37.

Hamilton, John T. *Music, Madness, and the Undoing of Language* (New York: Columbia University Press, 2008).

Harrán, Don. "Vicentino and His Rules of Text Underlay." *The Musical Quarterly* 59/4 (1973): 620–632.

Harrison, Carol. *On Music, Sense, Affect and Voice* (New York: T&T Clark, 2019).

Harrison, Peter. *The Territories of Science and Religion* (Chicago: University of Chicago Press, 2015).

Haynes, Bruce, and Geoffrey Burgess. *The Pathetick Musician: Moving an Audience in the Age of Eloquence* (Oxford: Oxford University Press, 2016).

Head, Matthew. "C. P. E. Bach 'In Tormentis': Gout Pain and Body Language in the Fantasia in A Major, h 278 (1782)." *Eighteenth-Century Music* 13 (2016): 211–234.

Heller, Wendy. *Emblems of Eloquence: Opera and Women's Voices in Seventeenth-Century Venice* (Berkeley: University of California Press, 2003).

———. *Music in the Baroque* (New York: Norton, 2014).

Heller-Roazen, Daniel. *The Inner Touch: Archaeology of a Sensation* (New York: Zone Books, 2007).

Helm, Jürgen. "Galen-Rezeption im 16. Jahrhundert am Beispiel Philipp Melanchthons." *European History Online*, 12 March 2010, http://www.ieg-ego.eu/helmj-2010-de.

Henderson, Judith A. *Translating Investments: Metaphor and the Dynamic of Cultural Change in Tudor-Stuart England* (New York: Fordham University Press, 2005).

Herdman, Jessica. "Songs Danced in Anger: Music and Violent Emotions in Late Sixteenth-Century Lyon." *French History* 32 (2018): 151–181.

Herissone, Rebecca. *Musical Creativity in Restoration England* (Cambridge: Cambridge University Press, 2013).

Herzfeld-Schild, Marie Louise. “Resonanz und Stimmung: Musikalische Paradigmen im historischen Spannungsfeld von Anthropologie, Ästhetik und Physiologie.” In *Resonanz—Rhythmus—Synchronisierung: Interaktionen in Alltag, Therapie und Kunst*, ed. Thiemo Breyer, Michael B. Buchholz, Andreas Hamburger, Stefan Pfänder, and Elke Schumann (Bielefeld: transcript, 2017), 127–144.

Heuss, Alfred. *Johann Sebastian Bachs Matthäuspassion* (Leipzig: Breitkopf & Härtel, 1909).

Hillman, David, and Carla Mazzio (eds.). *The Body in Parts: Fantasies of Corporeality in Early Modern Europe* (New York: Routledge, 2013).

Hinrichsen, Hans-Joachim. “Theologie, Ästhetik, Politik. Der Hamburger Opernstreit und die Frühaufklärung.” *MusikTheorie. Zeitschrift für Musikwissenschaft* 29 (2014): 197–208.

Hogg, Bennett. “Enactive Consciousness, Intertextuality, and Musical Free Improvisation: Deconstructing Mythologies and Finding Connections.” In *Music and Consciousness: Philosophical, Psychological, and Cultural Perspectives*, ed. David Clarke and Eric Clarke (New York: Oxford University Press, 2011), 79–93.

Holman, Peter. *Dowland: Lachrimae (1604)* (Cambridge: Cambridge University Press, 1999).

Holsinger, Bruce W. *Music, Body, and Desire in Medieval Culture: Hildegard of Bingen to Chaucer* (Stanford, CA: Stanford University Press, 2001).

Holzmüller, Anne. “Between Things and Souls: Sacred Atmospheres and Immersive Listening in Late Eighteenth-Century Sentimentalism.” In *Music as Atmosphere: Collective Feelings and Affective Sounds*, ed. Friedlind Riedel and Juha Torvinen (Abingdon: Routledge, 2020), 218–237.

Home-Cook, George. *Theatre and Aural Attention: Stretching Ourselves* (Basingstoke: Palgrave Macmillan, 2015).

Huizenga, Tom. “Bach’s St. Matthew Passion: Ritualized and Riveting.” NPR, 10 April 2012, https://www.npr.org/sections/deceptivecadence/2012/04/10/150346723/bachs-st-matthew-passion-ritualized-and-riveting?t=1593516820122.

Huron, David, and Elizabeth Hellmuth Margulis. “Musical Expectancy and Thrills.” In Patrik N. Juslin, *Handbook of Music and Emotion: Theory, Research, Applications* (Oxford: Oxford University Press, 2010), 591–597.

———. “Voice Denumerability in Polyphonic Music of Homogeneous Timbres.” *Music Perception: An Interdisciplinary Journal* 6 (1989): 361–382.

Hutcheon, Linda, and Michael Hutcheon. “Embodied Representation in Staged Opera.” In *The Oxford Handbook of Music and the Body*, ed. Youn Kim and Sander L. Gilman (New York: Oxford University Press, 2019), 294–305.

Hutchins, Barnaby R. “The Embodied Descartes: Contemporary Readings of *L’Homme*.” In *Descartes’ Treatise on Man and its Reception*, ed. Delphine Antoine-Mahut and Stephen Gaukroger (Cham: Springer, 2016), 287–304.

Ihde, Don. *Listening and Voice: Phenomenologies of Sound*, 2nd ed. (Albany: State University of New York Press, 2007).

Irving, David. *Colonial Counterpoint: Music in Early Modern Manila* (Oxford: Oxford University Press, 2010).

Jackson, Jean E. “Pain and Bodies.” In *A Companion to the Anthropology of the Body and Embodiment*, ed. Frances E. Mascia-Lees (Oxford: Wiley-Blackwell, 2011), 370–387.

James, Susan. *Passion and Action: The Emotions in Seventeenth-Century Philosophy* (Oxford: Clarendon Press, 1997).

Johnson, Julian. *After Debussy: Music, Language and the Margins of Philosophy* (New York: Oxford University Press, 2020).

Johnson, Lindsay. "Experiencing Alba Tressina's *Anima mea liquefacta est* through Bodily Humors and the Sacred Erotic." *Current Musicology* 96 (2013): 37–69.

Jolley, Nicholas. "The Reception of Descartes' Philosophy." In *The Cambridge Companion to Descartes*, ed. John Cottingham (Cambridge: Cambridge University Press, 1992), 393–432.

Jorgensen, Larry M. "Descartes on Music: Between the Ancients and the Aestheticians." *British Journal of Aesthetics* 52 (2012): 407–424.

Juslin, Patrik N. *Musical Emotions Explained: Unlocking the Secrets of Musical Affect* (Oxford: Oxford University Press, 2019).

Kane, Brian. "Sound Studies without Auditory Culture: A Critique of the Ontological Turn." *Sound Studies* 1/1 (2015): 2–21.

Kant, Immanuel. *Kritik der Urteilskraft* [1790]. In *Werke in zwölf Bänden*, ed. Wilhelm Weischedel, vol. 10 (Frankfurt: Suhrkamp, 1977).

Karant-Nunn, Susan. "'Gedanken, Herz und Sinn': Die Unterdrückung der religiösen Emotionen." In *Kulturelle Reformation: Sinnformationen im Umbruch 1400–1600*, ed. Bernhard Jussen and Craig Koslofsky (Göttingen: Vandenhoeck & Ruprecht, 1999), 69–95.

Kennaway, James. *Bad Vibrations: The History of the Idea of Music as a Cause of Disease* (London: Routledge, 2012).

Kennaway, James (ed.). *Music and the Nerves, 1700–1900* (Basingstoke: Palgrave Macmillan, 2014).

Kevorkian, Tanya. *Baroque Piety: Religion, Society and Music in Leipzig, 1650–1750* (Aldershot: Ashgate, 2007).

King, Elaine, and Caroline Waddington-Jones. "Performers' Perspectives on 'Feel' in Music." In *Music, Analysis, and the Body: Experiments, Explorations, and Embodiments*, ed. Nicholas Reyland and Rebecca Thumpston (Leuven: Peeters, 2018), 241–258.

Kivy, Peter. *Sound Sentiment: An Essay on the Musical Emotions* (Philadelphia: Temple University Press, 1989).

Klemm, Tanja. *Bildphysiologie. Wahrnehmung und Körper in Mittelalter und Renaissance* (Berlin: Akademie Verlag, 2013).

Knaup, Marcus. *Unity of Body and Soul or Mind-Brain-Being: Towards a Paradigm Shift in Modern Concepts of Personhood* (Stuttgart: Metzler, 2018).

Koelsch, Stefan. *Brain & Music* (Chichester: John Wiley & Sons, 2012).

Koelsch, Stefan, and Lutz Jäncke. "Music and the Heart." *European Heart Journal* 36 (2015): 3043–3049.

Koschorke, Albrecht. *Körperströme und Schriftverkehr: Mediologie des 18. Jahrhunderts* (Munich: Fink, 1999).

Kosovske, Yonit Lea. *Historical Harpsichord Technique: Developing La Douceur du Toucher* (Bloomington: Indiana University Press, 2011).

Kowalik, Jill Anne. *Theology and Dehumanization: Trauma, Grief, and Pathological Mourning in Seventeenth- and Eighteenth-Century German Thought and Literature*, ed. Gail K. Hart (Frankfurt: Peter Lang, 2009).

Kümmel, Werner Friedrich. *Musik und Medizin: Ihre Wechselbeziehung in Theorie und Praxis von 800–1800* (Freiburg: Alber, 1977).

———. "Puls und Musik (16.–18. Jahrhundert)." *Medizinhistorisches Journal* 3 (1968): 269–293.

Kuriyama, Shigehisa. *The Expressiveness of the Body and the Divergence of Greek and Chinese Medicine* (New York: Zone Books, 1999).

Lakoff, George, and Mark Johnson. *Metaphors We Live By* (Chicago: University of Chicago Press, 1980).

LaMay, Thomasin. "Composing from the Throat: Madalena Casulana's *Primo libro de madrigali, 1568*." In *Musical Voices of Early Modern Women: Many-Headed Melodies*, ed. Thomasin LaMay (London: Routledge, 2017), 365–397.

Lambert, Erin. *Singing the Resurrection: Body, Community, and Belief in Reformation Europe* (New York: Oxford University Press, 2017).

Laqueur, Thomas. *Making Sex: Body and Gender from the Greeks to Freud* (Cambridge, MA: Harvard University Press, 1990).

Larson, Katherine. *The Matter of Song in Early Modern England: Texts in and of the Air* (New York: Oxford University Press, 2019).

Leech-Wilkinson, Daniel. *The Changing Sound of Music: Approaches to Studying Recorded Musical Performances* (London: CHARM, 2009), https://www.charm.rhul.ac.uk/studies/chapters/intro.html.

Le Guin, Elisabeth. *Boccherini's Body: An Essay in Carnal Musicology* (Berkeley: University of California Press, 2006).

Leonard, Charlotte A. "The Role of the Trombone and Its *Affekt* in the Lutheran Church Music of Seventeenth-Century Saxony and Thuringia: The Mid- and Late Seventeenth Century." *Historic Brass Society Journal* 12 (2000): 57–93.

Leonardi, Susan J., and Rebecca A. Pope. *The Diva's Mouth: Body, Voice, Prima Donna Politics* (New Brunswick, NJ: Rutgers University Press, 1996).

Leopold, Silke. *Monteverdi: Music in Transition* (Oxford: Clarendon Press, 1991).

———. "Über die Inszenierung in der Musik. Einige grundsätzliche Überlegungen zur Interaktion von Verhaltensnormen und Personendarstellungen." *Basler Jahrbuch für historische Musikpraxis* 23 (1999): 9–40.

Leppert, Richard. *The Sight of Sound: Music, Representation, and the History of the Body* (Berkeley: University of California Press, 1993).

Levenberg, Jeffrey. "*Seconda Pratica* Temperaments, *Prima Pratica* Tempers: The Artusi-Monteverdi Controversy and the Retuning of Musica Moderna." *Acta Musicologica* 92 (2020): 21–41.

Levinson, Jerrold. *Music in the Moment* (Ithaca, NY: Cornell University Press, 2007).

Leys, Ruth. "The Turn to Affect: A Critique." *Critical Inquiry* 37 (2011): 434–472.

Li, Feng. "Taste Perception: From the Tongue to the Testis." *Molecular Human Reproduction* 19/6 (2013): 349–360.

Liester, Mitchell B. "Personality Changes Following Heart Transplantation: The Role of Cellular Memory." *Medical Hypotheses* 135 (2020): 1–7.

Lindemann, Mary. *Medicine and Society in Early Modern Europe* (Cambridge: Cambridge University Press, 2010).

Lock, Margaret, and Judith Farquhar (eds.). *Beyond the Body Proper: Reading the Anthropology of Material Life* (Durham, NC: Duke University Press, 2007).

Lockhart, Ellen. *Animation, Plasticity, and Music in Italy, 1770–1830* (Berkeley: University of California Press, 2017).

Maddox, Alan, and Jane W. Davidson. "Music." In *Early Modern Emotions: An Introduction*, ed. Susan Broomhall (London: Routledge, 2016), 173–176.

Malik, Bilal, Nadia Elkaddi, Jumanah Turkistani, Andrew I. Spielman, and Mehmet Hakan Ozdener. "Mammalian Taste Cells Express Functional Olfactory Receptors." *Chemical Senses* 44/5 (2019): 289–301.

Martin, Raymond, and John Barresi. *The Rise and Fall of the Soul and Self: An Intellectual History of Personal Identity* (New York: Columbia University Press, 2008).

Mascia-Lees, Frances E. "Aesthetic Embodiment and Commodity Capitalism." In *A Companion to the Anthropology of the Body and Embodiment*, ed. Frances E. Mascia-Lees (London: Blackwell, 2011), 3–13.

Maisano, Scott. "Infinite Gesture: Automata and the Emotions in Descartes and Shakespeare." In *Genesis Redux: Essays in the History and Philosophy of Artificial Life*, ed. Jessica Riskin (Chicago: University of Chicago Press, 2007), 63–84.

Marks, Thomas. *Sighs of the German People: An Emotional History of Musical Sigh-Compositions During the Thirty Years War (1618–1648)* (PhD diss., City University of New York, 2019).

McClary, Susan. *Desire and Pleasure in Seventeenth-Century Music* (Berkeley: University of California Press, 2012).

———. "Introduction: On Bodies, Affects, and Cultural Identities in the Seventeenth Century." In *Structures of Feeling in Seventeenth-Century Cultural Expression*, ed. Susan McClary (Berkeley: University of California Press, 2013), 14–29.

———. *Modal Subjectivities: Self-Fashioning in the Italian Madrigal* (Berkeley: University of California Press, 2004).

McClintock, Carol (ed. and trans.). *Readings in the History of Music in Performance* (Bloomington: Indiana University Press, 1979).

McDonald, Grantley. "Melanchthon's Theory of Spirit as a Bridge between Galen, Ficino and Luther." In *Aisthetics of the Spirits: Spirits in Early Modern Science, Religion, Literature and Music*, ed. Steffen Schneider (Göttingen: V&R unipress, 2015), 111–128.

McKean, John A. Hansmann. *Towards a Wahre Art: The Development of Keyboard Technique in the German Baroque* (PhD diss., University of Cambridge, 2016).

McKinnon, James (ed.). *Music in Early Christian Literature* (Cambridge: Cambridge University Press, 1987).

Mecke, Ann-Christine. "Johann Sebastian Bachs Sopranisten und Altisten: Untersuchungen zum Mutationsalter im 18. Jahrhundert." In *Geistliche Musik und Chortradition im 18. und 19. Jahrhundert: Institutionen, Klangideale und Repertoire im Umbruch*, ed. Anselm Hartinger, Christoph Wolff, and Peter Wollny (Wiesbaden: Breitkopf & Härtel, 2017), 189–206.

Melamed, Daniel R. *Hearing Bach's Passions* (Oxford: Oxford University Press, 2005).

———. "How Did J. S. Bach's 'Aus Liebe will mein Heiland sterben,' BWV 244/49, Get to Be So Slow?" *Nineteenth-Century Music* 43 (2019): 3–16.

Melrose, Susan. *A Semiotics of the Dramatic Text* (Basingstoke: Macmillan, 1994).

Merricks, Trenton. "The Word Made Flesh: Dualism, Physicalism and the Incarnation." In *Persons: Human and Divine*, ed. Peter van Inwagen and Dean Zimmerman (Oxford: Oxford University Press, 2007), 281–300.

Mollakazemi, M. J., D. Biswal, S. C. Elayi, S. Thyagarajan, and J. Evans. "Synchronization of Autonomic and Cerebral Rhythms During Listening to Music: Effects of Tempo and Cognition of Songs." *Physiological Research* 68/6 (2019): 1005–1019.

Morabito, Fulvia (ed.). *Musical Improvisation in the Baroque Era* (Turnhout: Brepols, 2019).

Morris, David B. *The Culture of Pain* (Berkeley: University of California Press, 1991).

Moser, Hans Joachim. *Heinrich Schütz: His Life and Work*, trans. Carl F. Pfatteicher (Saint Louis: Concordia, 1959).

Muchembled, Robert. *Orgasm and the West: A History of Pleasure from the Sixteenth Century to the Present*, trans. Jean Birrell (Cambridge: Polity, 2008).

Myers, David G. *Psychology*, 7th ed. (New York: Worth, 2004).

Nagel, Thomas. "What Is It Like to Be a Bat?" *The Philosophical Review* 83/4 (1974): 435–450.

Nancy, Jean-Luc. *Listening*, trans. Charlotte Mandell (New York: Fordham University Press, 2009).

Neufeld, Christine M. *Avid Ears: Medieval Gossips, Sound and the Art of Listening* (New York: Routledge, 2018).

Nussbaum, Charles O. *The Musical Representation: Meaning, Ontology, and Emotion* (Cambridge, MA: MIT Press, 2012).

Orden, Kate van. "Descartes on Musical Training and the Body." In *Music, Sensation and Sensuality*, ed. Linda Phyllis Austern (New York: Routledge, 2002), 17–38.

———. *Music, Discipline and Arms in Early Modern France* (Chicago: University of Chicago Press, 2005).

Ossi, Massimo, *Divining the Oracle: Monteverdi's Seconda Prattica* (Chicago: University of Chicago Press, 2003).

Palisca, Claude V. "The Artusi-Monteverdi Controversy." In *The New Monteverdi Companion*, ed. Denis Arnold and Nigel Fortune (London: Faber & Faber, 1984), 127–158.

———. "Vincenzo Galilei's Counterpoint Treatise: A Code for the 'Seconda Prattica.'" *Journal of the American Musicological Society* 9 (1956): 81–96.

Panksepp, Jaak. "The Emotional Sources of 'Chills' Induced by Music." *Music Perception: An Interdisciplinary Journal* 13 (1995): 171–207.

Pappa, Joseph. *Carnal Reading: Early Modern Language and Bodies* (Newark: University of Delaware Press, 2011).

Park, Katharine. "The Organic Soul." In *The Cambridge History of Renaissance Philosophy*, ed. Charles B. Schmitt and Quentin Skinner (Cambridge: Cambridge University Press, 1988), 464–484.

Paster, Gail Kern. *The Body Embarrassed: Drama and the Disciplines of Shame in Early Modern England* (Ithaca, NY: Cornell University Press, 1993).

———. *Humoring the Body: Emotions and the Shakespearean Stage* (Chicago: University of Chicago Press, 2004).

———. "Introduction: Reading the Early Modern Passions." In *Reading the Early Modern Passions: Essays in the Cultural History of Emotion*, ed. Gail Kern Paster,

Katherine Rowe, and Mary Floyd-Wilson (Philadelphia: University of Philadelphia Press, 2004), 1–20.

———. "Nervous Tensions." In *The Body In Parts: Fantasies of Corporeality in Early Modern Europe*, ed. David Hillman and Carla Mazzio (New York: Routledge, 1997), 112–116.

Peters, Deniz. "Introduction." In *Bodily Expression in Electronic Music*, ed. Deniz Peters, Gerhard Eckel, and Andreas Dorschel (New York: Routledge, 2012), 1–15.

Pirrotta, Nino. "Monteverdi's Poetic Choices." Reprinted in *Monteverdi*, ed. Richard Wistreich (New York: Routledge, 2016), 3–74.

Plamper, Jan. *The History of Emotions: An Introduction* (Oxford: Oxford University Press, 2017).

Price, Donald D. "Psychological and Neural Mechanisms of the Affective Dimension of Pain." *Science* 288 (2000): 1769–1772.

Radice, Mark A. *Chamber Music: An Essential History* (Ann Arbor: University of Michigan Press, 2012).

Rathey, Markus. *Bach's Major Vocal Works: Music, Drama, Liturgy* (New Haven, CT: Yale University Press, 2016).

Reardon, Colleen. *Holy Concord Within Sacred Walls: Nuns and Music in Siena, 1575–1700* (Oxford: Oxford University Press, 2002).

Reiss, Timothy J. *Mirages of the Selfe: Patterns of Personhood in Ancient and Early Modern Europe* (Stanford, CA: Stanford University Press, 2003).

Rifkin, Joshua. "Schütz and Musical Logic." *Musical Times* 113/11 (1972): 1067–1070.

Ringer, Mark. *Bach's Operas of the Soul: A Listener's Guide to the Sacred Cantatas* (Lanham, MD: Amadeus, 2020).

Riskin, Jessica. *The Restless Clock: A History of the Centuries-Long Argument over What Makes Living Things Tick* (Chicago: University of Chicago Press, 2016).

Roach, Joseph R. *The Player's Passion: Studies in the Science of Acting* (Newark: University of Delaware Press, 1985).

Robinson, Benedict S. "Thinking Feeling." In *Affect Theory and Early Modern Texts: Politics, Ecologies, and Form*, ed. Amanda Bailey and Mario DiGangi (New York: Palgrave Macmillan, 2017), 109–127.

Robinson, Jenefer. *Deeper Than Reason: Emotion and Its Role in Literature, Music and Art* (Oxford: Clarendon, 2005).

Rosand, Ellen. *Opera in Seventeenth-Century Venice: The Creation of a Genre* (Berkeley: University of California Press, 2007).

Rose, Stephen. "Bach and Material Culture." In *Rethinking Bach*, ed. Bettina Varwig (New York: Oxford University Press, 2021), 11–36.

———. "Memory and the Early Musician." *Early Music Performer* 13 (2004): 3–8.

Rosenwein, Barbara H., and Riccardo Cristiani. *What Is the History of Emotions?* (Balden: Polity, 2018).

Rousseau, George S. *Nervous Acts: Essays on Literature, Culture and Sensibility* (Basingstoke: Palgrave Macmillan, 2004).

Rublack, Ulinka. "Fluxes: The Early Modern Body and the Emotions." *History Workshop Journal* 53 (2002): 1–16.

Ruiter-Feenstra, Pamela. *Bach and the Art of Improvisation*, vol. 1 (Ann Arbor, MI: CHI Press, 2011).

Sanford, Sally A. "A Comparison of French and Italian Singing in the Seventeenth

Century." *Journal of Seventeenth-Century Music* 1/1 (1995), https://sscm-jscm.org/jscm/v1/no1/sanford_ex6.html.

Sawday, Jonathan. *The Body Emblazoned: Dissection and the Human Body in Renaissance Culture* (London and New York: Routledge, 1995).

Scarry, Elaine. *The Body in Pain: The Making and Unmaking of the World* (New York: Oxford University Press, 1985).

Schaefer, Donovan O. *Religious Affects: Animality, Evolution, and Power* (Durham, NC: Duke University Press, 2015).

Schäfer, Daniel. "More Than a Fading Flame: The Physiology of Old Age between Speculative Analogy and Experimental Method." In *Blood, Sweat and Tears: The Changing Concepts of Physiology from Antiquity Into Early Modern Europe*, ed. Manfred Horstmanshoff, Helen King, and Claus Zittel (Leiden: Brill, 2021), 241–266.

Scheer, Monique. "Are Emotions a Kind of Practice (And Is That What Makes Them Have a History)? A Bourdieuian Approach to Understanding Emotion." *History and Theory* 51 (2012): 193–220.

———. "Topographies of Emotion." In *Emotional Lexicons: Continuity and Change in the Vocabulary of Feeling 1700–2000* (Oxford: Oxford University Press, 2014), 32–61.

Schneider, Steffen. "Die aisthetische Dimension der Geistwesen in der frühen Neuzeit." In *Aisthetics of the Spirits: Spirits in Early Modern Science, Religion, Literature and Music*, ed. Steffen Schneider (Göttingen: V&R unipress, 2015), 9–18.

Schnell, Rüdiger. *Haben Gefühle eine Geschichte? Aporien einer History of Emotions* (Göttingen: V&R unipress, 2015).

Schoenfeldt, Michael. "The Unbearable Permeability of Bodies and Minds." In *Embodied Cognition and Shakespeare's Theatre*, ed. Laurence Johnson, John Sutton, and Evelyn Tribble (London: Routledge, 2014), 105–148.

Schulenberg, David. *Music of the Baroque* (New York: Oxford University Press, 2008).

Schulze, Hans-Joachim. *Die Bach-Kantaten: Einführungen zu sämtlichen Kantaten Johann Sebastian Bachs* (Leipzig: Evangelische Verlagsanstalt, 2006).

Seigworth, Gregory J., and Melissa Gregg. "An Inventory of Shimmers." In *The Affect Theory Reader*, ed. Melissa Gregg and Gregory J. Seigworth (Durham, NC: Duke University Press, 2010), 1–27.

Seow, Mark. *Sensing Corporeality in Bach's Communion Cantatas* (MPhil diss., University of Cambridge, 2018).

Serjeantson, Richard. "The Soul." In *The Oxford Handbook of Philosophy in Early Modern Europe*, ed. Desmond M. Clarke and Catherine Wilson (New York: Oxford University Press, 2011), 119–137.

Serres, Michel. *The Five Senses: A Philosophy of Mingled Bodies* (London: Bloomsbury, 2016).

Sevush, Steven. *The Single-Neuron Theory: Closing in on the Neural Correlate of Consciousness* (Cham: Palgrave Macmillan, 2016).

Shepherd, Simon. *Theatre, Body and Pleasure* (London: Routledge, 2006).

Shusterman, Richard. *Thinking Through the Body: Essays in Somaesthetics* (Cambridge: Cambridge University Press, 2012).

Small, Christopher. *Musicking: The Meanings of Performing and Listening* (Middletown, CT: Wesleyan University Press, 1998).

Smart, Mary Ann. Review of Gary Tomlinson, *Metaphysical Song: An Essay on Opera*. *19th-Century Music* 23 (1999): 103–109.

Smith, Bruce R. *The Acoustic World of Early Modern England: Attending to the O-Factor* (Chicago: University of Chicago Press, 1999).

———. "Hearing Green." In *Reading the Early Modern Passions: Essays in the Cultural History of Emotion*, ed. Gail Kern Paster, Katherine Rowe, and Mary Floyd-Wilson (Philadelphia: University of Pennsylvania Press, 2004), 147–168.

———. *Phenomenal Shakespeare* (Chichester: Wiley-Blackwell, 2010).

Smith, C. U. M. *The Animal Spirit Doctrine and the Origins of Neurophysiology* (Oxford: Oxford University Press, 2012).

Smith, Justin E. H. *Nature, Human Nature, and Human Difference: Race in Early Modern Philosophy* (Princeton, NJ: Princeton University Press, 2015).

Smith, Mark M. "Producing Sense, Consuming Sense, Making Sense: Perils and Prospects for Sensory History." *Journal of Social History* 40/4 (2007): 841–858.

Smith, Pamela H. *The Body of the Artisan: Art and Experience in the Scientific Revolution* (Chicago: University of Chicago Press, 2004).

Smith, Simon. *Musical Response in the Early Modern Playhouse, 1603–1625* (Cambridge: Cambridge University Press, 2017).

Souza, Jonathan De. *Music at Hand: Instruments, Bodies, and Cognition* (New York: Oxford University Press, 2017).

———. "Voice and Instruments at the Origins of Music." *Current Musicology* 97 (2014): 21–36.

Spitzer, Michael. *A History of Emotion in Western Music: A Thousand Years from Chant to Pop* (New York: Oxford University Press, 2020).

Stevens, Daniel B. "Rhythm and the Performer's Body." In *The Oxford Handbook of Music and the Body*, ed. Youn Kim and Sander L. Gilman (New York: Oxford University Press, 2019), 192–220.

Stiegler, Bernhard. *Technics and Time I: The Fault of Epimetheus* (Stanford, CA: Stanford University Press, 1998).

Stolberg, Michael. "Emotions and the Body in Early Modern Medicine." *emotion review* 11 (2019): 113–122.

———. *Experiencing Illness and the Sick Body in Early Modern Europe* (Basingstoke: Palgrave Macmillan, 2011).

Subotnik, Rose Rosengard. *Deconstructive Variations: Music and Reason in Western Society* (Minneapolis: University of Minnesota Press, 1996).

Sugg, Richard. *The Smoke of the Soul: Medicine, Physiology and Religion in Early Modern England* (New York: Palgrave Macmillan, 2013).

Sullivan, Erin. *Beyond Melancholy: Sadness and Selfhood in Renaissance England* (Oxford: Oxford University Press, 2016).

———. "The Role of the Arts in the History of the Emotions: Aesthetic Experience and Emotion as Method." *Emotions: History, Culture, Society* 2 (2018): 113–130.

Sutton, John. *Philosophy and Memory Traces: Descartes to Connectionism* (Cambridge: Cambridge University Press, 1998).

Taruskin, Richard. *The Oxford History of Western Music*, vol. 2: *Music in the Seventeenth and Eighteenth Centuries* (New York: Oxford University Press, 2005).

Taussig, Michael. *Mimesis and Alterity: A Particular History of the Senses* (New York: Routledge, 1993).

Thompson, Marie, and Ian Biddle. "Introduction: Somewhere Between the Signifying and the Sublime." In *Sound, Music, Affect: Theorising Sonic Experience*, ed. Ian Biddle and Marie Thompson (London: Bloomsbury, 2013), 1–23.

———. "Whiteness and the Ontological Turn in Sound Studies." *Parallax* 23 (2017): 266–282.

Toft, Robert. *With Passionate Voice: Re-Creative Singing in Sixteenth-Century England and Italy* (Oxford: Oxford University Press, 2014).

Tomlinson, Gary. "Fear of Singing (Episodes from Early Latin America)." In *Structures of Feeling in Seventeenth-Century Cultural Expression*, ed. Susan McClary (Berkeley: University of California Press, 2013), 117–146.

———. *Metaphysical Song: An Essay on Opera* (Princeton, NJ: Princeton University Press, 1999).

———. *A Million Years of Music: The Emergence of Human Modernity* (New York: Zone Books, 2015).

———. *Monteverdi and the End of the Renaissance* (Berkeley: University of California Press, 1987).

———. *Music and Renaissance Magic: Towards a Historiography of Others* (Chicago: University of Chicago Press, 1994).

———. "Sign, Affect, and Musicking Before the Human." *boundary 2* 43 (2016): 143–172.

———. *The Singing of the New World: Indigenous Voice in the Era of European Contact* (Cambridge: Cambridge University Press, 2007).

Trippett, David. "Music and the Transhuman Ear: Ultrasonics, Material Bodies, and the Limits of Sensation." *The Musical Quarterly* 100/2 (2017): 199–261.

Varela, Francisco J., Evan Thompson, and Eleanor Rosch. *The Embodied Mind: Cognitive Science and Human Experience*, rev. ed. (Cambridge, MA: MIT Press, 2016).

Varwig, Bettina. "Distributed Listening: Aural Encounters with Bach's Sacred Cantatas." *BACH: Journal of the Riemenschneider Bach Institute* 51 (2020): 210–240.

———. "Early Modern Voices." In *The Oxford Handbook of Timbre*, ed. Emily I. Dolan and Alexander Rehding (New York: Oxford University Press, 2018), 249–269.

———. "Embodied Invention: Bach at the Keyboard." In *Rethinking Bach*, ed. Bettina Varwig (New York: Oxford University Press, 2021), 115-140.

———. "Heart-Felt Musicking: The Physiology of a Bach Cantata." *representations* 143/1 (2018): 36–62.

———. "Metamorphosis and the Beast Within." *Journal of Musicological Research* 40 (2021): 262–269.

———. "Musical Expression: Lessons from the Eighteenth Century?" *Eighteenth-Century Music* 17/1 (2020): 53–72.

———. "'Mutato semper habitu': Heinrich Schütz and the Culture of Rhetoric." *Music & Letters* 90/2 (2009): 215–239.

Verwaal, Ruben E. "Fluid Deafness: Earwax and Hardness of Hearing in Early Modern Europe." *Medical History* 65 (2021): 366–383.

Vidal, Fernando. "Brainhood, Anthropological Figure of Modernity." *History of the Human Sciences* 22 (2009): 5–36.

Wald-Fuhrmann, Melanie. "Modell Orpheus: Die Erfindung des virtuosen Instrumentalisten aus den Bedingungen der Spiritus-Konzeption." In *Aisthetics of the Spirits: Spirits in Early Modern Science, Religion, Literature and Music*, ed. Steffen Schneider (Göttingen: V&R unipress, 2015), 213–243.

Waldron, Jennifer. *Reformations of the Body: Idolatry, Sacrifice, and Early Modern Theatre* (New York: Palgrave Macmillan, 2013).

Walker, D. P. "Joan Albert Ban and Mersenne's Musical Competition of 1640." *Music & Letters* 57 (1976): 233–255.

Warncke, Carsten-Peter. *Sprechende Bilder—sichtbare Worte: das Bildverständnis in der frihen Neuzeit* (Wiesbaden: Harrassowitz, 1987).

Watkins, Holly. *Musical Vitalities: Ventures in a Biotic Aesthetics of Music* (Chicago: University of Chicago Press, 2018).

Wels, Volkhard. *Manifestationen des Geistes: Frömmigkeit, Spiritualismus und Dichtung in der Frühen Neuzeit* (Göttingen: V&R unipress, 2014).

Weststeijn, Thijs. "Seeing and the Transfer of Spirits in Early Modern Art Theory." In *Renaissance Theories of Vision*, ed. John Shannon Hendrix and Charles H. Carman (Farnham: Ashgate, 2010), 159–169.

Wetherell, Margaret. *Affect and Emotion: A New Social Science Understanding* (Los Angeles: SAGE, 2012).

Wilbourne, Emily. "*Lo Schiavetto* (1612): Travestied Sound, Ethnic Performance, and the Eloquence of the Body." *Journal of the American Musicological Society* 63 (2010): 1–43.

———. *Seventeenth-Century Opera and the Sound of the Commedia dell'Arte* (Chicago: University of Chicago Press, 2016).

Williams, Bernard. *Descartes* (London: Penguin, 1978).

Williams, Raymond. *Marxism and Literature* (Oxford: Oxford University Press, 1977).

Winkler, Amanda Eubanks. "'Our Friend Venus Performed to a Miracle': Anne Bracegirdle, John Eccles and Creativity." In *Concepts of Creativity in Seventeenth-Century England*, ed. Rebecca Herissone and Alan Howard (Woodbridge: Boydell, 2013), 256–280.

Wistreich, Richard. "'Inclosed in This Tabernacle of Flesh': Body, Soul, and the Singing Voice." *Journal of the Northern Renaissance* 8 (2017), https://jnr2.hcommons.org/2017/5052/.

———. "'La voce è grata assai, ma . . .': Monteverdi on Singing." *Early Music* 2 (1994): 7–20.

———. "Of Mars I Sing: Monteverdi on Voicing Virility." In *Masculinity and Western Musical Practice*, ed. Ian Biddle and Kirsten Gibson (London and New York: Routledge, 2016), 67–94.

Wood, Jennifer Linhart. *Sounding Otherness in Early Modern Drama and Travel* (Cham: Palgrave Macmillan, 2019).

Wright, N. T. "Mind, Spirit, Soul and Body: All for One and One for All. Reflections on Paul's Anthropology in his Complex Contexts." https://ntwrightpage.com/2016/07/12/mind-spirit-soul-and-body.

Yearsley, David. *Bach and the Meanings of Counterpoint* (Cambridge: Cambridge University Press, 2002).

———. *Bach's Feet: The Organ Pedals in European Culture* (Cambridge: Cambridge University Press, 2012).

———. "Bach the Humorist." In *Rethinking Bach*, ed. Bettina Varwig (New York: Oxford University Press, 2021), 193–225.

Zohn, Stephen D. "Telemann's *Musique de table* and the *Tafelmusik* Tradition." *Oxford Handbooks Online*, April 2016, https://doi.org/10.1093/oxfordhb/9780199935321.013.120.

Zuckerkandl, Victor. *Man the Musician: Sound and Symbol Volume Two*, trans. Norbert Guterman (Princeton, NJ: Princeton University Press, 1976).

Recordings

All links accessible as of March 2023.

Bach Christmas Cantatas, Emmanuel Music, dir. Craig Smith, Koch International Classics 3–7462–2H1 (1999), https://www.youtube.com/watch?v=t5qhZeJDl3U.

Barbara Strozzi, Diporti di Euterpe, Emanuela Galli, Ensemble Galilei, dir. Paul Beier, Stradivarius STR33487 (2013), https://www.youtube.com/watch?v=w2lBnocuMC0.

Biber, Mensa Sonora, Sonata Representativa, Musica Antiqua Köln, dir. Reinhard Goebel, Archiv Production 423 701–2 (1988).

Canticum Canticorum, Les Voix Baroques, Atma Classique ACD2 2503 (2008), https://www.youtube.com/watch?v=R-JbZTLnYts.

"Dietrich Buxtehude: Quemadmodum desiderat cervus," Marc Mauillon (tenor), Ground Floor, live recording, Paradyz, 22 August 2015, https://www.youtube.com/watch?v=8nqPQ6v7a7Q.

Elin Manahan Thomas, Eternal Light, Universal Music 4765970 (2007).

Gasparo Zanetti: Il scolaro, Musica Antiqua, dir. Christian Mendoze, Disques Pierre Verany PV.792012 (1992).

Graupner, Partitas for Harpsichord, Vol. 1, Geneviève Soly (harpsichord), Analekta FL 23109 (2002), https://www.youtube.com/watch?v=orTSvHsNVSk.

Heinrich Schütz, Great Motets, Pro Cantione Antiqua, dir. Edgar Fleet, Alto ALC1118 (2010), https://www.youtube.com/watch?v=GbiDcjJFPeU.

Heinrich Schütz, Symphoniae Sacrae I, Concerto Palatino, Accent ACC 30078 (2004), https://www.youtube.com/watch?v=icAanVLJHKY.

Heinrich Schütz, Symphoniae Sacrae I, dir. Hans-Christoph Rademann, Carus 83.273 (2017).

Heinrich Schütz, Symphoniae Sacrae I, Musica Fiata, dir. Roland Wilson, Deutsche HM 88697524182 (2010), https://www.youtube.com/watch?v=vOtoTsLeHHQ.

Henry Purcell, King Arthur, dir. René Jacobs, Staatsoper Berlin, Schiller Theater, 21 January 2017, https://www.youtube.com/watch?v=gUETgs791tk.

J. S. Bach—"In Dir ist Freude" BWV 615, Ulf Norberg (organ), live recording, September 2015, https://www.youtube.com/watch?v=M5-8J9-2qaU.

J. S. Bach—Matthäus Passion—Aus Liebe—sopran aria, Christian Fliegner, https://www.youtube.com/watch?v=Ec40c_r-5s8.

J. S. Bach, Matthäus-Passion, Berliner Philharmoniker, Sir Simon Rattle, Peter Sellars, DVD recording (2014), BPHR 140021.

J. S. Bach, Matthäus-Passion, Collegium Vocale Gent, dir. Philippe Herreweghe, Harmonia Mundi France (1998).

Bach Cantatas, vol. 16, Monteverdi Choir, English Baroque Soloists, dir. John Eliot Gardiner, SDG 137 (2000), https://www.youtube.com/watch?v=1apvUSYvfgg.

Johann Sebastian Bach, Matthäus-Passion, Highlights, Rundfunkchor Leipzig, Staatskapelle Dresden, dir. Peter Schreier, Phillips (1987).

Johann Sebastian Bach, Matthew Passion, Dunedin Consort & Players, dir. John Butt, Linn Records (2008).

Like as the Hart: Music for the Templars Garden, The Choir of New College Oxford, dir. Robert Quinney, novum NCR1392 (2017).

A Purcell Collection, VOCES8, Les Inventions, Signum Classics SIGCD375 (2014), https://www.youtube.com/watch?v=Z7Sbx8tZUa4.

Purcell, King Arthur, Deller Consort & Choir, The King's Musick, Alfred Deller, Harmonia Mundi (1986), https://www.youtube.com/watch?v=kZhHpCrCMOY.

Reinhard Keiser: Der geliebte Adonis, Capella Orlandi Bremen, dir. Thomas Ihlenfeldt, cpo 999 636–2 (2001).

Reinhard Keiser, "Liebe, sag', was fängst du an?," Sandrine Piau, Akademie für Alte Musik Berlin, dir. Bernhard Forck, live recording, 20 October 2008, https://www.youtube.com/watch?v=Hbrrc3tu29g.

Une Passion et ils me cloueront sur le bois, Akadêmia Ensemble, dir. Françoise Lasserre, Bayard Musique B-308435–2 (2014).

Vivaldi, Vespri per L'Assunzione di Maria Vergine, Concerto Italiano, Rinaldo Alessandrini, Naïve OP30475 (2008), https://www.youtube.com/watch?v=lPevIrWRG1Q.

Youri Egorov plays Bach, Youri Egorov (piano), Pavane Records (1993), https://www.youtube.com/watch?v=rV29KqTGdPE.

Index